MW01618684

HOKUSAI

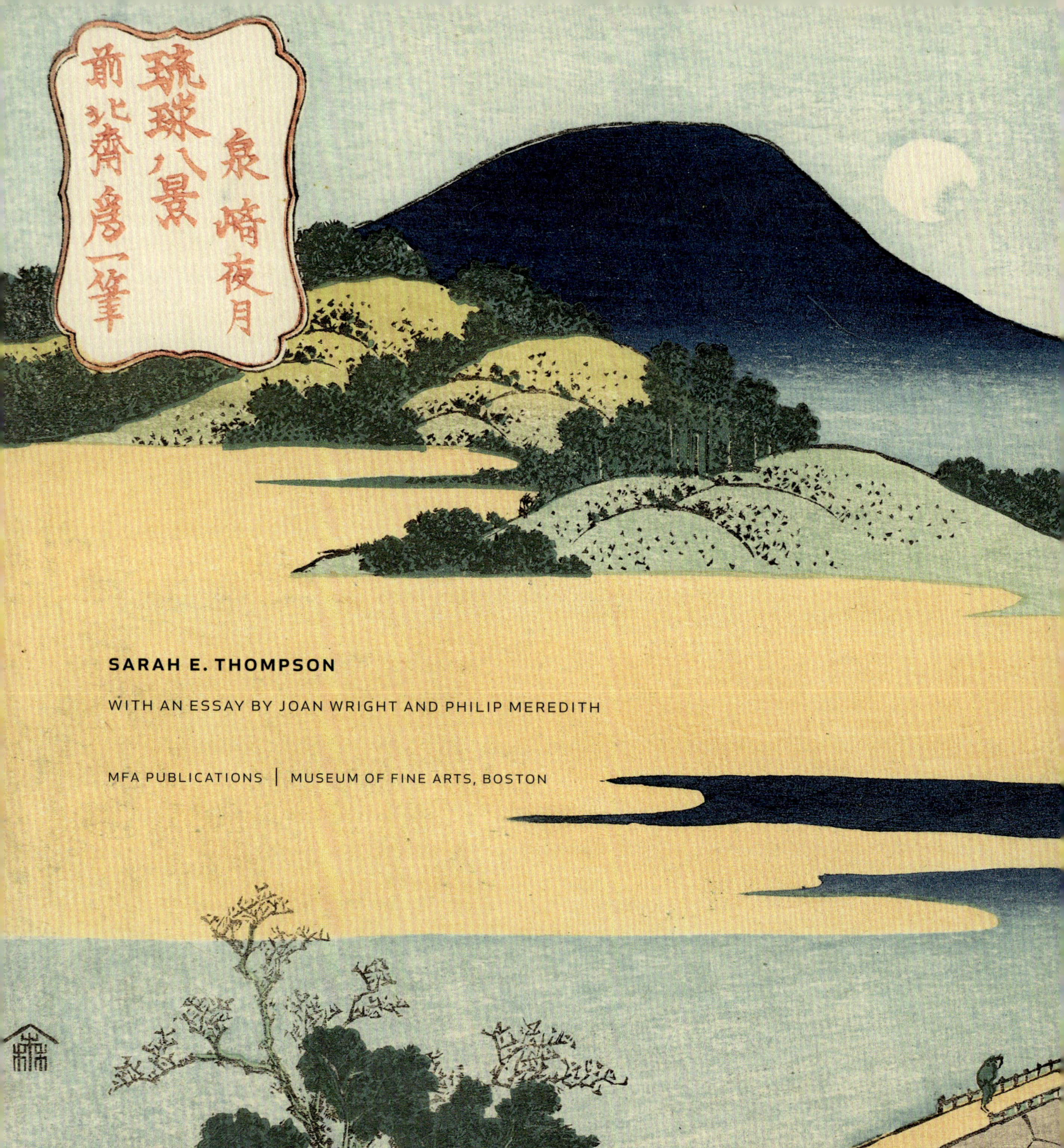

SARAH E. THOMPSON

WITH AN ESSAY BY JOAN WRIGHT AND PHILIP MEREDITH

MFA PUBLICATIONS | MUSEUM OF FINE ARTS, BOSTON

HOKUSAI

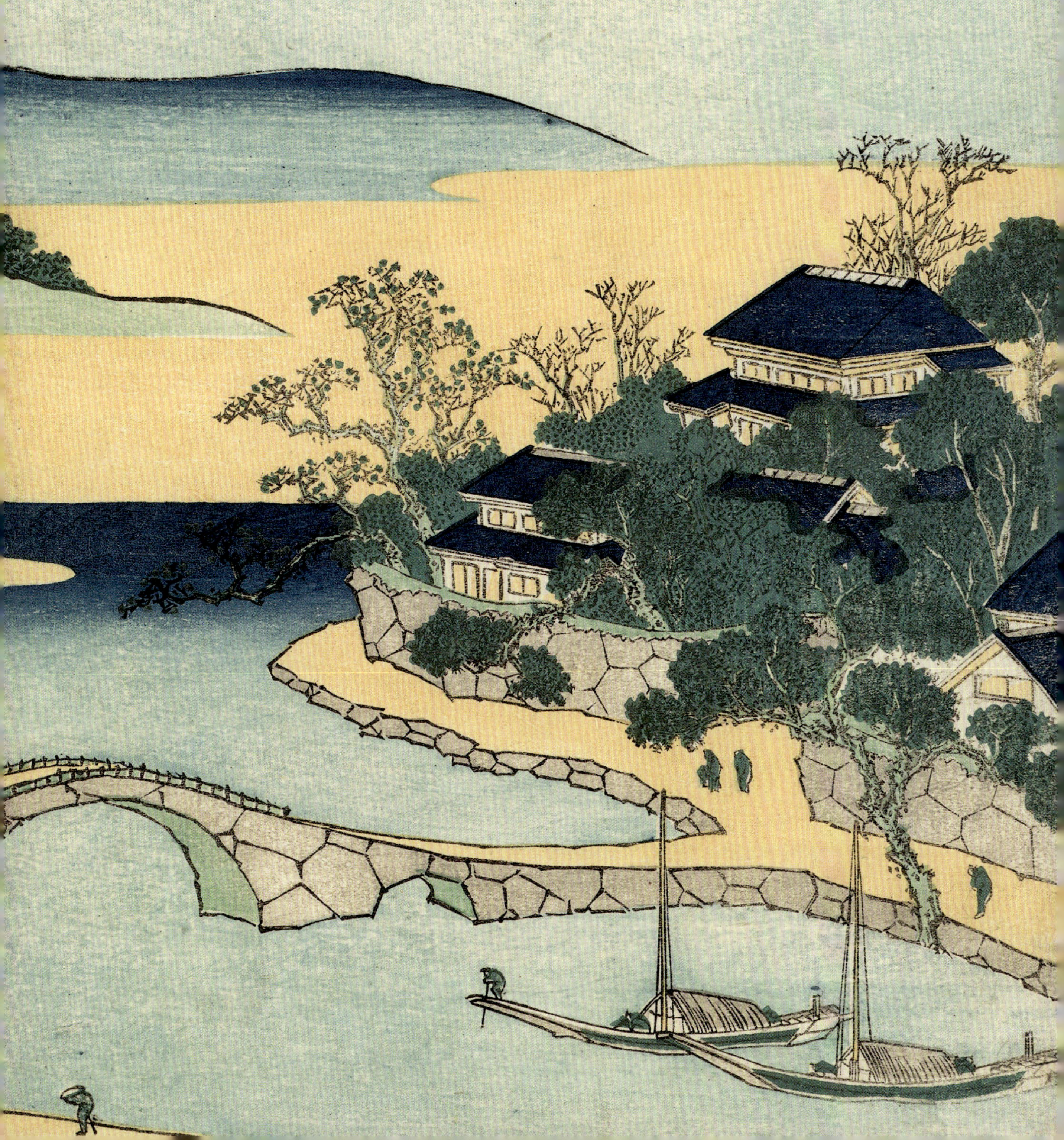

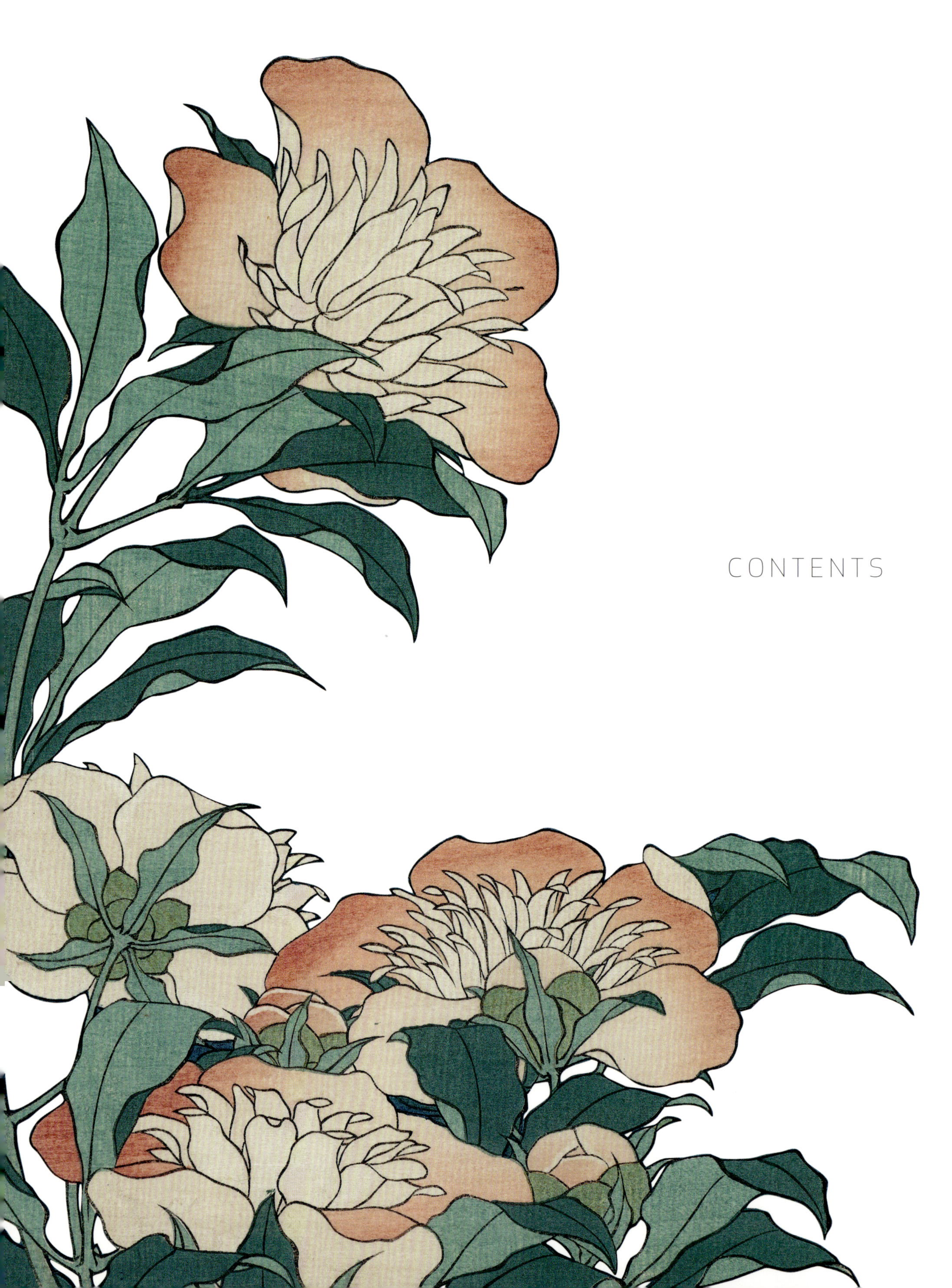

CONTENTS

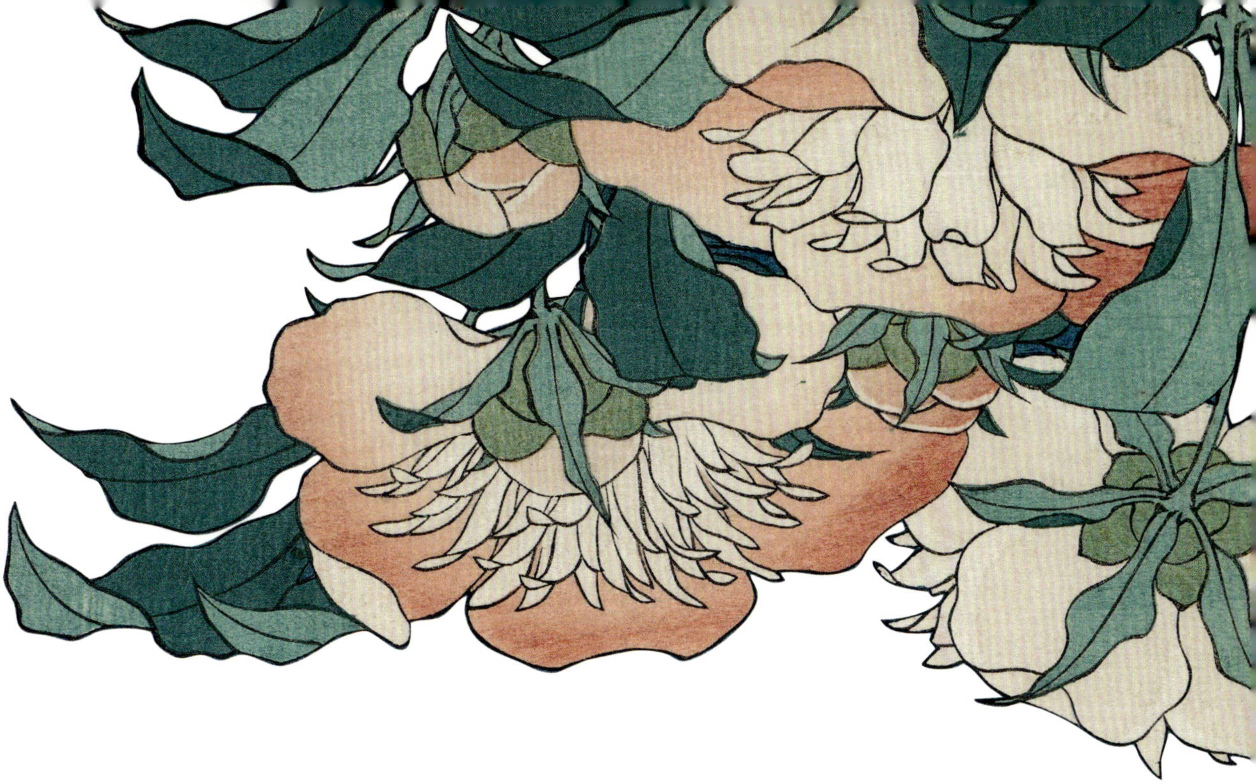

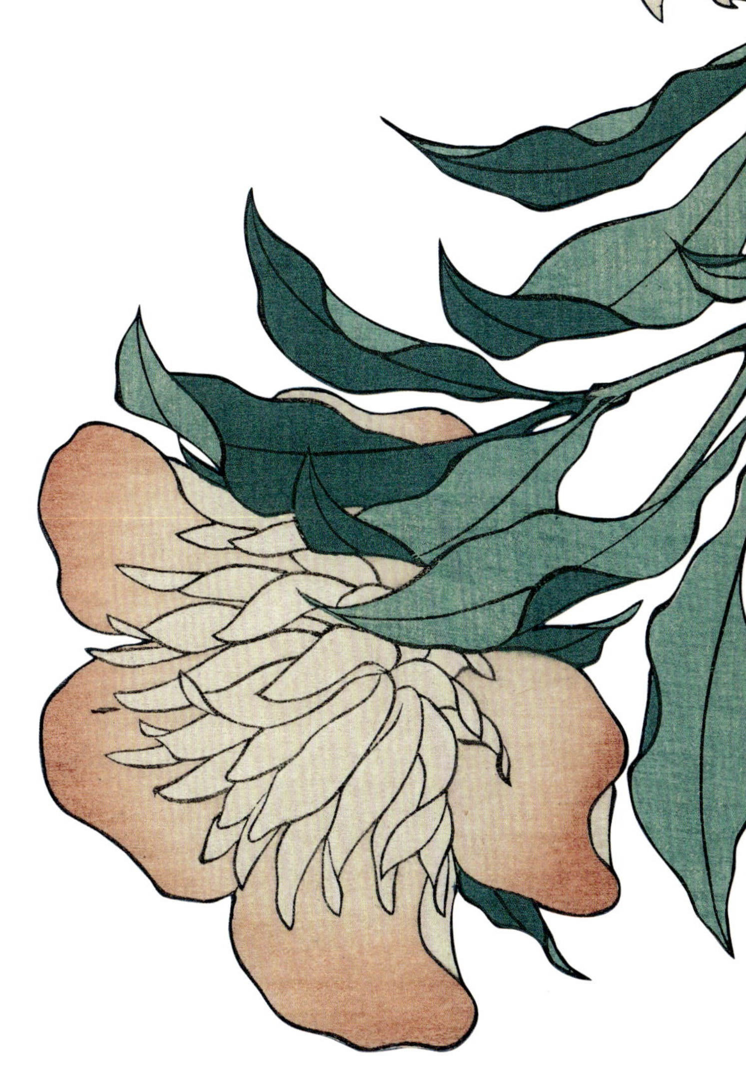

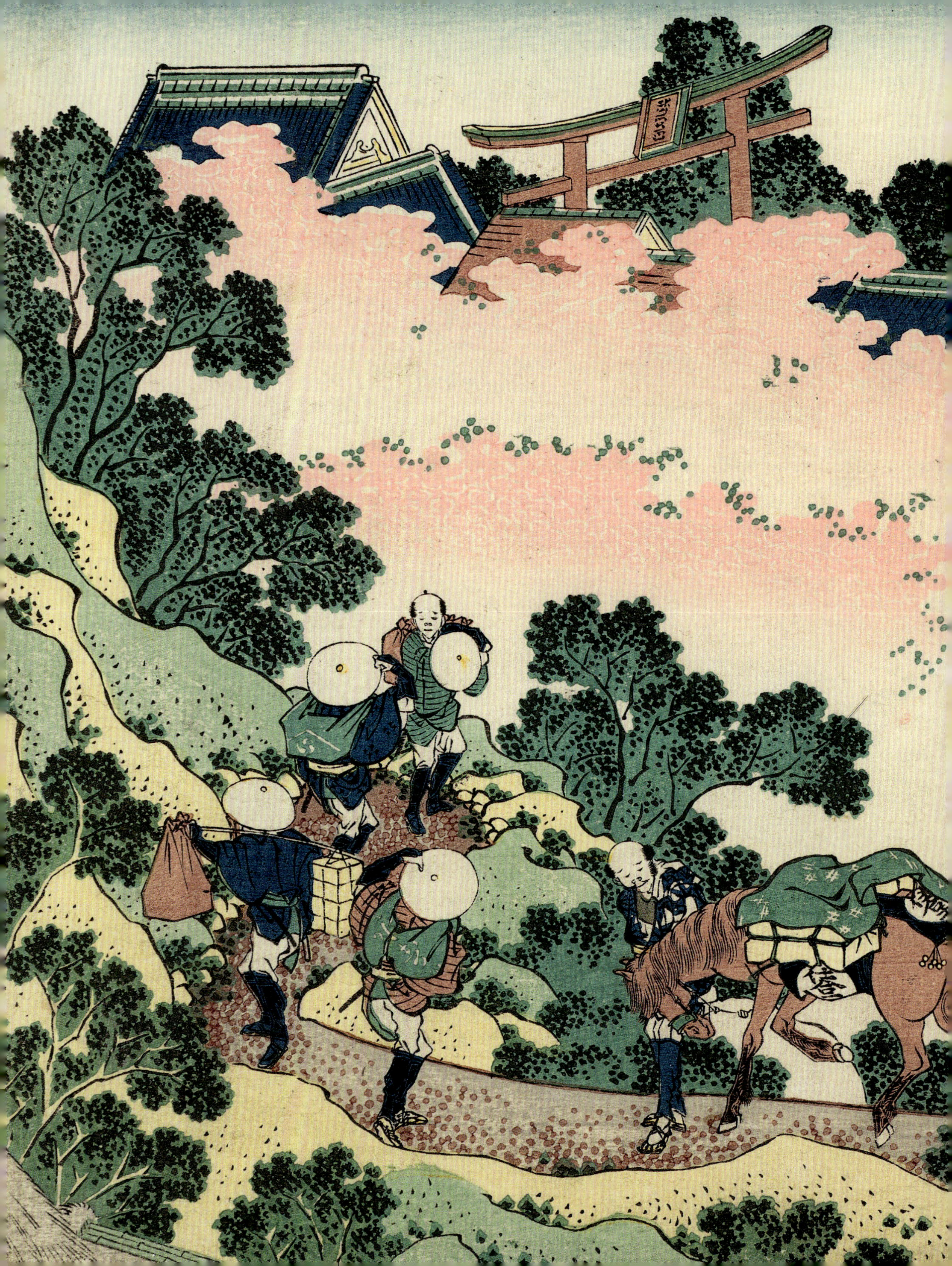

DIRECTOR'S FOREWORD

The remarkable achievements of Katsushika Hokusai, who created one of the world's indelible images in *The Great Wave*, include numerous paintings, woodblock prints, and book illustrations. The first museum exhibition of Hokusai's work anywhere in the world was *Hokusai and His School*, held at the Museum of Fine Arts, Boston, in 1892–93. Today, more than 120 years later, we are proud to present a comprehensive Hokusai retrospective drawn entirely from the MFA's own collection of Japanese art, the largest and finest outside Japan.

This publication and the exhibition it accompanies also commemorate the centennial of the largest gift of Japanese art ever made to the Museum, donated by Dr. William Sturgis Bigelow in 1911. Bigelow lived in Japan from 1882 to 1889, where he joined a congenial group of scholars and collectors with ties to Boston. Over the last century, more than two hundred additional donors have been inspired by Bigelow and other pioneer enthusiasts of Japanese art, and have further enriched our holdings through gifts of art and funds for acquisitions. For the book and exhibition, the most striking and unusual examples have been selected from some 150 paintings, 1200 woodblock prints, and 360 illustrated printed books by Hokusai at the MFA. This publication was generously supported by the Andrew W. Mellon Publications Fund. The exhibition was made possible thanks to generous support from the Jean S. and Frederic A. Sharf Exhibition Fund. We are proud to continue Boston's long tradition of delighting art lovers with the ingenious works of Hokusai.

MALCOLM ROGERS
Ann and Graham Gund Director
Museum of Fine Arts, Boston

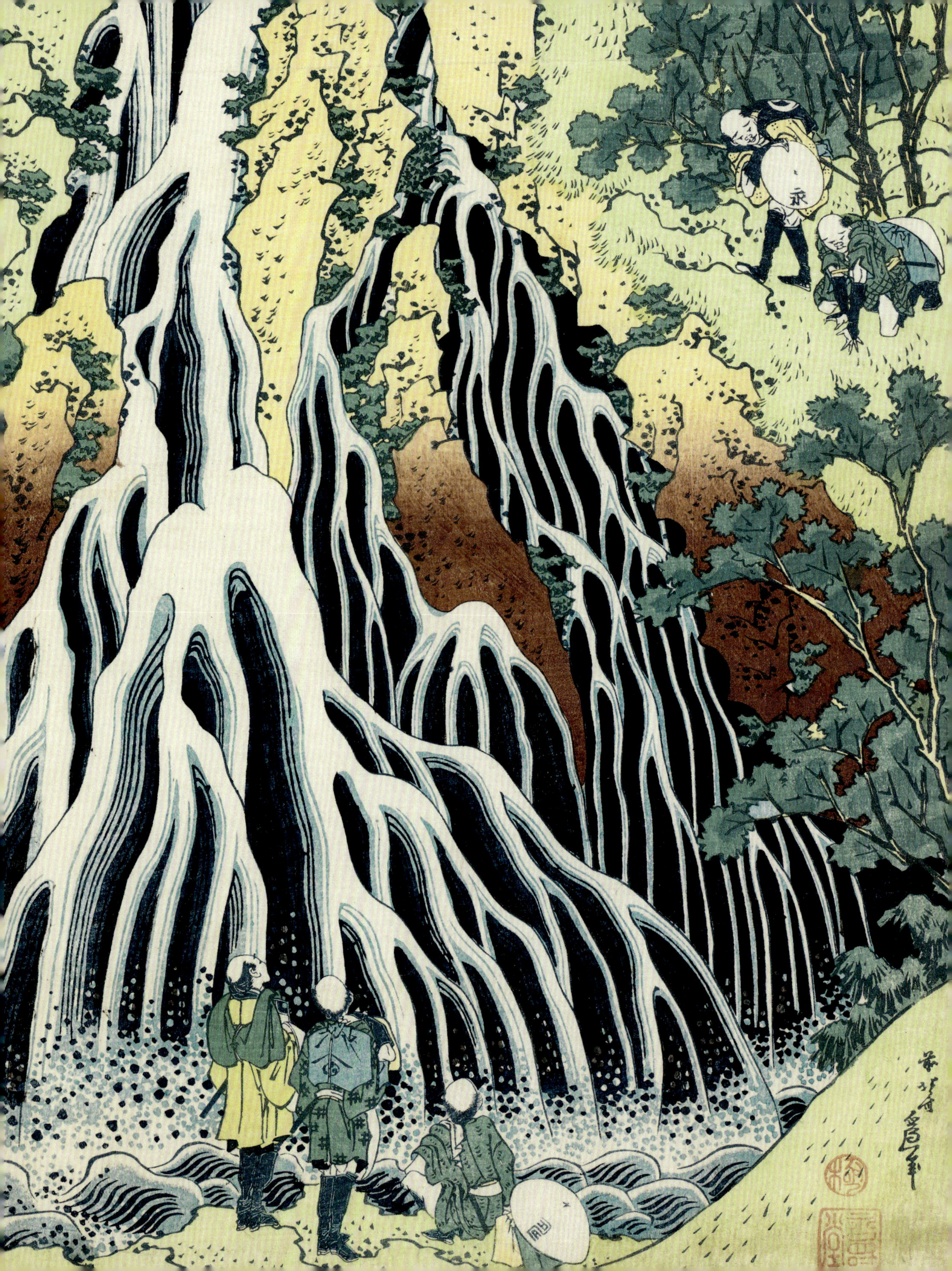

INGENIOUS HOKUSAI

Over a century and a half after his death, Katsushika Hokusai (1760–1849) is still by far the most popular of all Japanese artists. A major source of inspiration for the Japonisme craze in Europe and America in the late nineteenth century, his work continues to be known and loved around the world today. Contemporary artists make witty references to such iconic works as the color woodblock print nicknamed *The Great Wave* (cat. 20), from the series *Thirty-Six Views of Mount Fuji*, secure in the knowledge that the image will be understood by their own audiences. A prolific and versatile artist, Hokusai was not only a brilliant designer of single-sheet prints and illustrations for printed books, but also a superb painter and a gifted teacher, who passed on his skills directly to his many pupils and indirectly to the far more numerous readers of his how-to-draw books. This publication explores the wide range of Hokusai's artistic production in terms of one of his most remarkable characteristics: his intellectual ingenuity. As he drew, the self-styled "Man Mad about Drawing" must have been thinking constantly about how best to present his subjects—how to depict human bodies in motion, how to combine figures and landscapes, how to represent three-dimensional objects on two-dimensional surfaces, when to use the techniques of illusionism, and when to adjust reality for greater visual or emotional effect.

Hokusai lived at a time when Japan was still officially closed to the outside world; he had been dead for four years when Commodore Matthew Perry and his fleet arrived in Japan in 1853 to reopen the country to general trade. Nevertheless, Hokusai was keenly aware of the limited number of Western goods and concepts that the Dutch traders had been allowed to import to the city of Nagasaki while he lived. He was fascinated with mechanical devices, mathematics, and especially optical technology; lenses, eyeglasses, microscopes, and telescopes all appear in his prints. As a young man, he designed prints with exaggerated Western-style vanishing-point perspective, featuring receding lines converging on a low horizon, for use in toy peep shows. Decades later, he incorporated this way of seeing the world—by now thoroughly familiar to Japanese viewers—into his landscape prints, as did other artists of the ukiyo-e school. The enthusiastic reception of ukiyo-e landscape prints by Western artists and connoisseurs of the late nineteenth century must have had much to do with the fact that the treatment of space in the prints was easily understandable to them (as opposed to, for example, paintings using traditional Asian perspective with distant objects placed high in the picture plane, so that to Western eyes the ground seems to be tilted up).

The universal appeal of Hokusai's compositions also has much to do with their strong internal structure. Many prints in the *Fuji* series explicitly contrast the striking triangular shape of the mountain with triangles, rectangles, trapezoids, or curved shapes formed by other elements of the design. Careful examination of his nature studies and human figures shows that they, too, often have an underlying geometric structure. For example, the windblown flora in *Poppies* (cat. 33) form a spiral shape strongly reminiscent

Detail of cat. 30

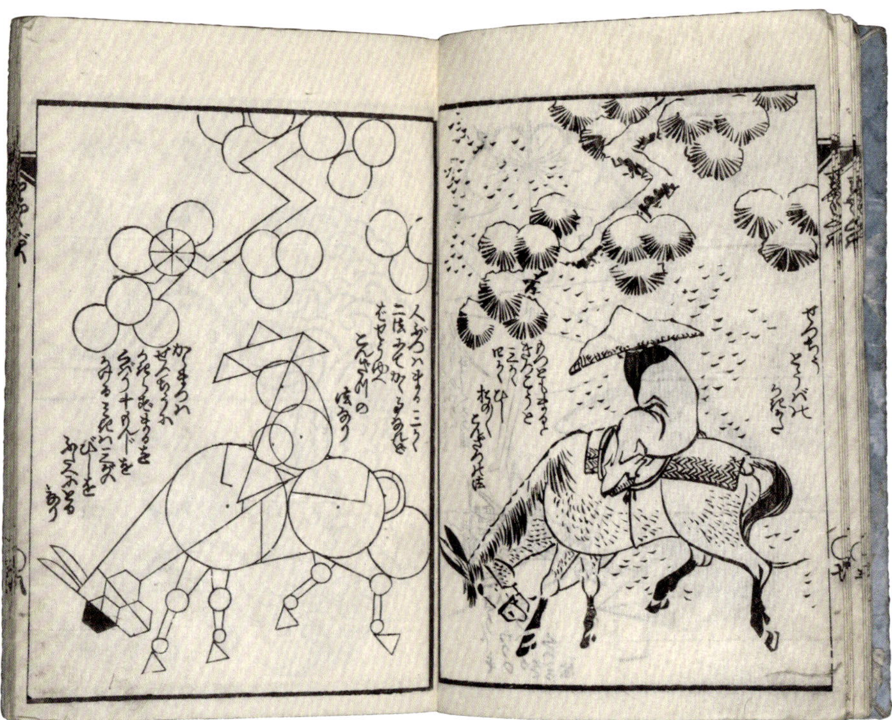

Fig. 1 | ***Quick Lessons in Simplified Drawing, Part One*** **(*Ryakuga haya-oshie, shohen*), 1812, woodblock-printed book, each page: 18.4 x 13 cm (7¼ x 5⅛ in.)**

of *The Great Wave*. The first volume of a book of instructions for self-taught artists, *Quick Lessons in Simplified Drawing* (*Ryakuga haya-oshie*, 1812), includes numerous examples of figures broken down into simplified geometric shapes to aid visual comprehension, showing that Hokusai did indeed envision images explicitly in geometric terms (fig. 1).[1]

Hokusai was constantly aware of the relationship between three-dimensional objects and two-dimensional pictorial surfaces, and he approached the problem from both directions. He painted not only on flat surfaces of paper or silk but on the rounded shapes of festival lanterns. In the early 1800s he was one of the leading designers of the toy prints known today as *tatebanko*, which were intended to be cut apart and glued together to form small three-dimensional dioramas. Just as his designs for the tatebanko moved from two dimensions into three, his landscape prints convincingly rendered three-dimensional scenes on flat, two-dimensional sheets of paper. (He would undoubtedly have scored an extremely high mark on the spatial reasoning section of a present-day aptitude test.)

The interplay of reality and illusion was also of great interest to Hokusai. He sometimes deliberately simplified or distorted landscape elements in the interest of creating a more interesting picture. Conversely, he applied his ability to draw convincing figures to the creation of wonderful ghosts and monsters that combine Japanese tradition with his own fertile imagination. The fabulous creatures in his paintings—dragons, lions, phoenixes—are plausible to the viewer because they are based on Hokusai's many years of observation and depiction of real animals moving in three-dimensional space.

The relationship between texts and images appealed to Hokusai on many levels. The brushstrokes used in Japanese calligraphy are exactly the same as those used in painting, and volume 2 of *Quick Lessons in Simplified Drawing*, published in 1814, includes examples of pictures built up from written characters, suggesting that anyone who can write can also draw (fig. 2). Pictures playfully constructed from words appear among Hokusai's own prints and paintings.

On a different level of text-image interaction, Hokusai was famous in his own time as a book illustrator. Extensive experience in book illustration may have given rise to another one of Hokusai's interests, the creation of a lengthy series of related images. He seems to have been

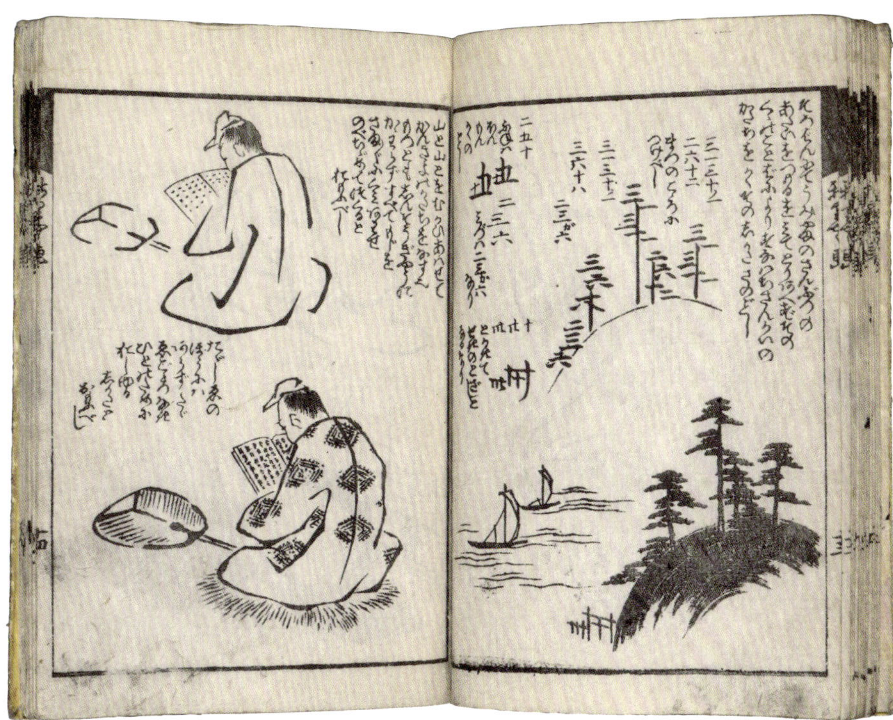

Fig. 2 | ***Quick Lessons in Simplified Drawing, Part Two (Ryakuga haya-oshie, kōhen)*, 1814, woodblock-printed book, each page: 18.6 x 13.2 cm ($7\frac{5}{16}$ x $5\frac{3}{16}$ in.)**

the first artist to design single-sheet prints showing the fifty-three stations of the Tōkaidō Road, a theme later made famous by his younger colleague and rival Utagawa Hiroshige (1797–1858). Likewise, his designs for toy prints included a travel board game with small landscape designs in a series. The concept came to fruition in 1830 with the *Fuji* series—forty-six separate scenes connected by the unifying motif of the great mountain—which made landscape a major theme in ukiyo-e prints for the first time.

Hokusai's cleverness manifested itself not only in his artistic productions but also in his approach to publicizing his work and pleasing his fans. The most outstanding examples of his gift for publicity are his public performances of gigantic paintings several stories tall, each made (with the help of his pupils) in a single day before a large audience. Hokusai gave private performances as well and was often invited to create paintings on the spot in commissioned appearances at gatherings of the intellectual elite. The most famous of the many tales of Hokusai's wit and resourcefulness is the anecdote of his appearance before the shogun himself. Hokusai is said to have brought a chicken with him to the event. When his turn came to demonstrate his painting skills, he first painted a long blue streak on a sheet of paper, then dipped the chicken's feet in red paint and let it run across the paper. The result, he announced, was a painting of the traditional poetic theme of Maple Leaves on the Tatsuta River. Of course, only an artist who was already famous for his skills (and his eccentricity) could have garnered praise for displaying his wit instead.

Throughout his long life, Hokusai was intensely aware of the world around him. He constantly sketched scenes of nature and of human activity, publishing his drawings on their own in works such as *Hokusai Sketchbooks* (*Hokusai manga*) and incorporating scenes of daily life into his landscape prints as well. He paid attention to technological developments in the printing industry, most notably the introduction of a new colorant, Prussian blue, which greatly facilitated the production of color landscape prints because of its resistance to fading. He was well aware of the work of other artists and was willing to copy their ideas, but he always added personal touches, so that his work outshines its sources. The wit, charm, and skill of Hokusai's works, and his ability to provide his viewers with pleasing surprises, captured the attention and admiration both of his contemporaries and of millions more viewers distant from him in space and time but united in visual delight.

HOKUSAI'S WORLD

At the time of Hokusai's birth in 1760, his home city of Edo (modern Tokyo) had a population of roughly one million and was probably the largest city in the world. Edo was the seat of government of the shogun, the hereditary military dictator who ruled in the name of the figurehead emperor in Kyoto, the ancient capital located some 230 miles to the west. According to the Confucian philosophy of the shogunate, Japanese society was divided into four classes: the ruling class of the samurai, formerly warriors but now hereditary bureaucrats; the peasantry, who in theory comprised the second most important group because they produced food, a basic necessity of life; the artisans; and finally the merchants, who were ranked at the bottom because they did not produce anything but lived off of the work of others. In practice, however, the more successful merchants were rapidly becoming as affluent as the lower-ranking samurai, and sometimes more so. The tension between the regulations of the class system and the realities of the new cash economy was a major influence on the art of the Edo period (1615–1868).

The shoguns of the Tokugawa clan, which came to power in 1615, instituted two major policies that had far-reaching effects on the society of the Edo period. To consolidate and strengthen their control of Japan, the Tokugawa shoguns limited contact with the outside world to a very narrow window centered on the city of Nagasaki. A series of edicts issued in the 1630s strictly banned Christianity and expelled all Europeans except the Dutch, putting an abrupt end to a century of extensive contact with Europe that had begun in the 1540s. Even the Dutch—who were deemed acceptable as trading partners because they had never engaged in religious proselytizing—were confined to the island of Dejima in Nagasaki Harbor, traveling to Edo just once a year to report to the shogun on events in the outside world.

Merchants from Korea and China were also required to stay in Nagasaki, and official embassies from Korea and the semi-independent Ryukyu Islands occasionally visited Edo. (Japan did not, however, have official diplomatic relations with China because the Tokugawa shogunate did not recognize the legitimacy of the Qing dynasty, which had overthrown the Ming dynasty in 1644.) Other than these very limited contacts, no foreigners were allowed to enter Japan, and no Japanese were permitted to travel abroad. The laws were strictly enforced. For Hokusai and his contemporaries, imported foreign goods and ideas had a special glamour in part because they came from mysterious, forbidden places.

The second Tokugawa policy that profoundly affected the social development of the Edo period was the policy of "alternate attendance" (*sankin kōtai*), requiring all of the feudal lords (daimyo) who governed the provinces on behalf of the shogun to spend alternate years administering their domains and attending the court of the shogun. The wives and children of the daimyo remained in Edo at all times, as de facto hostages of the shogun. The need to maintain two suitably impressive households and to travel back and forth between them in lavish style consumed much of the daimyo's wealth and thereby discouraged them from raising armies to oppose the shogun, just as the ban on contact with the outside world prevented them from seeking foreign allies.

A side effect of the alternate attendance policy was that travel throughout Japan was greatly facilitated. The Tokugawa government maintained five major highways leading from Edo to various parts of the country; the most famous of these was the Tōkaidō, or Eastern Sea Road, the coastal route from Edo to Kyoto that is still the most heavily used artery of transportation in Japan. Each of the major highways offered officially designated rest stops at frequent intervals where travelers could eat, spend the night, perhaps hire a palanquin or a packhorse with a driver for the next stage of the trip, and shop for souvenirs. Tourism became increasingly popular during Hokusai's lifetime; he himself traveled on a number of occasions and frequently depicted travelers visiting famous scenic spots.

The daimyo were expected to travel with large retinues, which consisted largely of young, unmarried samurai, leading to a gender imbalance in the population of Edo. To promote orderly conduct in sexual matters as in other areas of life, the shogunate established official, licensed brothel quarters in all major cities, most notably the Yoshiwara in Edo. The patrons of the pleasure districts were not only samurai but also urban commoners of the artisan and merchant classes, called *chōnin*, or "town people." Forbidden to participate in government or to travel abroad, the newly affluent commoners spent their money on the entertainments available in large cities, including the Kabuki theater, sumo wrestling matches, carnivals and special exhibitions on the grounds of Buddhist temples, restaurants, stores

Cut-out facsimile of cat. 15

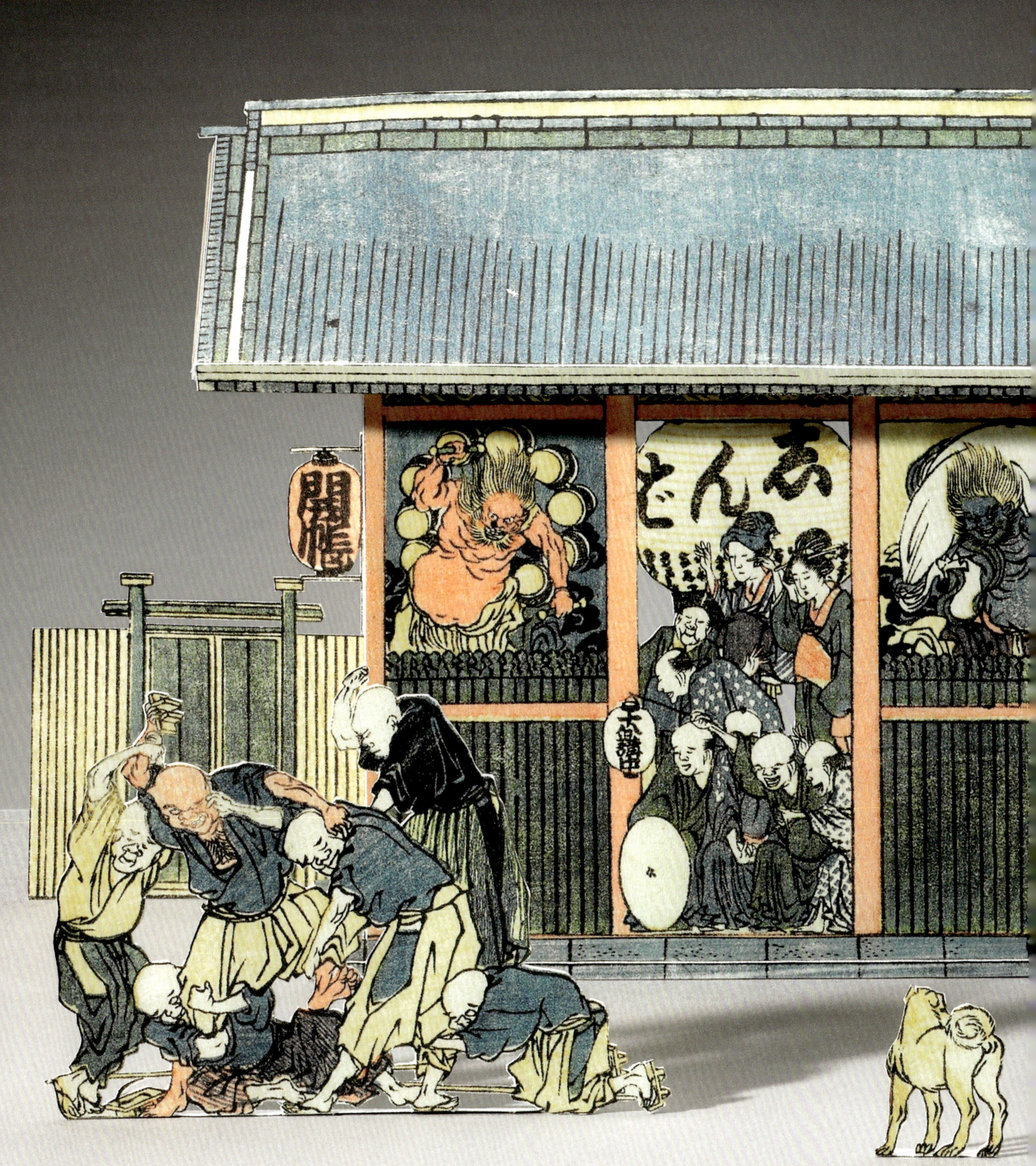

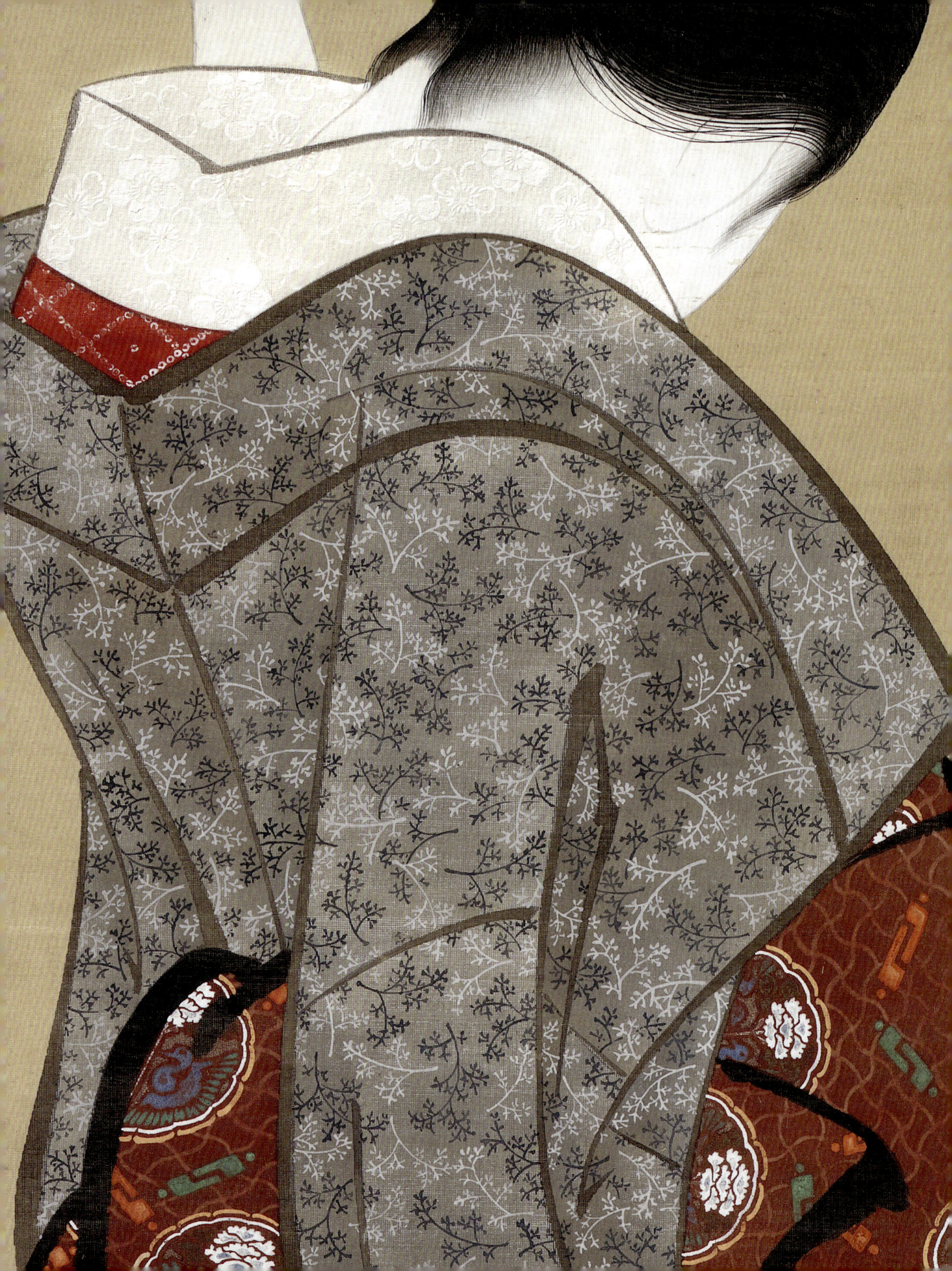

selling fashionable clothing and accessories, and so on. The term Floating World (*ukiyo*) was originally applied to the specific areas of the cities where such amusements could be found, but it soon came to refer to the world of urban pleasures in general. Ukiyo-e, or Pictures of the Floating World, was the name of the school of art—which included paintings, illustrated printed books, and woodblock prints—that depicted this chic new lifestyle.

Hokusai was trained in the traditions of the ukiyo-e school, and his early works included numerous examples of the two subjects most often depicted by ukiyo-e artists of the eighteenth century: Kabuki actors and beautiful women. Later, during Hokusai's mature period, the repertoire of ukiyo-e artists expanded, so that subjects that had previously been of only minor importance became prominent subgenres in a new, broader field of ukiyo-e. Hokusai himself was responsible for the sudden popularity of both landscapes and nature subjects (known in East Asia as bird-and-flower pictures), and he contributed significantly to the rise of historical subjects, especially those featuring great warriors of the past. The later work of Hokusai and his younger contemporaries of the nineteenth century expanded the boundaries of the Floating World far beyond the amusement centers of Edo in both space and time, depicting not just the immediate surroundings of the citizens of Edo but the realms of their imaginations as well.

HOKUSAI'S LIFE

The main sources of information about Hokusai's life are his own words, especially the prefaces and colophons of his picture books, and the biography published in 1893, *Katsushika Hokusai den* by Iijima Kyoshin. Written just over forty years after Hokusai's death in 1849, it includes reminiscences by people who had met the artist in person. Hokusai is also listed in the later editions of *Thoughts on Ukiyo-e* (*Ukiyo-e ruikō*, notes by various authors originally compiled in manuscript form between about 1800 and 1868), the standard source of biographical information on ukiyo-e artists, and anecdotes about his activities as a famous artist appear in assorted memoirs and histories of the Edo period. The sources do not always agree with each other, but the general outline of his life has emerged.[2]

Hokusai was born in 1760 in the Honjō district of Edo. His original family name was Kawamura, and his childhood name was Tokitarō. At an early age, he was adopted by his uncle Nakajima Ise, a mirror polisher in the service of the shogun, who wanted an heir to succeed him in his prestigious position. Hokusai took a new, more adult personal name as well and was known as Nakajima Tetsuzō during his teens. Hokusai's lifelong fascination with reflections and optical effects of many kinds may well be related to his early experience with mirrors. It is also likely that he received a good education, since if he had succeeded his uncle, he would have associated with people of high rank.

The education of the child who would become Hokusai would have begun with reading and writing, a complicated matter in Japan, since two different writing systems were (and are) used simultaneously: the set of forty-seven phonetic symbols known as *kana*, each representing one syllable of the Japanese language, and the thousands of Chinese characters known as *kanji* in Japanese, in which each symbol represents an entire word. In Japan, written Chinese—read aloud with Japanese pronunciation—played a role somewhat similar to that of Latin in Europe; it was the language of Buddhist liturgy and of all official and legal matters, and many words derived from Chinese became part of the everyday Japanese language. Stories from ancient China were familiar to educated Japanese, just as Greek and Roman mythology and history were known to their European counterparts.

Learning to write automatically meant learning to draw, for the materials used were exactly the same: ink, brush, and paper. Hokusai noted in the preface to the first volume of his picture book *One Hundred Views of Mount Fuji* (*Fugaku hyakkei*, 1834) that he had been drawing enthusiastically since the age of six, the age when his formal education would have begun and he would have been trained to hold a brush.[3] In all of the East Asian cultures, the relationship between the arts of calligraphy and painting is an especially close one, since the fluid brushstrokes that form the written characters are the basis for pictorial art as well. Hokusai explicitly invoked the close relationship between letters and pictures in a number of his later works.

Given Hokusai's early display of drawing talent and the relatively high status of his adopted family, it is somewhat surprising that he did not receive training from the Kano school of art, the official painters to the shogun and the dominant force in art education in Edo-period Japan. As far as we know, however, young Nakajima Tetsuzō had no formal training in drawing and painting until he joined

Detail of cat. 1

the studio of the ukiyo-e artist Katsukawa Shunshō (1726–1792) at the age of nineteen. By that time, the future Hokusai had already parted ways with his uncle, or at least with his uncle's profession. For some reason, the prospect of becoming a professional mirror polisher, despite the status and security of the position, did not appeal to him. Perhaps he thought that metal mirrors were becoming an obsolete technology, given the increasing popularity in Edo of the silvered glass mirrors imported by the Dutch. He may also have had a personality clash with his uncle, since personal relationships seem to have been important to him and to have affected his career choices on other occasions.

As a teenager, Hokusai found jobs in the flourishing publishing business. The changes that occurred in Japanese society under Tokugawa rule—increased urbanization, the development of a cash economy, the rise of the middle class—led to an increase in the rate of literacy and to the production of woodblock-printed books catering to the newly literate urban commoners. The books included popular versions of classic works, retellings of historical tales, and modern stories of fashionable life in the Floating World, as well as nonfiction works such as travel guides and how-to books. Both fiction and nonfiction works were heavily illustrated, and books consisting largely of pictures were popular as well. In the late seventeenth century, canny publishers realized that printed pictures could be sold separately as a new product line in addition to books, and the ukiyo-e print was born.

The 1893 biography by Iijima stated that in his early teens Hokusai worked for a lending library, and several other sources confirm that from the age of sixteen to nineteen, he was employed as a block carver. Given these early experiences, Hokusai was perhaps even more aware than most ukiyo-e artists of the collective nature of print production. The artist's drawing for a book page or single-sheet print was turned over to the block carver, who would glue it facedown to a wooden block and carve through the thin paper, following the ink lines that were clearly visible when the paper was dampened. In the case of a color woodblock print, impressions taken from the main block would be used to carve a separate printing block for each color, a method that came into commercial use in 1765, just as little Hokusai was learning to hold a brush. The block or blocks then went to a professional printer, who laid a sheet of paper on the inked block and rubbed the back of the sheet with a pad to make a clear impression; no printing press was needed. The entire process was controlled by the publisher, who employed the artist, carver, and printer, and sold the finished works in his store.

Hokusai officially became an ukiyo-e artist in 1779, when he joined the studio of Katsukawa Shunshō, the most prominent print designer of the time. Shunshō had made the Katsukawa school the leader in prints of Kabuki actors by drawing actors with recognizable, individual facial features, not just generic handsome faces. The new member of the school quickly mastered the art of drawing likenesses and designed a number of actor prints with the signature Shunrō, using, as was customary, one written character taken from the name of his teacher (the Shun of Shunshō) and one different character (rō). During his years as a Katsukawa artist, from 1780 to 1794, the future Hokusai also drew illustrations for about fifty books.[4]

During the 1780s, Shunshō let his senior pupils such as Shunkō (1743–1812) and Shun'ei (1762–1819) take over much of the business of designing actor prints while he concentrated on his other specialty, exquisitely detailed paintings of beautiful women in sumptuous kimonos, painted on silk using gorgeous, expensive mineral colors. Already in 1775, a playful poem had described a painting by Shunshō as worth a thousand pieces of gold.[5] While this amount was probably poetic exaggeration, it is clear that these paintings were very expensive, luxurious works. Only a few, relatively modest paintings with Hokusai's early signature Katsukawa Shunrō have survived, but the mastery of technique that Hokusai displays in his later paintings must surely have been learned from Shunshō during this time.

In addition to prints of actors, sumo wrestlers, beautiful women in urban settings, children at play, historical warriors, and Chinese scenes, during his Shunrō period Hokusai designed a number of perspective prints, a genre that was not a specialty of the Katsukawa school but rather was associated with the Utagawa school founded by Utagawa Toyoharu (1735–1814). These prints, known as "floating pictures" (*uki-e*), used an exaggerated form of Western vanishing-point perspective to create startlingly realistic scenes. The origin of the term *uki-e* is uncertain, but it may be related to the fact that such works were sometimes viewed in toy peep shows; the viewer looked through an imported lens to see the scene "floating" as if in a small window to an imagined world. Perspective prints had been introduced to Japan around 1740 and went through several cycles of popularity. By designing these prints, Hokusai became thoroughly familiar with the principles of Western-style perspective, which he later incorporated into his landscape prints.

Very little is known about Hokusai's personal life, but he seems to have been married, widowed, and married again during his Shunrō period. His two wives gave him a total of five children, two sons and three daughters (and possibly, according to some sources, a fourth daughter who died young), but the exact dates of their lifespans are unknown.

Shunshō died in 1792, and Hokusai's position as a Katsukawa school artist deteriorated. He left the Katsukawa school altogether and ceased to use the name Shunrō at the end of 1794. The reasons are unclear but may have had to do with friction with the senior pupils of Shunshō, as several anecdotes suggest. Fortunately for Hokusai — and for his wife and children — he found a congenial new position with another family of artists, the Tawaraya.[6] The head of the family, Tawaraya Sōri I, had died in 1782, leaving a very young heir. Hokusai was apparently hired by the family to train this young heir, now approaching adulthood, and was permitted to use the Sōri name himself until the heir was ready to assume his responsibilities. From 1794 to 1798, under the name Sōri, Hokusai became a very successful designer of *surimono*, privately commissioned prints. He also produced many excellent paintings, using fine materials that were presumably provided by the Tawaraya family, and passed on to his new pupil the skills that he had learned from the late Katsukawa Shunshō.

Because they were not sold commercially but were produced to order for private patrons, surimono were not subject to the sumptuary regulations that applied to other prints and could therefore be printed as lavishly as the patron desired. The patrons were most often members of amateur poetry clubs who competed with each other in composing *kyōka*, a kind of playful verse that used the same form as classical *waka* poetry — five lines in a pattern of 5, 7, 5, 7, and 7 syllables each — but used lighthearted, up-to-date topics and words instead of the strictly limited subjects of classical poetry. Small prints with poems and illustrations were exchanged between the club members at parties on special occasions, especially at New Year, then and now the most important holiday in Japan. Other surimono, with pictures in a long, narrow format that was folded into a small pamphlet, were illustrated programs for musical performances and various cultural events. In both the poetry and the pictures, innovation and cleverness were highly prized. Hokusai does not seem to have designed commercial prints during his Sōri period. This omission may have been due to a restriction imposed by the Tawaraya family; possibly they considered ordinary prints déclassé, although the elegant surimono were acceptable.

In the spring of 1798, the Tawaraya heir assumed the leadership of his family school and reclaimed the name Sōri. Hokusai announced the change of his own name to Hokusai Tokimasa in a surimono issued in the third month of 1798.[7] Like other Japanese artists of his time, Hokusai used multiple art names. The name Hokusai, literally Northern Studio, which had already been used as an alternate name during the Sōri period, now became his main art name. It was this name that was established as a household word, familiar to the general public as the name of a famous artist. Even after moving on to other art names, such as Taito (used 1810–1819), Iitsu (1819–1834), and Manji (1834–1849), he often included in his signatures the phrase "The Former Hokusai" (*Saki no Hokusai*) as a prefix to the current name.

Hokusai seems to have prospered not only professionally but also financially during his Sōri period. A 1798 city map indicated that someone named Kawamura owned two houses in Hokusai's home district of Warigesui in Honjō; however, we do not know whether this person was Hokusai, his elderly father, or some other individual who happened to have the same surname. Since Hokusai's financial fortunes went downhill in later years, despite his success as an artist, this may have been the most affluent period of his life. Certainly his many friendships among the kyōka poets, wealthy and well-educated men who fully appreciated his talents, had given him a solid basis for his future career.

Hokusai's middle years were a time of great creativity and exploration of artistic possibilities. While continuing to produce paintings, surimono, and book illustrations, he began to design commercial prints again. Some of the ideas that he had initially developed for surimono now started to appear in prints and books for the general public, such as the views of the city of Edo in his *Picture Book of the Two Banks of the Sumida River at a Glance* (*Ehon Sumidagawa ryōgan ichiran*), published about 1804, and the seven different small-format series that he designed around the same time, showing the fifty-three stations of the Tōkaidō road, the main highway between Edo and Kyoto (cats. 11 and 41). The earliest of these Tōkaidō series was a set of surimono with kyōka poems, later reissued as commercial prints

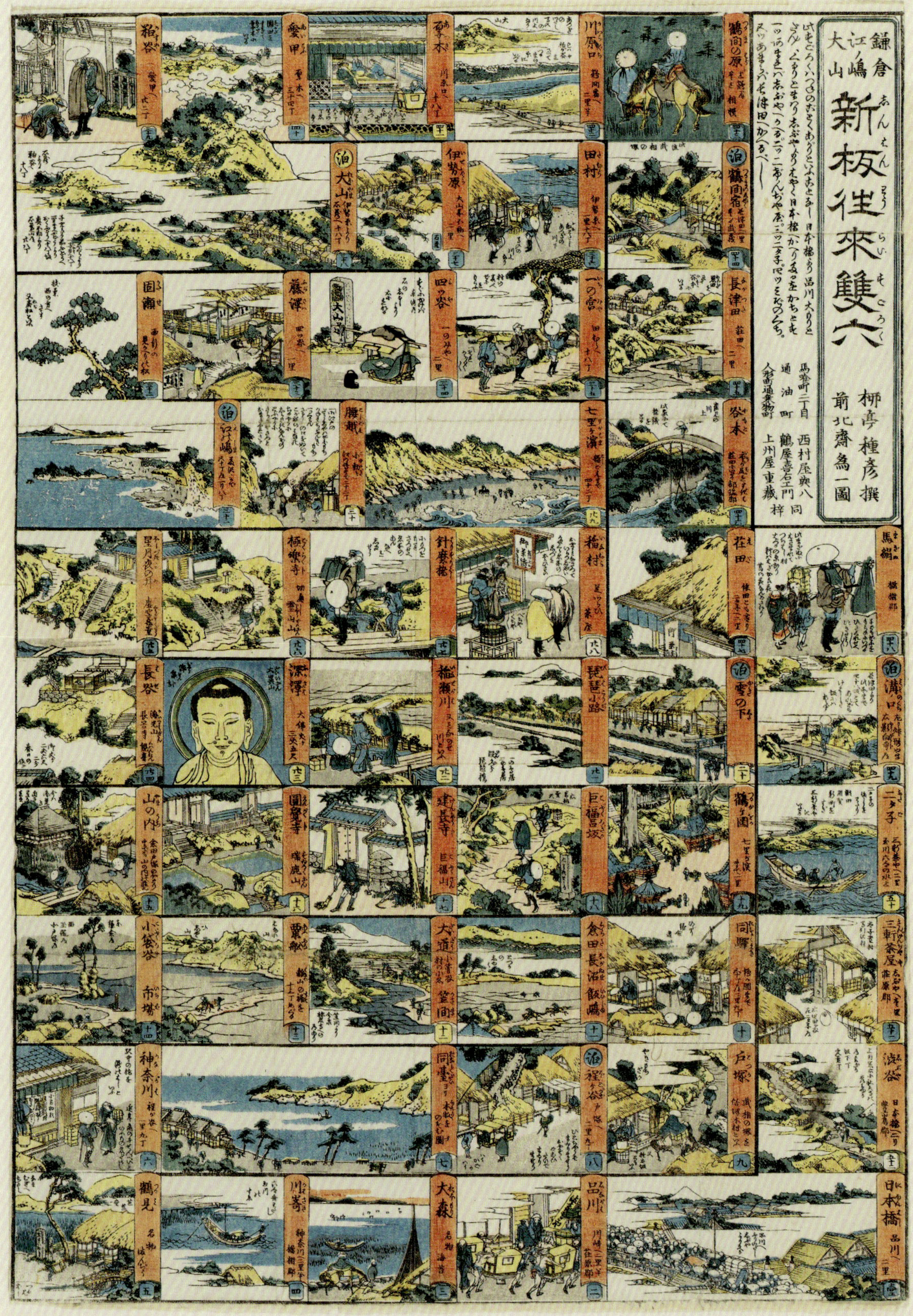
鎌倉
江ノ嶋
大山
新板往来雙六
柳亭種彦撰
前北斎為一圖
馬喰町二丁目 西村屋與八
通油町 鶴屋喜右エ門 同
人形町通乗物町 上州屋重蔵 梓
日本橋
品川
大森
川崎
鶴見
神奈川
戸塚
長谷
建長寺
圓覺寺
山の内
極樂寺
江ノ嶋
藤澤
大山
伊勢原
田村
一の宮
四ッ谷
長津田

without the poems. Also appearing as both surimono and commercial prints were landscapes that explicitly emulated the small Western-style etchings that were being sold in Edo at the time.

Hokusai also designed a board game focused around the motif of a journey, with one scene after another, showing the route of a pilgrimage from Edo to the pilgrimage sites of Kamakura, Enoshima, and Ōyama, and back to Edo again (fig. 3). The instructions inscribed on the game board explain that whereas most games show only a route going in a single direction, this one takes you back to the starting point; this realistic twist in game design may have been invented by Hokusai as a way of making his product distinctive. The game board, dating from the 1820s, represents another aspect of the same problem that Hokusai was considering in the cityscape book illustrations and the Tōkaidō prints: how to present a series of images that, while thematically related to each other, are different enough to hold the viewer's interest throughout the series.

Other examples of Hokusai's toy prints include puzzle pictures, such as the portraits of classical poets with the characters for their names hidden in their costumes, and a set of playing cards for a game based on the fifty-four chapters of *The Tale of Genji*, the eleventh-century novel long considered the greatest work of Japanese literature.[8] Above all, he became one of the top designers of cut-out dioramas. Methods for turning flat sheets of paper into three-dimensional scenes were as intriguing to him, it seems, as methods for rendering real-life, three-dimensional scenes on flat sheets of paper: the same sort of transformation operating in opposite directions.

In book illustration, Hokusai produced notable works in the genres of poetry books, adventure fiction, and instruction books for would-be artists. He continued to illustrate the short, graphic works of humorous fiction known as *kibyōshi* (literally "yellow covers") and even tried his hand at writing a few of them under the pseudonym Tokitarō Kako, using his childhood name. He also became very successful as an illustrator for a new type of fiction known as *yomihon* (literally "books for reading"), long, multivolume works in which text pages were more numerous than illustrations, with plots typically featuring fantastic adventures set in past centuries, often with supernatural elements. The leading author of this new type of fiction was Takizawa Bakin (1767–1848), and Hokusai illustrated many of his books. Hokusai's skill in drawing human figures in action and historical details of costumes and settings in both China and Japan made him the ideal choice for this work. The best-selling author and his illustrator were such a well-known combo that they appeared together in a publication of about 1845, *Extraordinary Persons of Japan* (*Nihon kijin den*), a picture book of noted eccentrics of Japan from ancient times to the present (fig. 4).[9]

Fig. 3 | ***Newly Published Board Game of a Journey to and from Kamakura, Enoshima, and Ōyama* (*Kamakura Enoshima Ōyama shinpan ōrai sugoroku*), 1820s, woodblock print, 62.2 x 43.2 cm (24 1/2 x 17 in.)**

In addition to teaching his own pupils, Hokusai began to produce how-to-draw books for the general public. The earliest examples, such as *Quick Lessons in Simplified Drawing*, presented clever tricks for creating pictures from written words or geometric shapes; but most were simply model books presenting a wide assortment of pictures for aspiring artists to copy. Several of Hokusai's picture books were specifically intended as sources of inspiration for craftsmen creating works such as decorated pipes or combs — and perhaps for customers who might wish to commission such elegant objects.

By far the most popular of all the picture books, considered one of his great masterpieces, was the multivolume series *Hokusai Sketchbooks* (*Hokusai manga*), published in ten volumes from 1814 to 1819, with five volumes added in 1834 to 1878 (cat. 39). The word *manga*, which has come to mean "comics" (i.e., stories told in pictures) in modern Japanese, was used in the Edo period to mean informal drawings, possibly preparatory sketches for paintings (the English word "cartoon" has a somewhat similar history). Each volume contains an assortment of human figures, nature studies, landscapes, illustrations of well-known stories, and other subjects; every viewer is likely to find something of special pleasure and interest. Not only were the books a huge success in Japan, they were taken to Europe by Philipp Franz von Siebold (1796–1866), a German physician employed by the Dutch who had some of the landscape scenes copied as illustrations for the influential book on Japan that he published in 1832. Some years later, around 1859, the "discovery" of a volume of *Hokusai Sketchbooks* by French artists began the Japonisme craze.[10]

Although Hokusai had no idea that his work would someday become popular in foreign countries, he was keenly aware of his audience at home in Japan and sought

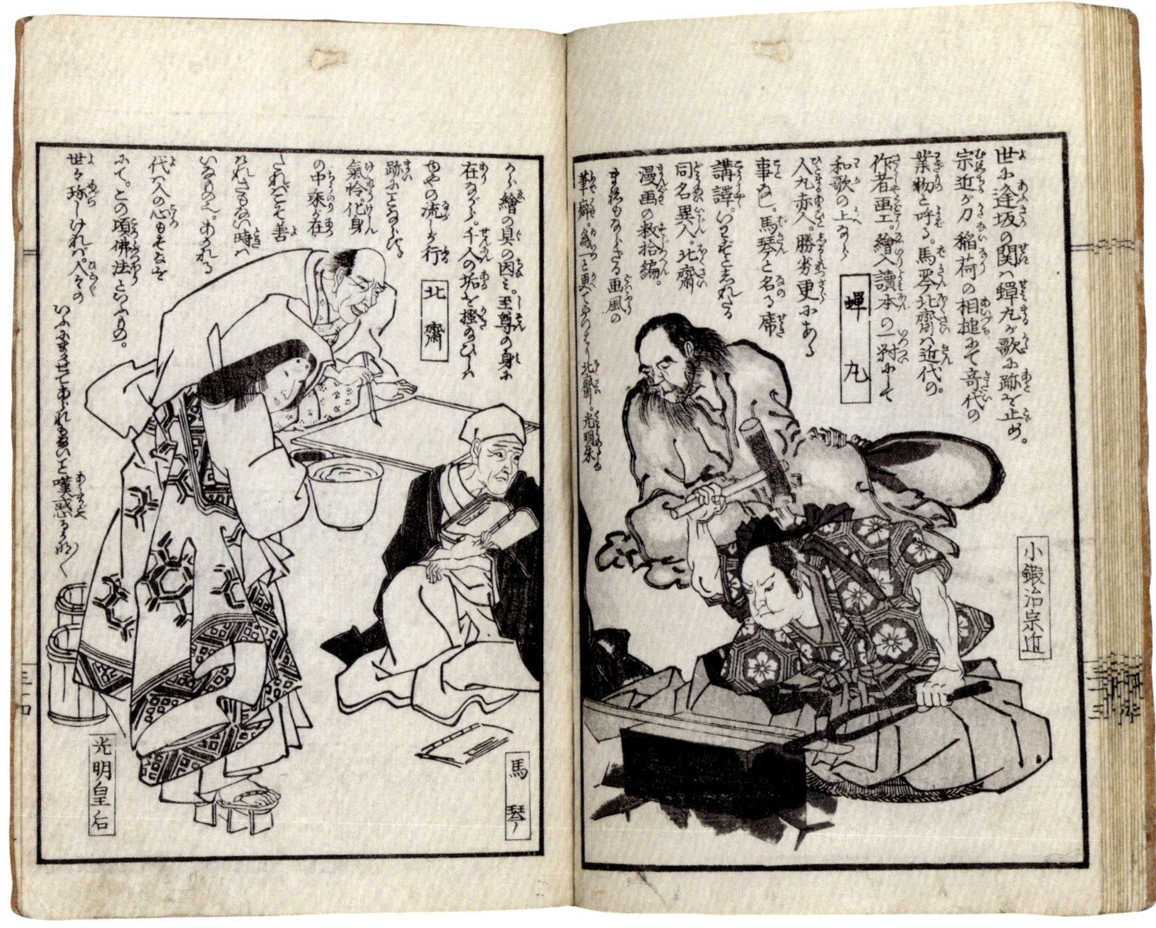

Fig. 4 | **Hokusai (at the upper left, drawn as he would have appeared several decades earlier) and Bakin (center) are shown together with the benevolent empress Kōmyō (701–760) and two legendary figures of the Heian period (794–1185), the blind poet Semimaru and the master swordsmith Kokaji Munechika. *Extraordinary Persons of Japan* (*Nihon kijin den*), illustrated by Utagawa Kuniyoshi (1797–1861), about 1845, woodblock-printed book, each page: 22.6 x 14.2 cm (8⅞ x 5 9/16 in.)**

clever ways to please them. In addition to cultivating a reputation for eccentricity, he was happy to promote himself still further by performing for large audiences. In 1804 he and his pupils created a gigantic painting of Bodhidharma (Daruma), the founder of Zen Buddhism, at the Gokoku-ji Temple in Edo (cat. 38). An even larger picture of the same subject was painted in 1817 in Nagoya, where his best-selling *Hoksuai Sketchbooks* had originated, as part of a publicity campaign for the ongoing publication of the series. The painting itself has not survived, but illustrations in the 1893 biography, based on drawings made at the time, show the completed painting, some three stories tall, being hauled up onto scaffolding for display. Hokusai is said to have done several other giant paintings as well.

In 1820 Hokusai changed his art name to Iitsu (literally "One Again") to mark his completion of a full sixty-year calendrical cycle and the beginning of a new one. The new cycle began well, with commissions for major surimono series in 1821 and 1822, but over the course of the decade, a number of misfortunes befell Hokusai and his family. In 1822 the marriage between his eldest daughter and his pupil Yanagawa Shigenobu ended in divorce. In 1826 Hokusai himself was seriously ill, and in 1827 his wife died. In 1829 and 1830 unspecified but serious misbehavior on the part of his grandson, the son of Shigenobu and his eldest daughter, led to financial disaster for Hokusai. Hokusai's response to these troubles seems to have been to pour his energy into his work. In 1830, at the age of seventy, he began the project for which he is best known, the color print series *Thirty-Six Views of Mount Fuji* (*Fugaku sanjūrokkei*).

One major source of inspiration for the *Fuji* series seems to have been the introduction of a new pigment to the printmakers' palette, the synthetic color known to the Japanese as Berlin blue and to Europeans as Prussian blue. Invented in the eighteenth century, the pigment had already been known in Japan for some time, but when the Chinese as well as the Dutch began to import it, the price dropped sufficiently to make it practical for use in prints. Around 1830 there was a craze for "blue-printed pictures" (*aizuri-e*) done entirely, or almost entirely, in shades of blue.[11]

Either Hokusai or his publisher, Nishimuraya Yohachi of the Eijudō publishing house, must have realized that a blue pigment that did not fade easily was ideal for producing color landscape prints. Hokusai, with his years of experience designing uki-e and landscape scenes for book illustrations, was the perfect choice for this bold new experiment in commercial publishing, offering the public a new kind of single-sheet print: full-size landscape prints issued as a series, with multiple variations on a unifying theme, focusing sometimes on the landscape itself and sometimes on the figures inhabiting it. The first designs in the series were printed almost entirely in shades of blue, to capitalize on the fad for the newly introduced pigment. A little later, when the public had become accustomed to the new colorant, additional colors were used for subsequent designs in the series, and for reprints of the earlier ones.

The great success of the *Fuji* series, with ten additional designs added as supplements to the first thirty-six, established landscape as a major new genre comparable to Kabuki prints and depictions of beautiful women. While Hokusai himself continued to design landscape series, such as the *Waterfalls*, he soon had competition from younger artists such as Hiroshige and Keisai Eisen (1790–1848). In particular, Hiroshige's series *Fifty-Three Stations of the Tōkaidō Road* (*Tōkaidō gojūsan tsugi*) of 1833–34 became the second great hit of the new landscape genre, comparable in popularity to Hokusai's *Thirty-Six Views of Mount Fuji*. Several decades earlier, Hokusai had pioneered the subject of the Tōkaidō as the basis for prints in series, but it is Hiroshige's version, printed in full color in the same horizontal *ōban* format as the *Fuji* series (about 10 by 15 inches), that became the most famous.

Two additional genres rose to popularity at around the same time as the landscape prints, and in both cases Hokusai played a key role. The new, brilliant color palette was ideal not only for landscapes but also for bird-and-flower prints, a minor area of subject matter that became a major one as a result of two series by Hokusai, untitled in Japanese, the *Large Flowers* in the horizontal ōban format and the *Small Flowers* in the vertical *chūban* format (half the size of ōban; about 10 by 7.5 inches). As in the case of the landscapes, other artists, especially Hiroshige, soon followed Hokusai's lead in designing nature studies.

The popularity of the genre known as warrior prints (*musha-e*), including not only actual battle scenes but various vignettes from both Japanese and Chinese history, began around 1827 when Utagawa Kuniyoshi (1797–1861) issued the first designs of a series showing the heroes of the great Chinese novel known in English as *The Water Margin*, or *Outlaws of the Marsh* (*Shui Hu Zhuan*; *Suikoden* in Japanese), the ancestor of all martial arts stories. Kuniyoshi's hit series was based on a new, popular Japanese translation of the Chinese novel intended for the general public, written by Bakin and illustrated by none other than Hokusai, who thus had a hand, indirectly, in the rise of a third genre of ukiyo-e print as well. Hokusai himself designed just one series of warrior prints in the ōban format, in the same burst of creativity that resulted in his landscapes and bird-and-flower prints.

The landscape prints that are the best-known part of Hokusai's prodigious output were produced in a relatively short span, from 1830 to about 1836. His final landscape series, *One Hundred Poems Explained by the Nurse* (*Hyakunin isshu uba ga etoki*), was never published in full, although Hokusai probably did complete all of the drawings for the series (cats. 47 and 48). The problem seems to have been primarily economic, and perhaps also a matter of personal relations. From 1833 to 1837, Japan suffered a severe economic depression. Crop failures due to flooding and cold weather led to widespread starvation in rural areas, particularly in northern Japan, and the effects were felt in Edo as well. The first five prints of the *One Hundred Poems* series were published in 1835 by Nishimuraya Yohachi of the Eijudō publishing house, the publisher of the *Fuji* series and many of Hokusai's books. In the following year, twenty-two prints in the series were issued, but with a slightly different form of the Eijudō trademark. The most likely explanation seems to be that Nishimuraya went

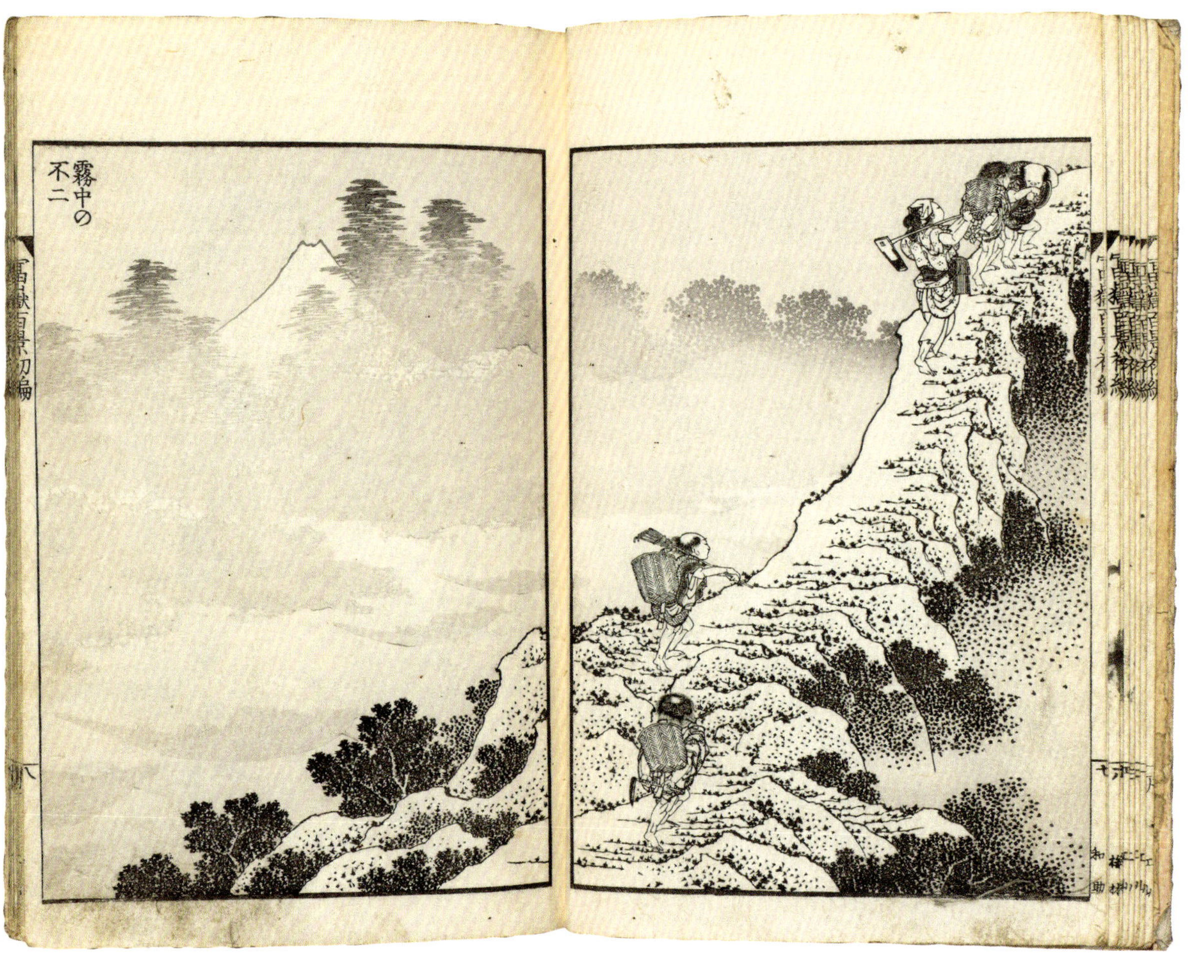

Fig. 5 | ***Fuji in Mist (Muchū no Fuji)*** **from volume 1 of** ***One Hundred Views of Mount Fuji*** **(*****Fugaku hyakkei*****), 1834, woodblock-printed book, each page: 22.5 x 15.5 cm (8 ⅞ x 6 ⅛ in.)**

bankrupt and his business, the Eijudō house, was taken over by another publisher, probably Iseya Sanjirō, who for some reason decided not to continue the series.

Similar problems befell the third volume of the book *One Hundred Views of Mount Fuji*, in which Hokusai continued to work out the visual ideas he had explored in the *Fuji* series of color prints. Volumes 1 and 2 had appeared in 1834 and 1835 (fig. 5), and the blocks for volume 3 were, according to one of Hokusai's letters, carved in 1835, but the third volume was not published at that time, presumably due to Nishimuraya's bankruptcy. Fortunately, it was eventually published by Eirakuya Tōshirō of Nagoya, who had been the copublisher, with Nishimuraya and others, of the first two volumes.

With the collapse of the plans for the *Hundred Poems* series, Hokusai gave up designing commercial prints almost completely. The market for privately commissioned surimono prints also disappeared as a result of the depression, depriving Hokusai of yet another source of income. In 1835–36 he was living just south of Edo in the town of Uraga (today a suburb of Yokohama), partly to avoid the conditions in the city and also to try once more to bring order to the life of his wayward grandson, for whom he arranged a marriage and a business as a fishmonger, all at his own expense at a time when finances were very tight. Hokusai's notoriously easygoing attitude toward money in his old age may have had something to do with the fact that he had lost so much of it over the years, not altogether through his own fault.

In 1834, with the publication of volume 1 of the book *One Hundred Views of Mount Fuji*, Hokusai had taken a new primary art name, Manji (previously one of his minor names), which he used for the rest of his life. In the Manji period he concentrated on book illustrations and especially paintings, often including his impressive age in the signatures. He was famous for moving frequently from one rented residence to another and commented toward the end of his life that he had moved ninety-three times. His third daughter, who had been married to another artist but had divorced him, lived with her father and assisted him in his work. She herself was a gifted painter using the name Katsushika Ōi.

Hokusai's remarkable creativity continued to the very end of his life. During the 1840s, when he was well into his eighties, he and Ōi made several extended visits to the town of Obuse in Shinano Province (modern Nagano Prefecture), where they were provided with lodging, food, and painting materials by the wealthy local sake merchant and amateur painter Takai Kōzan (1806–1883). Among Hokusai's numerous works still extant in Obuse are paintings for the double ceilings of two festival floats showing a dragon and a phoenix, and a pair of "male" and "female" waves. Furthermore, one of the floats contains a wooden sculpture of a dragon and a Chinese hero from the martial-arts novel *The Water Margin*, for which Hokusai had illustrated the Japanese translation. It is the only known example of a sculpture designed by Hokusai, demonstrating that his interest in three-dimensional forms, apparent in his cutout toys of the early 1800s, was still very much on his mind many decades later.

In the first volume of *One Hundred Views of Mount Fuji*, published when he was seventy-five, Hokusai famously expressed his desire to live to be a hundred years old so that at last he might become a truly skilled painter. By the end of his life, with seven full decades of outstanding work as a professional artist, he had come remarkably close to his goal, and his long lifespan did indeed make it possible for him to produce spectacular works in the final quarter of his life. He died in Edo in the fourth month of 1849, aged ninety by the Japanese count and eighty-nine by the Western system. His last words are said to have been a plea for just five or ten more years to paint.

1. Hokusai may have been aware of European book illustrations utilizing this technique. See Tsuji Nobuo, "The Impact of Western Book Illustrations on the Designs of Hokusai — The Key to His Originality," in John T. Carpenter, ed., *Hokusai and His Age: Ukiyo-e Painting, Printmaking, and Book Illustration in Late Edo Japan* (Amsterdam: Hotei Publishing, 2005), 340–51.
2. The most current biographical information on Hokusai in English can be found in two essays in Ann Yonemura et al., *Hokusai* (Washington, DC: Freer Gallery of Art and Arthur M. Sackler Gallery, Smithsonian Institution, 2006): Seiji Nagata, "Hokusai's Artistic Career and Topics for Research," 2:1–7, and Tadashi Kobayashi, "The Real Hokusai, Artist 'Mad about Drawing,'" 2:9–15.
3. A full translation of this famous autobiographical statement appears in Katsushika Hokusai, *Hokusai: One Hundred Views of Mount Fuji*, introduction and commentary by Henry D. Smith II (New York: George Braziller, 1988), 7.
4. A chronological list of books illustrated by Hokusai is included as an appendix in Jack Hillier, *The Art of Hokusai in Book Illustration* (Los Angeles: University of California Press, 1980), 263–80.
5. Timothy Clark, "Katsukawa Shunshō: Ukiyo-e Paintings for the Samurai Elite," in Julia Meech and Jane Oliver, eds., *Designed for Pleasure: The World of Edo Japan in Prints and Paintings, 1680–1860* (Seattle: Asia Society and Japanese Art Society of America in association with University of Washington Press, 2008), 102.
6. For a comprehensive study of this period of Hokusai's career, see Roger Keyes, "'My Master Is Creation': Prints by Hokusai Sōri (1795–1798)," *Impressions* 20 (1998): 38–51.
7. Illustrated in ibid., 38.
8. Seiji Nagata, *Hokusai: Genius of the Japanese Ukiyo-e*, trans. John Bester (Tokyo: Kodansha International, 1995), 76.
9. John M. Rosenfield, *Extraordinary Persons: Works by Eccentric, Nonconformist Japanese Artists of the Early Modern Era (1580–1868) in the Collection of Kimiko and John Powers* (Cambridge, MA: Harvard University Art Museums, 1999), 1:34–5.
10. On Siebold's illustrations, see Hillier, *The Art of Hokusai in Book Illustration*, 107–11. A brief summary of the introduction of Hokusai's work to the French art world appears in Sarah E. Thompson, "Hokusai in Boston: The Formation of the Collection," in Seiji Nagata, Sarah E. Thompson, et al., *Hokusai from the Museum of Fine Arts, Boston*, exh. cat. (Tokyo: Nihon Keizai Shimbun, 2013), 220–1. For fuller details, see Toshio Watanabe, *High Victorian Japonisme*, Swiss Asian Studies 10 (Bern: Peter Lang, 1991).
11. On the history of the use of Prussian blue in Japanese prints, see Henry D. Smith II, "Hokusai and the Blue Revolution in Edo Prints," in John T. Carpenter, ed., *Hokusai and His Age*, 234–61.

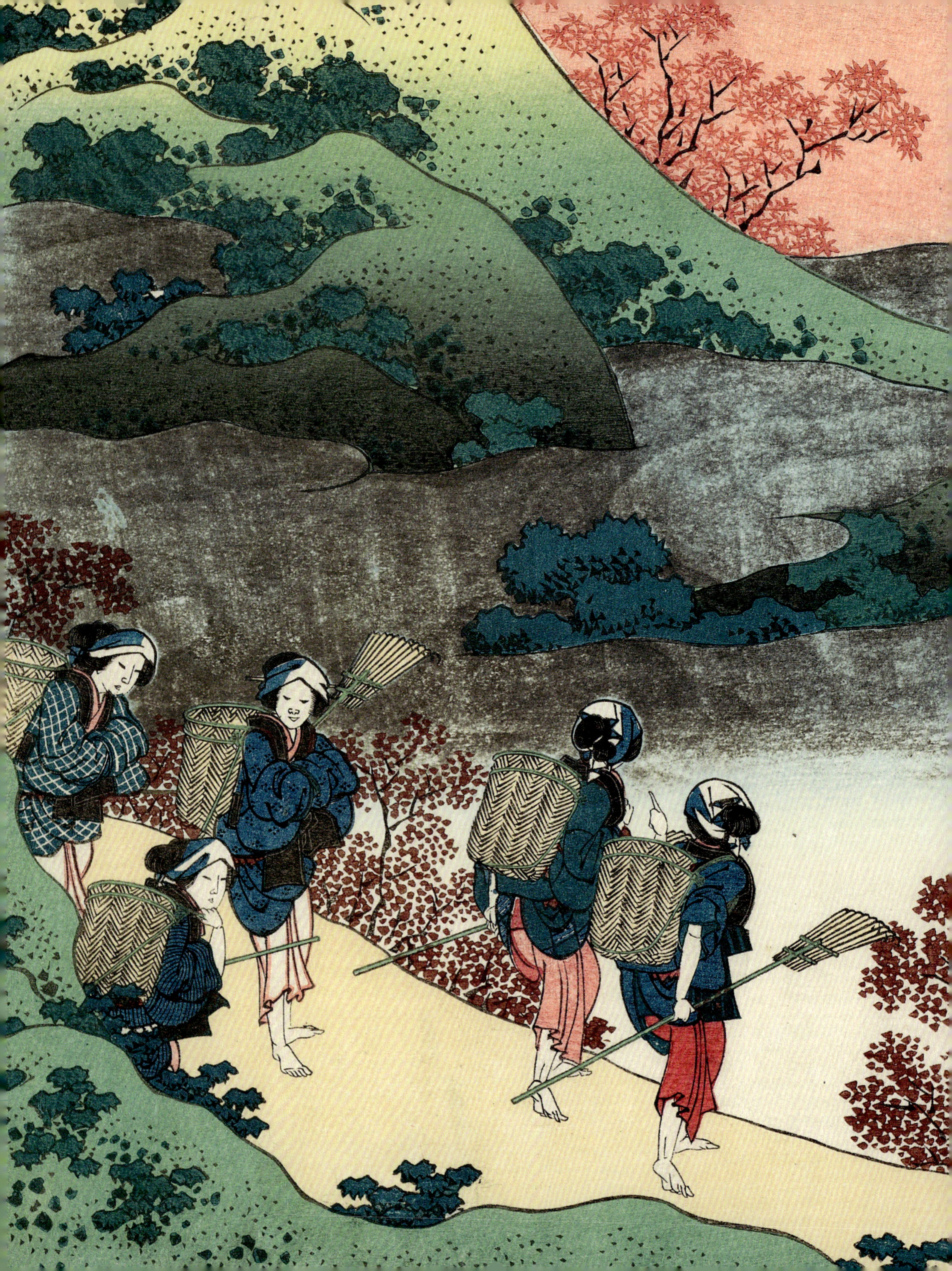

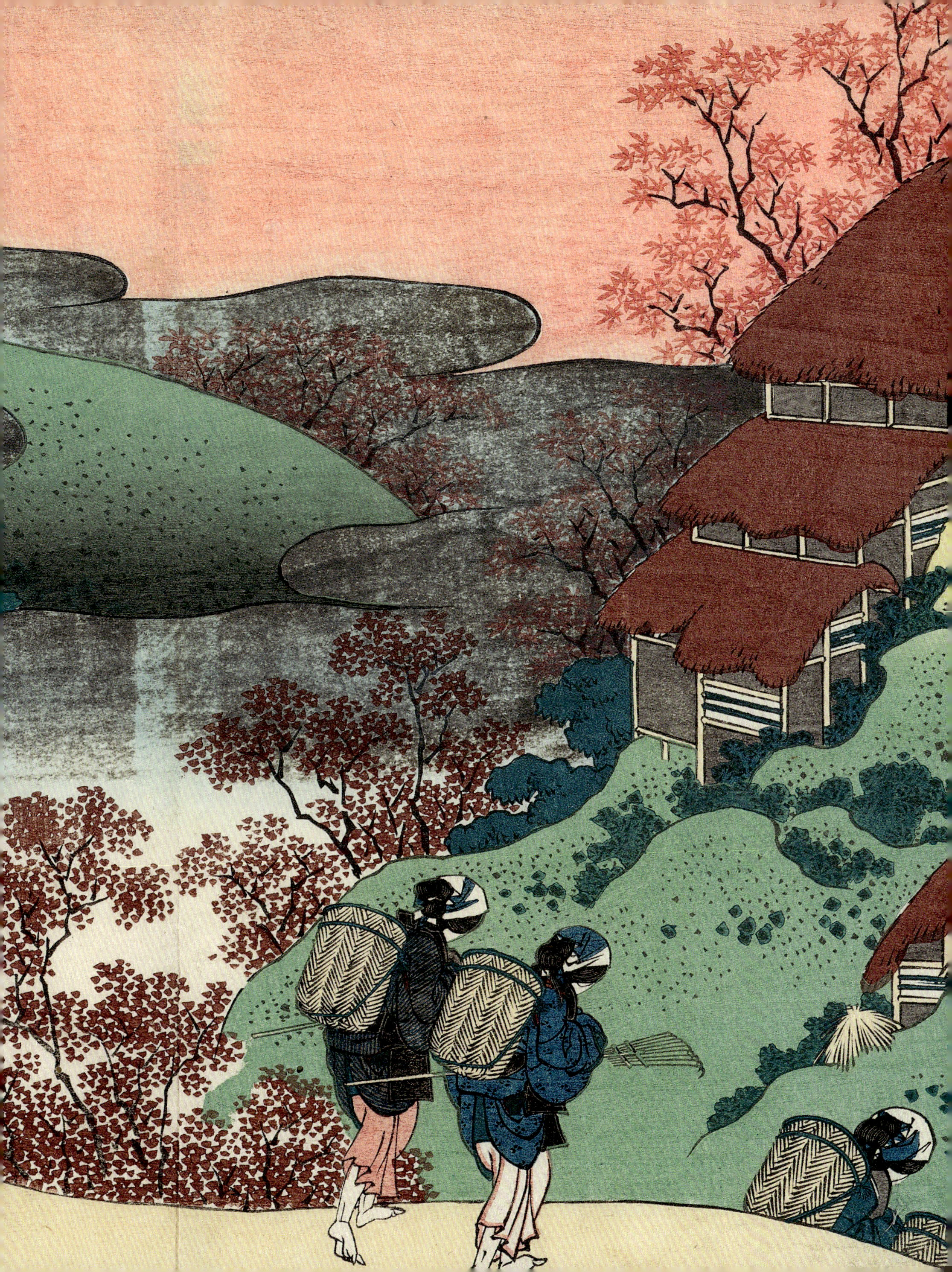

1 | **Woman Looking at Herself in a Mirror**, about 1805

The motif of a beautiful woman studying her reflection in a mirror was a favorite in ukiyo-e paintings and prints. Not only does the image convey a sense of behind-the-scenes intimacy—perhaps even of voyeurism, if the beauty who observes herself at her toilette does not realize that she in turn is observed by the viewer—but it also provides simultaneous glimpses of both the face and the nape of the neck, which was considered a particularly attractive and alluring part of the female body. Hokusai used similar poses in several of his paintings of women, of which this is the finest example.

The woman's body forms a gentle S curve as she steps back onto her right foot, with the lower part of her kimono draping elegantly over her raised heel. She holds her shoulders slightly back while leaning her head forward at just the right angle to see herself in the mirror as she adjusts the back of her hairstyle. A small chest of drawers serves as a dressing table, propping up the mirror with an open drawer, filled with cosmetics. The sumptuous fabrics and furnishings are rendered in high-quality pigments with loving detail.

Hokusai must have learned these techniques from his teacher Katsukawa Shunshō, whose luscious paintings of beauties were in great demand during the 1770s and 1780s. In the 1790s tall, slim figures became the ideal, and Hokusai drew slender girls with delicate, waiflike faces. In his mature style, as seen here, the women are still elegantly attenuated but have a new solidity and vitality.

The round object held daintily in the figure's mouth is a trademark Hokusai touch also seen in some of his other depictions of beauties. It is the fruit of the *hoozuki*, or ground cherry, a traditional symbol of summer; the round, hollow skin of the fruit could be manipulated by the tongue to make a sound. Hokusai's beauty may be whistling softly to herself as she admires her red lipstick, with a green shimmer on the lower lip where it is applied most thickly, and teeth neatly blackened for maximum contrast with her white-powdered face.

The letter held in her right hand suggests a reason to take special care with her makeup. A poem by Shima Tokki inscribed above the mirror hints at its contents: "Does that letter from / the man she waits for promise / a summer's night out?"

Signature: Dokuryū Kukushin Hokusai ga
Hanging scroll; ink, color, gold, and mica on silk
138.7 x 57.5 cm (54 5/8 x 22 5/8 in.)
William Sturgis Bigelow Collection, 11.7424

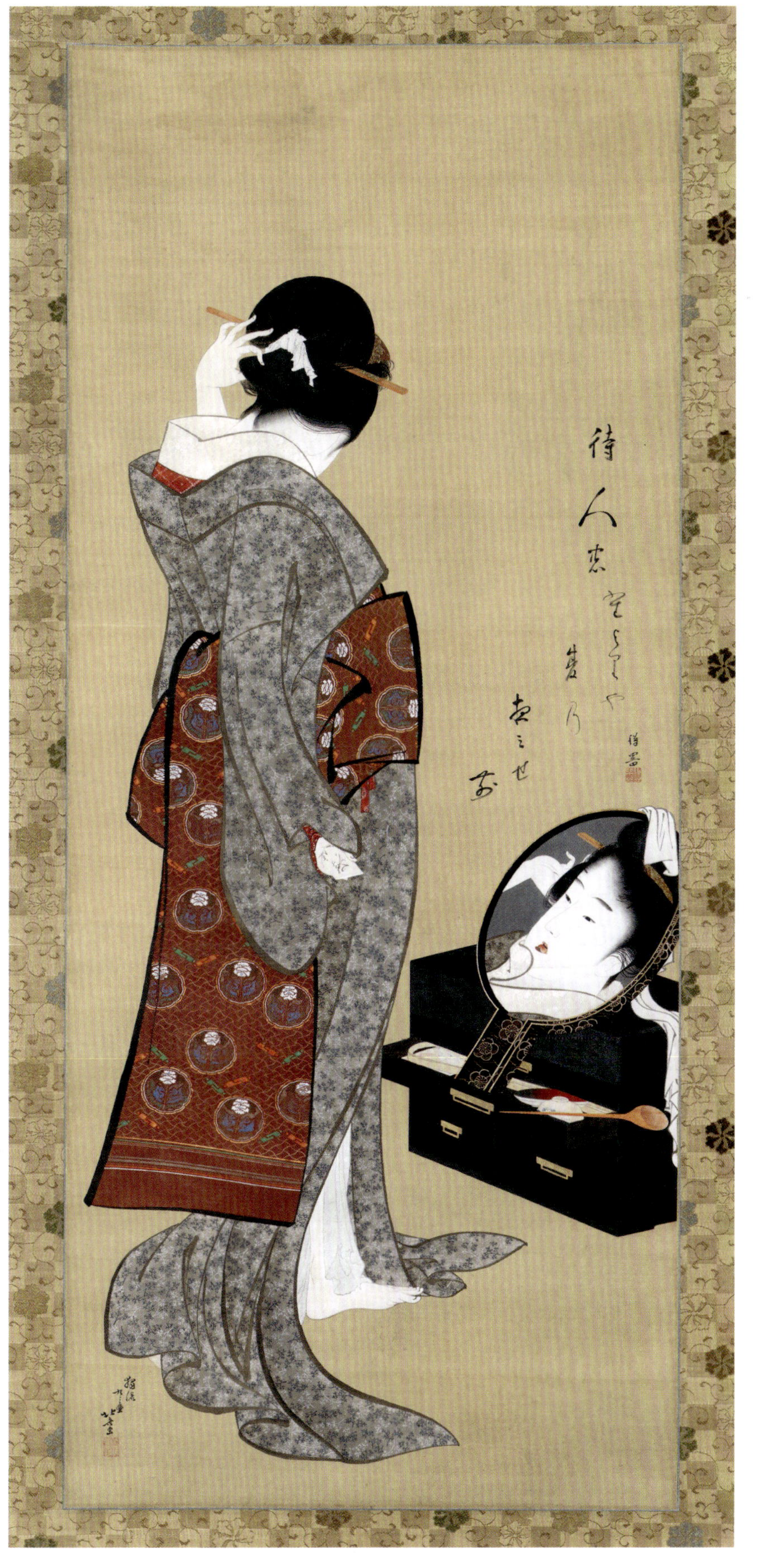

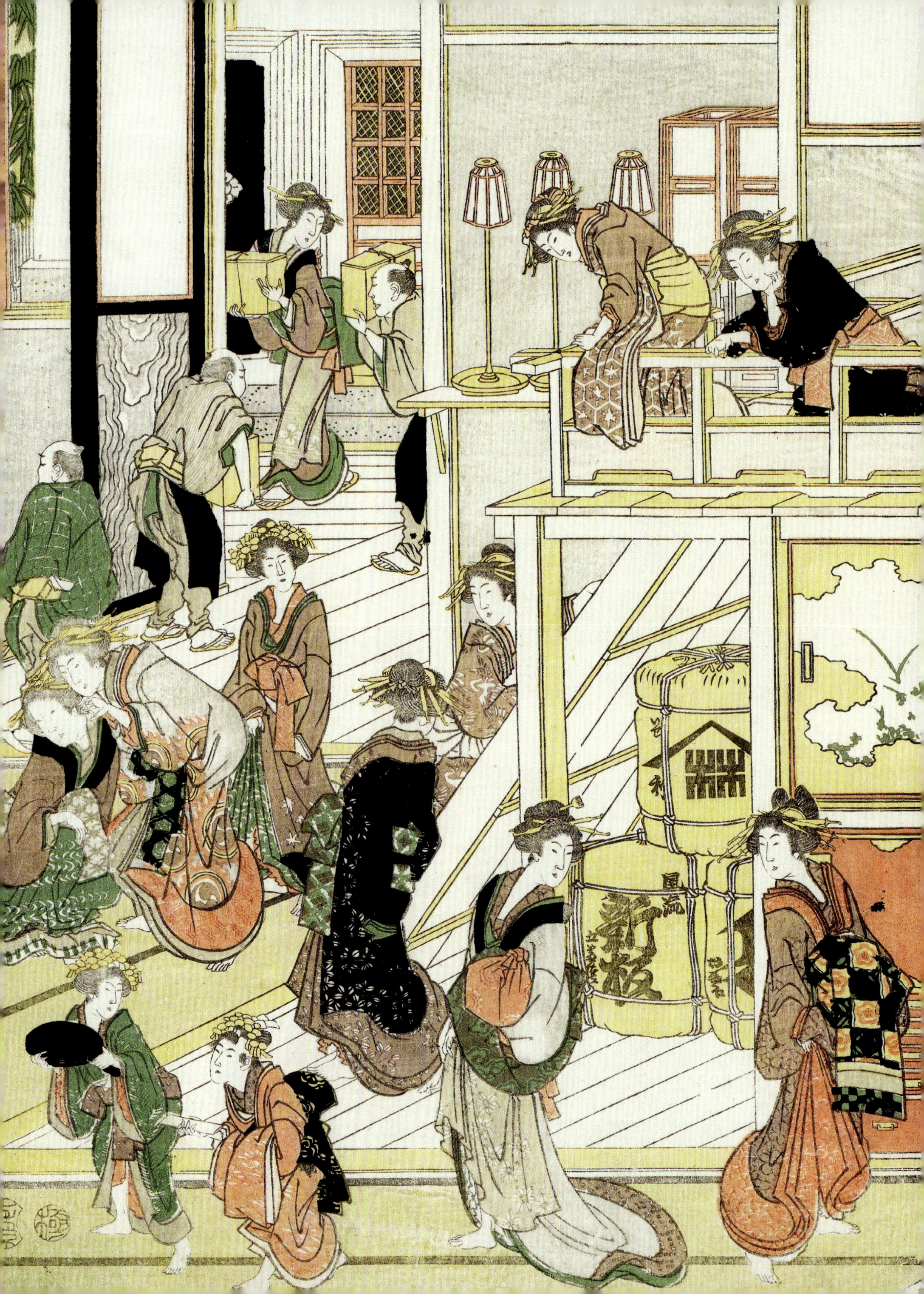
風流
新板

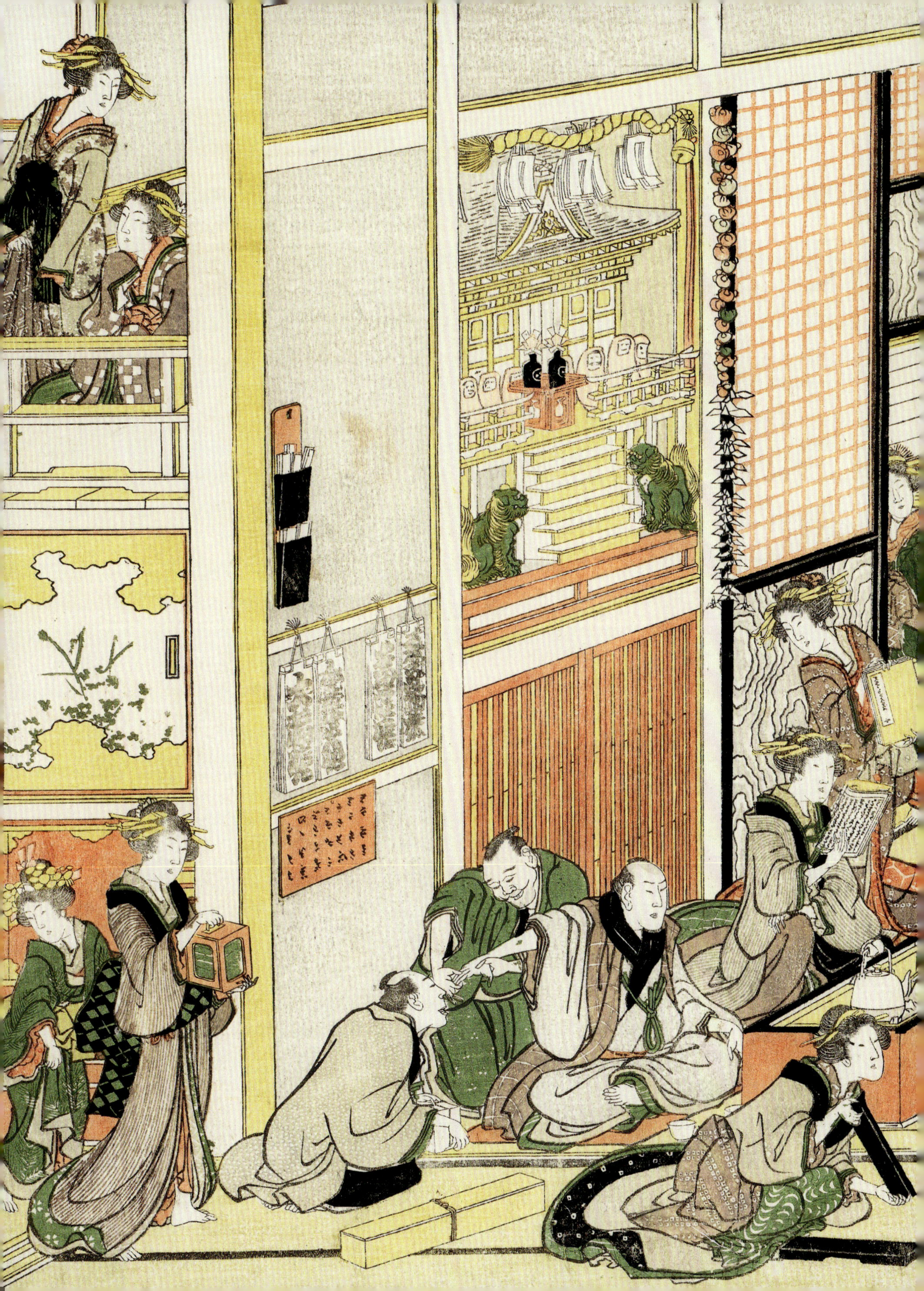

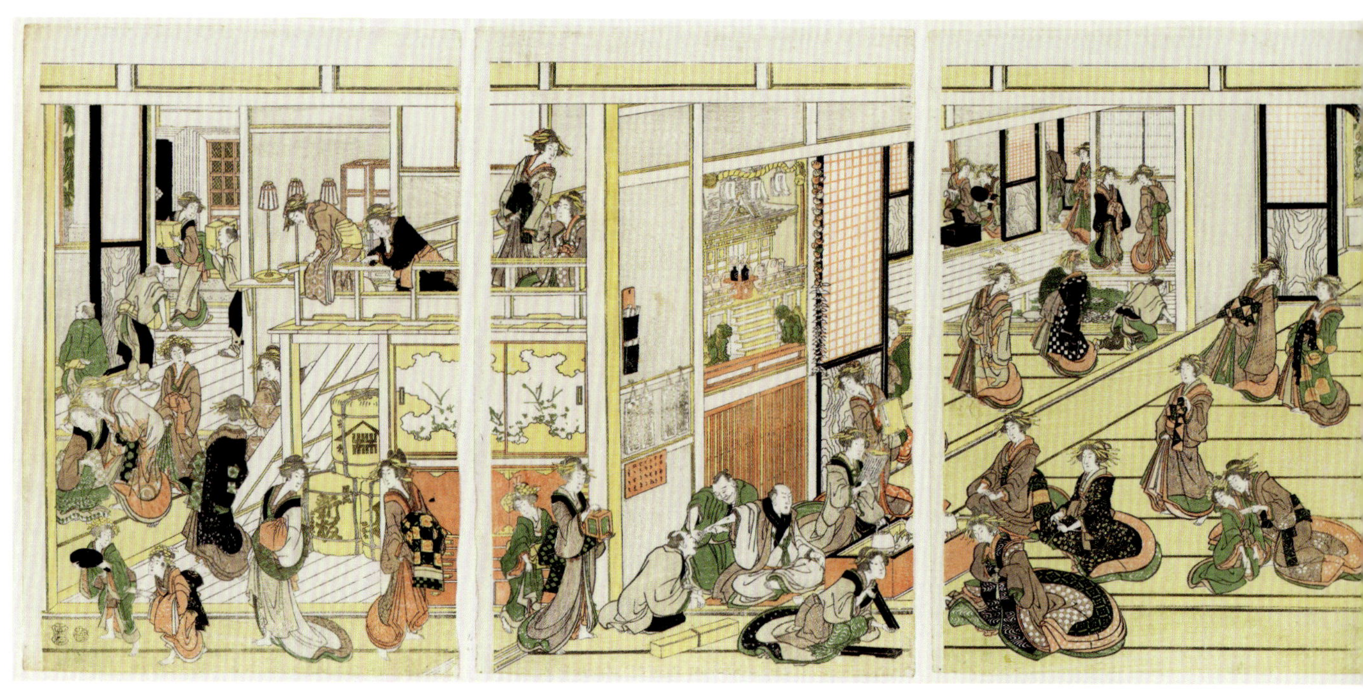

2 | **Interior of a House of Pleasure**, about 1808–13

The complex, carefully drawn interior architecture and variety of figures in realistic poses mark this rare five-sheet design as a Hokusai masterpiece. Preparations are underway for a banquet at one of the great houses of the Yoshiwara pleasure district, entertainment centers that functioned as restaurants and cabarets as well as brothels. Employees—some of whom have the character "Hayashi," part of the publisher's trademark, concealed in their clothing—ready food, clean tables, and unpack boxes containing utensils for special occasions. In the fourth sheet from the right, the owner and his wife sit in front of a large, elaborate household shrine that includes not only a *shimenawa* (sacred rope with paper streamers), offerings of sake, and guardian lions, but also a string of monkey toys and origami cranes symbolizing vows and wishes. Rows of Daruma dolls with both eyes painted in, indicating wishes that have been granted, flank the sake bottles.

The doorway in the upper right corner has a large curtain with characters that presumably give the name of the house, but the pillar that obscures most of the writing makes it difficult, if not impossible, to read. The large wall painting of a phoenix visible in the background of the second sheet from the right could provide a clue. The Ōgiya house is known to have had such a painting; however, a triptych by Utamaro shows courtesans of the Matsubaya house in front of a similar phoenix painting, so the identification of the house is not certain.

Under the staircase in the left-most sheet are barrels of sake, including one that displays the trademark of the publisher Iseya Rihei and another marked "Fashionable New Publication in Five Sheets." Hokusai often portrayed the courtesans of the Yoshiwara and other beauties of Edo in his paintings and deluxe, privately commissioned surimono prints; but the theme of beautiful women and their surroundings is only occasionally treated in his commercial prints. Hokusai did not design many multisheet images. Only a few diptychs and triptychs are known, and this is his only five-sheet design.

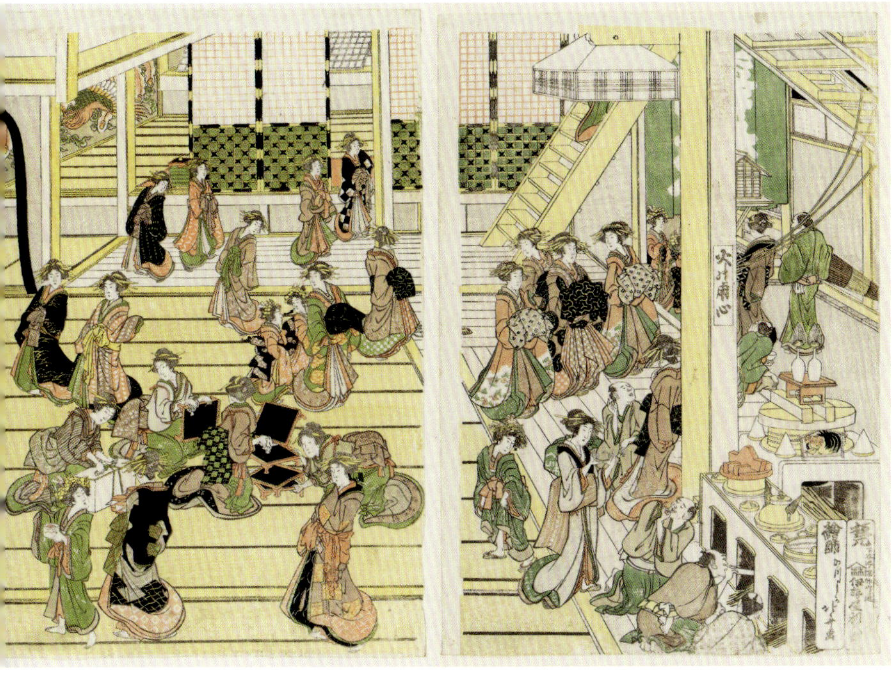

Signature (on right-most sheet only): Katsushika Hokusai ga
Publisher: Iseya Rihei
Woodblock print (*nishiki-e*); ink and color on paper
Pentaptych (overall): 38.5 x 130 cm (15 3/16 x 51 3/16 in.)
William Sturgis Bigelow Collection, 11.17688, 11.17689, 11.17695, 11.17696, 11.17697

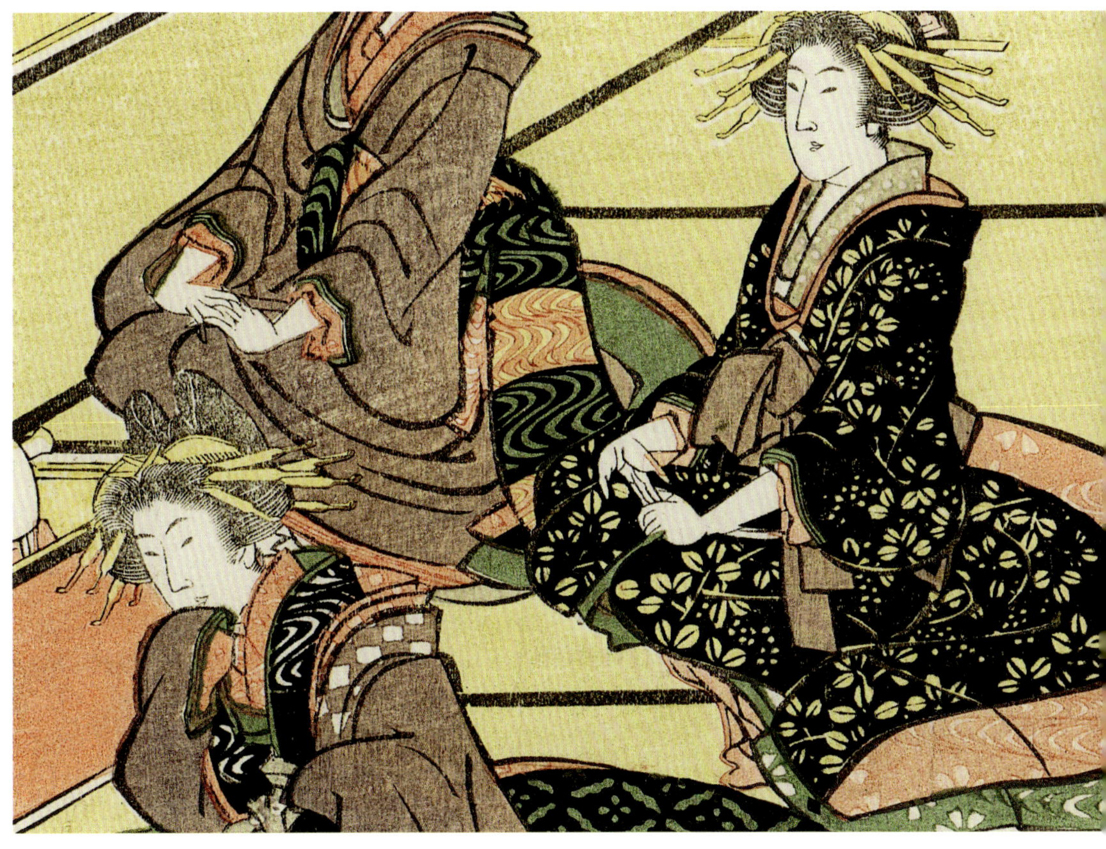

3 | **Actor Sakata Hangorō III as a Traveling Priest, Actually Minamoto Chinzei Hachirō Tametomo**, 1791

The brawny actor Sakata Hangorō III, who specialized in portraying villains and action heroes, strikes a pose in a graveyard at night. In a dramatic confrontation with another actor, who is depicted on a matching print that once formed a diptych with this one, he has just cast off his disguise as a traveling priest to reveal himself to be none other than Minamoto Chinzei Hachirō Tametomo, one of the last survivors of a faction that was defeated during the civil wars of the twelfth century. The real, historical Tametomo was killed in battle, but during the Edo period he became a legendary character in fiction and drama, said to have lived on in secret after his side's defeat.

The scene is from a play called *The Golden Sword Decoration and the Square Sword Guard of the Minamoto Family* (*Kin no Menuki Genke no Kakutsuba*), which was the season-opening production at the Ichimura Theater in Edo. The skull held by Tametomo is that of his deceased lord, a symbol of his determination to seek vengeance for his lost cause.

Hokusai's earliest actor prints with the Shunrō signature are often unimpressive in appearance, partly because he was still learning his trade and partly because, as a very junior artist in the Katsukawa school, he was less likely to be assigned the best block cutters and printers for his designs. But as works such as this one show, by the early 1790s, after over ten years of apprenticeship, he had developed into an outstanding designer of actor prints, with a talent for capturing both facial likenesses and dynamic poses. It is surprising, therefore, that he left the Katsukawa school and gave up designing actor prints almost completely after the death of his teacher, Katsukawa Shunshō (1726–1792). One theory suggests that older Katsukawa-school artists were jealous of the talented younger man, and that he turned to other areas of art as a result of their hostility.

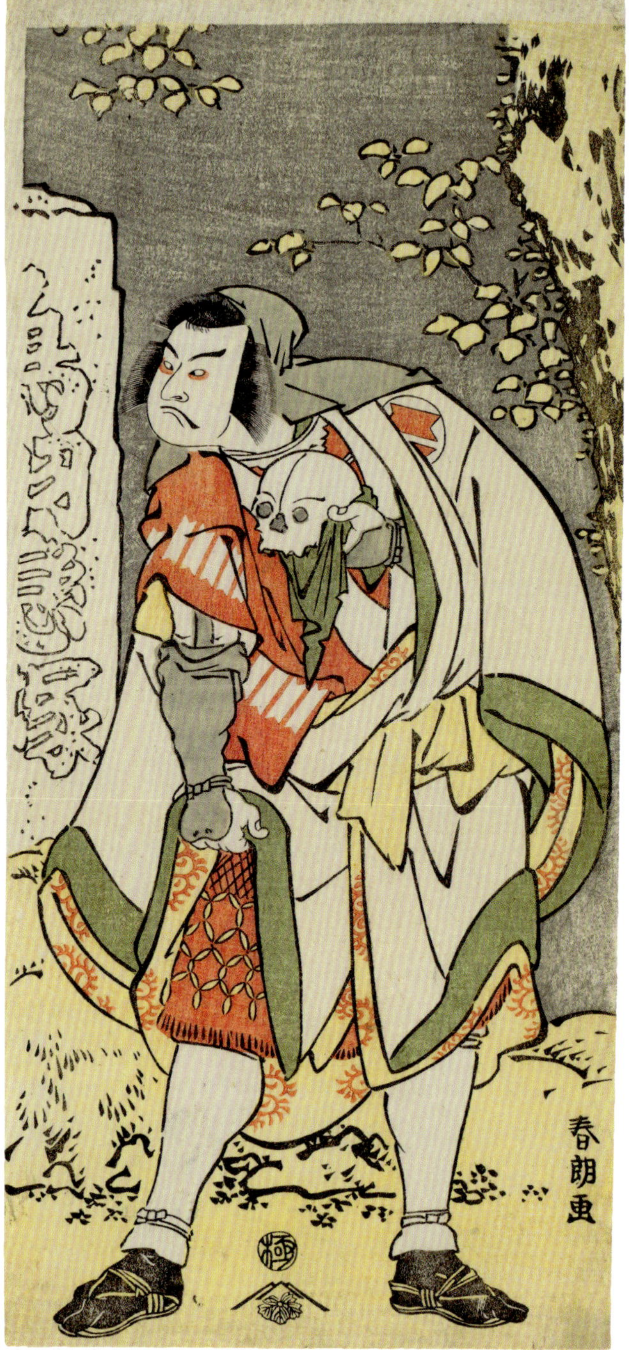

Signature: Shunrō ga
Publisher: Tsutaya Jūzaburō (Kōshodō)
Woodblock print (nishiki-e); ink and color on paper
31.4 x 14.2 cm (12 3/8 x 5 9/16 in.)
William Sturgis Bigelow Collection, 11.19925

4 | **Zhong Kui, the Demon Queller**, about 1805

The demon queller known in Japan as Shōki, or Zhong Kui in the original Chinese, was a figure from Chinese legend who became enormously popular in Japan as well. He was said to be the ghost of an unsuccessful candidate for an official position in the Chinese bureaucracy who committed suicide after he was unfairly disqualified in the imperial examinations, but in his afterlife became a benevolent guardian. Supposedly, he appeared in a dream to the Chinese emperor and vowed to fight all demons, especially those that cause disease. A picture of this supernatural warrior was considered an auspicious object that would promote the health and well-being of everyone in the home in which it was displayed, particularly that of children, and so he became the subject of numerous paintings and woodblock prints in both China and Japan.

Artists depicted the demon queller as a large, fierce-looking man with a bushy black beard and glaring eyes. He is often seen holding a sword and wearing either a Chinese official's cap or a large round hat. Many such representations were done in the Chinese ink-monochrome style, but as seen here, cinnabar red was sometimes used instead of ink because it was believed to be a magical color that would enhance the image's efficacy in warding off disease demons.

This decoration was created for the Tango Festival, also known as the Boys' Festival, celebrated on the fifth day of the fifth month. At this time, families with young sons displayed windsock streamers in the shape of a carp, which are still used today, and large banners with appropriate motifs. Shōki was a favorite subject because he was both a protector of children and a warrior whose bravery and determination provided a model of ideal masculine behavior. The loops at the side and top of the banner were used to attach it to a pole in the shape of an inverted L. When the fabric fluttered in the wind, Shōki would appear to stride boldly forward, pursuing his ongoing battle against evil.

Banner; color with ink on cotton
236 x 94 cm (92 15/16 x 37 in.)
William Sturgis Bigelow Collection, 11.9240

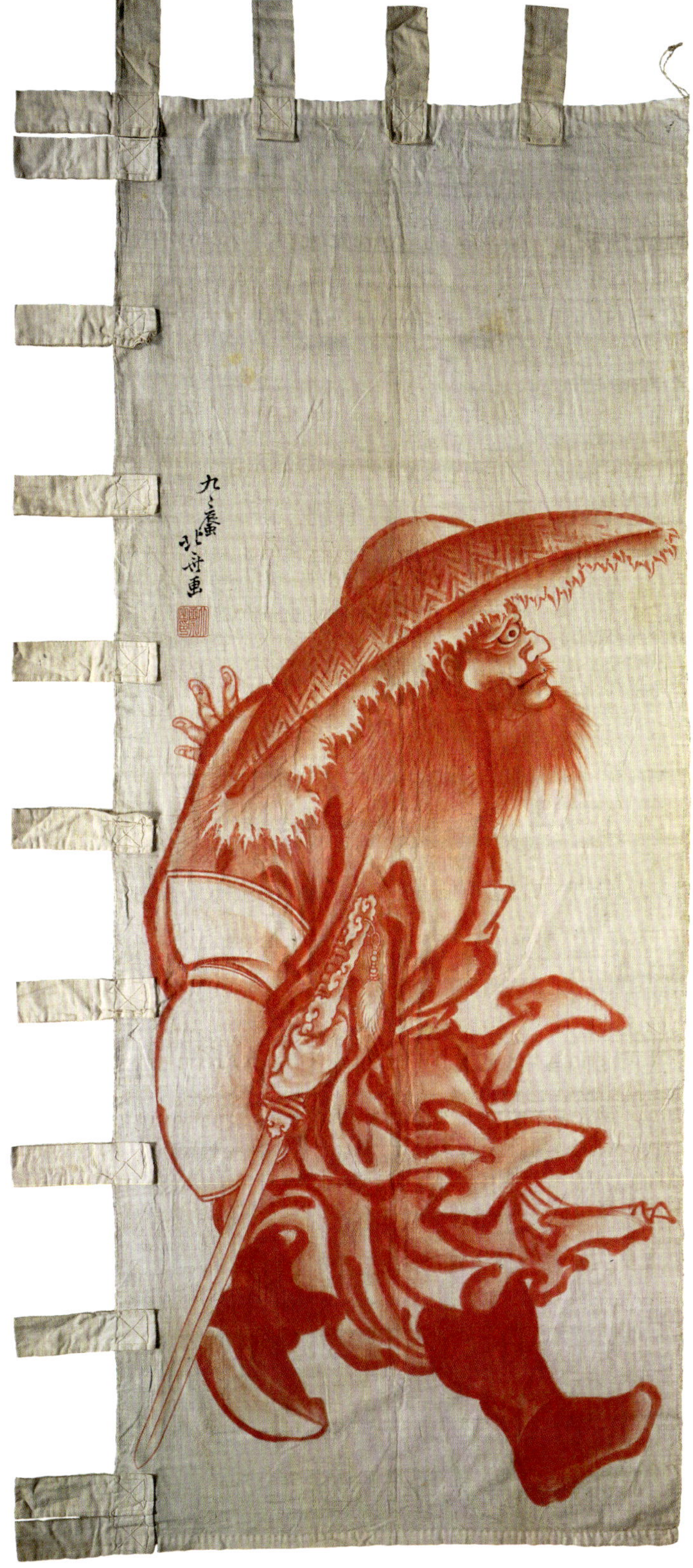

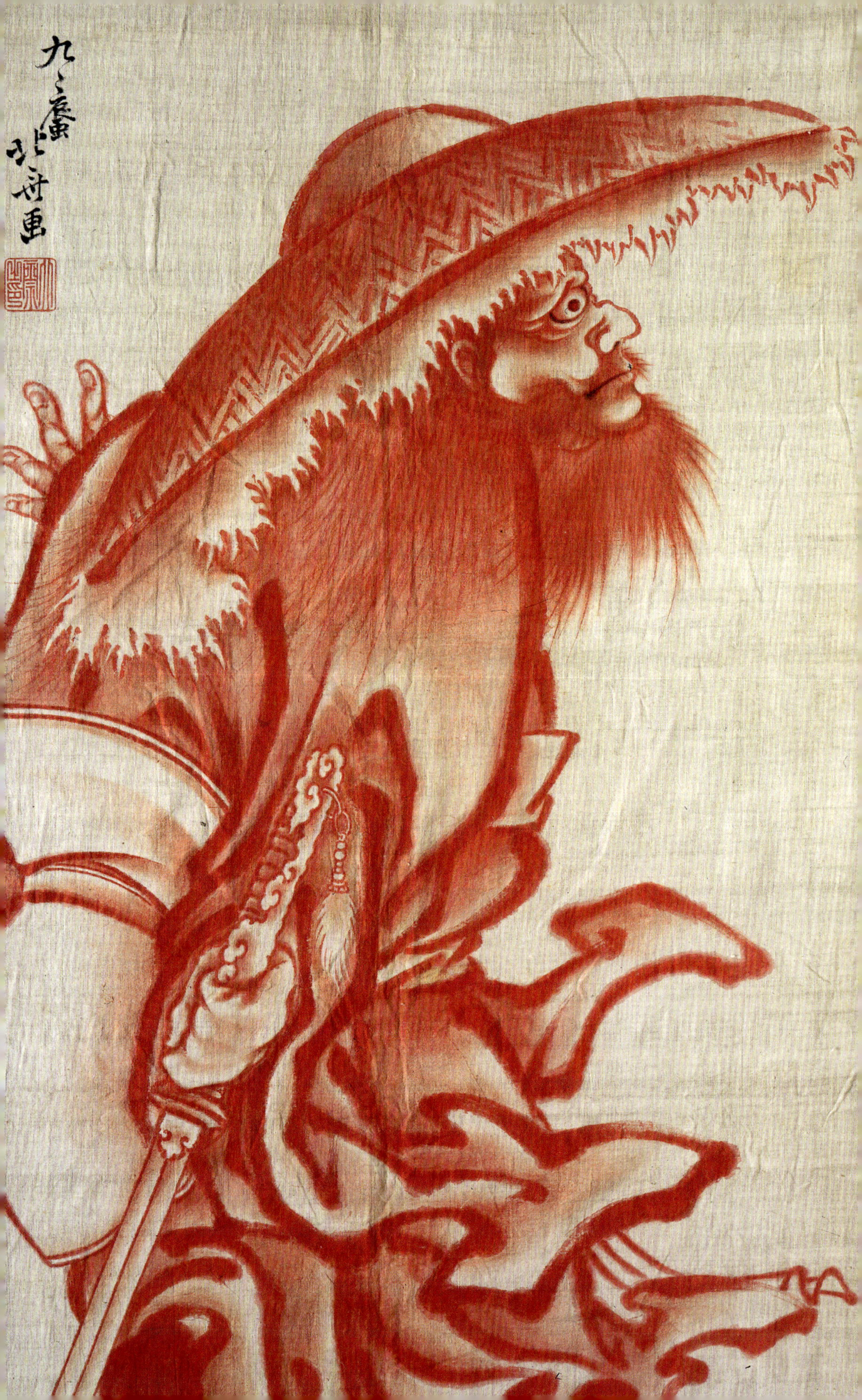
九々蜃
北斎画

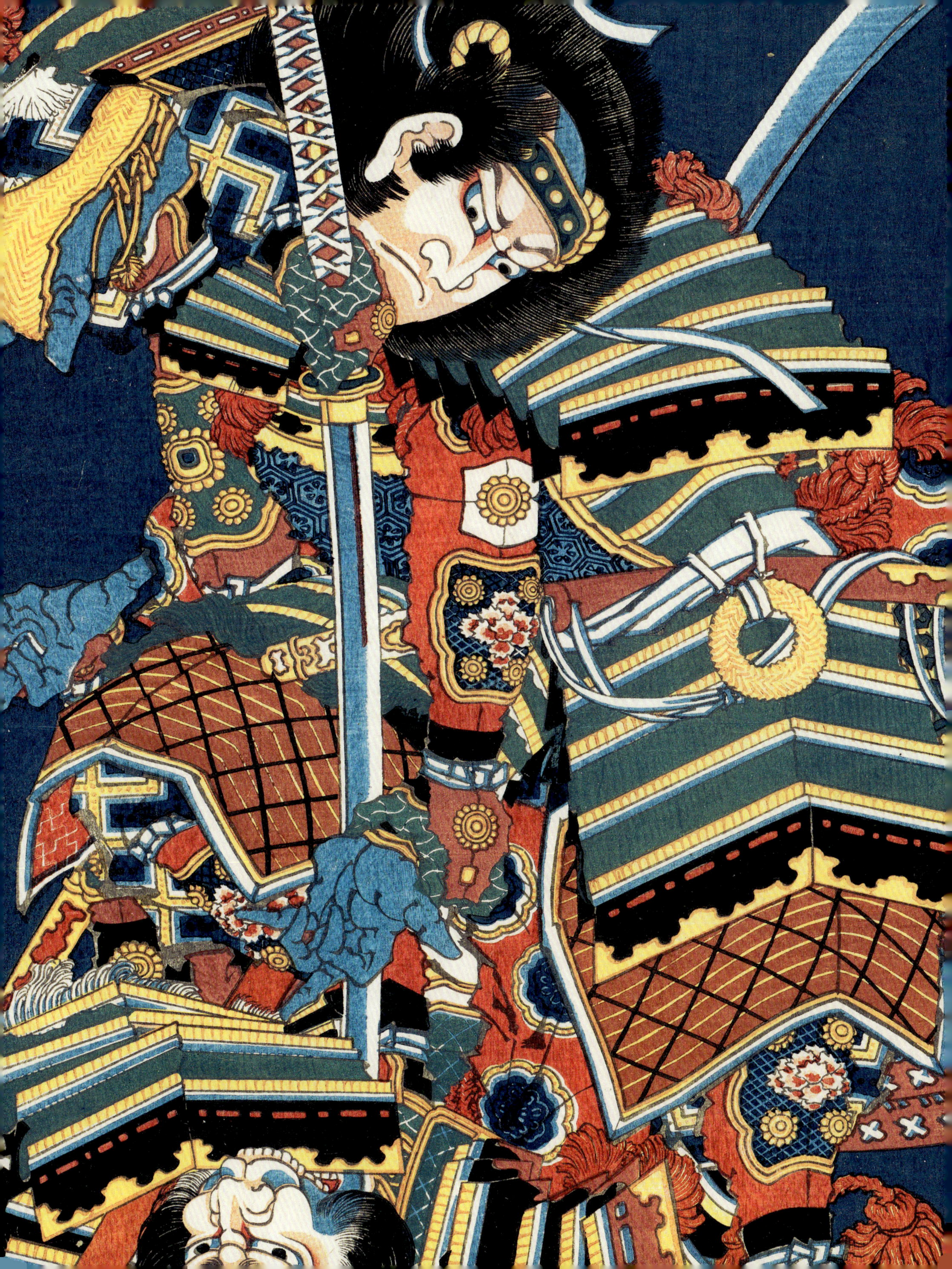

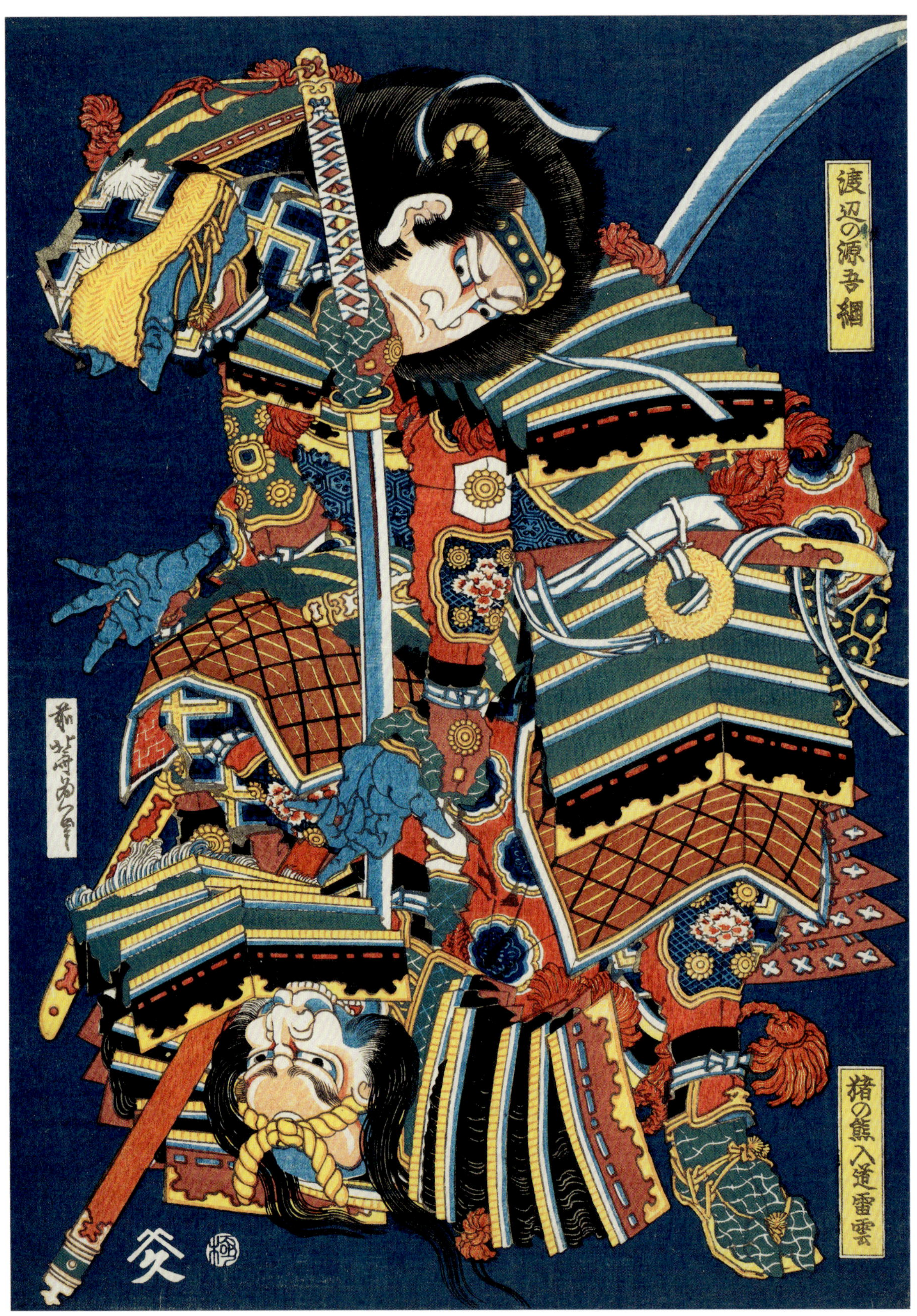
渡辺の源吾綱
猪の熊入道雷雲
前北斎為一筆

5 | **Watanabe no Gengo Tsuna and Inokuma Nyūdō Raiun** from an untitled series of warriors in combat, about 1833–35

Watanabe no Tsuna was a retainer of the tenth-century general Minamoto no Yorimitsu (Raikō). Like his master, he was a historical warrior whose real-life adventures took on mythological dimensions in later legends. He is especially famous for his battle with the Ibaraki demon at Rashomon Gate in Kyoto, in which he cut off the demon's arm. Later, he joined Raikō and the other retainers in demon-killing expeditions against supernatural monsters. He was a popular character in Edo-period fiction and drama and appears in manga, anime, and fantasy novels even today. His adversary, Inokuma Nyūdō Raiun, seems to be an entirely fictional character. He is drawn as a warrior monk with a shaved head and comical "catfish" sideburns that dangle upside down as the hero keeps him at bay. Still fighting, even though he is clearly about to be defeated, Raiun has pulled off one sleeve of his opponent's armor with his teeth. The composition is very complicated, but the different colors worn by the two antagonists help the viewer decipher who is doing what to whom.

Hokusai emphasizes the size and power of the heroes by pushing the design to the edges of the paper, making the figures so tall that they could not stand up straight within the height of the picture. The effect is of a close-up view of intense, deadly, one-on-one combat, accentuated by the brilliant Prussian blue that fills in all the remaining space not occupied by the figures.

Although Hokusai included many designs featuring noted warriors from Japanese and Chinese history in book illustrations and deluxe surimono prints, the untitled series of five prints of which this work is a part is his only known commercial print series in the genre of warrior prints (*musha-e*). Like landscape and bird-and-flower subjects, warrior prints had previously been a minor genre within ukiyo-e but became a major subject from the 1830s on. Although Hokusai was the pioneer artist for print series of landscapes and bird-and-flower designs, the first major series of warrior prints was Utagawa Kuniyoshi's *Suikoden*, which began publication in about 1827. But Hokusai was still closely connected with the development of this new genre, since Kuniyoshi's series was inspired in part by Hokusai's illustrations for Takizawa Bakin's new Japanese translation of the Chinese classic martial arts novel *The Water Margin* (*Shui Hu Zhuan*, or *Suikoden* in Japanese).

Signature: Saki no Hokusai litsu hitsu
Publisher: Yamamotoya Heikichi (Eikyūdō)
Woodblock print (nishiki-e); ink and color on paper
37.4 x 26.5 cm (14 3/4 x 10 7/16 in.)
William Sturgis Bigelow Collection, 11.17552

6 | **Sketch of Figures Prepared for Instruction of a Pupil**, 1830s

Although this highly informal sketch is unsigned, the drawing style and the handwriting are definitely those of Hokusai. In words and pictures, the master explains to an unidentified pupil his method for drawing figures that, even while performing energetic actions such as the dance moves here, retain their balance. At the left edge of the sheet is part of another drawing, showing what appears to be a fragment of a garment. Apparently the dancing figures were cut from a larger sheet of sketches.

According to Hokusai, the artist should drop an imaginary vertical line from the head of the figure to either the left or the right foot. In the text at the upper right, Hokusai does not write the characters for "an imaginary vertical line" but rather draws the line itself, making his meaning absolutely clear. This rebuslike play with words can also be seen in Hokusai's personal correspondence.

Ink on paper
27.7 x 20.2 cm (10 15/16 x 7 15/16 in.)
Gift of Edward S. Morse, 22.400

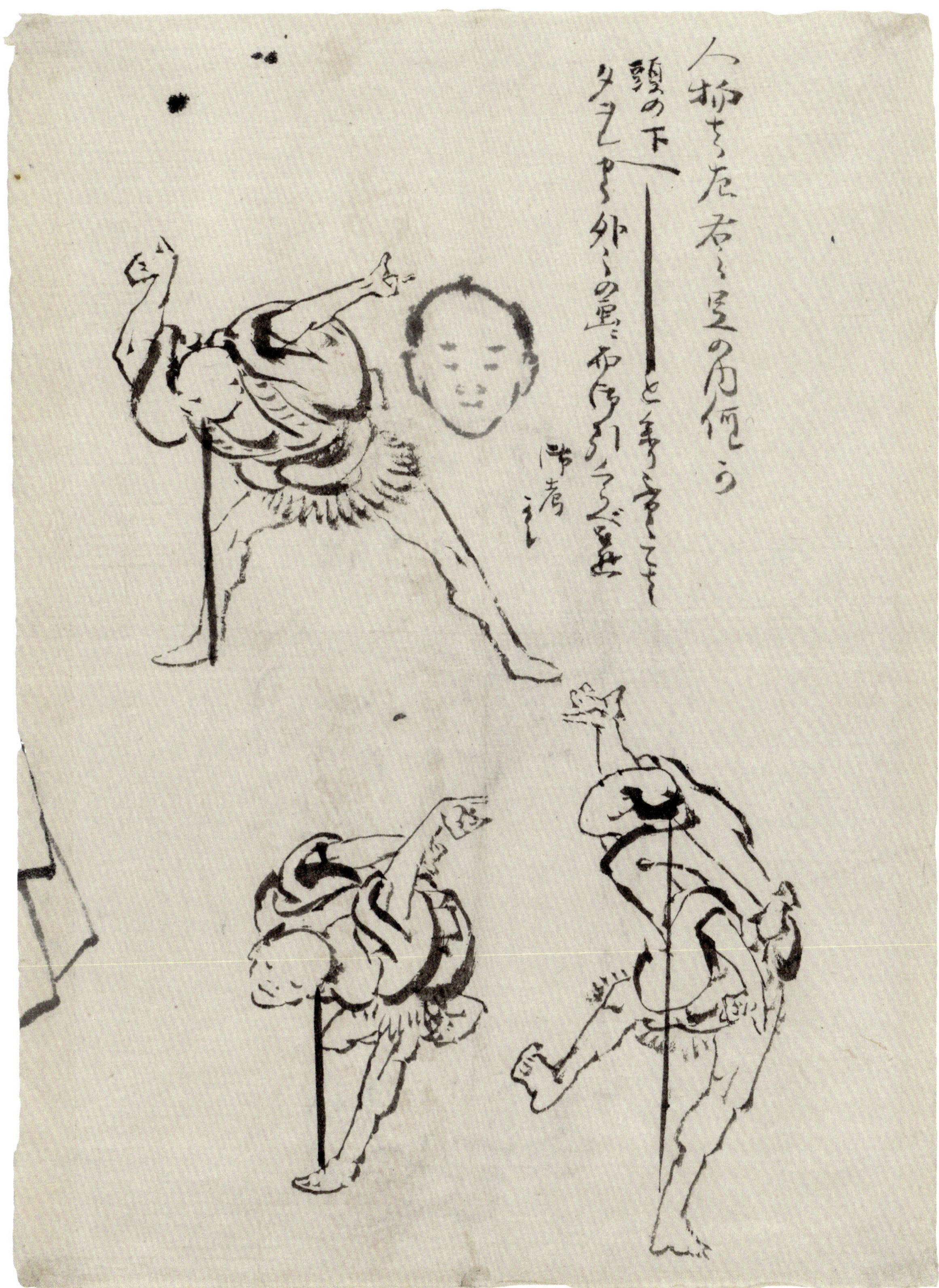

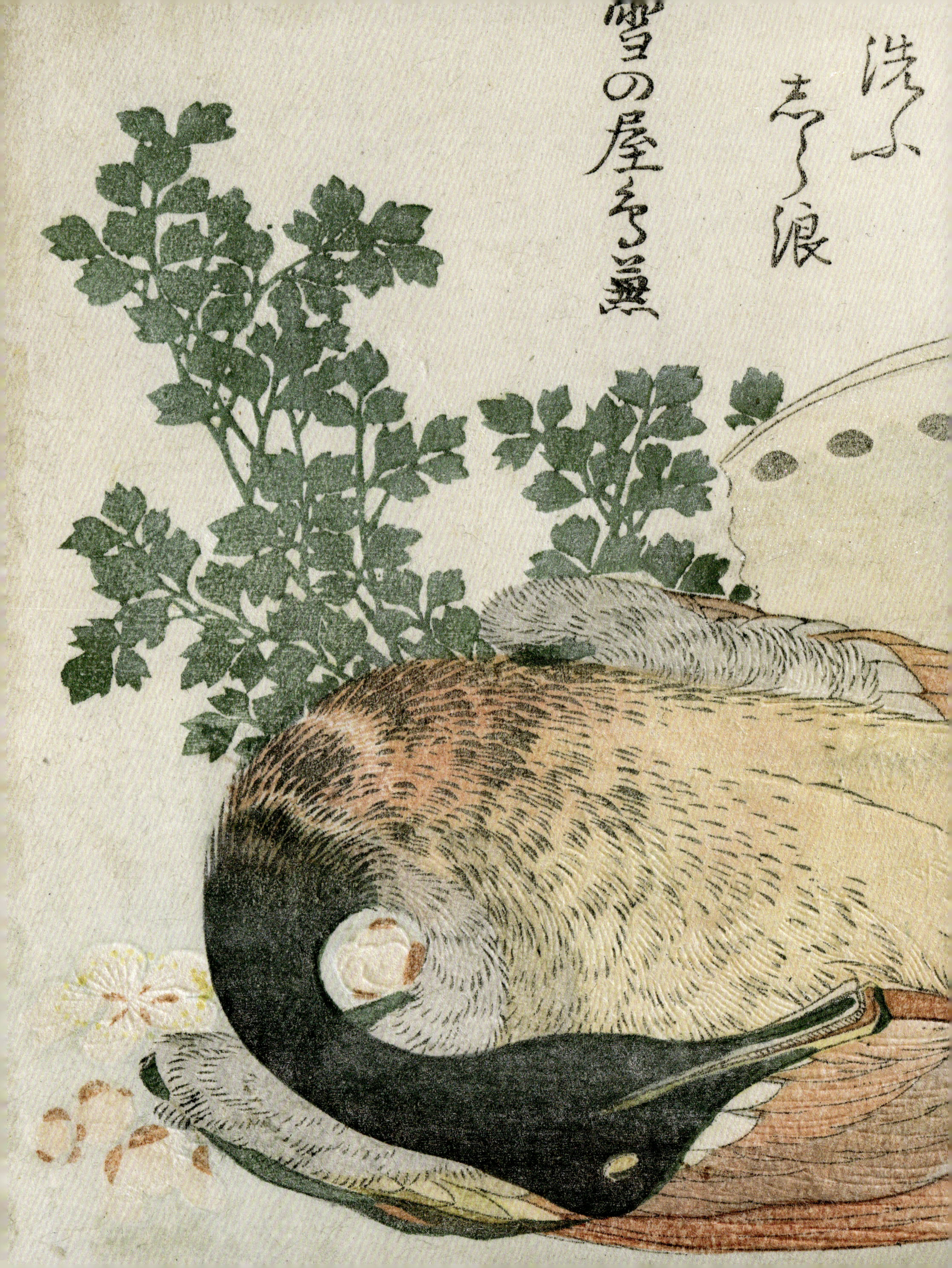

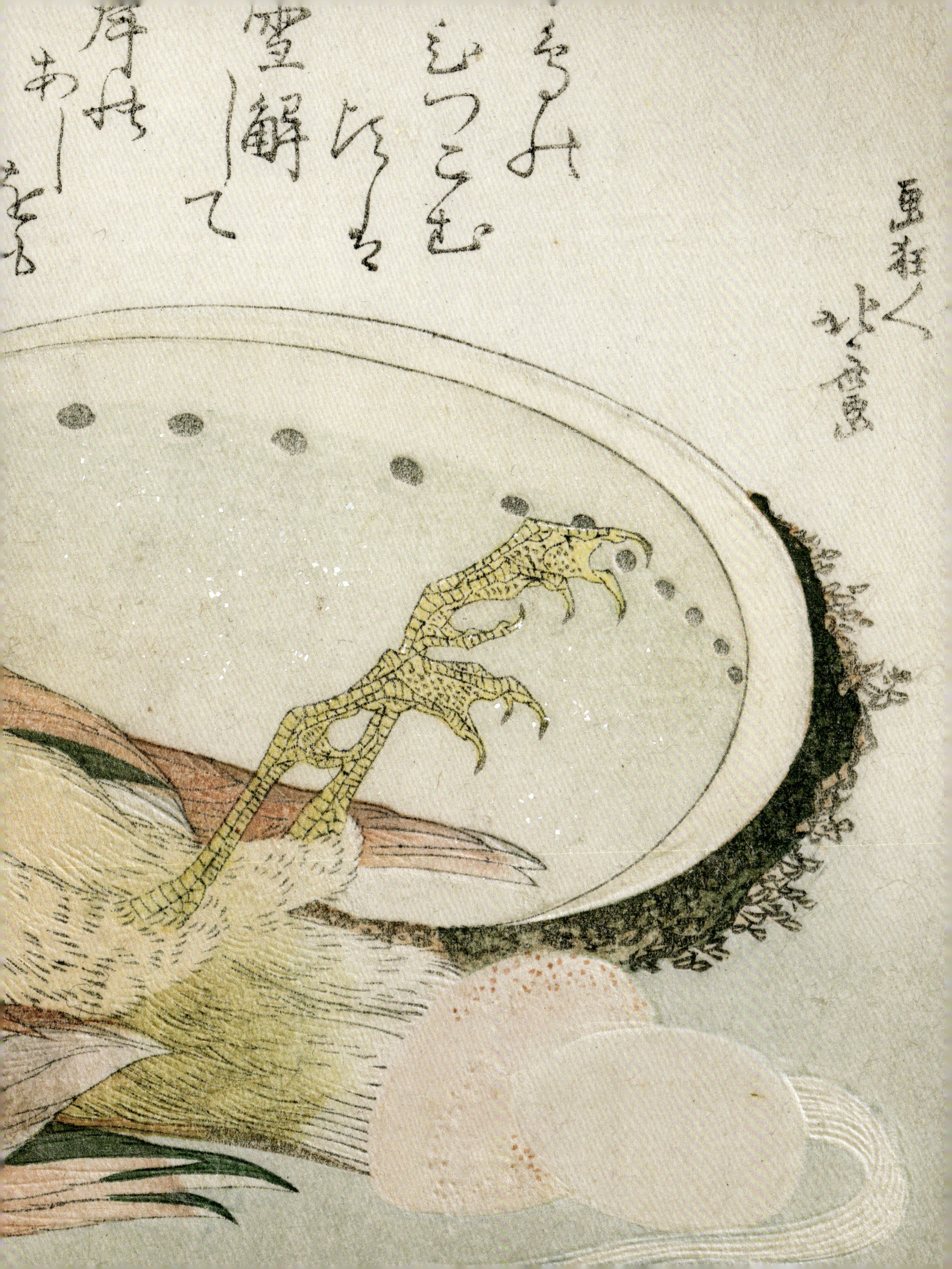

7 | ***Duck, Abalone Shell, and Parsley***, about 1805–10

In the 1790s and early 1800s, Hokusai gained a reputation as one of the leading designers of the deluxe, privately commissioned prints called surimono. Since these prints were made to order, and were not sold commercially, they were not subject to government sumptuary restrictions and so could be as lavishly produced as the customer could afford. Most surimono were made for the members of amateur poetry clubs, who exchanged them as gifts on special occasions, especially New Year's.

The amateur poets were well-educated men (and occasionally women) who valued erudition and ingenuity. As a result, surimono have the widest range of subject matter seen in any form of ukiyo-e. They depict figures, landscapes, and even still lifes, formerly an uncommon subject in Japanese art. It is uncertain whether Japanese artists such as Hokusai were influenced by Dutch still lifes they encountered in the form of imported prints or book illustrations, or whether they reinvented the genre on their own.

In this print, the dead duck and surrounding vegetables are the ingredients for a gourmet soup. Buddhist-inspired laws dating back many centuries prohibited the Japanese from raising animals for food, but wild game was legally acceptable (if morally dubious) and was available at restaurants in Edo. The iridescent abalone shell that forms a decorative accent behind the duck may refer to abalone as an ingredient in the duck soup, or—since the shell seems to be empty—it may be intended for use as a kitchen bowl to hold chopped ingredients.

The inscribed poem by Yukinoya Torikane recalls the duck as it appeared in life and suggests that the season is early spring: "Just when water birds / are returning north again, / the snow starts to thaw, / and reeds along the bank / are washed by white-capped waves."* Apparently the poem was written first, and Hokusai's print was designed as a witty visual play on the wording. The word for reeds (*ashi*) is a homophone for feet, and so the reeds mentioned in the poem are indicated by the prominently depicted feet of the duck. The duck will soon be "washed" not by white-capped waves but by the boiling water of the stewpot when it is cooked.

Signature: Gakyōjin Hokusai ga
Woodblock print (surimono); ink and color on paper
13.9 x 19.3 cm (5 1/2 x 7 5/8 in.)
William Sturgis Bigelow Collection, 11.16798

*Translated by John T. Carpenter

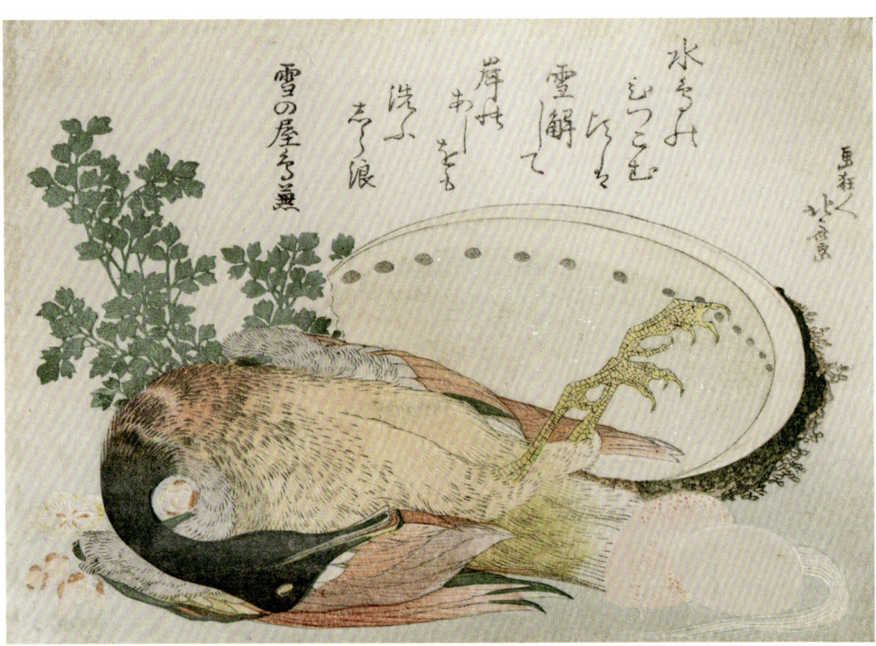

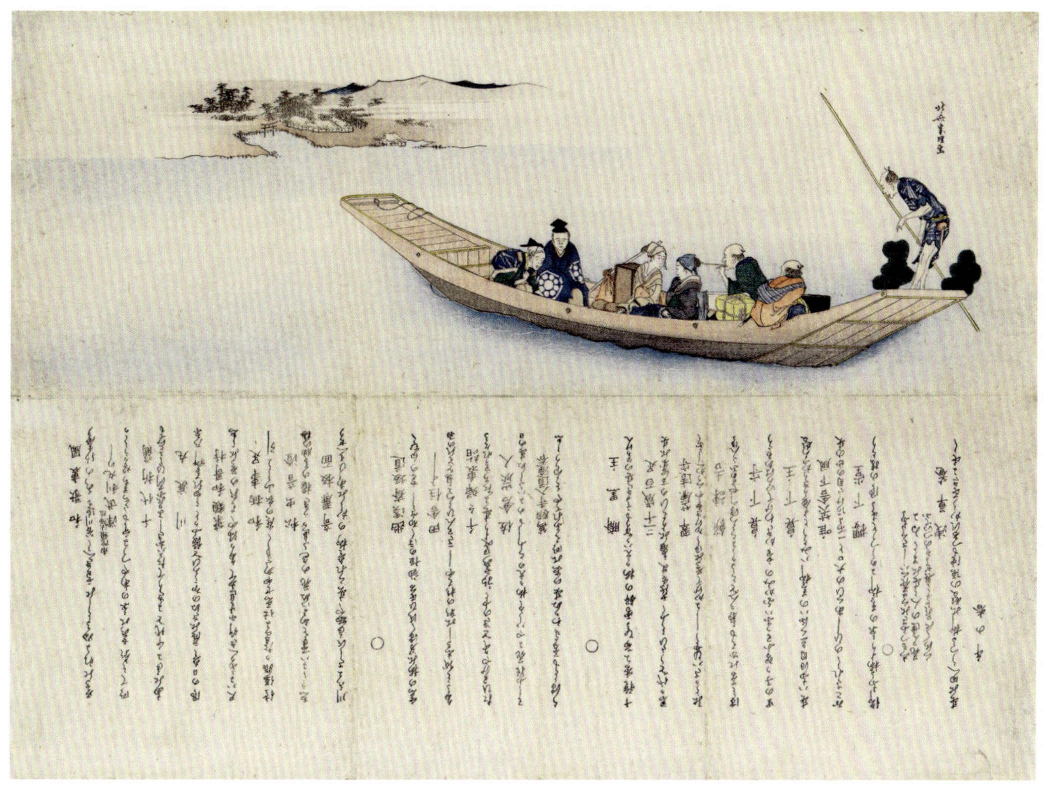

8 | **Ferryboat**, 1798

This print is unusual not only for the beauty of its design but also because it has survived intact. Surimono in the long horizontal format were originally printed on a large sheet of paper, which was divided lengthwise with the picture on one half and the text upside down on the other half. The sheet would be folded in half, with the fold on the bottom — thus turning the text right side up — and then folded three times to make a small pamphlet with the picture outside and the text inside. Sometimes the text consisted of lighthearted kyōka poems, as on most other surimono; but the long format was also used for souvenir programs of musical performances and other special events. People who saved the long surimono often kept only the picture and cut off the text, but in this case the text was left folded under the image.

Hokusai took advantage of the long format to show a ferryboat at New Year. Passengers smoke, chat quietly with each other, or simply watch the scenery go by. The boatman poles the boat, which is decorated with pine branches for the holiday, toward a Shinto shrine on the far bank, possibly the Masaki Inari Shrine on the Sumida River in Edo. When the sheet was folded, a viewer would see first the blue expanse of the river with the shrine in the upper right corner; then, when the first page was opened, the boatman and the back of the boat; and finally, if the pamphlet was turned over, the front of the boat. Viewing the print in its original format thus replicated the experience of a passenger in the boat, looking in different directions. The twenty-two poems celebrating New Year are by members of the amateur poetry club known as the Hanami-ren (Cherry-Blossom-Viewing Circle), and at the end of the text is the occasion, "New Year of the Horse" (1798).

Signature: Hokusai Sōri ga
Woodblock print (surimono); ink and color on paper
40.2 x 53.7 cm (15 13/16 x 21 1/8 in.)
William Sturgis Bigelow Collection, 11.19657

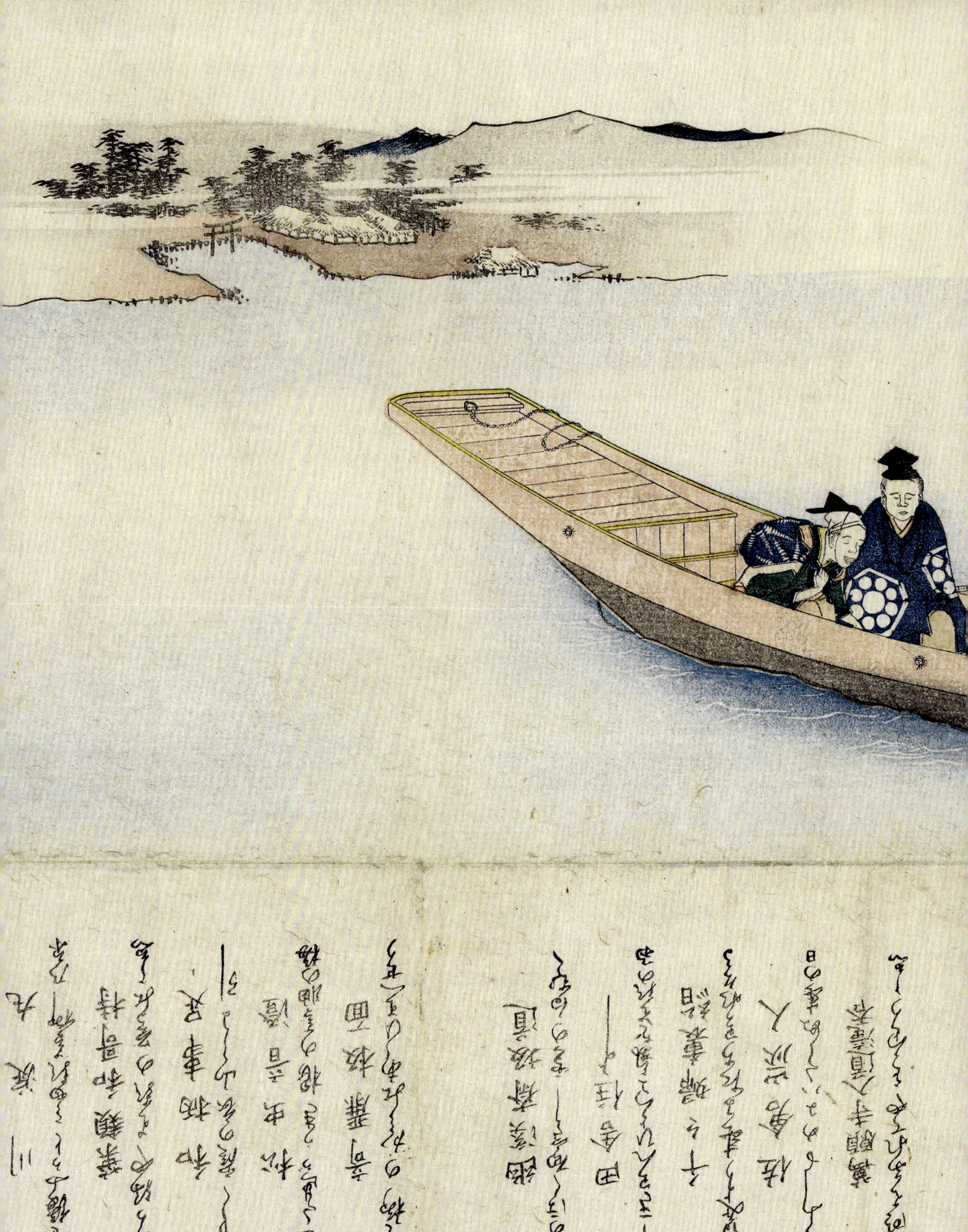

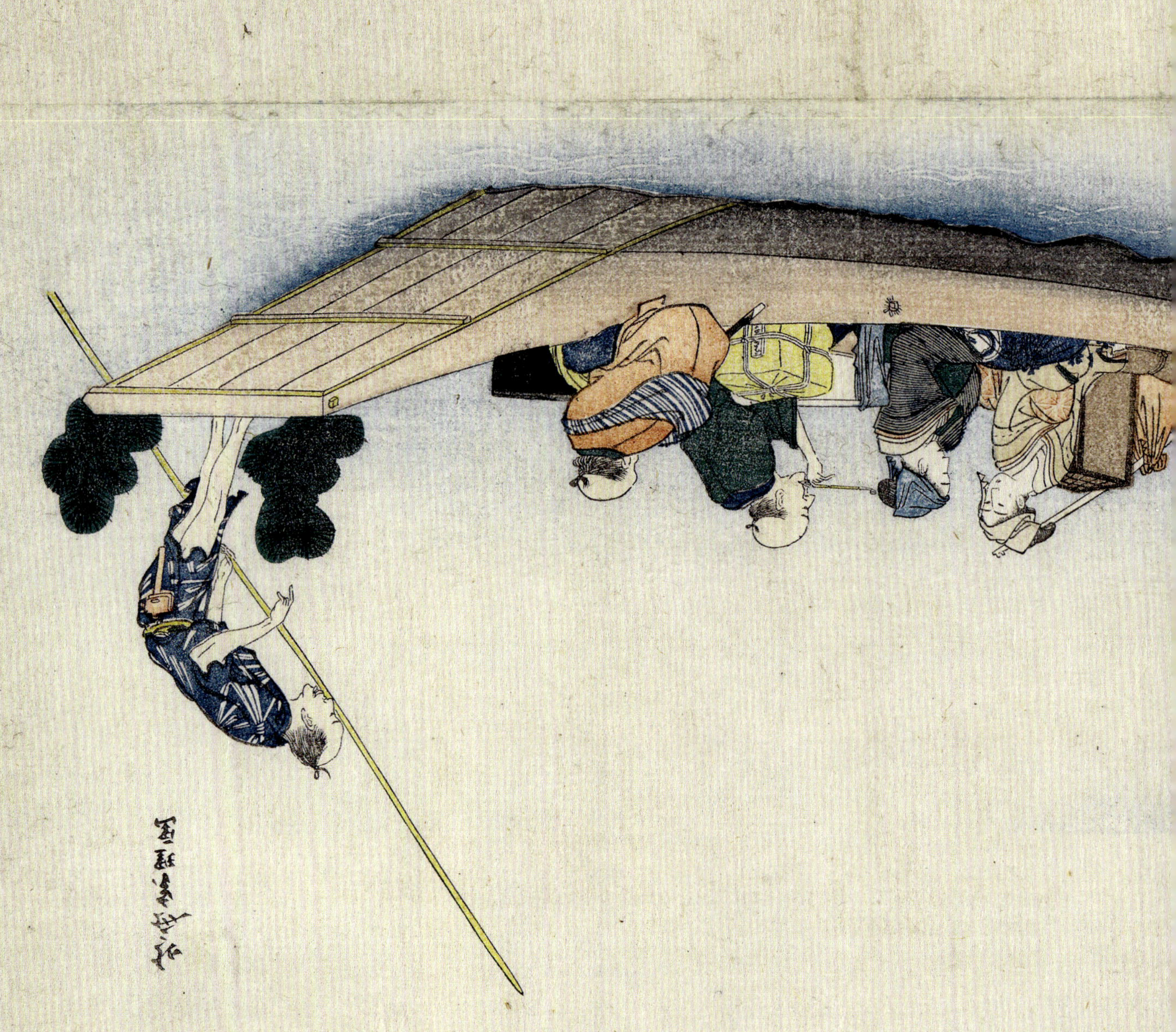

…わらんハかめりもこゑまき舟の日のけん

瞞黒主

…ま亀井よりひの万里帆挟

三千歳百足

…るはほしかけさ…やうかれ…

翠簾遠守

…るうらよころろほうやよあふらん…

飯練吉

…の音かきわけていろはあさうり

臯下守

…ハみどりとよ…きりかかる…

臯下主

大口と一両にたけさ月の西の夷

唯笑舎下風

…よめつつそまる風の請とり

櫻下堂

…かしさくらある
…れまとぬよ
…せるそのついでふ

浅草菴

…泊もつあれかしさきよなく

9 | **Stone** (*Ishi*) from the series *Three Pictures for a Children's Hand Game* (*Osana asobi ken sanbantsuzuki no uchi*), 1823

One of a set of three prints based on the hand game rock-paper-scissors, this surimono cleverly represents stone in two forms. A lovely young lady, whose floral hair decorations identify her as the pampered daughter of an upper-class household, uses pebbles and sand to make a tray landscape. On the wall behind her is a painting showing the Chinese Taoist immortal Huang Zhuping, who had the magical ability to change stones into goats and goats into stones. The print was most likely made to celebrate 1823, the Year of the Goat.

The mountain created by the young lady has sometimes been identified as a model of Mount Fuji, but its asymmetrical shape suggests that it may represent some other peak instead, or perhaps simply a generic mountain. Of the three kyōka poems inscribed on the print, one suggests a resemblance to Mount Tsukuba, which dominated the horizon north of Edo, much as Fuji did to the south; a second poem does not specify the mountain; and a third makes a joking reference to Ishiyama near Kyoto, based not on the appearance of that mountain but on its name, literally Stone Mountain. In this case, it seems likely that the picture was drawn first (or at least, the concept of the picture was described to the poets) and the poems were written to accompany it.

Signature: Hokusai aratame Iitsu hitsu
Woodblock print (surimono); ink and color on paper
21.8 x 18.4 cm (8 9/16 x 7 1/4 in.)
William Sturgis Bigelow Collection, 11.20413

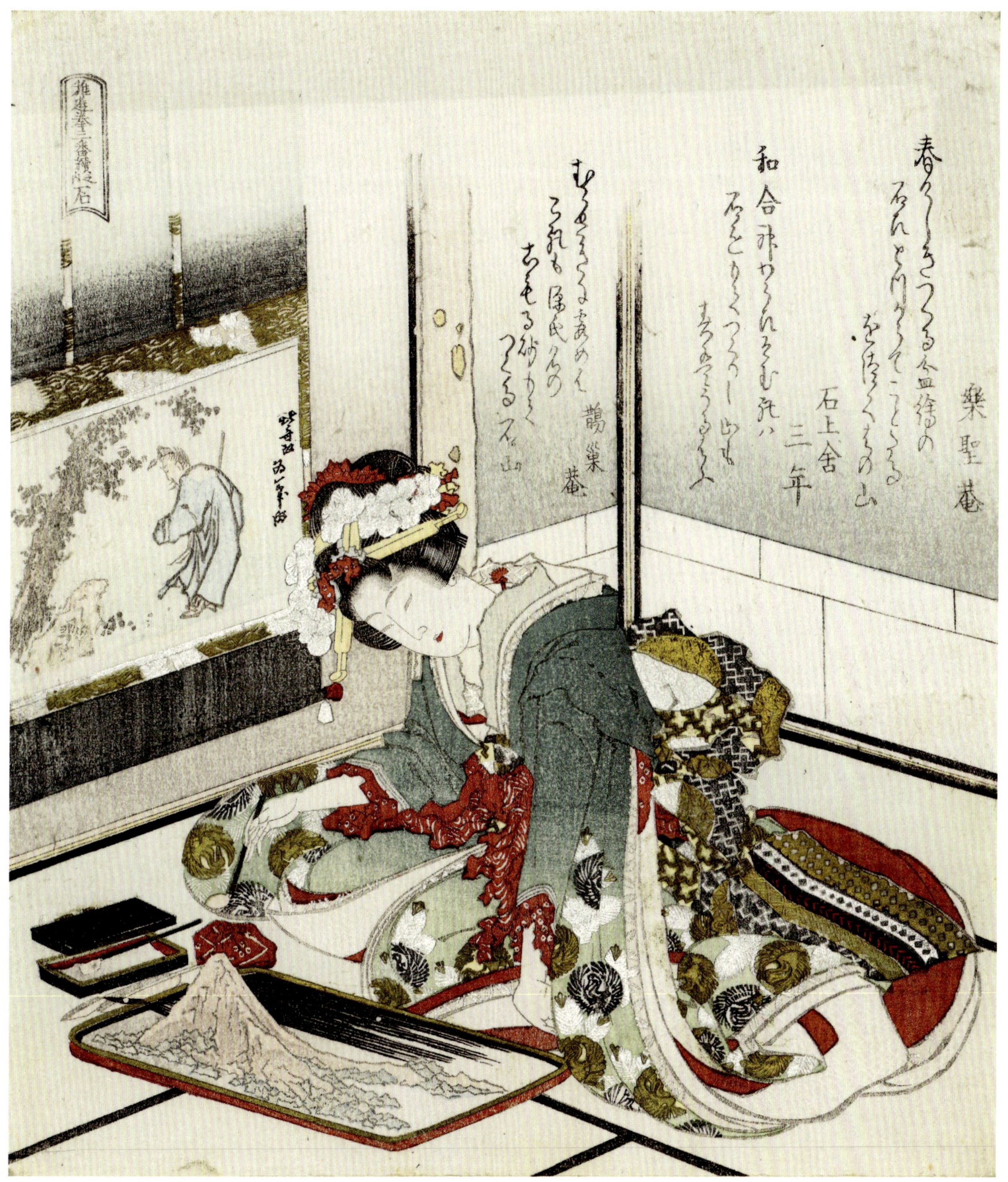

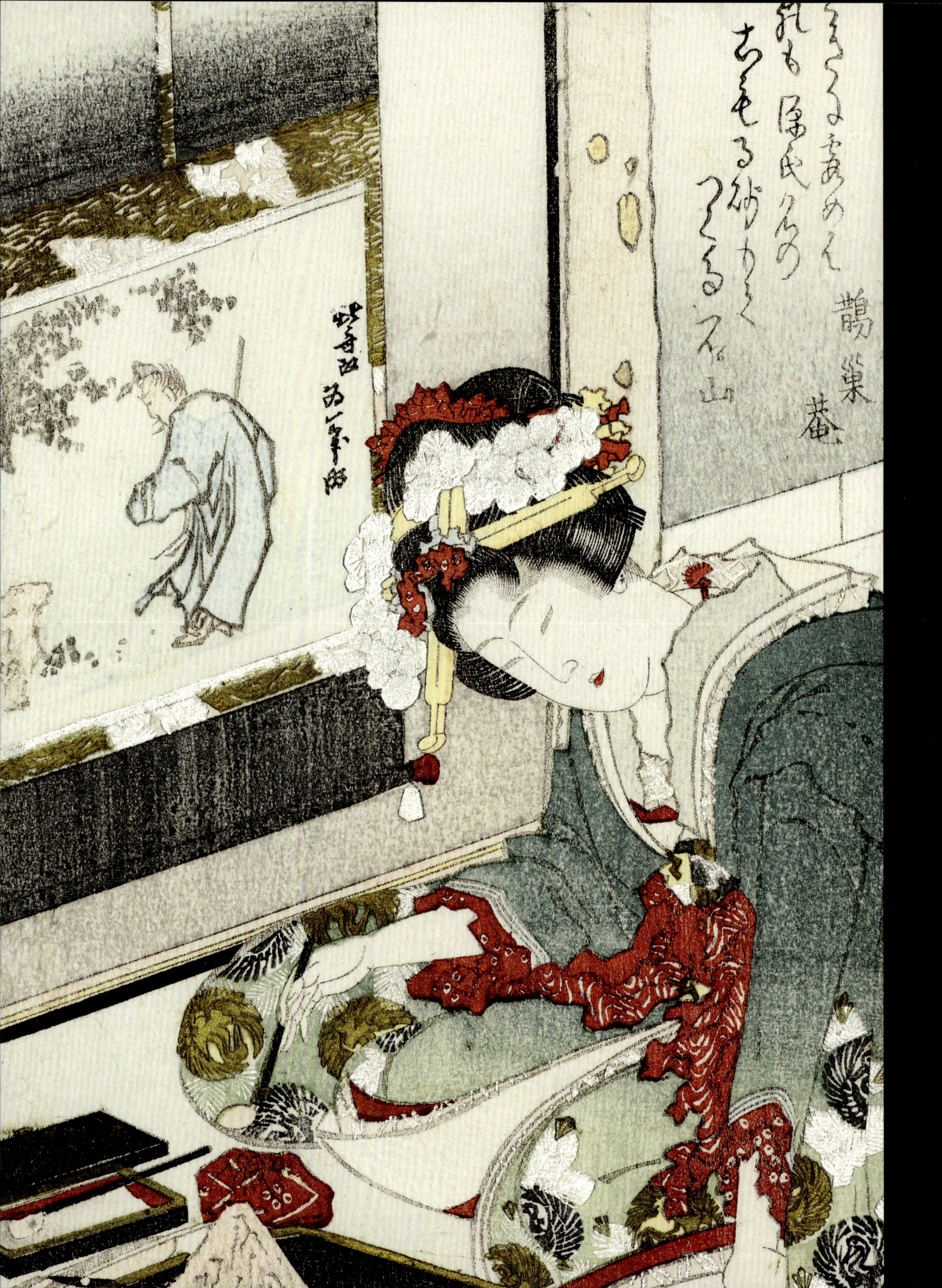
鵲巣菴

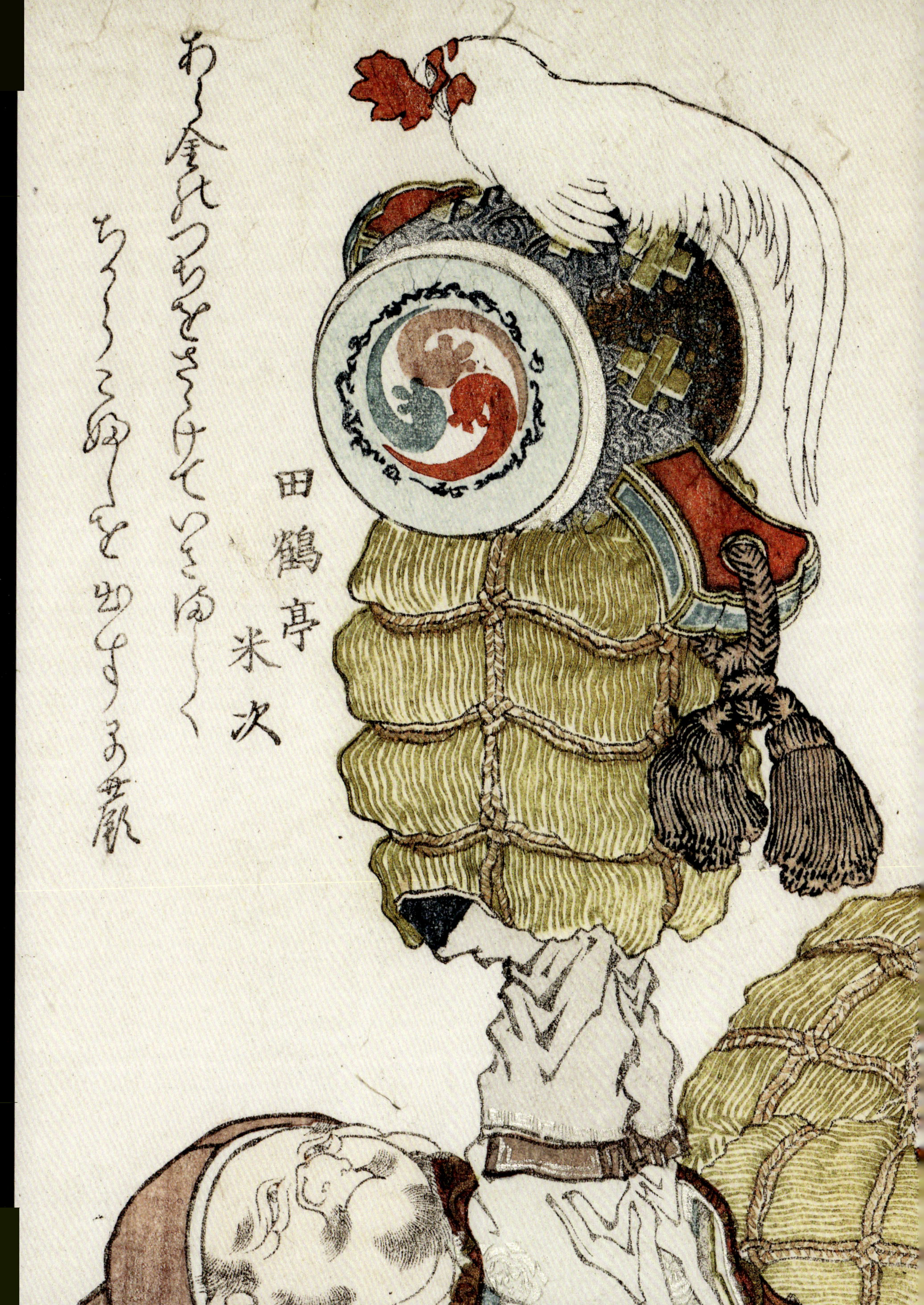
田鶴亭
米次

10 | **Daikoku Lifting Rice Bales, with Chickens,** 1825

Daikoku, the god of wealth, was a natural choice for the subject of a New Year surimono. As one of the Seven Gods of Good Fortune, he wears a Chinese-style costume and has a plump face and very large earlobes, an indication of prosperity according to physiognomists. He often appears seated on a stack of rice bales, the traditional measure of wealth in pre-modern Japan. Because mice are found where grain is found, they are usually associated with Daikoku, but since this surimono was made for 1825, the Year of the Chicken, Hokusai instead shows a rooster, with two chicks on the ground below, and a hen pecking hopefully at a rice bale.

Daikoku himself has taken on the role of an acrobatic performer and weight lifter. He uses his legs to lift a heavy bale of rice, on top of which balances another of his attributes: the magic mallet that he uses to pound out gold coins. The head of the mallet is decorated with a variation of the lucky three-comma symbol, which was also used on drumheads, inspiring Hokusai to create a visual pun. The white rooster perched on top of the mallet, his feathers beautifully embossed and his red comb waving like a flag, brings to mind the then familiar image of a chicken roosting on a drum as a symbol of peace. In ancient Chinese literature, an ideal, peaceful society was one in which the war drums were so seldom beaten that they became perches for chickens.

The two kyōka poems inscribed in the upper left corner are signed with the pen names Dengakutei Yoneji and Yomo Utagaki Magao. The first poem refers to the weight-lifting theme, describing a curled fern shoot pushing up the heavy earth like a tiny fist (fern shoots were a traditional New Year delicacy). The second poem also utilizes auspicious New Year motifs, describing triangular stacks of rice bales that resemble evergreen trees. In this case, it is not clear which was created first, the picture or the poems. The interplay of verbal and visual imagery—related but not identical—would have been a major source of pleasure for the original viewers of the print.

Signature: Saki no Hokusai Iitsu hitsu
Woodblock print (surimono); ink and color on paper
21.1 x 18.3 cm (8 5/16 x 7 3/16 in.)
Julia Bradford Huntington James Fund, 00.1948

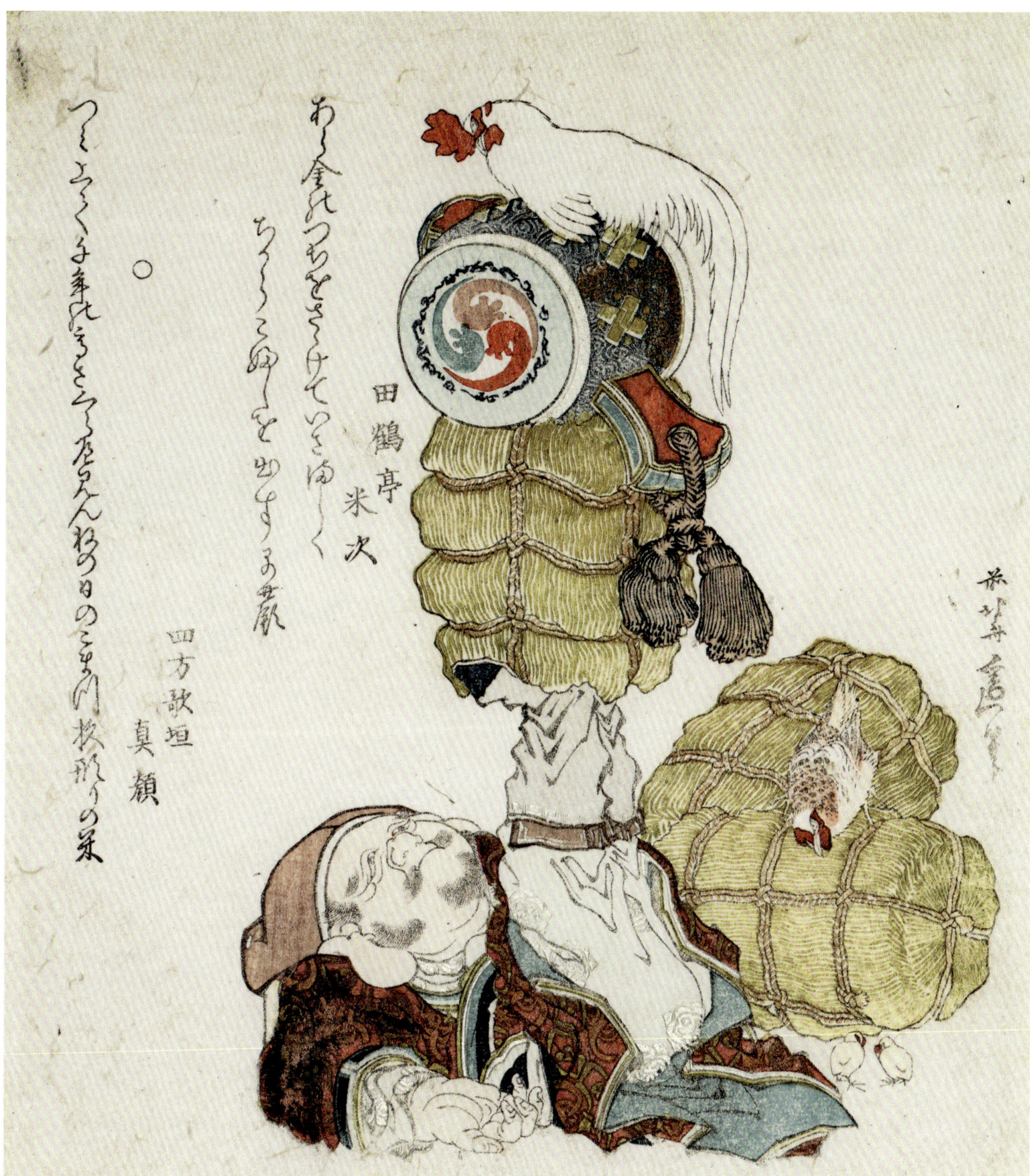
田鶴亭
米次
四方歌垣
真顔

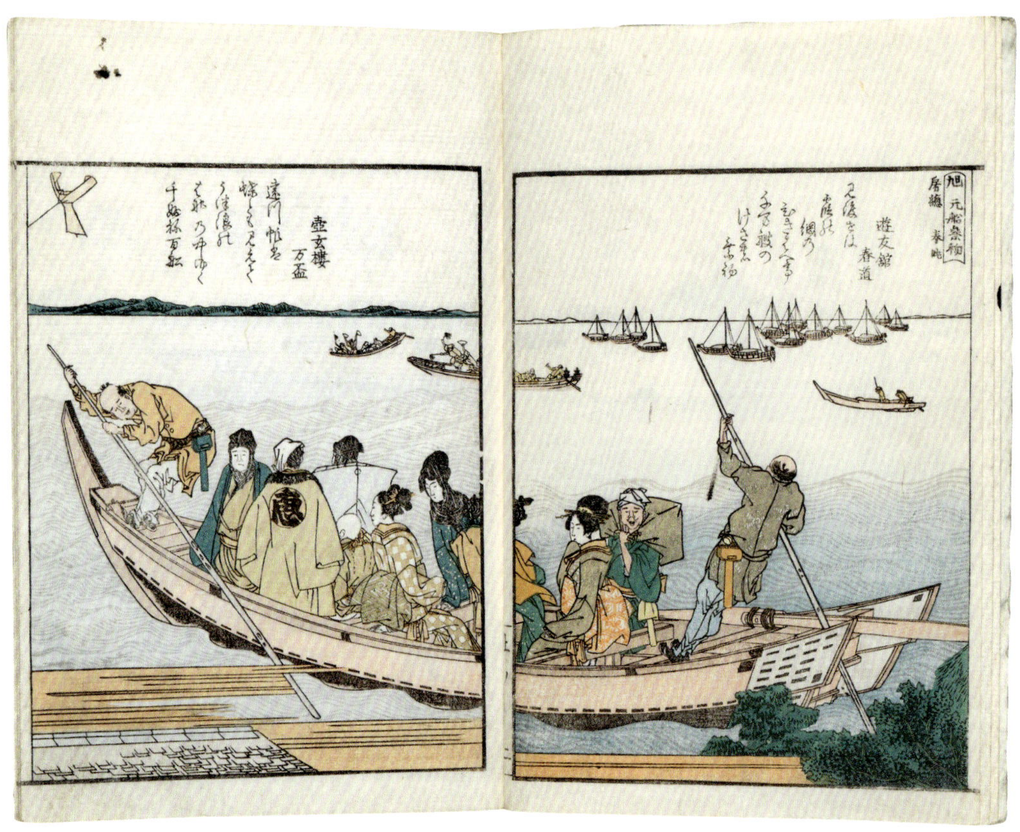

11 | **Picture Book of the Two Banks of the Sumida River at a Glance** (*Ehon Sumidagawa ryōgan ichiran*), about 1804

In the early 1800s, Hokusai began to produce picture books with kyōka poems that were intended not only for the poets themselves but also for the general public. Considered the finest of all his poetry books, *The Two Banks of the Sumida River at a Glance* presents a journey through space and time along the great river that runs through the city of Edo, beginning in the harbor district of Takanawa on New Year's Day and moving upstream to conclude at the end of the year in the Yoshiwara pleasure quarter.

Each two-page vignette is linked directly to the next so that the scene unfolds continuously as in a handscroll painting. This idea had already been used by other artists, but Hokusai employed it with great skill, combining scenes of human activity along the river with panoramic views of the landscape in ways that foreshadow his landscape prints of the 1830s. The unifying motif of the river also suggests Hokusai's later use of themes linking the individual prints in his later landscape series *Mount Fuji*, *Waterfalls*, and *Bridges*.

In a preface to the book, the kyōka poet Kojūrō Nariyasu explains that he asked his fellow poets and drinking companions to compose poems based on Hokusai's illustrations. *The Two Banks of the Sumida River* is undated, but it resembles other works by Hokusai published around 1804.

Publisher: Tsuruya Kiemon (Senkakudō)
Woodblock-printed book; ink and color on paper
26.6 x 18.2 cm (10½ x $7\frac{3}{16}$ in.)
Source unidentified, 1997.694.1–3

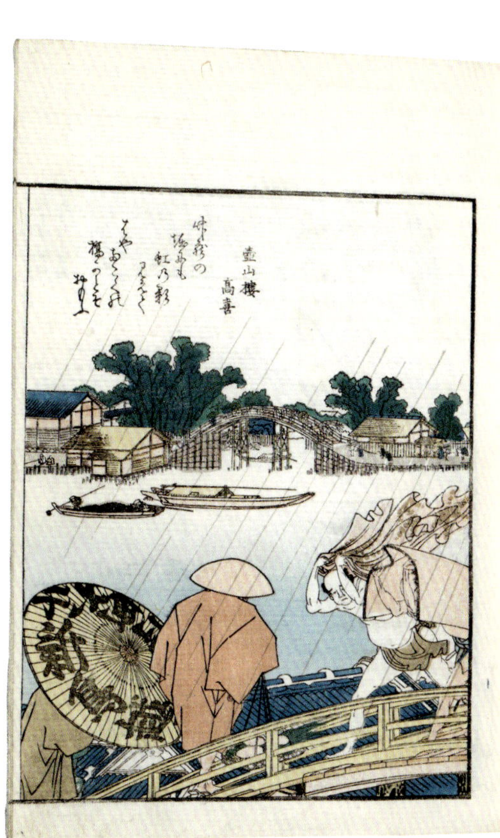

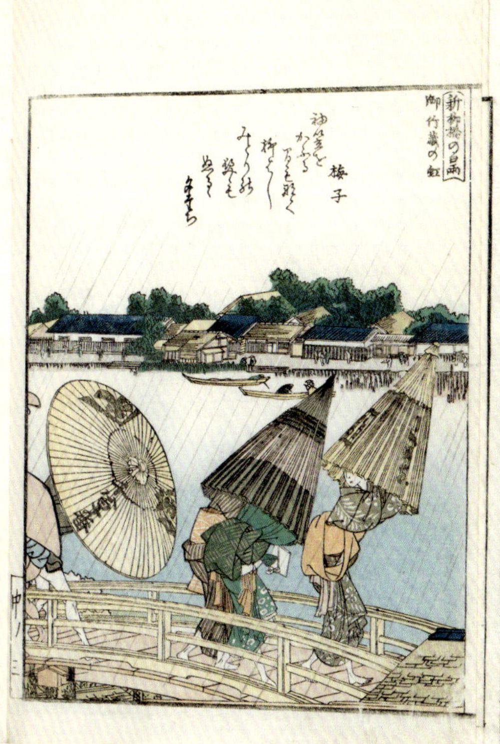
新大橋の白雨
御竹蔵の虹

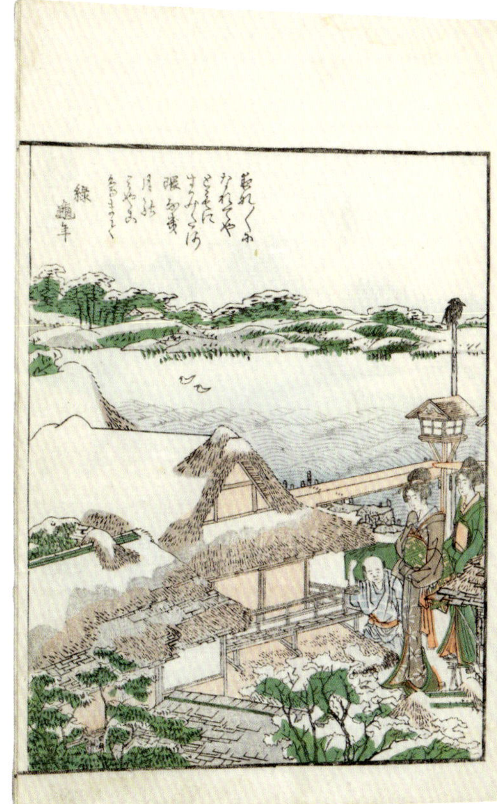

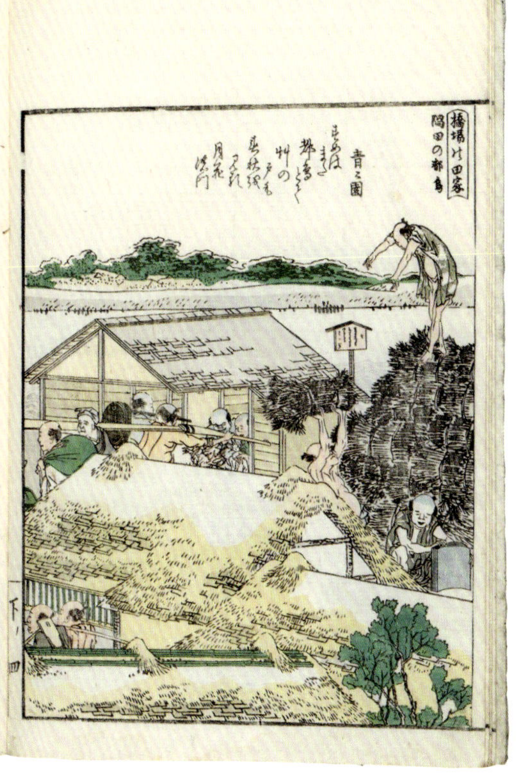
隅田の都鳥

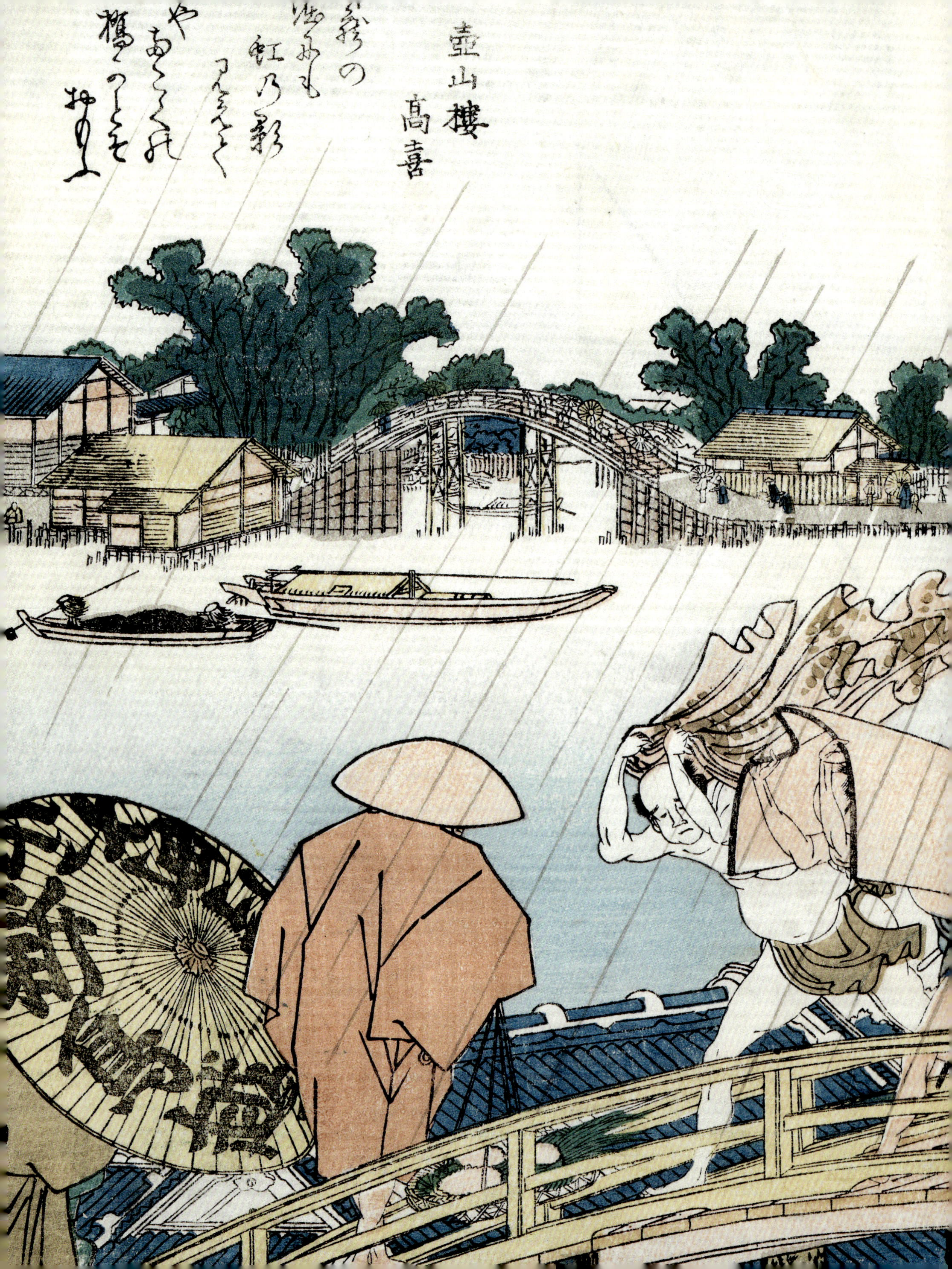
壺山樓
高喜

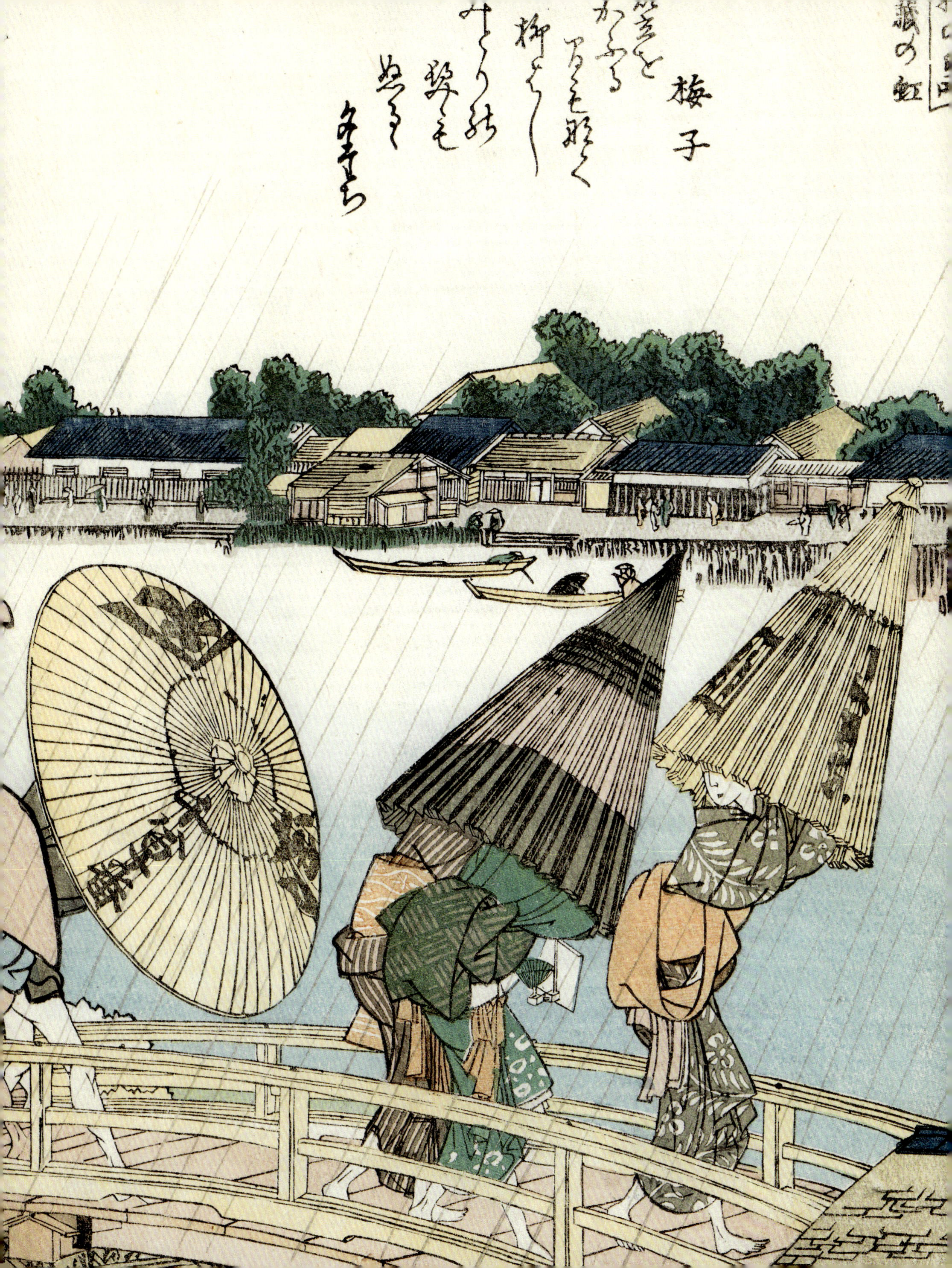
梅子

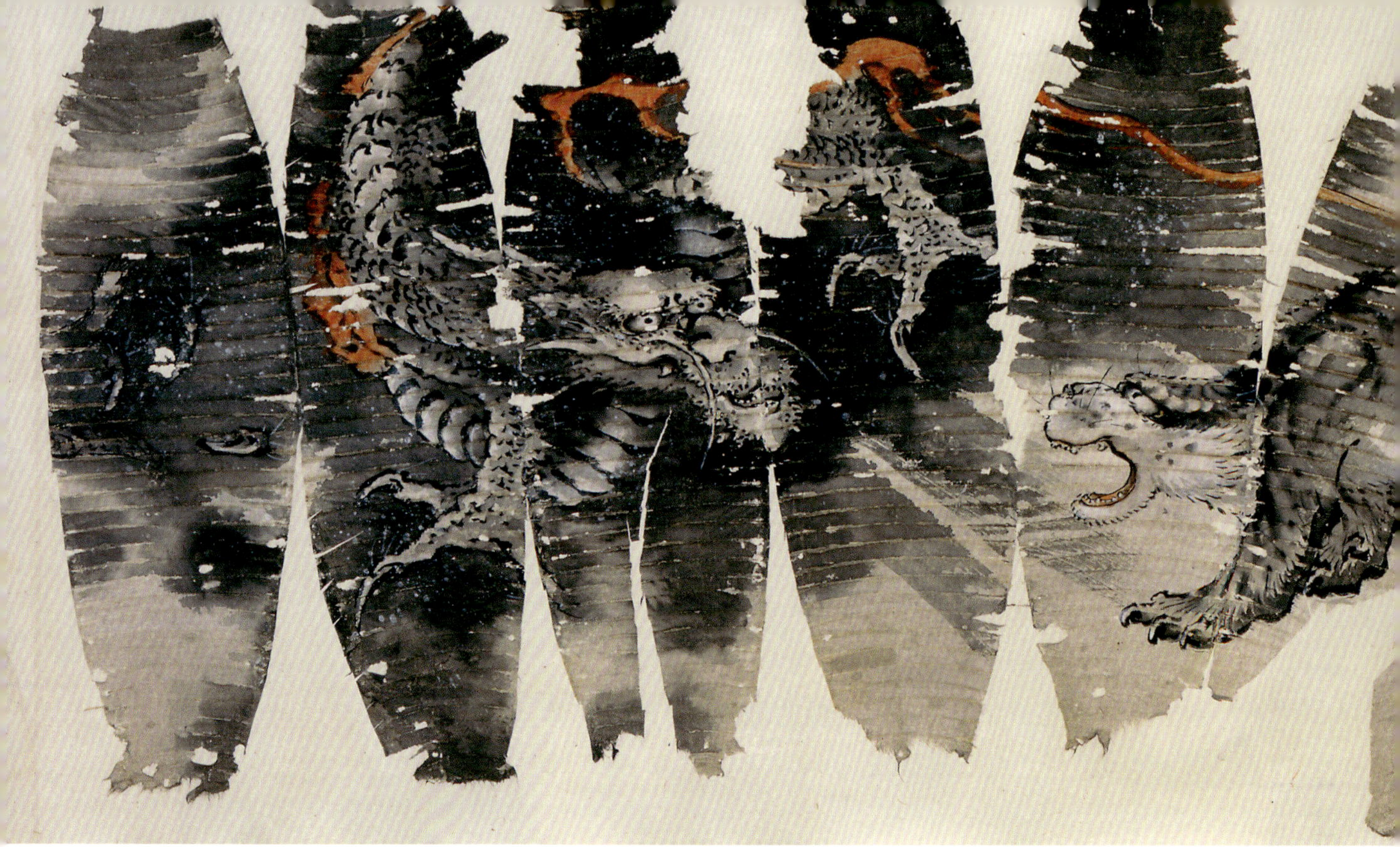

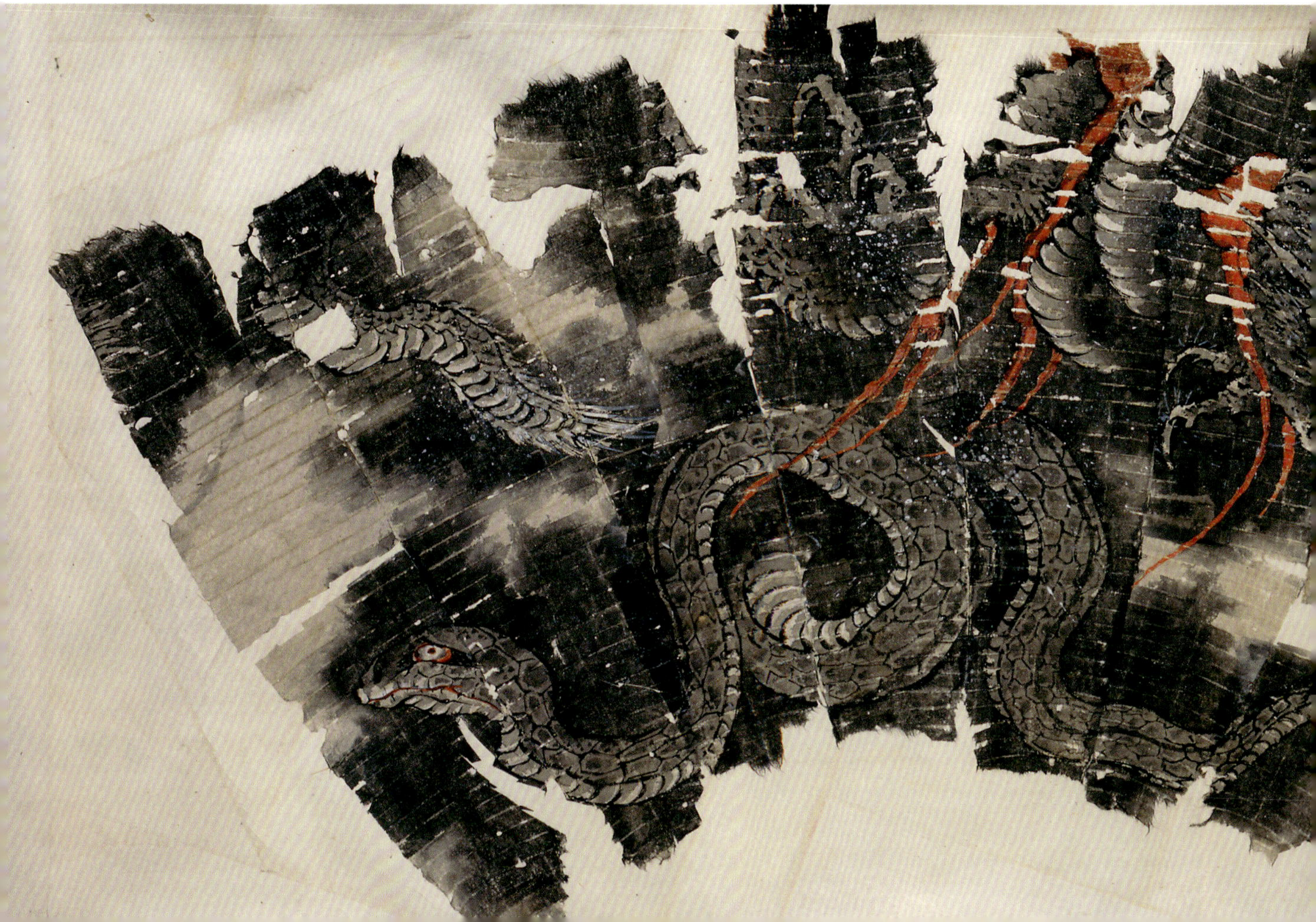

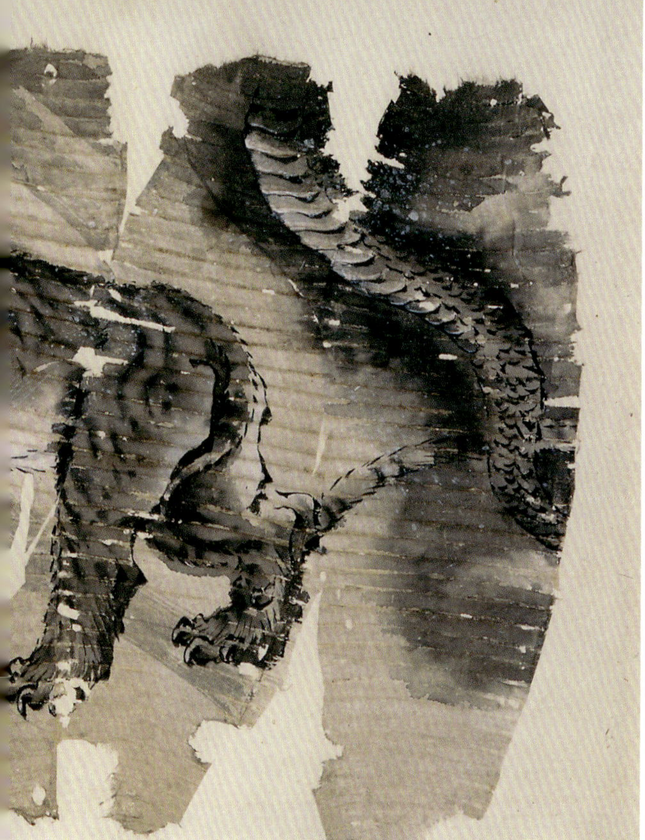

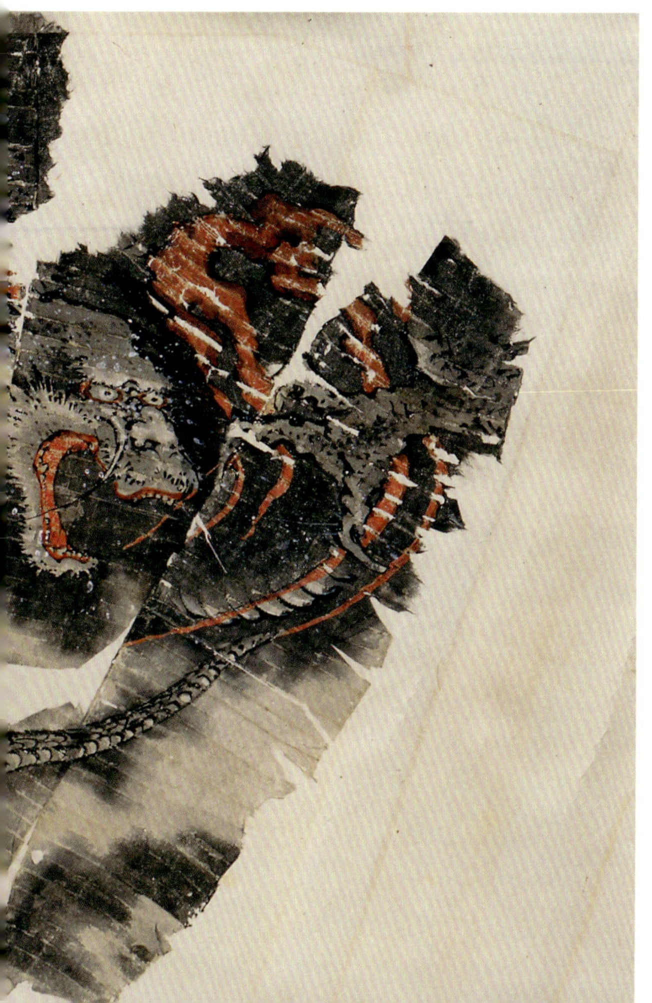

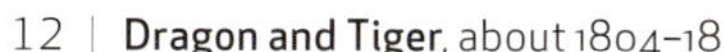

12 | **Dragon and Tiger**, about 1804–18

13 | **Dragon and Snake**, about 1804–18

Most of Hokusai's paintings were done on flat surfaces of paper or silk, but he was also highly skilled at painting three-dimensional objects and at creating special designs to take advantage of these unusual exteriors. The lanterns that he painted for display at festivals and other special occasions are mentioned in contemporary sources, and two of them have survived at the MFA. Lanterns such as these, originally constructed of paper over a bamboo framework, could be hung from the eaves of buildings or carried on a short pole to light the way when walking at night. When not in use, the lantern (minus the candle or small oil lamp inside) could be collapsed flat for storage.

Both lanterns show animals with deep mythological significance. The dragon and tiger represent the forces of nature; in the ancient lore imported from China, the dragon controlled rainstorms while the tiger's roar generated the wind. Since real tigers were not found in Japan, both the dragon and the tiger were imaginary creatures to Hokusai, although there was a long tradition of paintings of the subject. On one side of the lantern, they confront each other with ferocious expressions, but on the other side, their overlapping tails imply their close relationship.

The dragon and snake shown on the second lantern are two of the twelve animals of the East Asian zodiac, a cycle that in Hokusai's time could be used to represent years, months, days, hours, or spatial directions. These animals are adjacent to each other in the cycle, and so the combination of the two could imply the transition from a Year of the Dragon to a Year of the Snake. They could also be a geographic reference to the Fukagawa area in the southeast part of the city, sometimes nicknamed Tatsumi (Dragon-Snake) because it lay in the direction associated with the two reptiles.

12
Lantern painting; ink and light color on paper
H. 40.6, diam. 30.5 cm (H. 16, diam. 12 in.)
William Sturgis Bigelow Collection, 11.9100

13
Lantern painting; ink and light color on paper
H. 50.8, diam. 30.5 cm (H. 20, diam. 12 in.)
William Sturgis Bigelow Collection, 11.9113

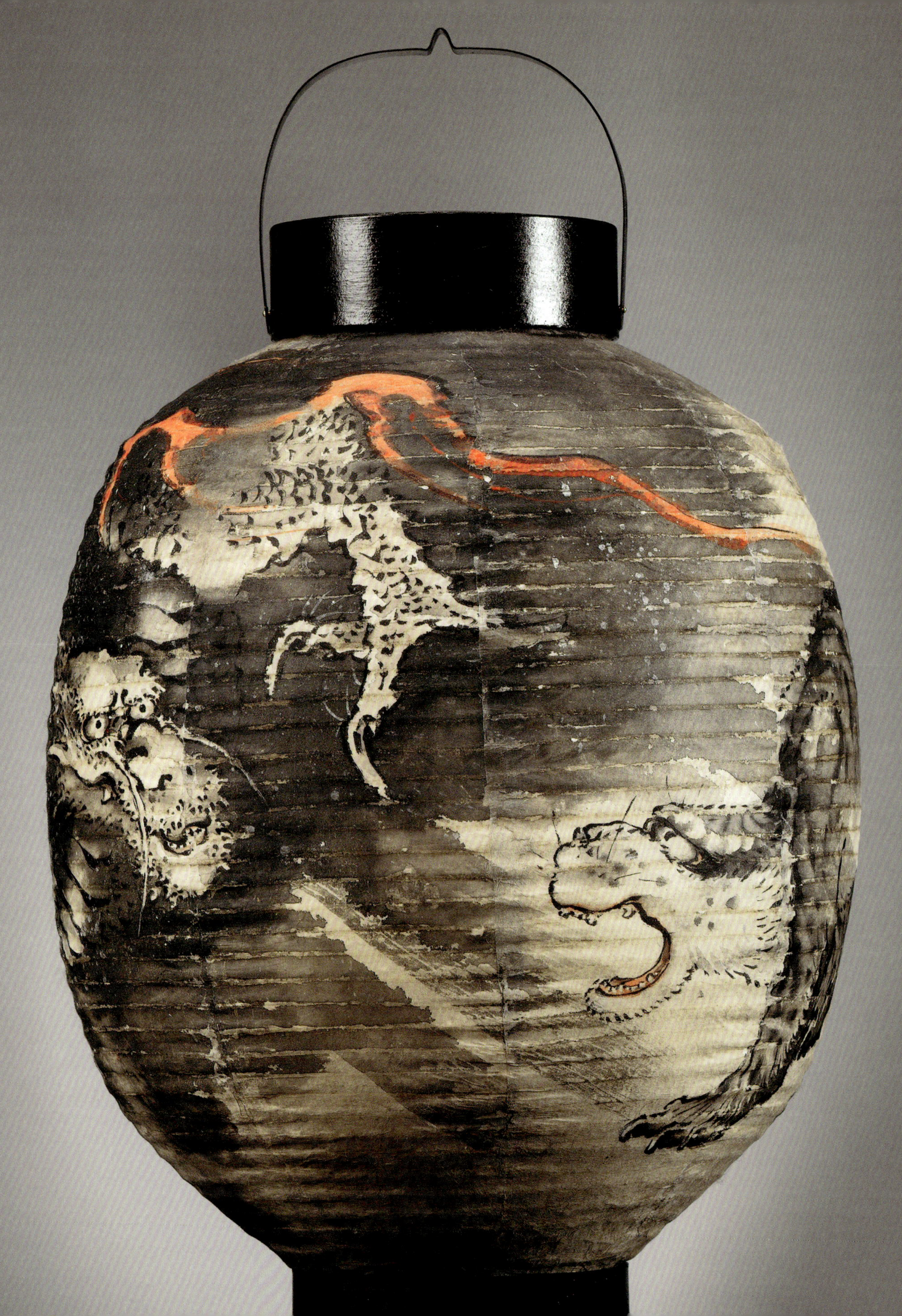

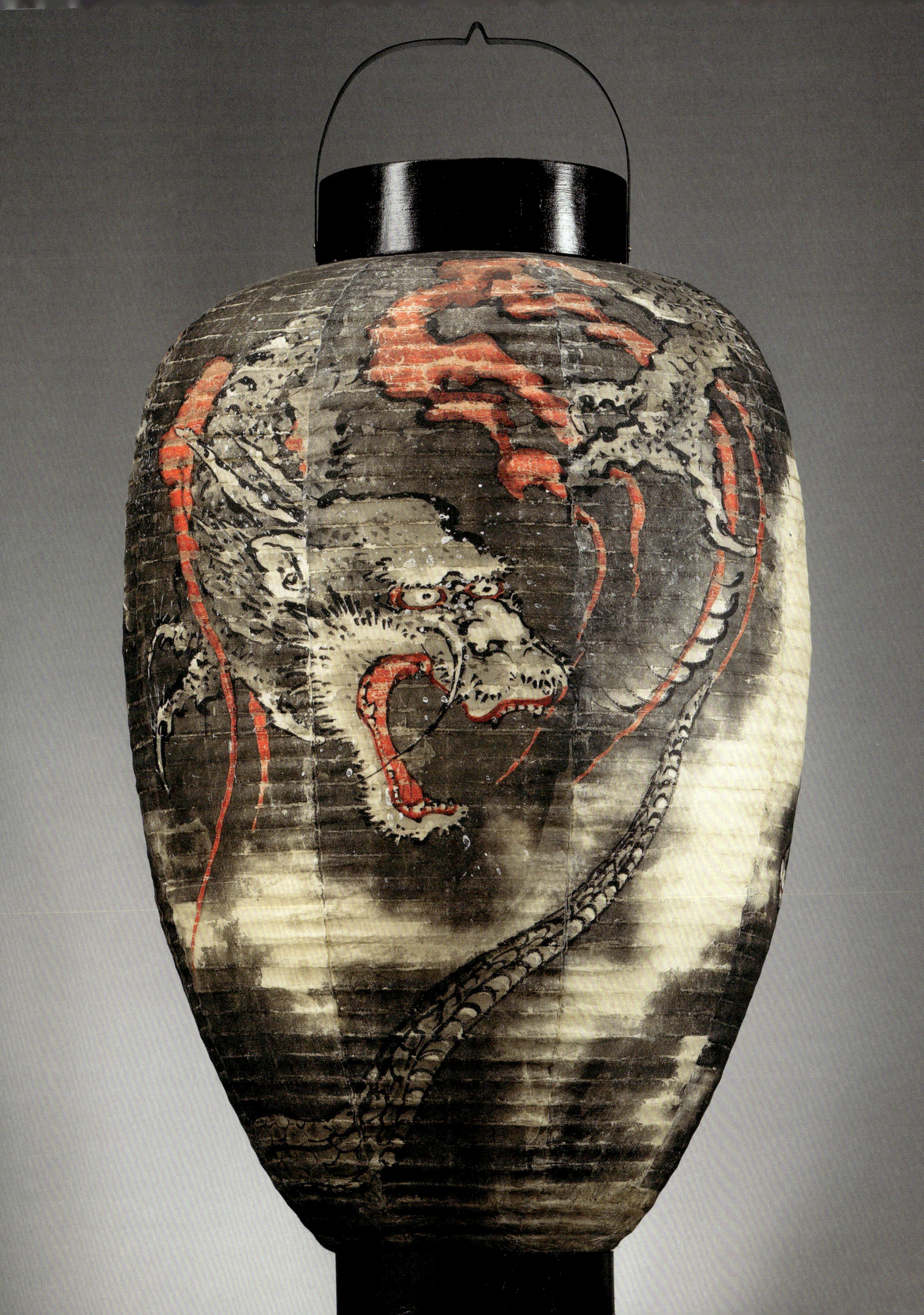

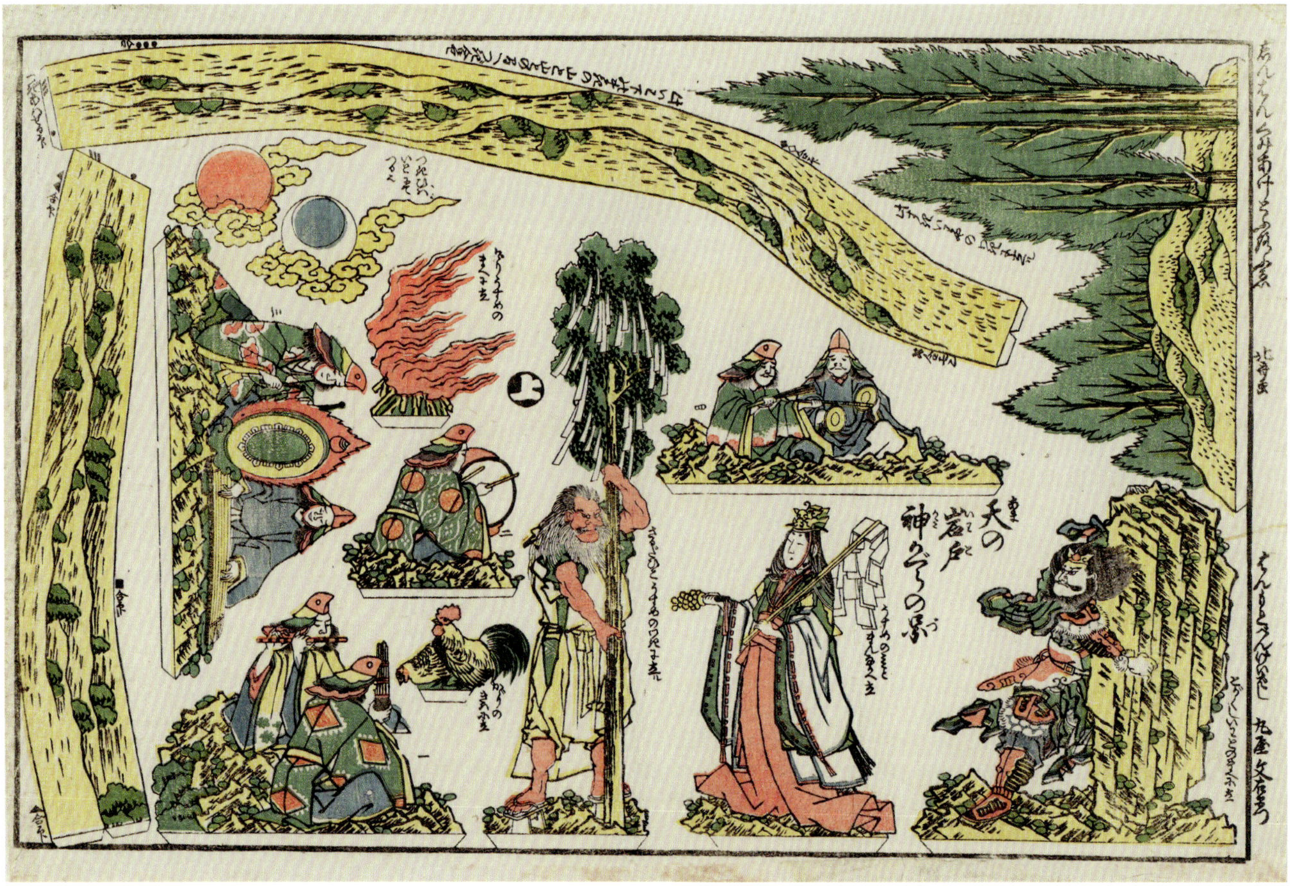

14 | **Newly Published Cut-Out Lantern Pictures: Dance of the Gods at the Heavenly Cave**
(*Shinpan kumiage tōrō-e, Ama no iwato kami kagura no zu*), part 1 (*jō*) and part 2 (*ge*), about 1808–13

Hokusai was one of the leading designers of cut-out prints, which were cut apart with scissors and pasted together into small paper dioramas. The engineering aspect of their construction must have appealed to the artist's interests in mechanical devices and in convincingly rendering three-dimensional objects. Since most of these toys were cut apart, played with, and discarded, intact examples are rare today.

Cut-out prints, which became popular in Edo in the early years of the nineteenth century, were said to have originated in the Kamigata area (Kyoto and Osaka), the traditional center for making paper lanterns. The modern word for them is *tatebanko*

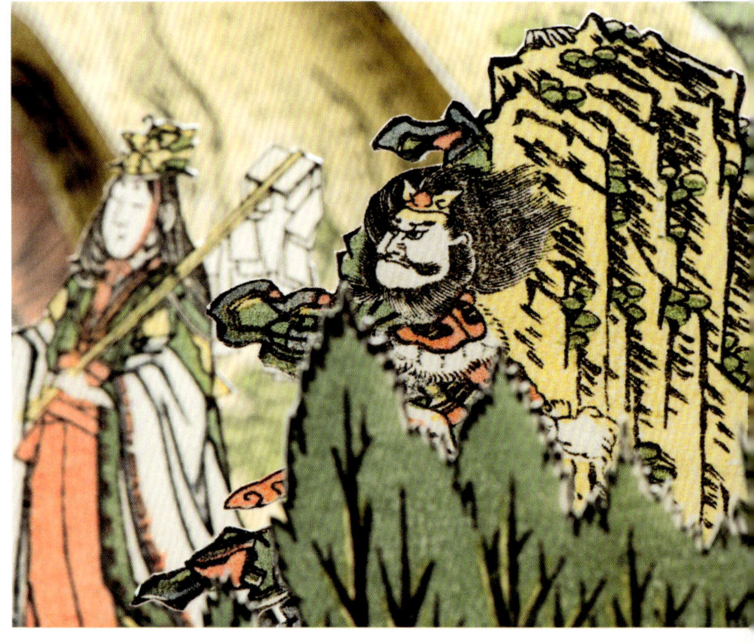

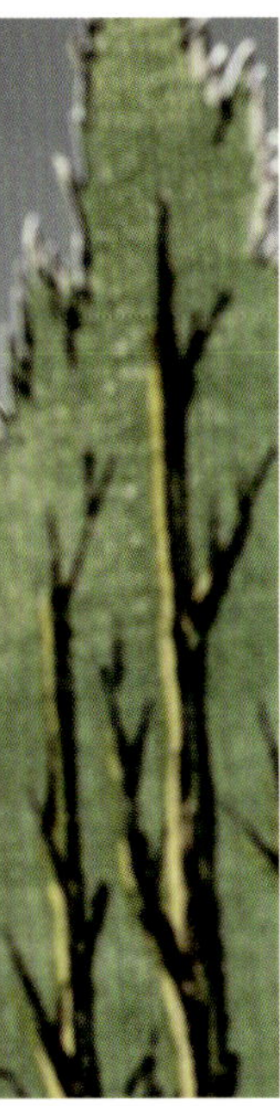

(literally "construction prints"), but one of the older terms, which appears on this example, translates as "lantern pictures." This latter expression may mean that the scenes were similar to cut-out pictures used to decorate the tops of festival lanterns, or it may refer to the fact that they were often enjoyed with tiny lamps or candles illuminating the completed scene from behind, shining through cut-out windows and doors.

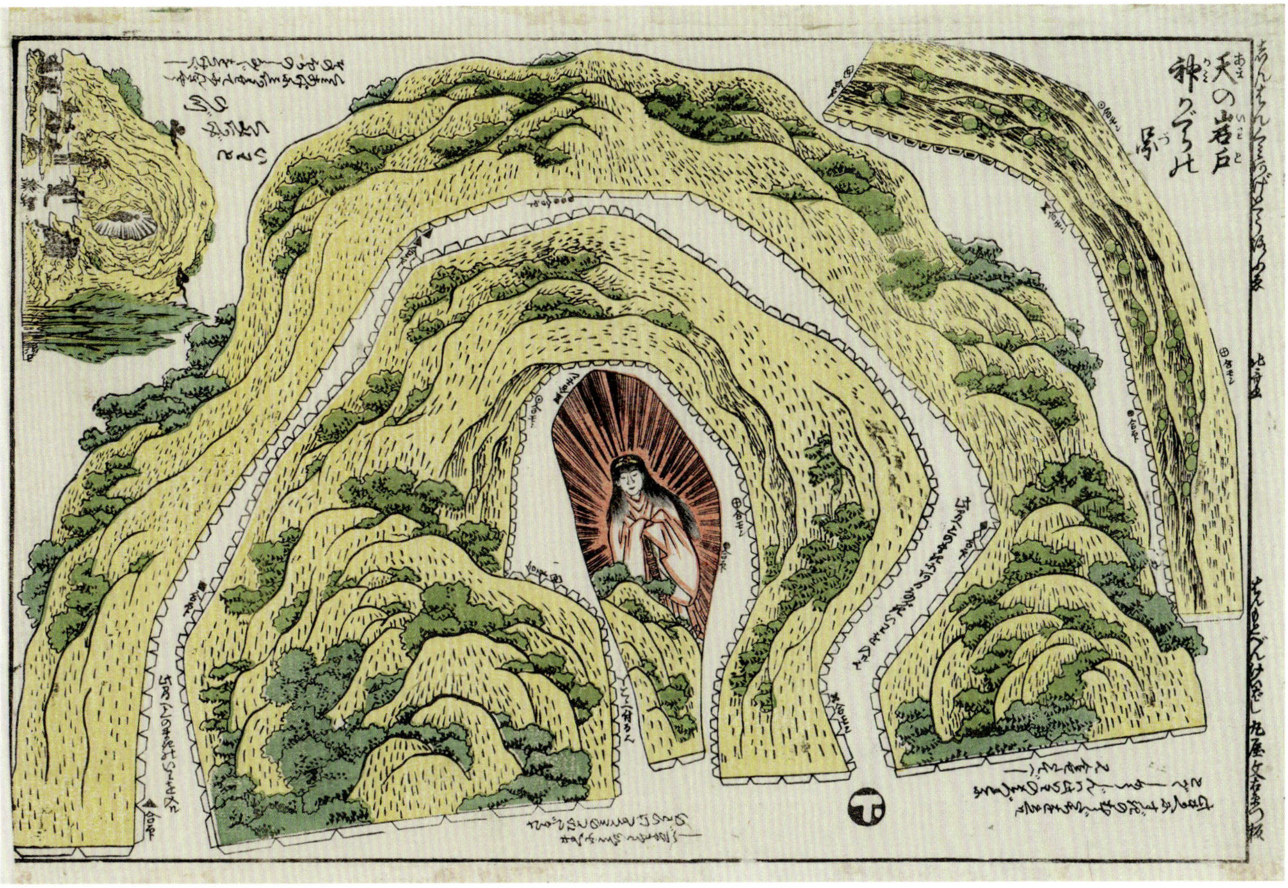

This two-sheet design would have been an especially challenging one for the model maker because it involves not the square, easily folded shapes of buildings but the irregular shapes of a natural landscape. The sacred dances performed at Shinto shrines were said to have originated in the distant past, during the Age of the Gods. The Sun Goddess, Amaterasu, was so offended by the misbehavior of her bratty little brother that she retreated into the Heavenly Cave (Ama no Iwato) and deprived the world of light and warmth. To lure her out, the other gods held a noisy party with music and dancing. When the Sun Goddess came out of the cave to see what was happening, a powerful god placed a large rock over the entrance to keep her from going back inside.

A small sketch on the second sheet shows how the completed scene should be assembled, with the radiant goddess deep inside the central cave and the other figures arranged in front. Additional instructions on the assembly of the scene and the placement of the figures are written beside the relevant components.

Signature: Hokusai ga
Publisher: Maruya Bun'emon (Bunjudō)
Woodblock print (nishiki-e); ink and color on paper
26.5 x 38.3 cm (10 7/16 x 15 1/16 in.)
William Sturgis Bigelow Collection, 11.20433, 11.20434

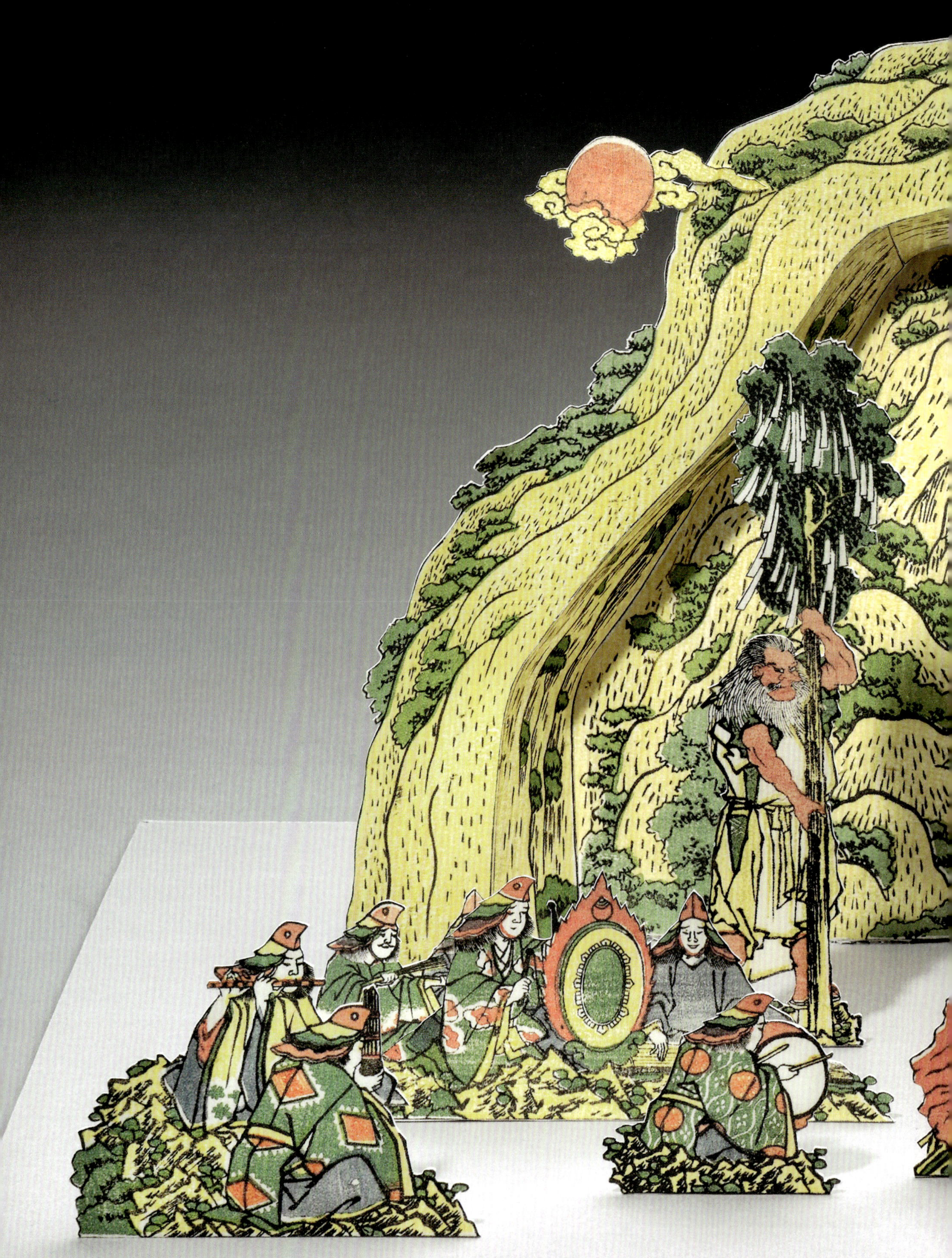

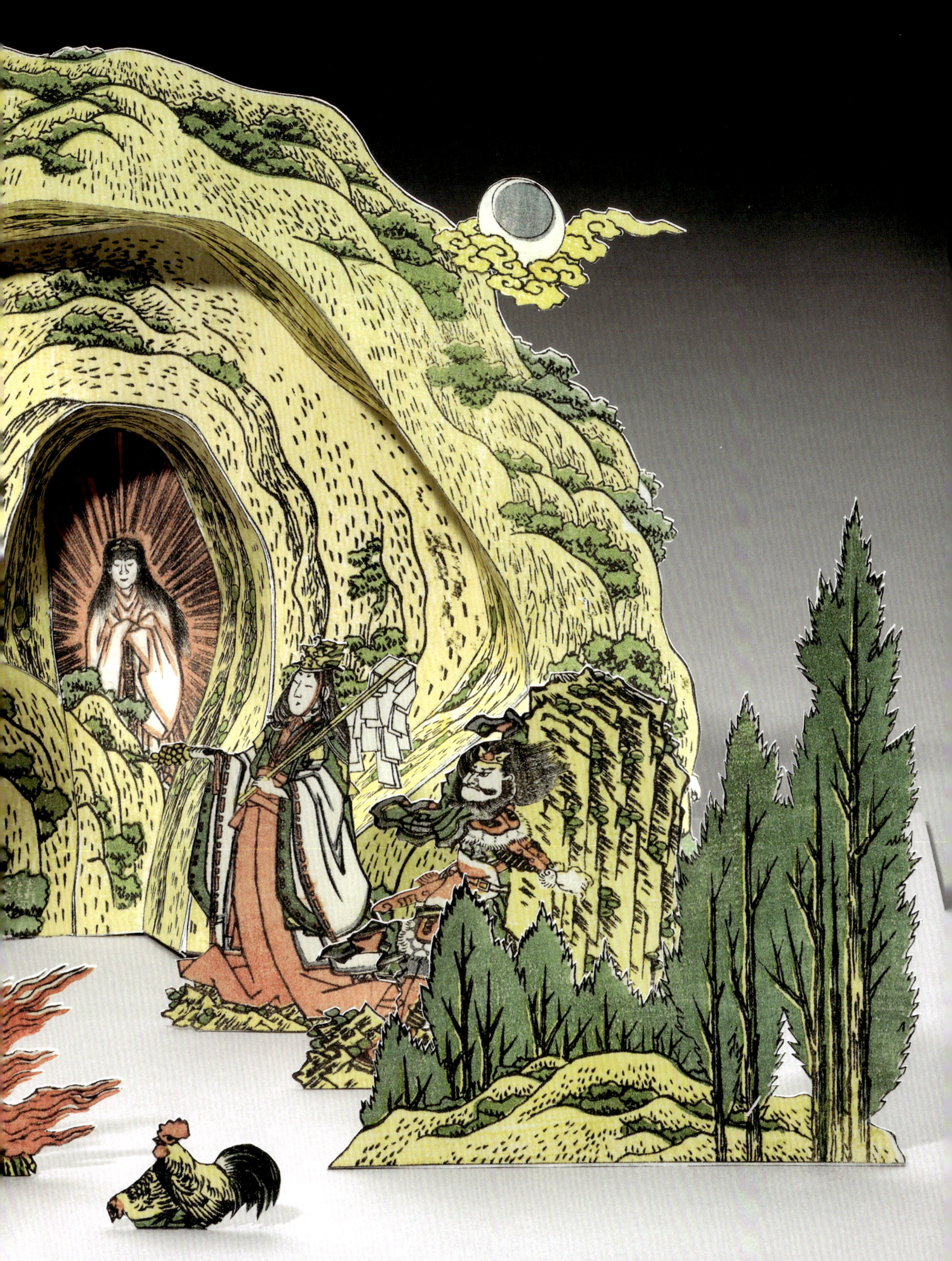

15 | **The Kaminarimon Gate at Sensō-ji Temple in Asakusa**, about 1808–13

The front gate of the Sensō-ji Temple in Asakusa is famous because the sculptures inside it are not the usual guardian figures but rather the Wind God (at the right, holding a bag of wind) and the Thunder God (at the left, with a circle of small drums that he beats to create thunder). This print is untitled except for the expression "Newly Published" in the upper right corner, but an inscription next to the group of brawling men reads "Stand [these figures] in front of the Gate of the Thunder God," confirming the identification.

For this cut-out toy, the size of the human figures relative to the gate has been scaled up considerably, so that the actions and expressions of the figures can be seen more clearly. The fully shaven heads of the fighting men indicate that they are members of the guild of blind masseurs and musicians. The central figure is bright red with rage (and perhaps also alcohol); five men attempt to restrain him, observed by human and canine spectators. The humorous expressions of the bystanders watching the fight from the safety of the gate building are typical of Hokusai's style.

The portable lanterns held by one of the female onlookers and by one of the male figures inside the gate indicate that the scene takes place in the evening. At the side of the gate building, a red lantern bears the words "Special Exhibition," a possible explanation for why so many people are still on the grounds of the temple even at this late hour. The gigantic round lantern hanging inside the gate has the first part of the word *Shinba[shi]*, the name of the area whose residents donated the lantern to the temple; the names of the individual donors were on the lower part of the lantern, here represented by illegible scribbles. The smaller inscribed portable lantern below identifies its holder as a member of a Buddhist confraternity (*kō*).

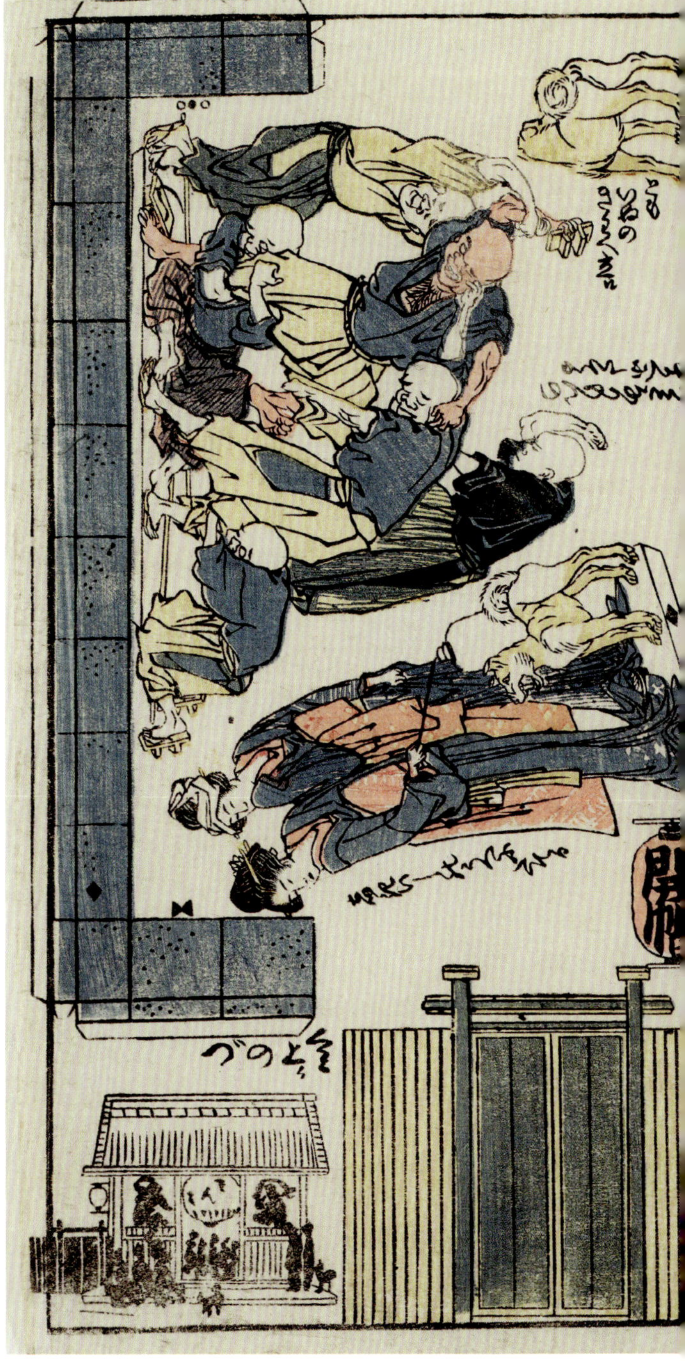

Woodblock print (nishiki-e); ink and color on paper
24.4 x 36.6 cm (9 5/8 x 14 7/16 in.)
William Sturgis Bigelow Collection, 11.19640

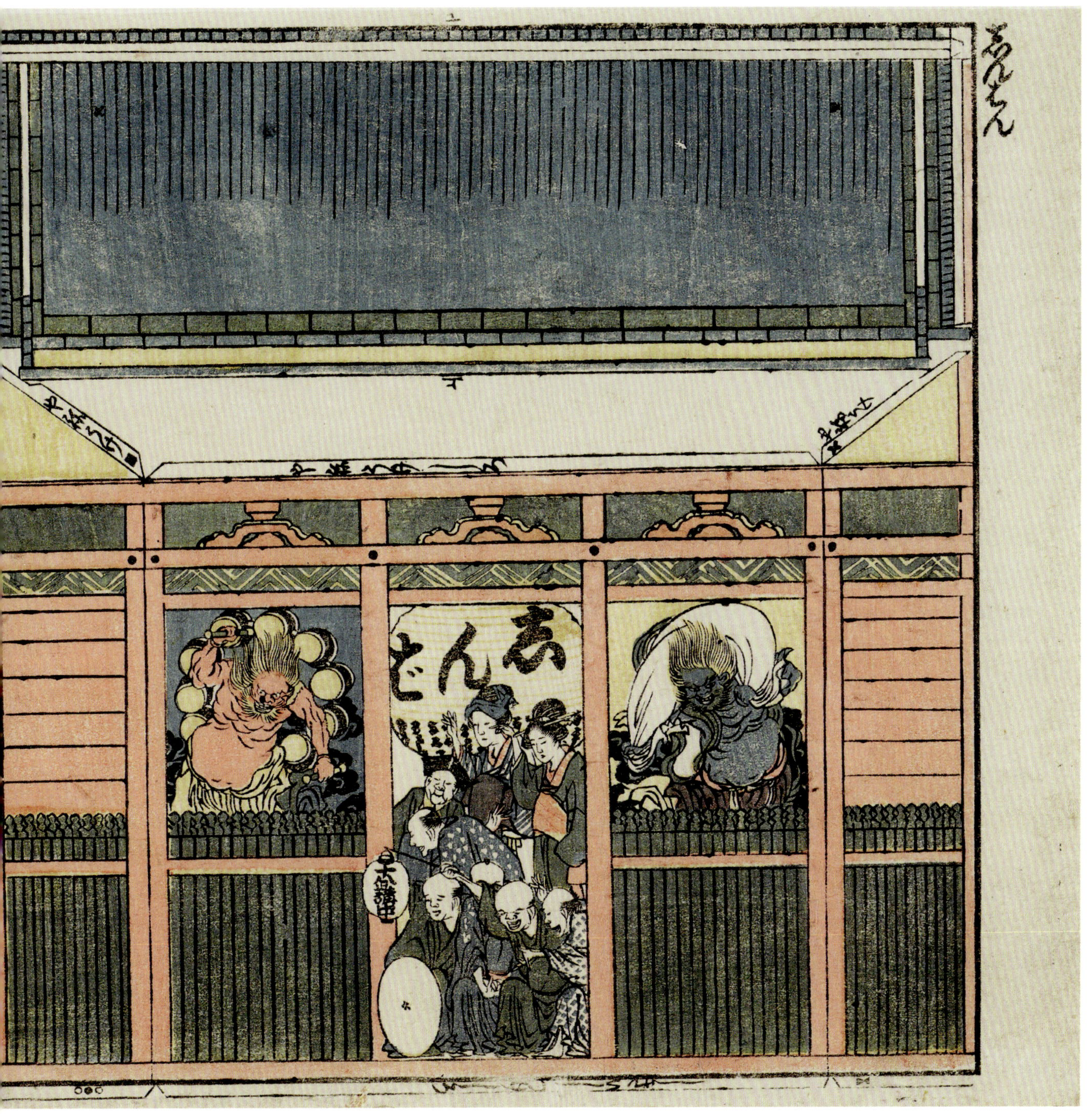

らいでん

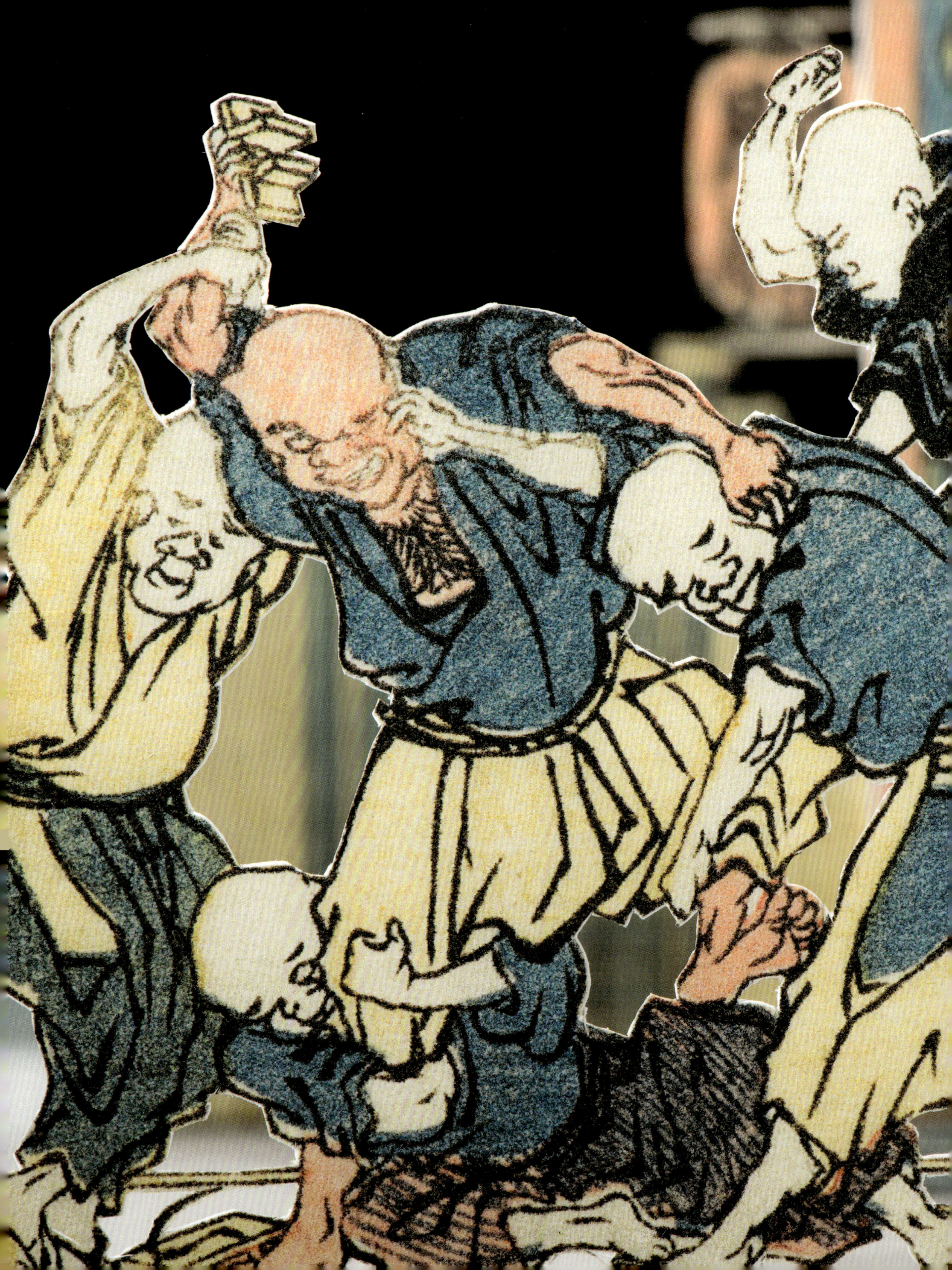

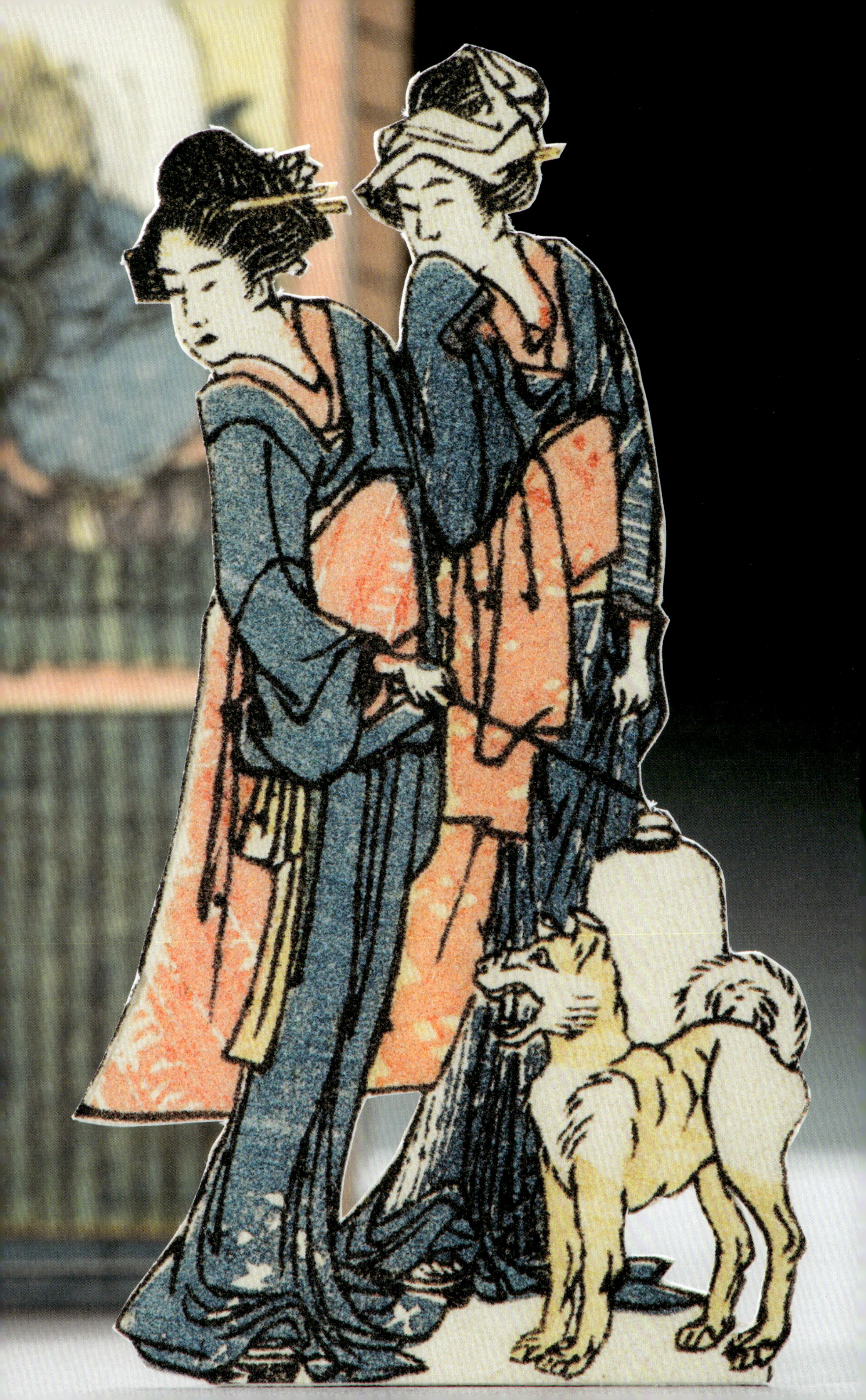

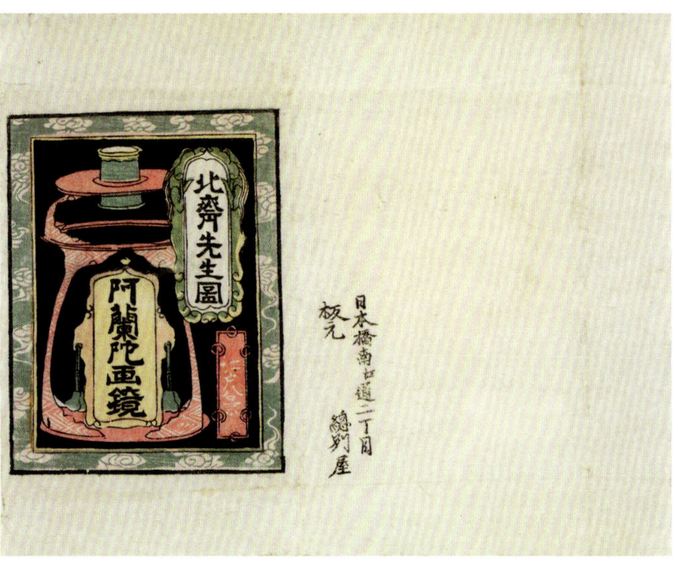

16 | Wrapper for the series **The Dutch Picture Lens: Eight Views of Edo** (*Oranda gakyō, Edo hakkei*), about 1802

17 | **Suruga-chō** from the series *The Dutch Picture Lens: Eight Views of Edo* (*Oranda gakyō, Edo hakkei*), about 1802

18 | **Shinobazu** from the series *The Dutch Picture Lens: Eight Views of Edo* (*Oranda gakyō, Edo hakkei*), about 1802

In the early nineteenth century, Hokusai designed two sets of miniature landscape prints for the publisher Sōshūya Yohei, both of which deliberately imitate the style of Western copperplate prints. Western-style copperplate etching had first been practiced in Japan by Shiba Kōkan (1747–1818) in 1783, and from 1798 on, etchings of Japanese scenes rendered in a Western style were sold in Edo by Aōdō Denzen (1748–1822). Two sets of Hokusai's woodblock prints, *Eight Views of Ōmi in Copperplate Style* and *The Dutch Picture Lens: Eight Views of Edo*, closely imitate some of the genuine copperplate prints made by Denzen, which were small, included printed frames, and were apparently sold in sets in paper wrappers. The vanishing-point perspective, low horizon line, and clouds drawn as irregular, outlined shapes, derived from Western etching, recurred many years later in Hokusai's great landscape series. Especially interesting in the *Eight Views of Edo* is his extensive use of parallel lines for shading, a technique that was unnecessary in Japanese woodblock printing because shading (*bokashi*) could be indicated by gradations of color when the block was inked.

When pictures with vanishing-point perspective were introduced to Japan in the mid-eighteenth century, they were sometimes viewed through an optical device that was made with an imported lens (Japan did not yet have lens-grinding technology) as a peephole to view the image, so that it would look like a real landscape floating in a tiny window, as in a telescope, another popular optical device made from imported lenses. By the time Hokusai made this series, the perspective prints were more likely to be viewed on their own, but the title nonetheless refers to a "Dutch mirror" or a "Dutch lens." The device shown on the wrapper for the series, however, is not a peep show at all, but rather a microscope—and Hokusai certainly knew the difference, since a similar microscope appears in one of his surimono. The implication may be that Hokusai is making the city of Edo itself the subject of a careful, scientific investigation and inviting his viewers to share in the results.

16
Signature: Hokusai sensei zu
Publisher: Sōshūya Yohei
Woodblock print (nishiki-e); ink and color on paper
18.4 x 22.5 cm (7 1/4 x 8 7/8 in.)
William Sturgis Bigelow Collection, 11.37810

17
Woodblock print (nishiki-e); ink and color on paper
8.6 x 11.4 cm (3 3/8 x 4 1/2 in.)
William Sturgis Bigelow Collection, 11.20162

18
Woodblock print (nishiki-e); ink and color on paper
8.6 x 11.4 cm (3 3/8 x 4 1/2 in.)
William Sturgis Bigelow Collection, 11.20163

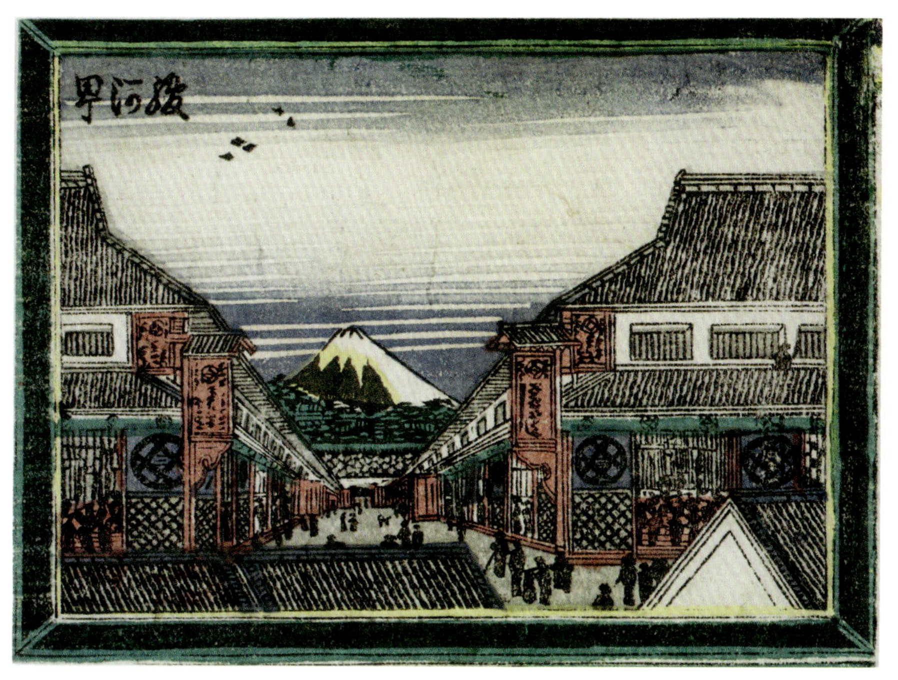
駿河町

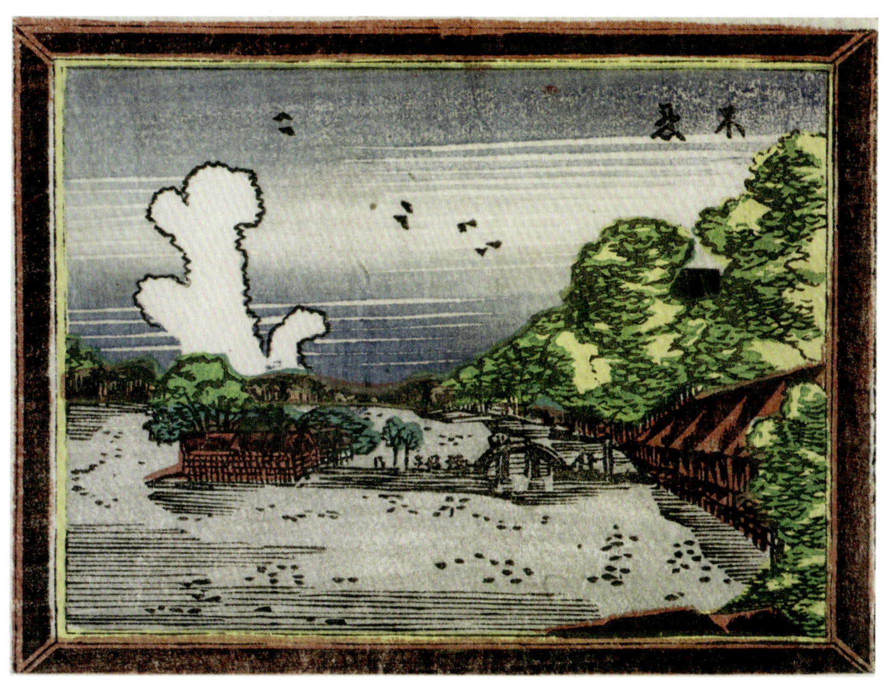
不忍

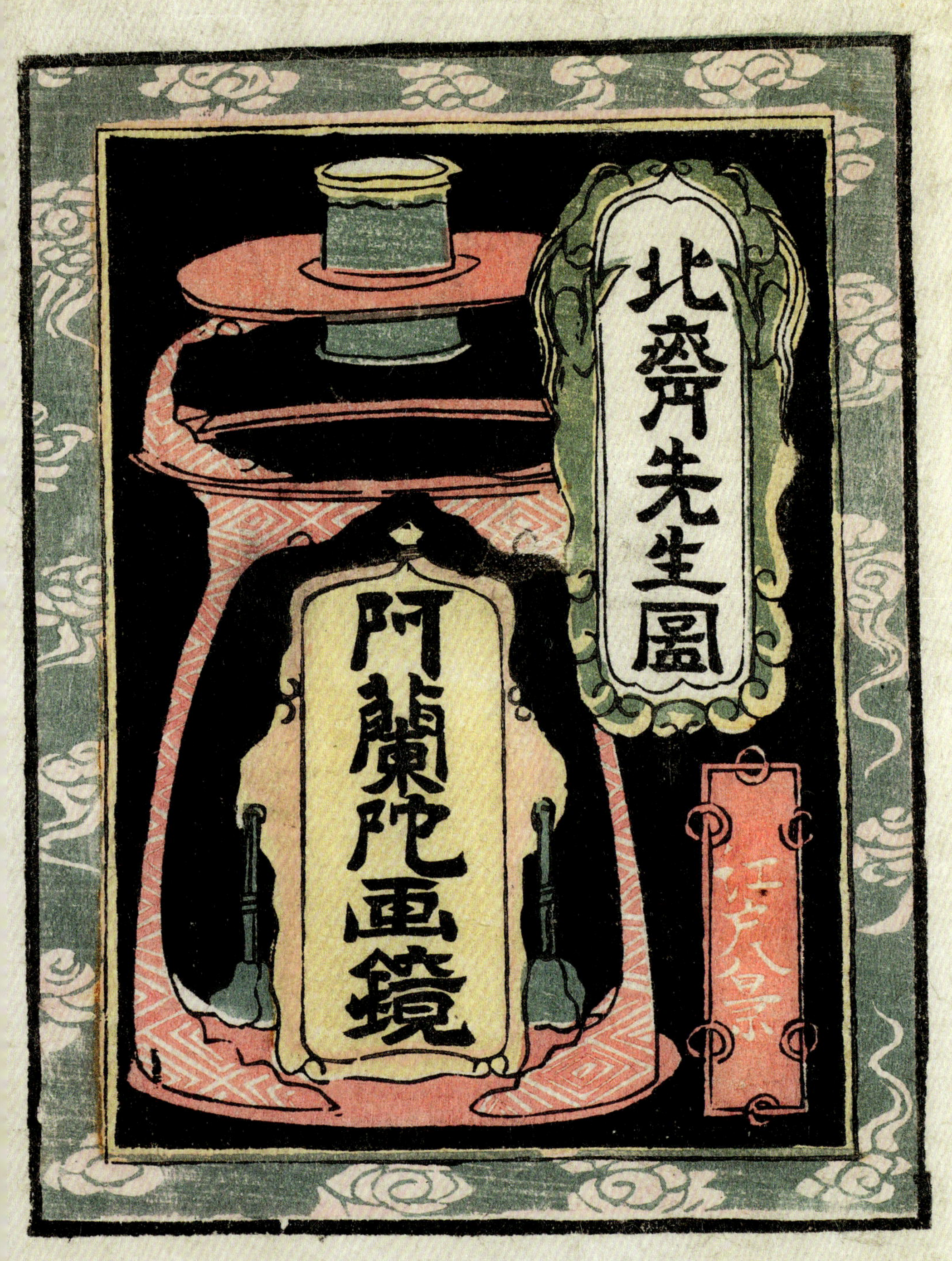

日本橋南壱通二丁目
板元
總州屋

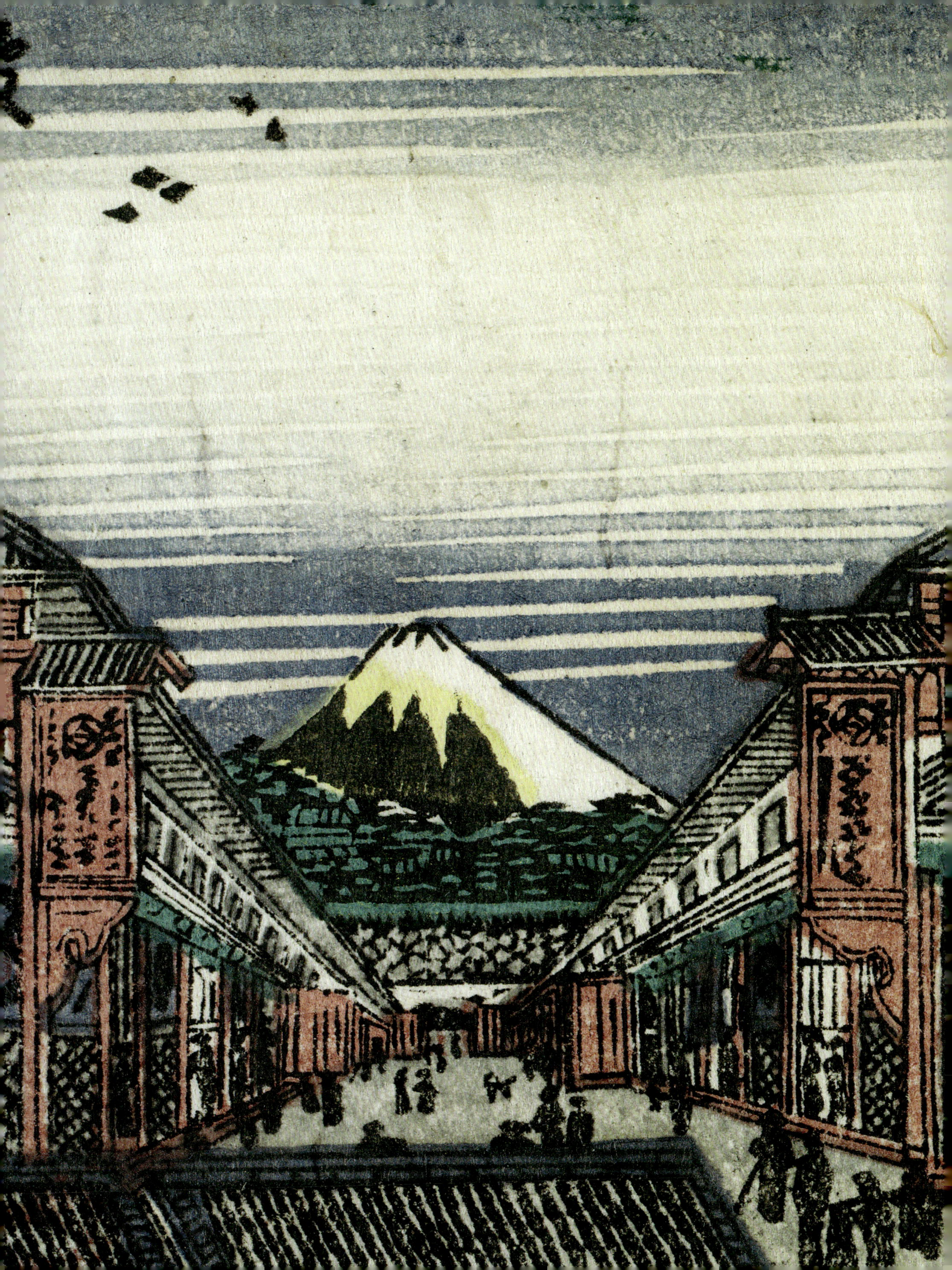

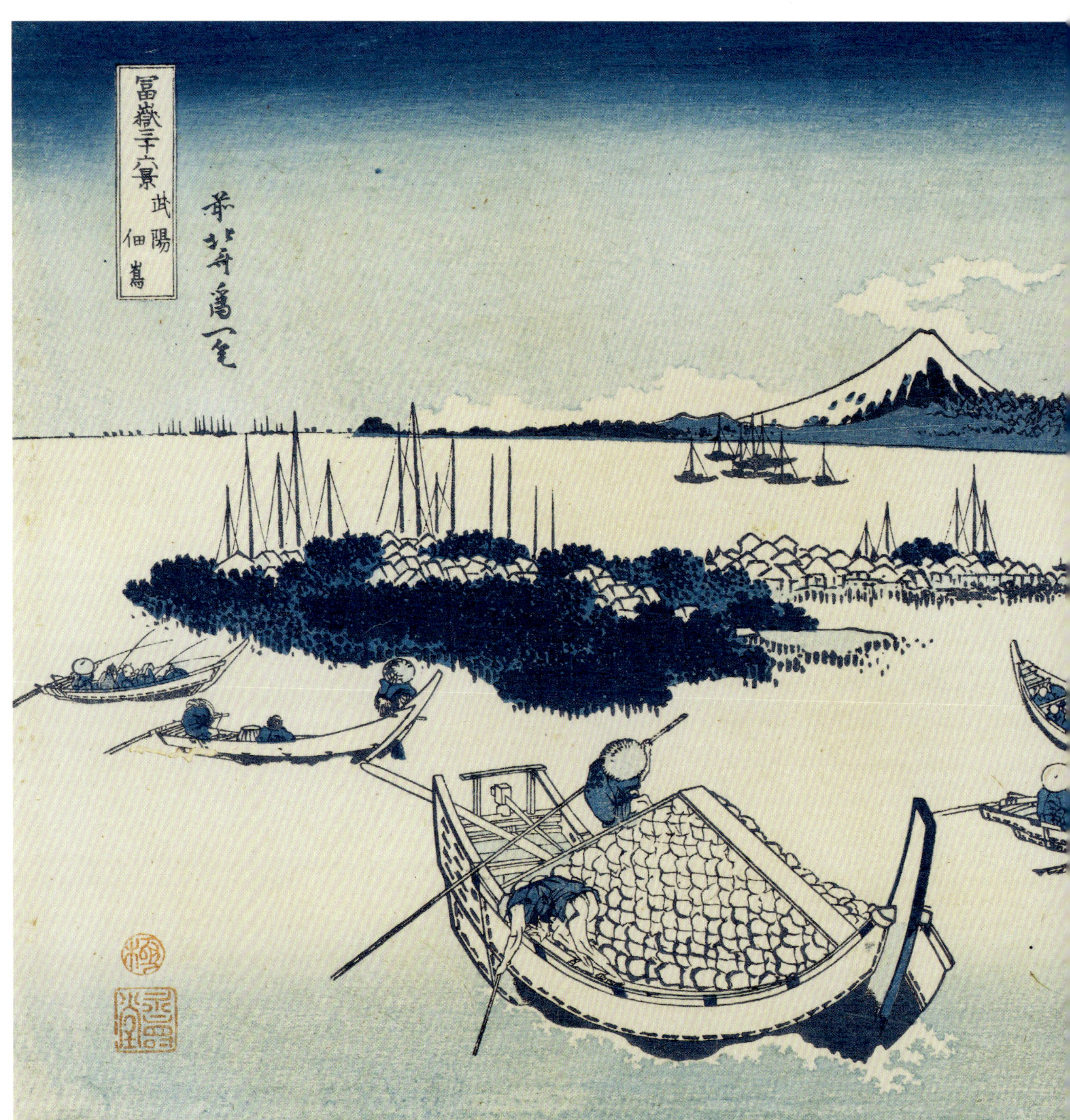
冨嶽三十六景
武陽佃嶌
前北斎為一筆

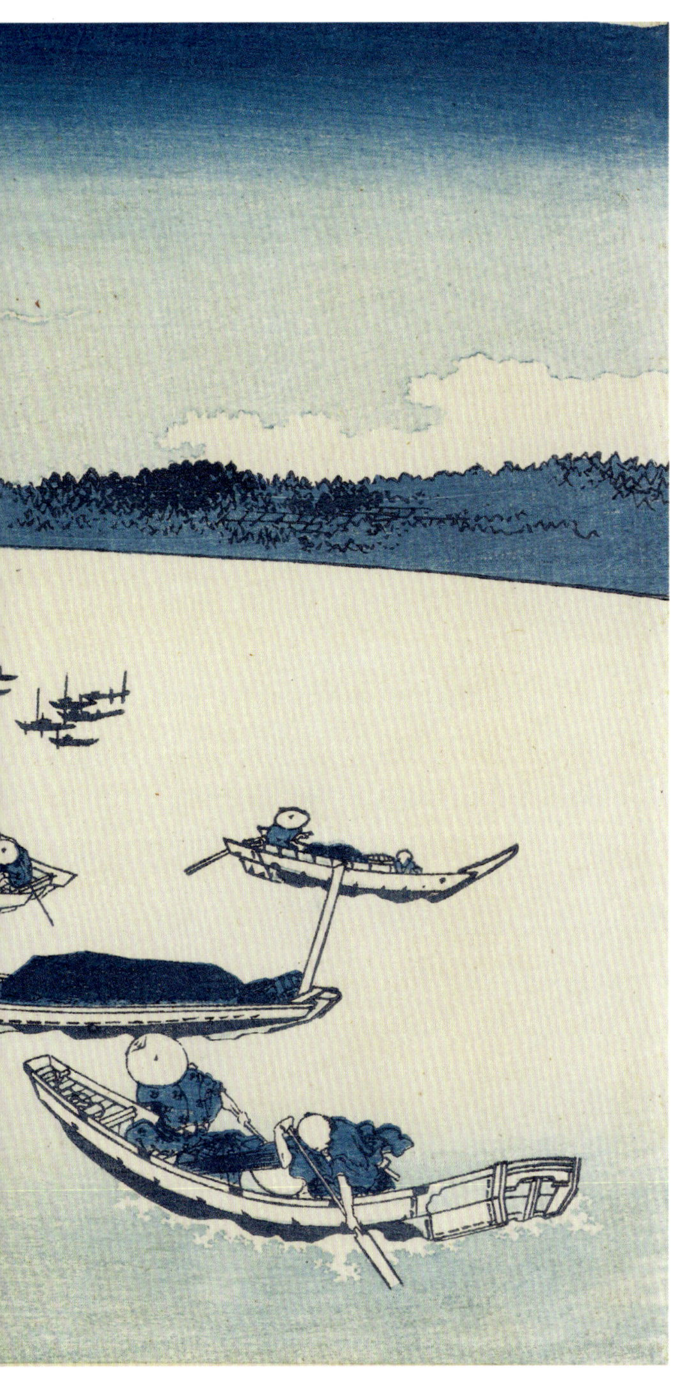

Signature: Saki no Hokusai Iitsu hitsu
Publisher: Nishimuraya Yohachi (Eijudō)
Woodblock print (nishiki-e); ink and color on paper
25.7 x 38.1 cm (10 1/8 x 15 in.)
Gift of Mr. and Mrs. Yves Henry Buhler, 52.950

19 | **Tsukudajima in Edo in Musashi Province** (*Buyō Tsukudajima*) from the series *Thirty-Six Views of Mount Fuji* (*Fugaku sanjūrokkei*), about 1830–31

Thirty-Six Views of Mount Fuji was the first of the great landscape series, which are now the most highly regarded of all nineteenth-century ukiyo-e prints. The exact date of publication is still uncertain, but the earliest documentary evidence for the series is an advertisement in a book printed near the end of 1830, suggesting that the series had debuted earlier that year. The prints sold so well that following the completion of the first thirty-six designs, ten extra ones were added, for a total of forty-six.

The introduction of a new colorant, the imported European synthetic pigment known as Prussian blue, was a major source of inspiration for Hokusai when he began to design the series. Prussian blue was a bright color highly resistant to fading that had recently become cheap enough to be applied in woodblock prints as well as in paintings. Scientific testing has shown that Hokusai also made use of indigo, traditionally used in Japan for fabric dyeing. Some designs in the series were originally printed entirely in shades of blue (*aizuri*), and all thirty-six of the first group had outlines printed in indigo blue rather than the usual black ink in the first editions.

The 1830 advertisement specifically mentions the view of Fuji from Tsukudajima as one of the designs, so this print must have been one of the first in the series. The only other color besides blue is the red used for the censor's seal and publisher's mark in the lower left corner.

In Hokusai's time, the fishing fleet of the island was a major source of food for the city of Edo, one of the main suppliers of the fish market at Nihonbashi. Hokusai's viewers would also have been aware of the rumor that the fishermen of Tsukudajima were spies keeping an eye on the harbor on behalf of the Tokugawa shogunate, which had brought them to Edo from Tsukuda in Osaka in 1590.

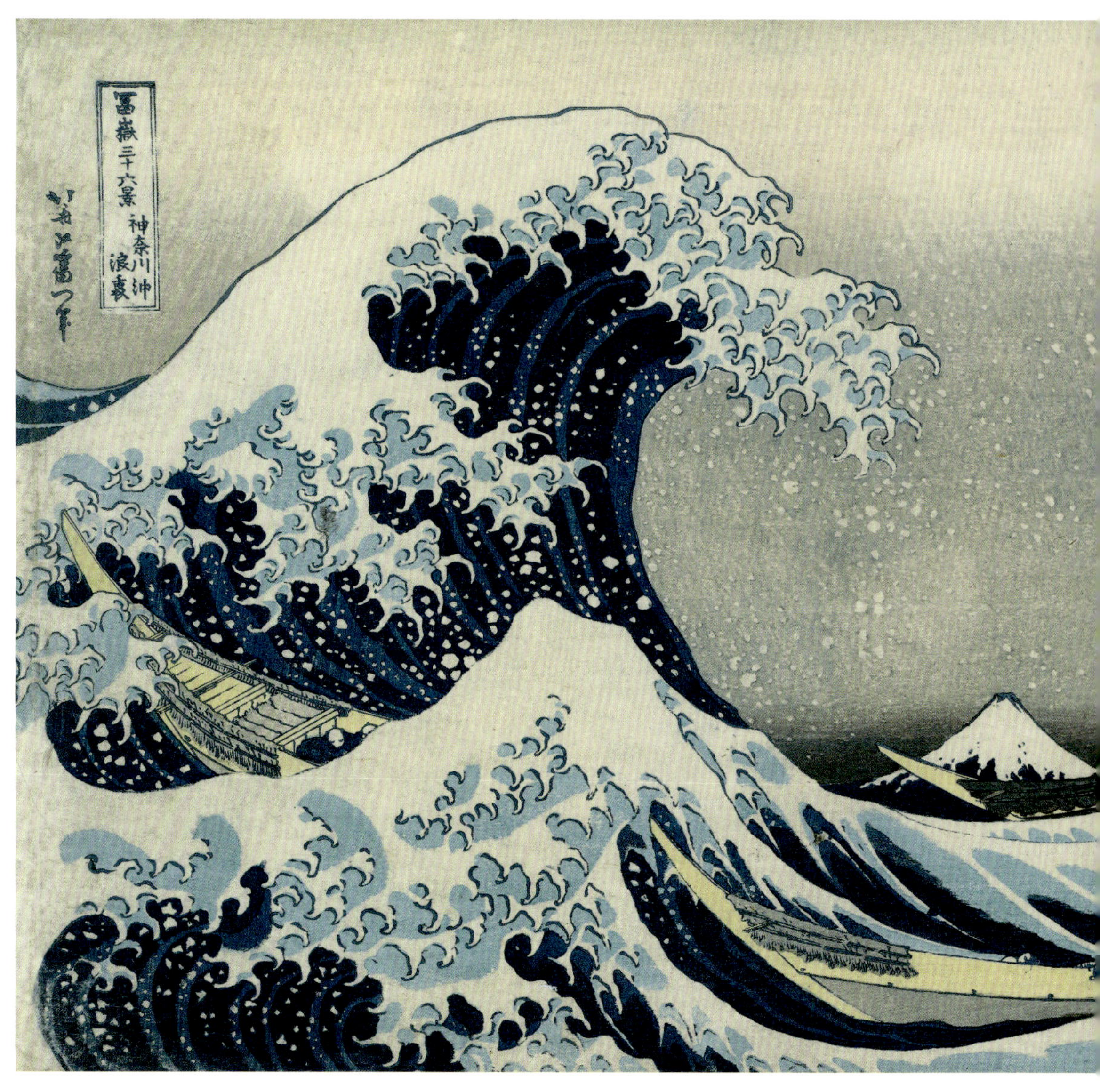

20 | **Under the Wave off Kanagawa**
(*Kanagawa-oki nami-ura*), also known as *The Great Wave*, from the series *Thirty-Six Views of Mount Fuji* (*Fugaku sanjūrokkei*), about 1830–31

This print, nicknamed *The Great Wave*, is not only the most famous of all ukiyo-e prints, but arguably the most famous image in all of Japanese art in the eyes of the world. The majestic curve of the towering wave has inspired hundreds, if not thousands, of visual references, both humorous parodies and serious homages. No other image evokes the beauty

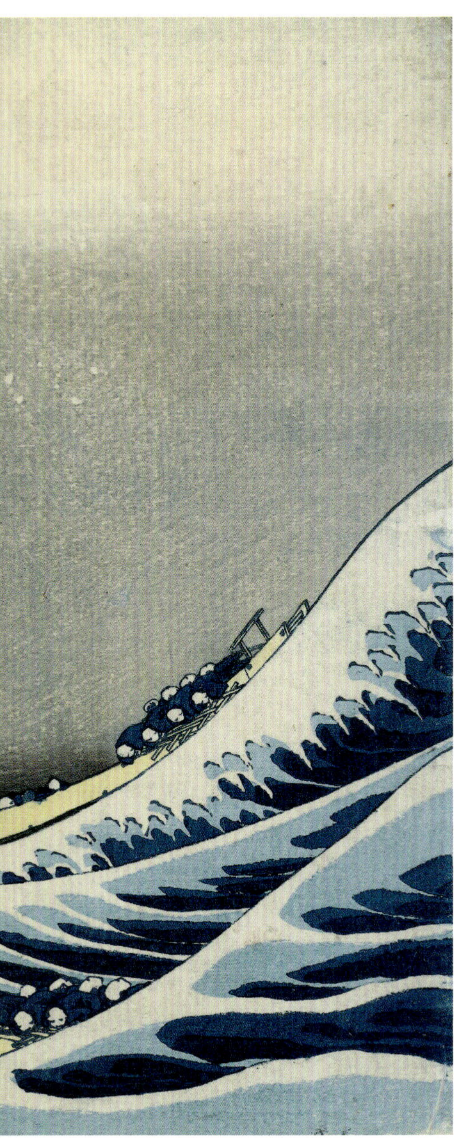

Signature: Hokusai aratame Iitsu hitsu
Publisher: Nishimuraya Yohachi (Eijudō)
Woodblock print (nishiki-e); ink and color on paper
25.8 x 38 cm (10 3/16 x 14 15/16 in.)
William S. and John T. Spaulding Collection, 21.6765

Fig. 6 | ***Express Delivery Boats Rowing through Waves* (*Oshiokuri hatō tsūsen no zu*), about 1800–5, woodblock print, 18.5 x 24.5 cm (7 5/16 x 9 5/8 in.)**

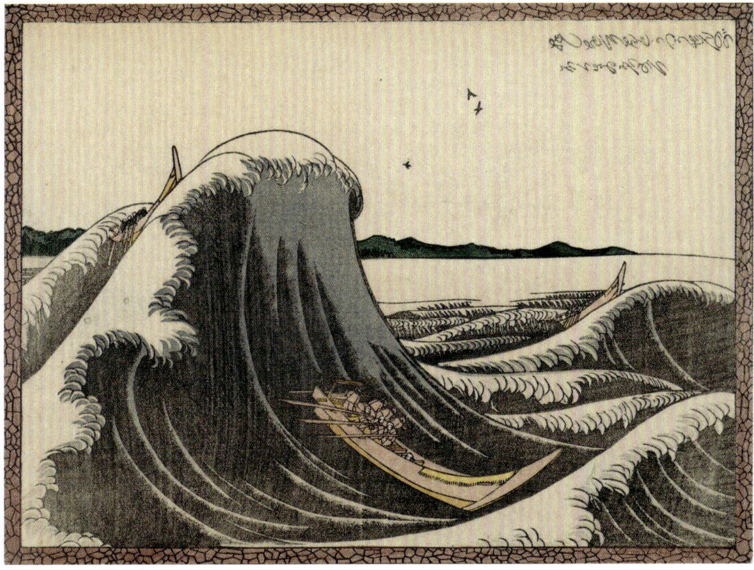

and terror of nature as this one does. Hokusai's print has even affected the popular image of a tsunami, which many people around the world picture as the gigantic breaking wave seen here, although a real tsunami is similar to an extremely high, rapid tide—hence the older term *tidal wave*.

Hokusai had been thinking about the pictorial problem of depicting an enormous wave for some thirty years. Two similar scenes can be found among his early Western-style landscapes: *Express Delivery Boats Rowing through Waves* (*Oshiokuri hatō tsūsen no zu*) and *View of Honmoku off Kanagawa* (*Kanagawa oki Honmoku no zu*), both made around 1804. All three prints show the express cargo boats that crossed the bay from the fishing grounds of Awa Province at the tip of the Bōsō Peninsula (modern Chiba Prefecture) to bring fresh fish to the city of Edo, braving rough water to deliver the perishable cargo in good time. Since speed was of the essence, the boats generally relied on rowers rather than sails.

Only this version of the scene, however, includes a view of Fuji. The glimpse of the great mountain beyond the curve of the wave—the only visible land in the picture—is both the perfect finishing touch to the composition and a symbol of hope that the boats will come through safely.

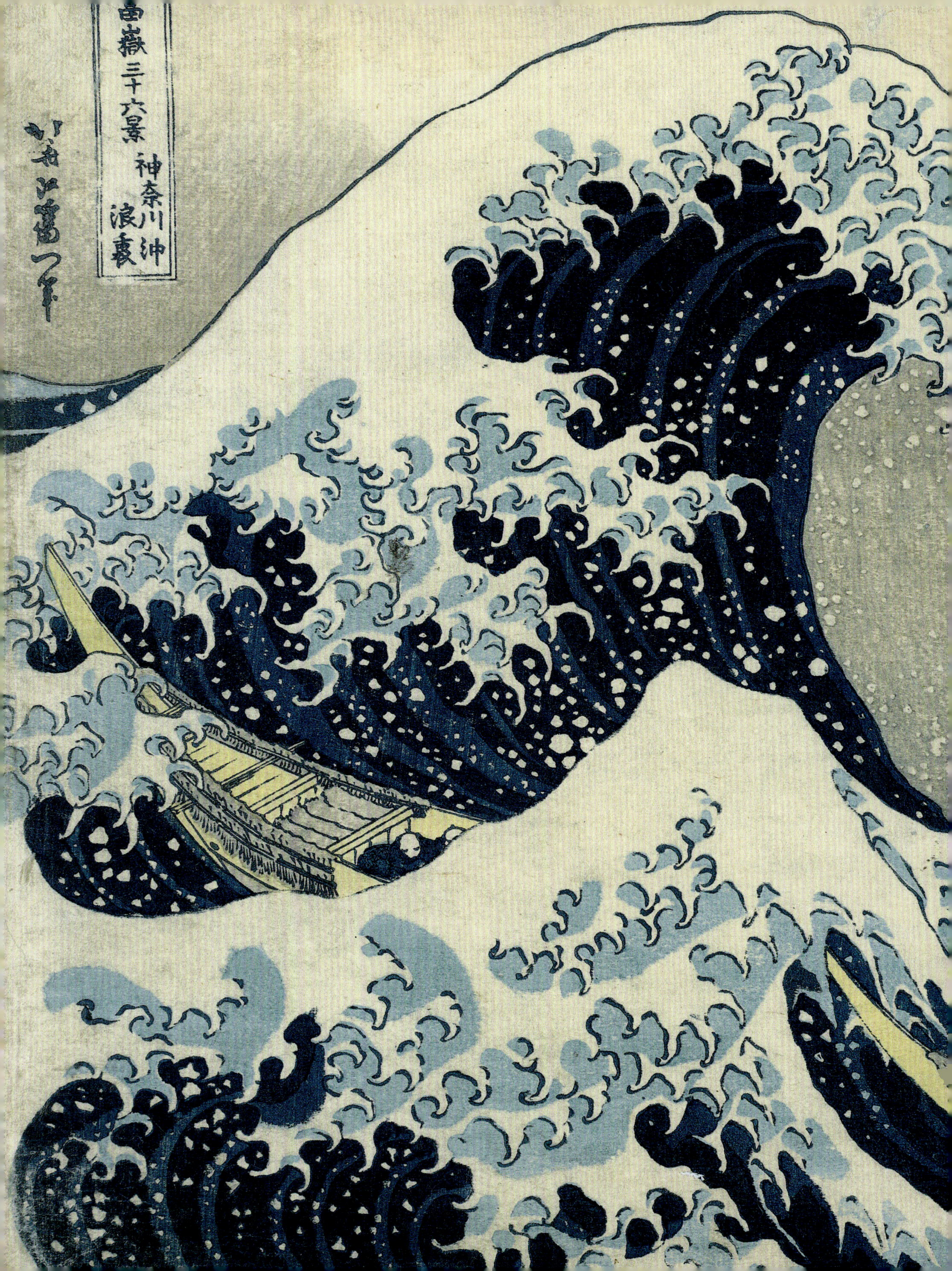
冨嶽三十六景
神奈川沖
浪裏

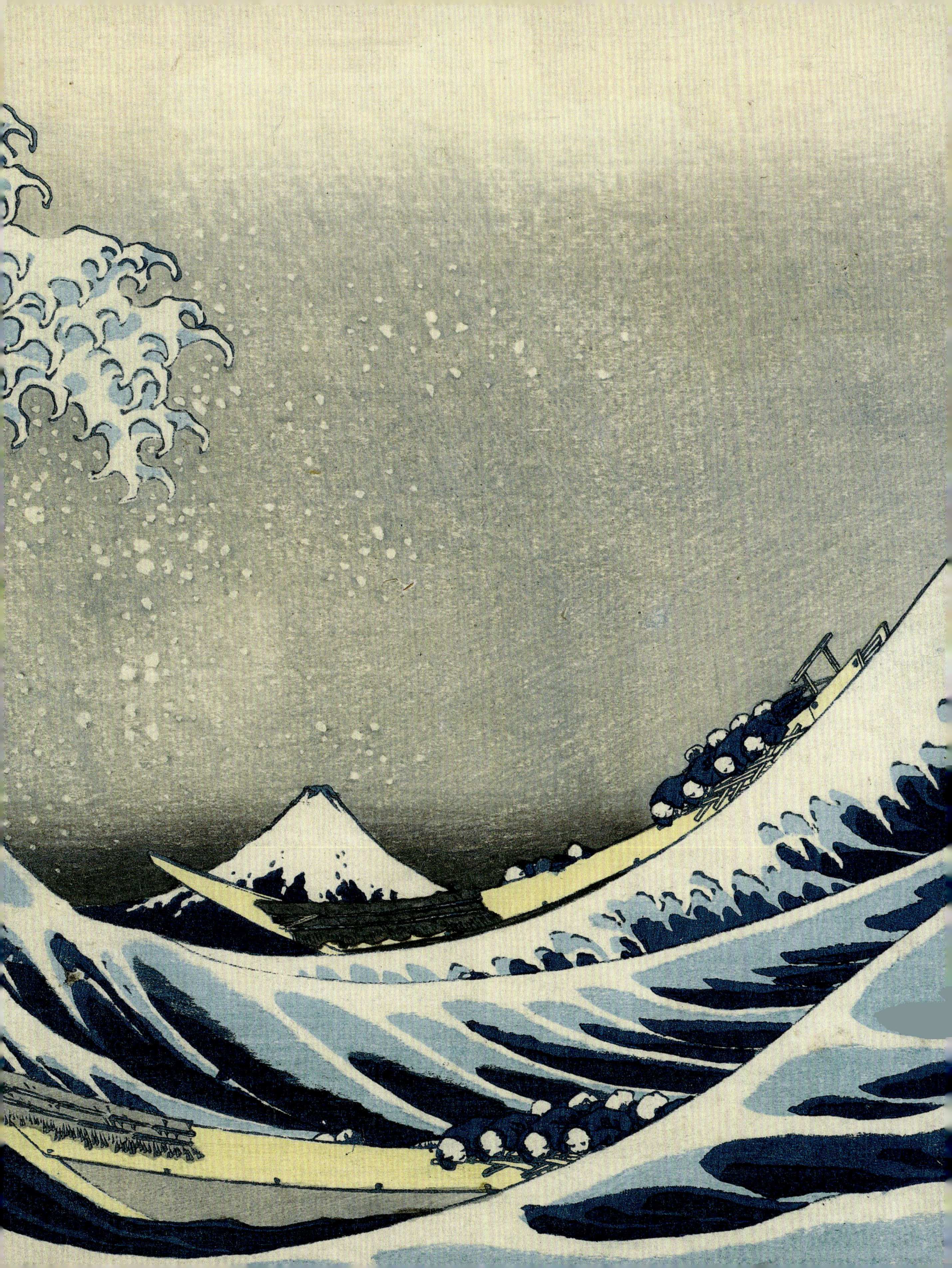

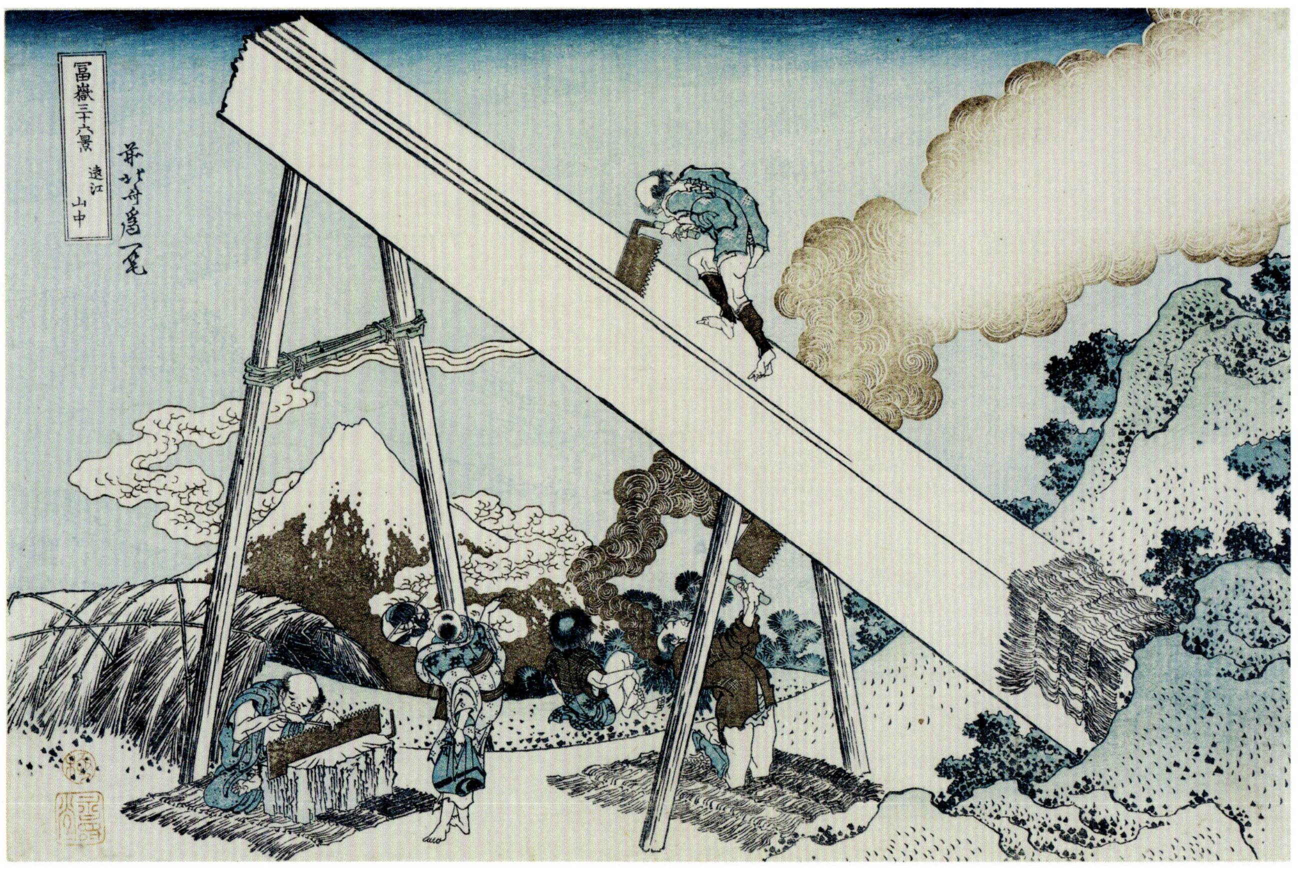

21

21 | **In the Mountains of Tōtōmi Province** (*Tōtōmi sanchū*) from the series *Thirty-Six Views of Mount Fuji* (*Fugaku sanjūrokkei*), about 1830–31

22 | **In the Mountains of Tōtōmi Province** (*Tōtōmi sanchū*) from the series *Thirty-Six Views of Mount Fuji* (*Fugaku sanjūrokkei*), about 1830–31

23 | **In the Mountains of Tōtōmi Province** (*Tōtōmi sanchū*) from the series *Thirty-Six Views of Mount Fuji* (*Fugaku sanjūrokkei*), about 1830–31

The *Fuji* series was so popular that it was frequently reprinted; many surviving examples of later impressions show evidence of wear on the blocks. As the use of Prussian blue gradually lost its novelty, designs that had originally been printed primarily in blue were reprinted with additional colors. In still later printings, even the outlines that had originally been printed in indigo blue were printed in black. Three impressions of *In the Mountains of Tōtōmi Province* show this progression clearly. The earliest printing was done with the aizuri (blue-printed) technique, with black ink cleverly used as a "color" for the smoke of the fire and the slopes of the distant mountain. In a slightly later printing, the outlines are still blue but some green has been added; and in the third example, the design is printed in full color with black outlines, with some small breaks in the fine lines indicating wear and tear on the blocks.

The exact location of this scene has not been identified, and it may be that no specific place was

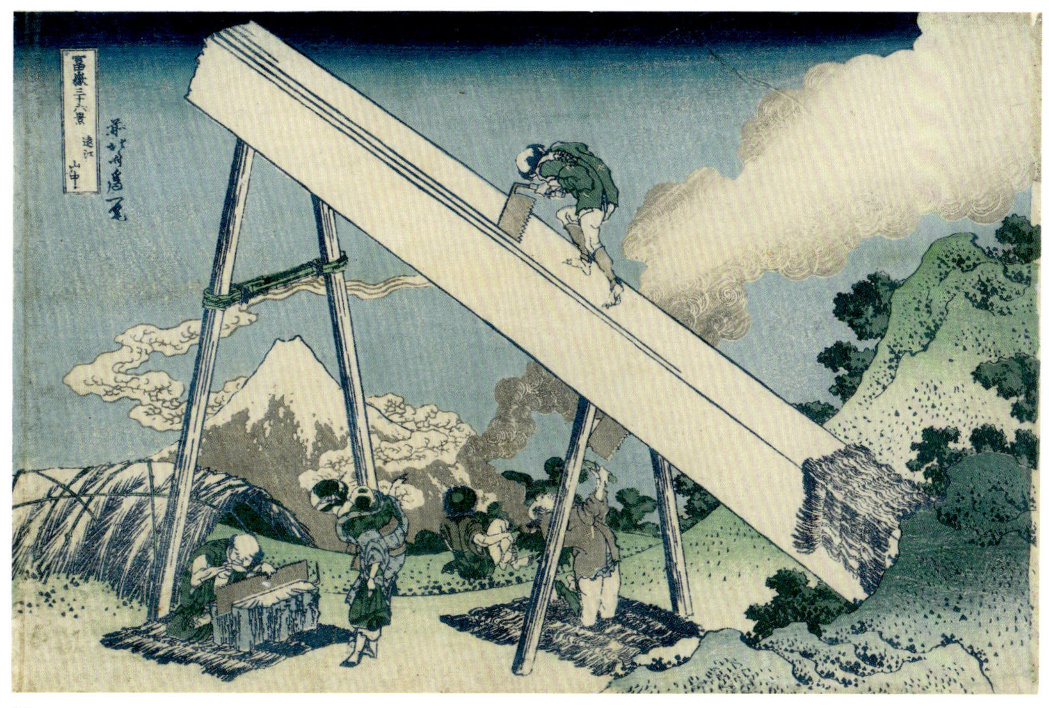

22

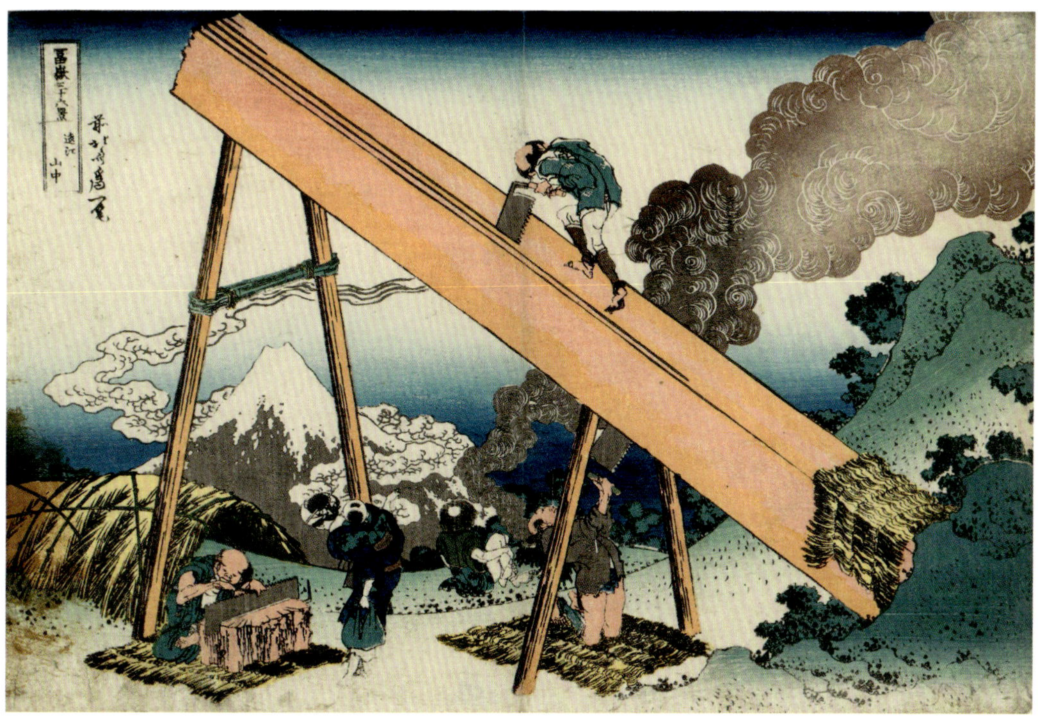

23

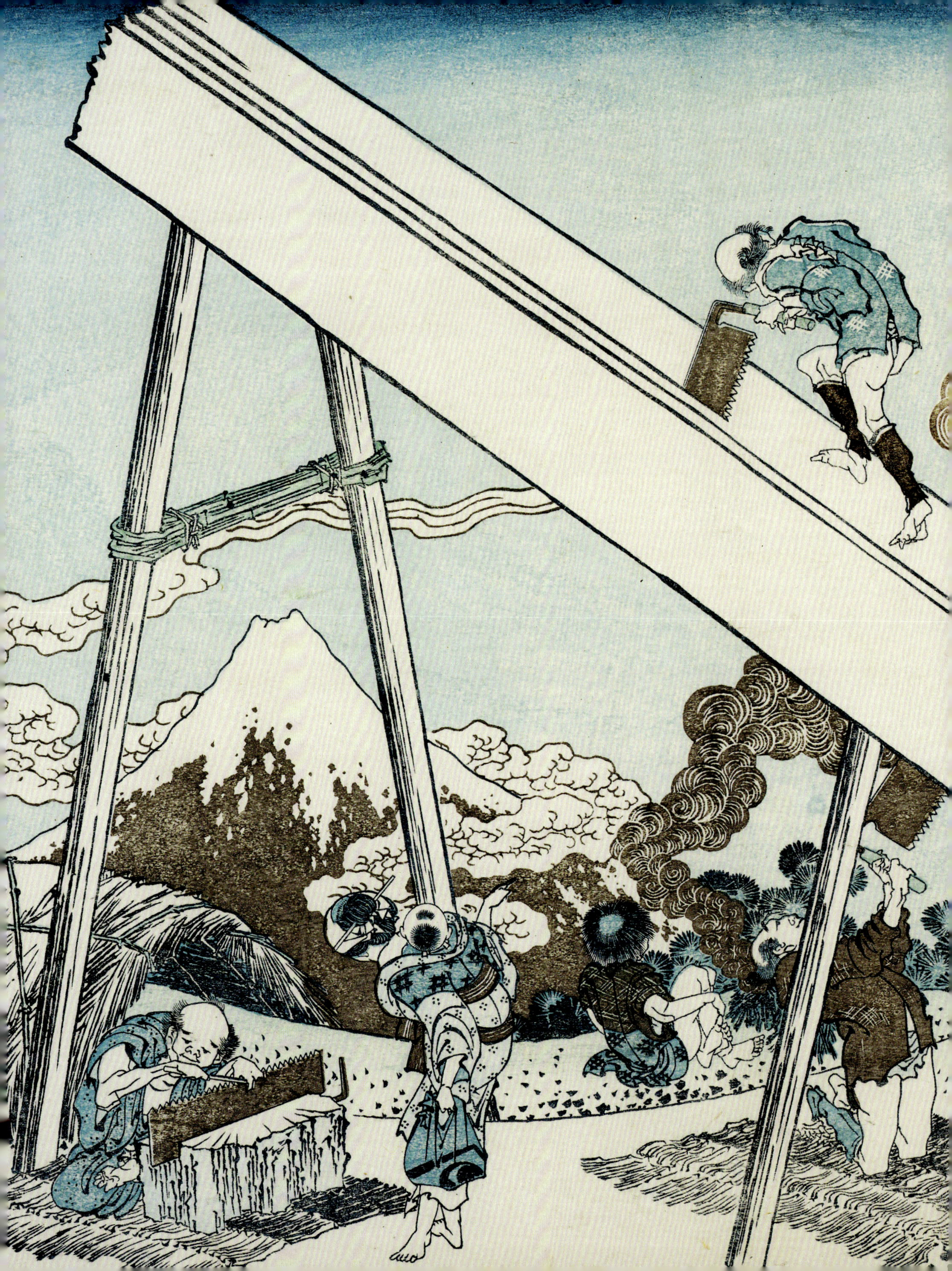

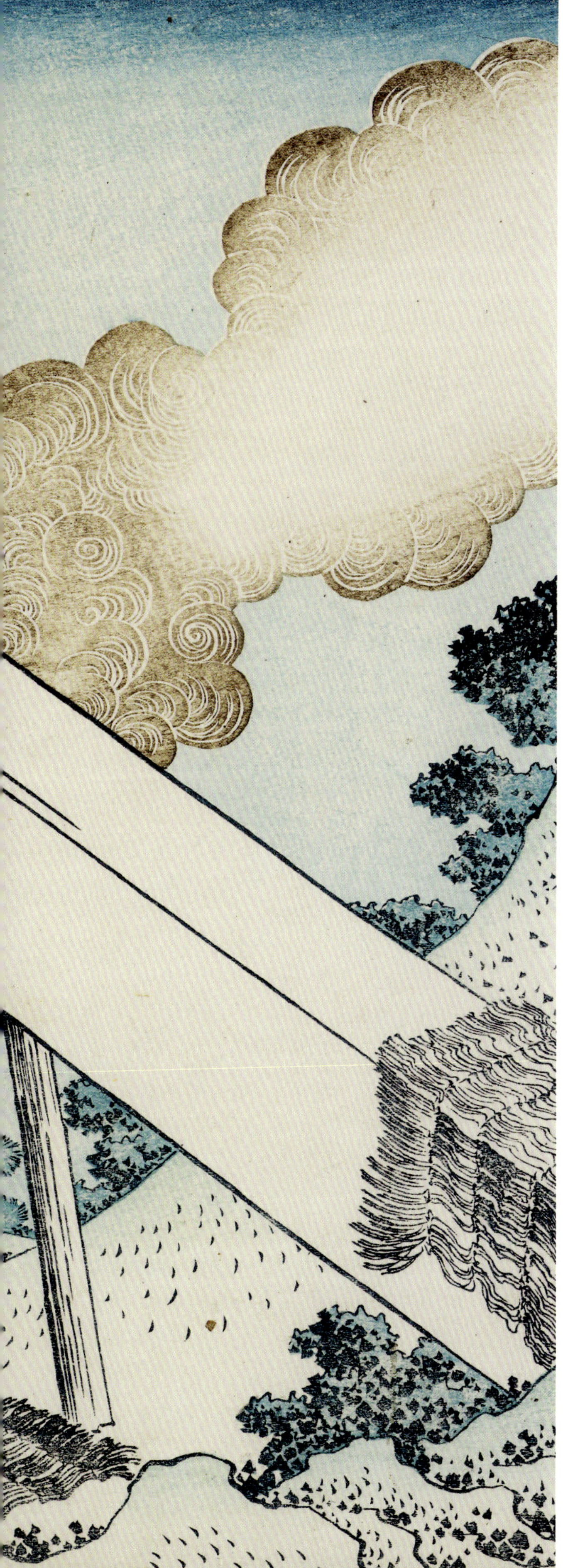

intended. The woodcutters are hard at work somewhere in Tōtōmi Province, which corresponds to the western part of modern Shizuoka Prefecture. The presence of a woman with a baby on her back indicates that this is a family business and emphasizes the contrast between the busy scene of everyday life in the foreground and the stately peak of Fuji, wreathed in ribbons of mist that reinforce its spiritual importance. In the foreground, the mist is echoed by the smoke of the woodcutters' fire, which crosses behind the line of the plank in an X shape. The view of woodcutters sawing a gigantic plank from both above and below was based on a painting by Kuwagata Keisai (also known as Kitao Masayoshi, 1764–1824). Keisai was very displeased with Hokusai for stealing his composition, but the clever idea of a view of Fuji seen through the tall supports of the plank appears to have been Hokusai's own invention. Hokusai also altered the picture to make it less realistic but more interesting. Where Keisai had painted two planks being sawed side by side, Hokusai combined them into one plank with two carpenters working on it at once, something that would probably not have been done in real life.

21
Signature: Saki no Hokusai Iitsu hitsu
Publisher: Nishimuraya Yohachi (Eijudō)
Woodblock print (nishiki-e); ink and color on paper
25.1 x 37.7 cm (9 7/8 x 14 13/16 in.)
William Sturgis Bigelow Collection, 11.19717

22
Signature: Saki no Hokusai Iitsu hitsu
Publisher: Nishimuraya Yohachi (Eijudō)
Woodblock print (nishiki-e); ink and color on paper
25.7 x 38.5 cm (10 1/8 x 15 3/16 in.)
William S. and John T. Spaulding Collection, 21.6778

23
Signature: Saki no Hokusai Iitsu hitsu
Publisher: Nishimuraya Yohachi (Eijudō)
Woodblock print (nishiki-e); ink and color on paper
25.3 x 37 cm (9 15/16 x 14 9/16 in.)
William Sturgis Bigelow Collection, 11.17658

24 | **The Kintai Bridge in Suō Province**
(*Suō no kuni Kintaibashi*) from the series
Remarkable Views of Bridges in Various Provinces
(*Shokoku meikyō kiran*), about 1834

The Kintai Bridge, sometimes translated as Bridge of the Brocade Sash, is located in the modern Yamaguchi Prefecture. It was originally part of the main road to Iwakuni Castle, crossing the Nishiki River to Mount Yokoyama, where the castle was located. The castle had been completed in 1608, only to be largely dismantled in 1615 at the order of the Tokugawa shogunate, but some parts of it remained in use as administrative buildings and the residence of the Kikkawa daimyo clan. After earlier bridges were destroyed by floods, the new bridge was built in its present form in 1673. Four stone piers are connected by three arched wooden spans, with two more wooden spans forming approach ramps at each end. The interaction between the arcs of the bridge and the triangular shape of the mountain in the background is an especially complex example of Hokusai's technique of using geometrical forms to build a pleasing composition.

The name of the bridge referred to its elegant shape, suggesting a decorative sash across the river. It was originally intended for use only by samurai and their retinues, and so Hokusai shows a figure with an umbrella and two swords, accompanied by several other men who are probably his attendants, making their way over the bridge in the rain.

An advertisement for this series of prints appears for the first time in the back of a book published in 1834, in a list of Eijudō publications that also includes the *Thirty-Six Views of Mount Fuji* and the *Waterfalls* series, both of which had already been mentioned in earlier advertisements. As in the case of the waterfalls, the bridges have been selected to show the greatest possible variety in their locations and construction. There are eleven known designs in this series, an unusual number. Possibly there were originally twelve prints, the most common number for a series, or it may have been begun as a set of ten prints, with the scene of Tenpōzan, which is somewhat different from the others, added at the end as an extra.

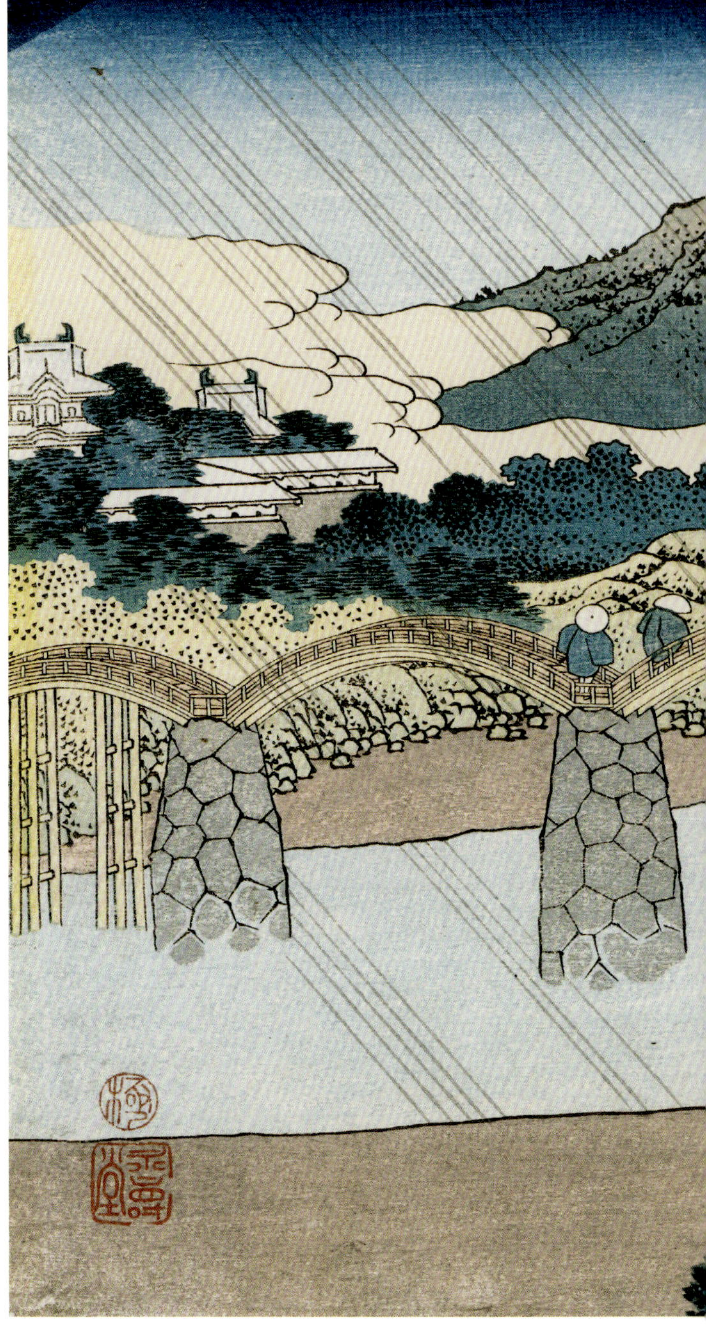

Signature: Saki no Hokusai Iitsu hitsu
Publisher: Nishimuraya Yohachi (Eijudō)
Woodblock print (nishiki-e); ink and color on paper
24.3 x 36.7 cm (9 9/16 x 14 7/16 in.)
William Sturgis Bigelow Collection, 11.25221

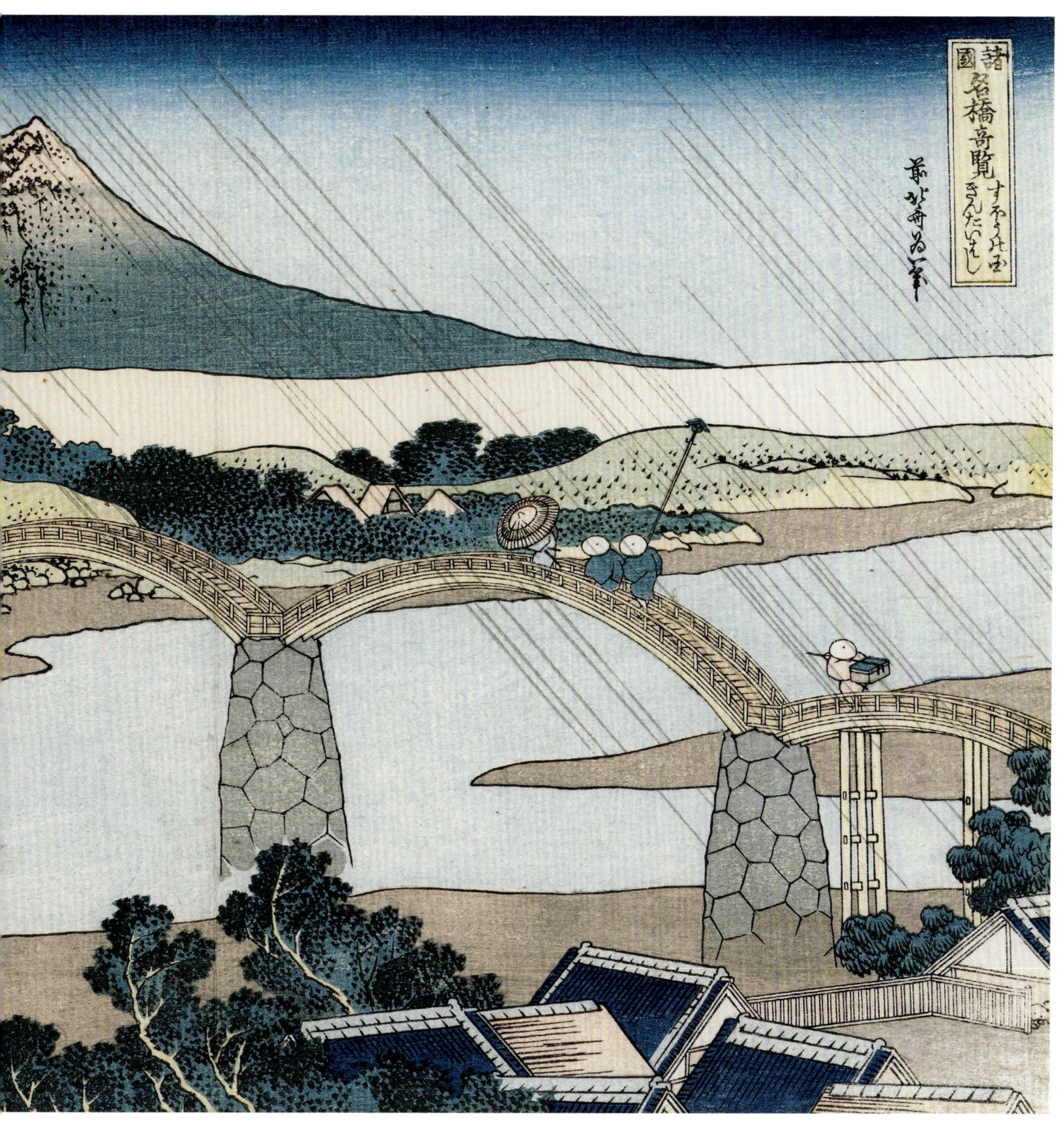
諸國名橋奇覧
きんたいはし
前北斎為一筆

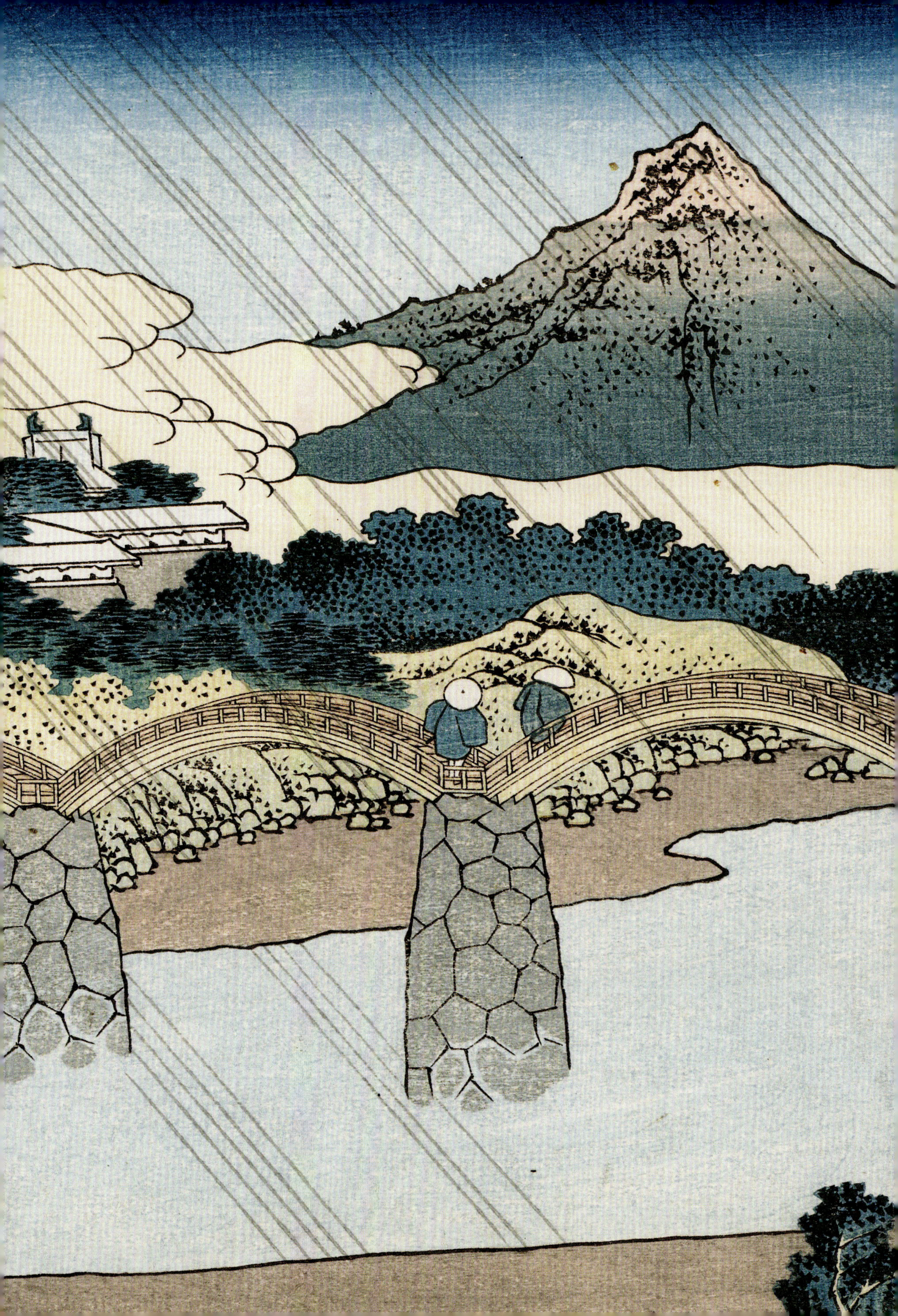

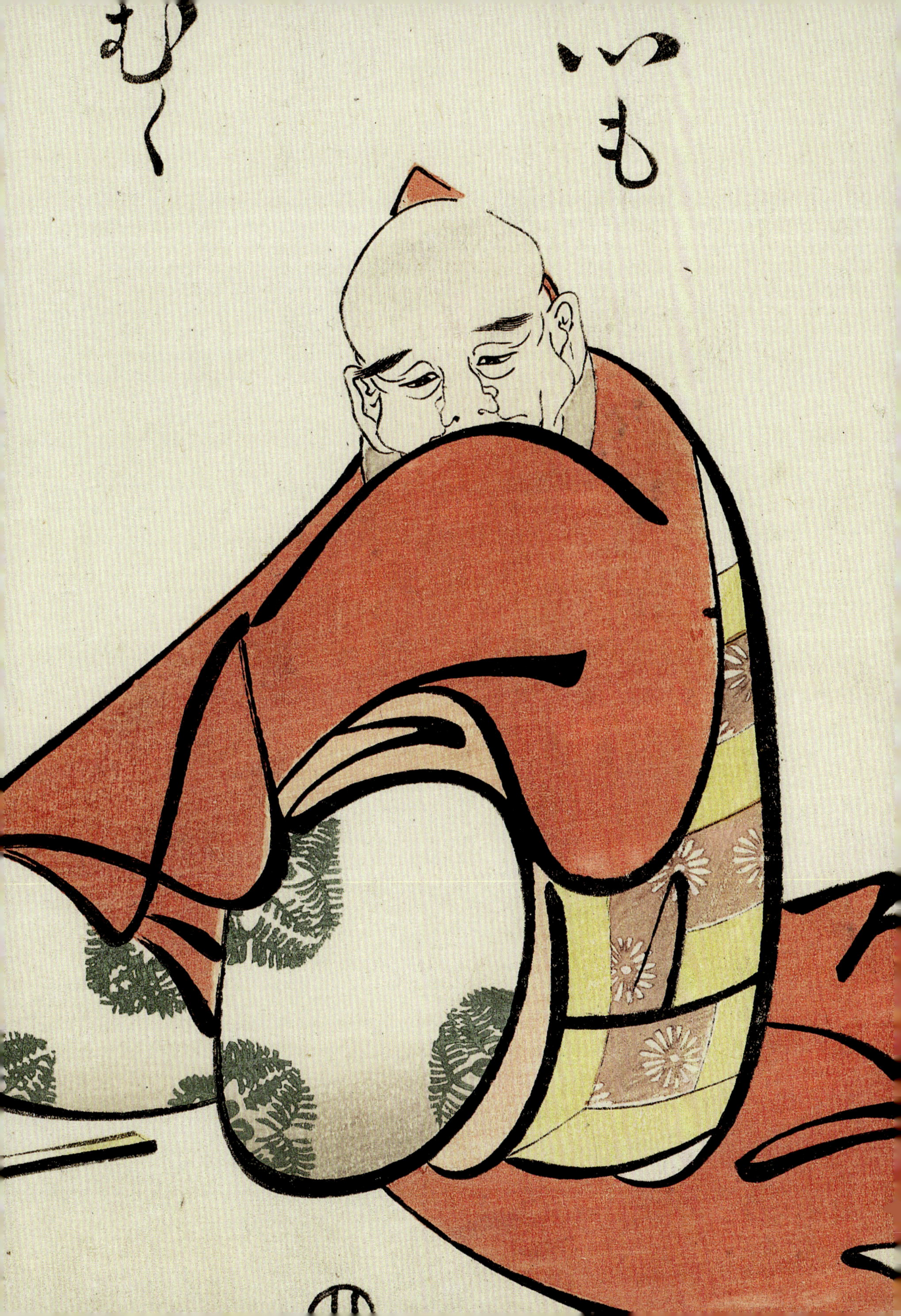
いつも
むく

25 | **Sōjō Henjō** from an untitled series of Six Poetic Immortals (Rokkasen) formed by the characters for their names, about 1810

An entire genre of traditional Japanese painting is devoted to imaginary portraits of the great poets of classical times. Such paintings are known as Pictures of Poetic Immortals. Here the Chinese Taoist term is applied to both supernatural beings and successful alchemists and to Japanese historical figures who had achieved immortality through the brilliance of their poetry. Foremost among them were the Six Poetic Immortals, mentioned in the preface to the first imperial anthology of Japanese poetry, *Collection of Poems Old and New* (*Kokinshū*, compiled around 920).

Hokusai's series of prints, showing the traditional Six Poetic Immortals with samples of their poetry, has an amusing twist that is apparent only on close examination: the name of each poet is concealed in the lines of his or her garments. Sōjō Henjō (816–890) is recognizable by his red robes and high pointed collar, the mark of elevated rank in the Buddhist priesthood; his title Sōjō is often translated as "Bishop." Bishop Henjō holds one red sleeve to his mouth in a polite gesture meant to conceal the fact that he is smiling broadly, perhaps laughing at the joke. His face looks somewhat like self-portraits by Hokusai, so there may be a second joke as well.

Most of the letters concealed in the costume are from the hiragana syllabary, whose flowing forms adapt well to this game. For the last part of the name, however, Hokusai chose a Chinese kanji character because its angular shape is perfect for the rectangular patchwork of the stole worn by Buddhist priests over their robes.

The poem above the figure is written over a decorative background of dripped colors that suggest the decorated paper traditionally used for fine Japanese calligraphy. It is signed by the calligrapher Tonan, who has not, however, been identified. Appropriate to the priestly status of its author, the poem describes the beauty of an unblemished lotus blossom, sprinkled with gemlike dewdrops, as it rises above the muddy water (by implication, like the teachings of the Buddha in this impure world).

Signature: Katsushika Hokusai ga
Publisher: Ezakiya Kichibei
Woodblock print (nishiki-e); ink and color on paper
38.2 x 26.1 cm (15 1/16 x 10 1/4 in.)
William Sturgis Bigelow Collection, 11.17497

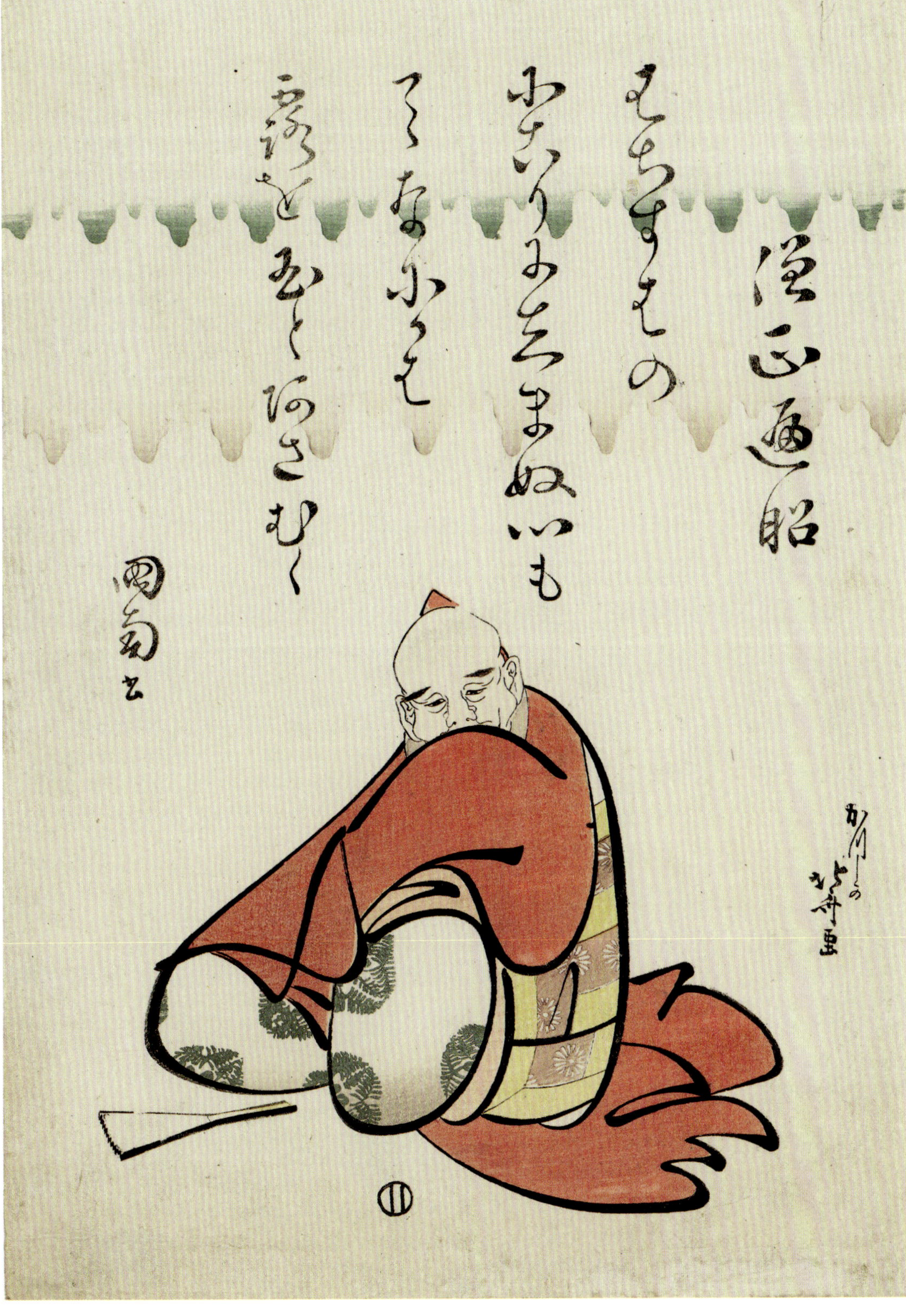
僧正遍昭

26 | **The Character "Long Life" and Chinese Boys**, 1845

Made late in Hokusai's life, this painting demonstrates a very different way of turning words into images. Rather than concealing written characters within the brushstrokes of a picture, the artist treats the character for "long life" as if it were a concrete, physical object, on which two little boys in Chinese costumes perform acrobatic tricks. One does a precarious handstand at the very top of the character, clinging unevenly to the vertical and horizontal strokes, while the other balances on a tiny ink stroke, holding on with his left hand while he waves a tasseled fan with his right.

The work is a collaboration between Hokusai and an even longer-lived friend who did the calligraphy. Below the large character, the text continues: "With best wishes for good luck, and boundless felicitations, by the ninety-eight-year-old man, Hanai Hakusō." Since the characters are centered on the sheet, it is unclear whether Hakusō intended from the beginning to collaborate with Hokusai or whether Hokusai spontaneously added the figures (signed "Chinese children by eighty-six-year-old Manji") to the finished calligraphy. There are several other known examples of similar works done by Hokusai in his mid- to late eighties in collaboration with calligraphers of similar age or even older.

The chronicle *Annals of Edo* (*Bukō nenpyō*) by Saitō Gesshin records that in 1844 the oldest men in Edo gathered to celebrate their advanced age. In his mid-eighties, Hokusai was one of the younger members of the group, and Hakusō was by no means the oldest. The attendees ranged in age from eighty to one hundred and five, calculated according to the Japanese method of counting the number of calendar years lived in, rather than the time elapsed since birth. It was probably this social event that led to ongoing friendships between Hokusai and other long-lived residents of Edo.

Signature (figures): Karako wa yowai hachijūrokusai Manji hitsu
Signature (calligraphy): Kyūjūhassai ō Hanai Hakusō sho
Hanging scroll; ink and color on paper
59.6 x 31.6 cm (23 7/16 x 12 7/16 in.)
William Sturgis Bigelow Collection, 11.7420

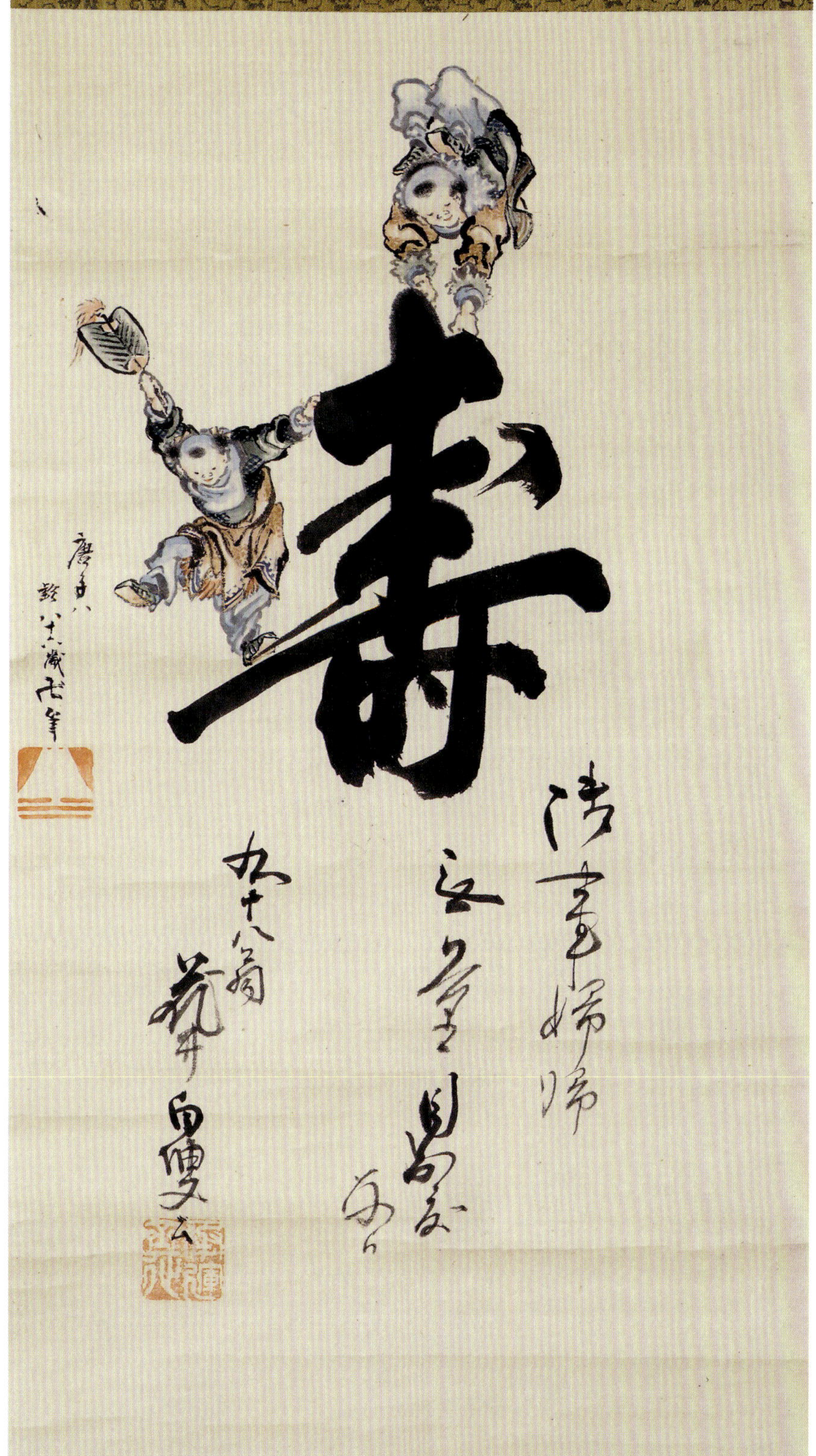

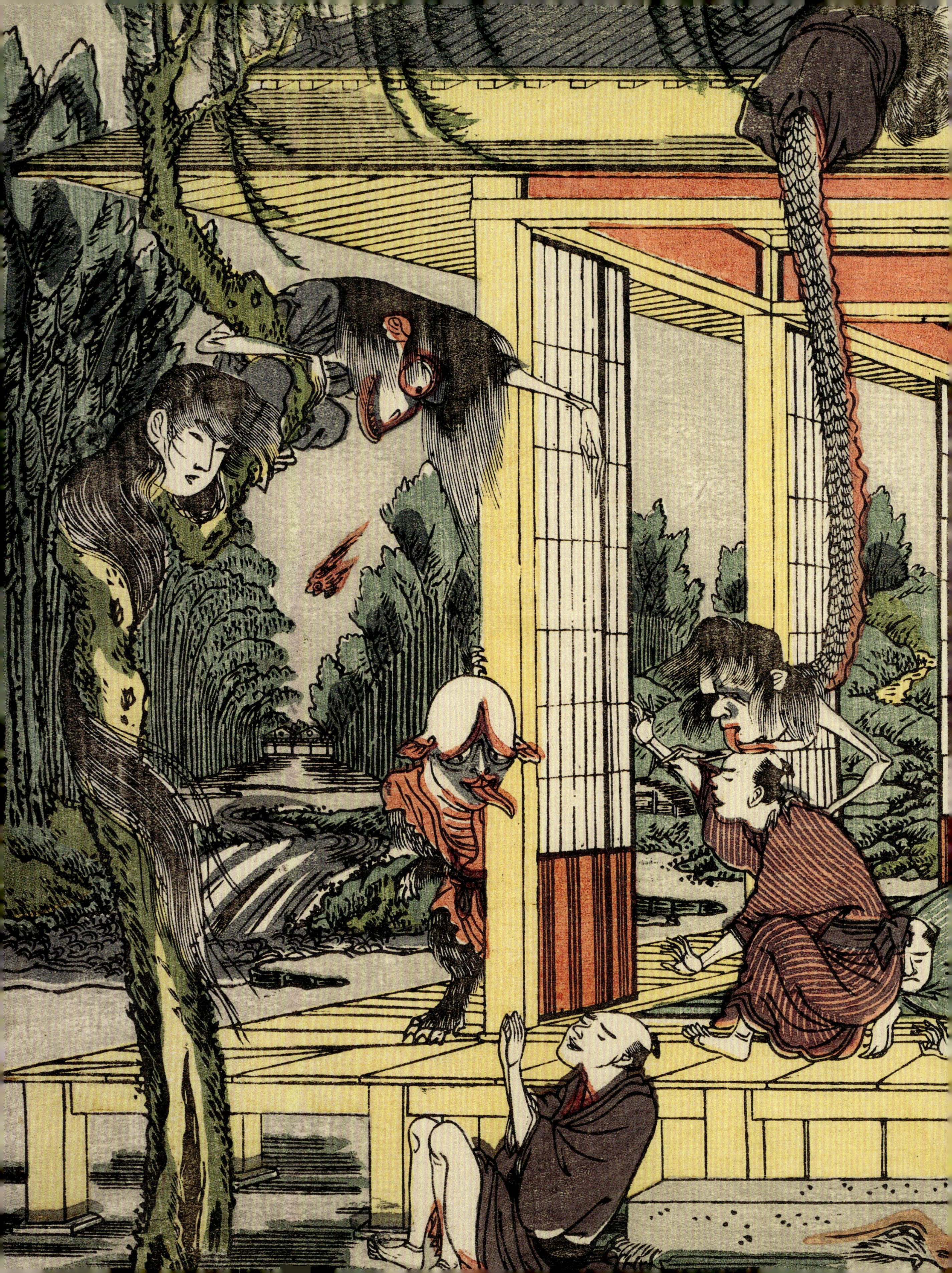

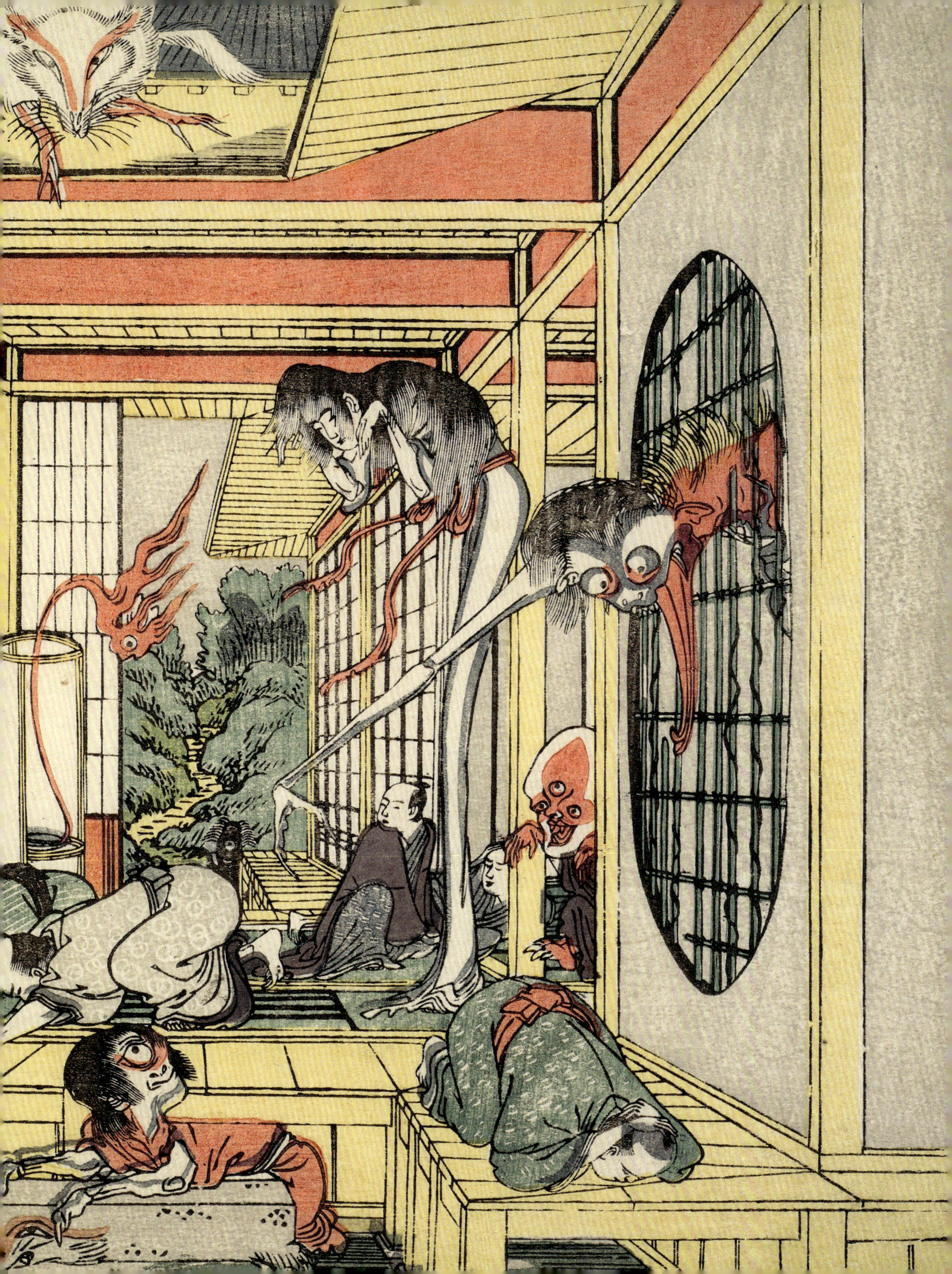

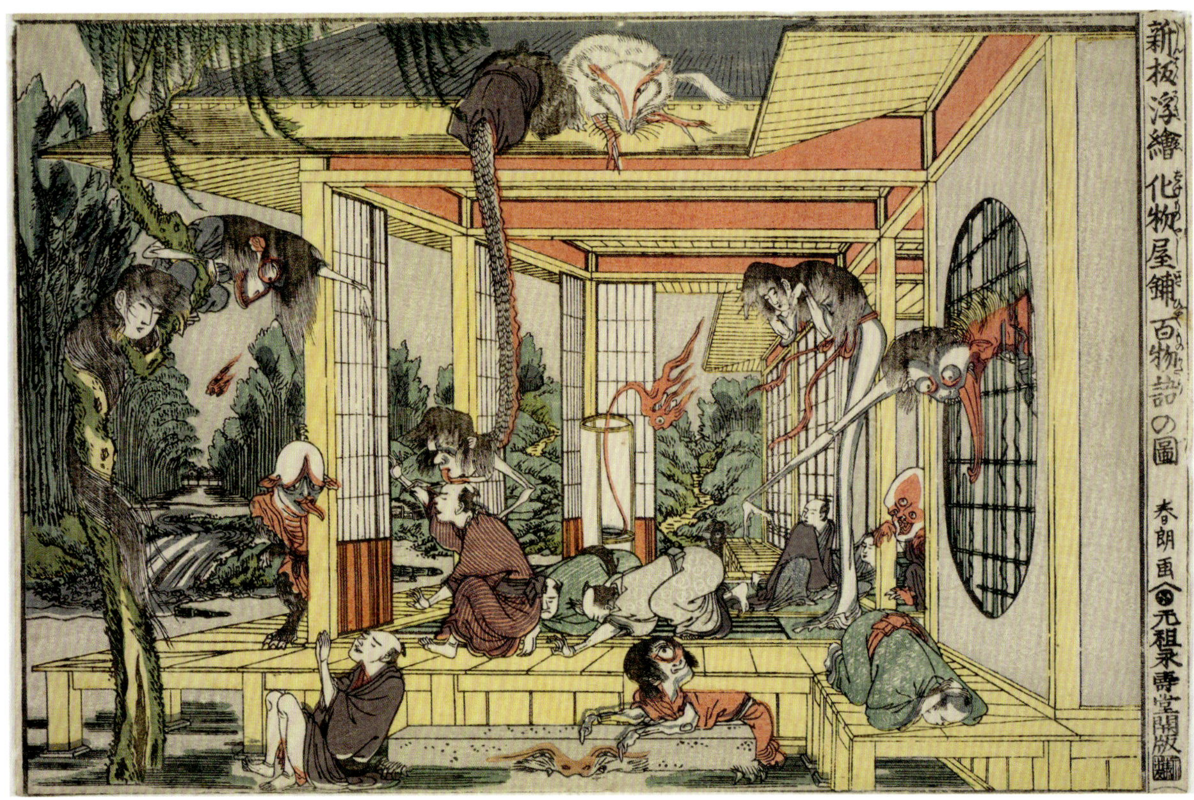

27 | **Newly Published Perspective Picture: One Hundred Ghost Stories in a Haunted House**
(*Shinpan uki-e bakemono yashiki hyaku mono gatari no zu*), about 1781–89

This delightful print is perhaps the most successful of all of Hokusai's early uki-e prints. It combines the illusionistic effect of Western-style vanishing-point perspective with fantastical and bizarre monsters drawn as if they, too, really existed—rather like a horror movie with extremely good special effects. The title refers to a popular Edo-period pastime in which a group of people took turns telling ghost stories at night, putting out the lights one by one at the end of each story. When all the tales were told and all the lights were out, ghosts would supposedly appear. In Hokusai's print, the well-dressed men gathered on the veranda of an elegant mansion may have been playing the game, little realizing what creatures they would summon. Later, in the 1830s, haunted houses, featuring dolls or costumed actors representing the ghosts, became popular tourist attractions in Edo. But at the time Hokusai designed this print, such scenes existed only in the imagination of the artist and his viewers. Hokusai continued to produce wonderfully creative images of ghosts throughout his career, most notably in various scenes in his best-selling picture book series *Hokusai Sketchbooks* (*Hokusai manga*) and in another famous series also titled *One Hundred Ghost Stories*.

Signature: Shunrō ga
Publisher: Nishimuraya Yohachi (Eijudō)
Woodblock print (nishiki-e); ink and color on paper
23.7 x 35.4 cm ($9\frac{5}{16} \times 13\frac{15}{16}$ in.)
Gift of C. Adrian Rübel, 46.1417

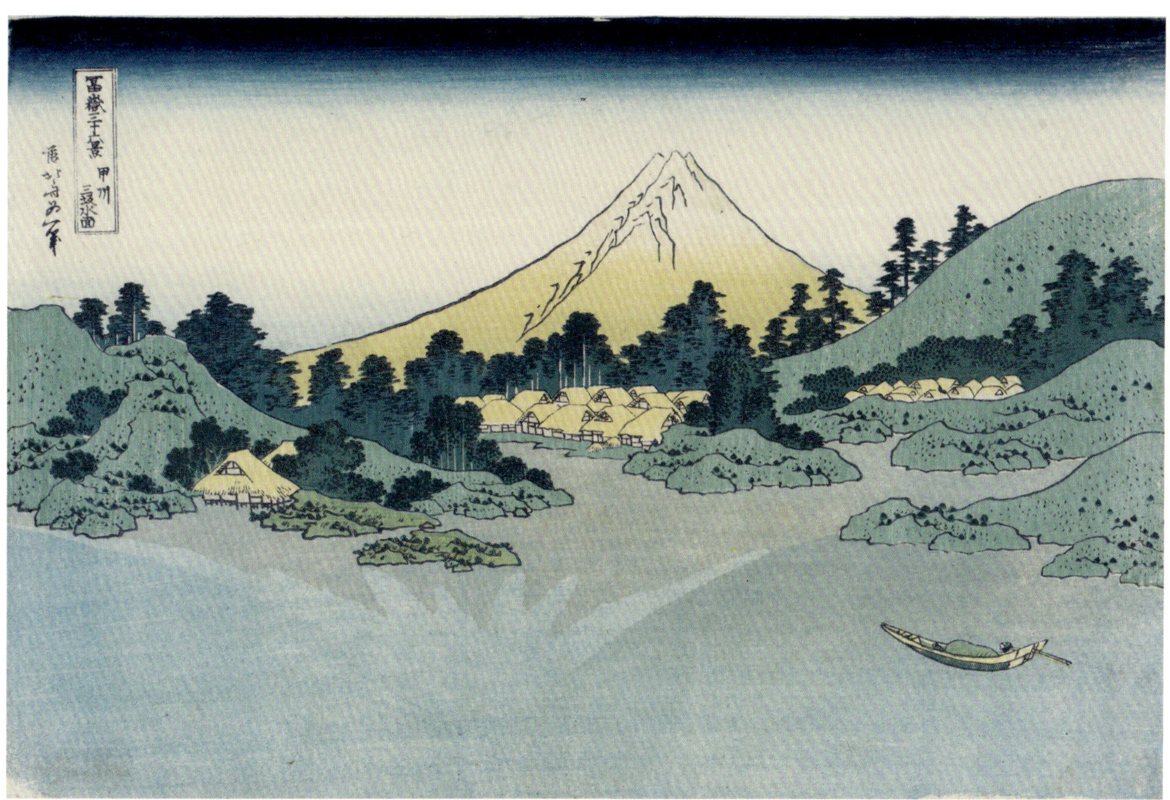

28 | **The Surface of the Lake at Misaka in Kai Province** (*Kōshū Misaka suimen*) from the series *Thirty-Six Views of Mount Fuji* (*Fugaku sanjūrokkei*), about 1830–31

The only humans in this tranquil scene are two tiny figures in the boat at the lower right. But the serenity is deceptive, for Hokusai is playing with the idea of reality versus illusion. The mountain that towers over the lakeside village is shown as it appears in high summer, without any snow. But its reflection in the smooth water of the lake shows the classic view of the mountain in the other three seasons, with its peak covered with snow. Furthermore, the reflection does not appear directly under the real mountain, as it would in real life, but is displaced slightly to one side, perhaps as a metaphor for the disjunction between mental images and real objects.

The lake is Lake Kawaguchi, as seen in a sudden, spectacular panorama from Misaka Pass near modern Fuefuki City, formerly Isawa Station on the Kōshūkaidō, one of the five great highways maintained by the Tokugawa shogunate. On this side of the mountain, facing away from Edo, the summit is more irregular in shape, with three distinct peaks.

Signature: Saki no Hokusai Iitsu hitsu
Publisher: Nishimuraya Yohachi (Eijudō)
Woodblock print (nishiki-e); ink and color on paper
26.3 x 38.3 cm (10 3/8 x 15 1/16 in.)
William Sturgis Bigelow Collection, 11.17544

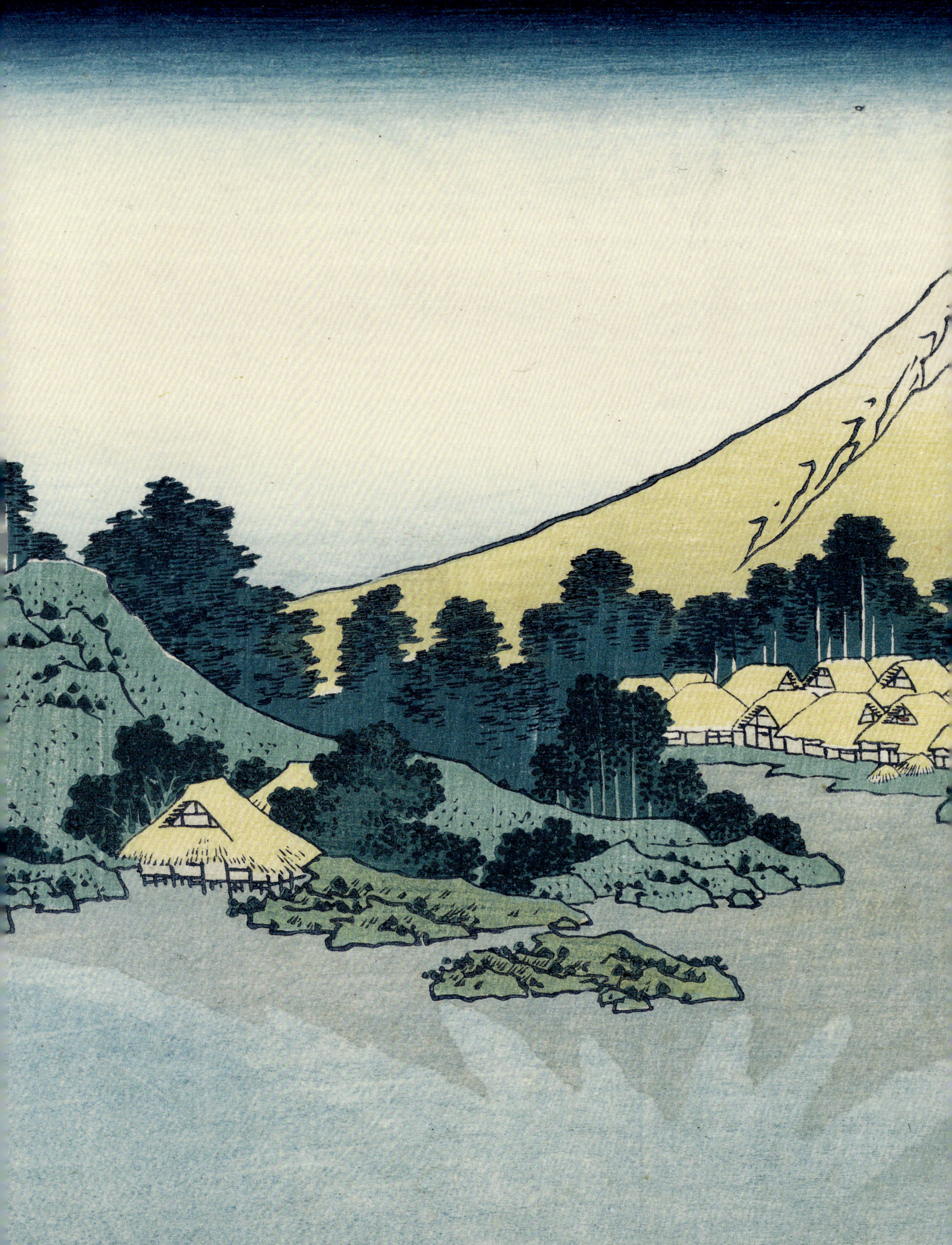

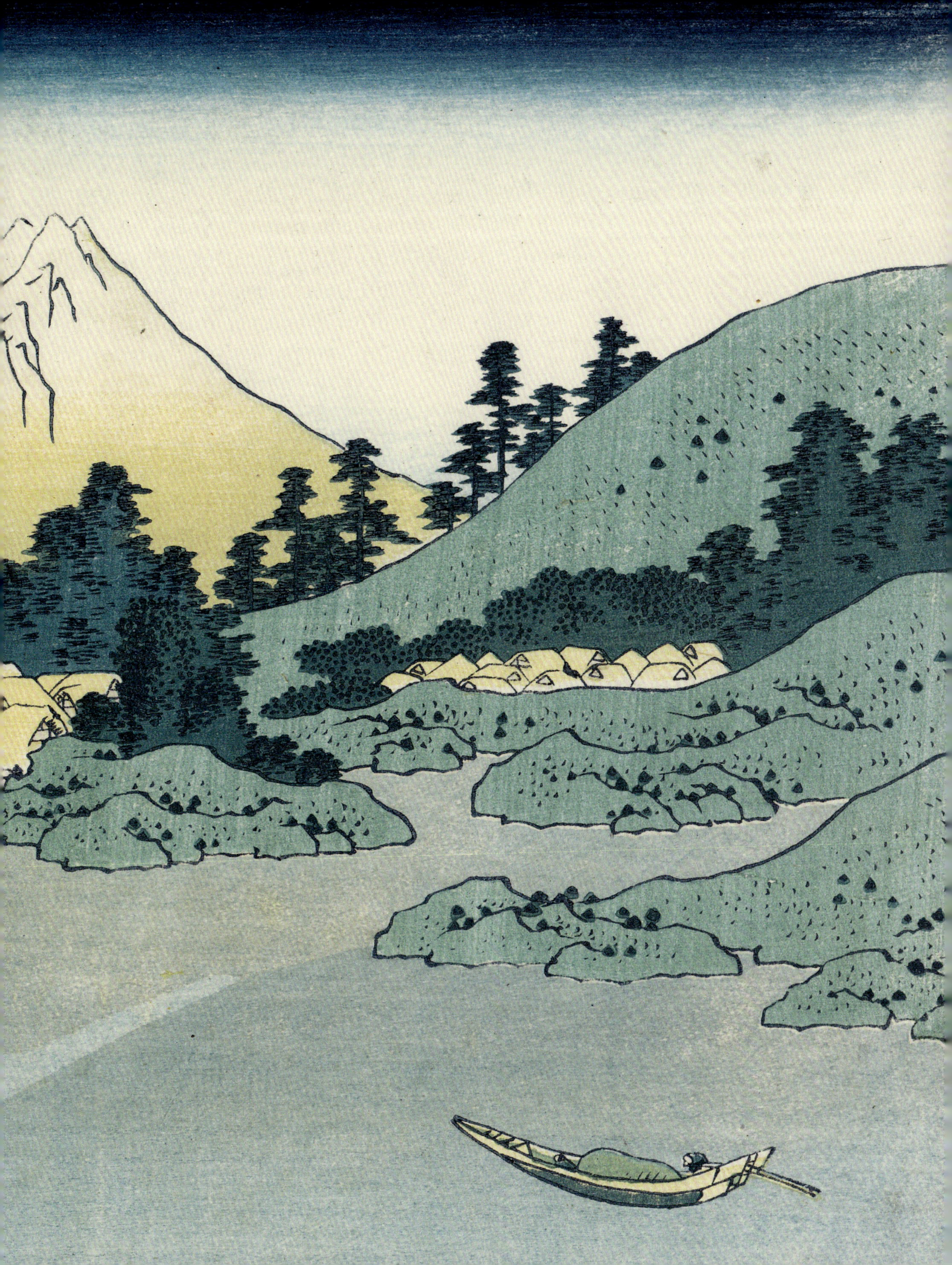

29 | **Mount Myōgi in Kōzuke Province**

(*Jōshū Myōgi-san*) from the series *Rare Views of Famous Landscapes* (*Shōkei kiran*), about 1834–35

In the steamy, humid heat of a Japanese summer, fans are essential for personal comfort. Prints such as this one were intended to be cut out and pasted to a flat bamboo framework to create an attractive, inexpensive fashion accessory featuring the latest in popular design. Of the eight known designs in the series, some are printed primarily in shades of blue, and others, like this one, are in full color. The scenes depicted are a mix of mountain landscapes and horizontally oriented views of lake or ocean shorelines.

Mount Myōgi in present-day Gunma Prefecture is noted for its unusual, dramatic rock formations, which are only slightly exaggerated in Hokusai's depiction. Today the mountain is a favorite destination for photographers and mountaineers, although the climb is considered dangerous. In real life, however, the buildings of the Myōgi Shrine are near the foot of the mountain rather than among the high peaks. Preliminary sketches for two designs in the series, including this one, have been preserved in an album of drawings by Hokusai. The sketches are rectangular, suggesting that the series may not originally have been intended for fans. Furthermore, the drawing for Mount Myōgi was a vertical design, which was rearranged when it was altered to fit the fan format. The shrine buildings were originally placed farther below the jagged peaks, as they appear in real life. Hokusai changed the geographic layout to fit the fan format and created a stronger, more recognizable image in the process.

Signature: Saki no Hokusai Manji
Woodblock print (nishiki-e); ink and color on paper
22.2 x 29 cm (8 3/4 x 11 7/16 in.)
Gift of L. Aaron Lebowich, 53.508

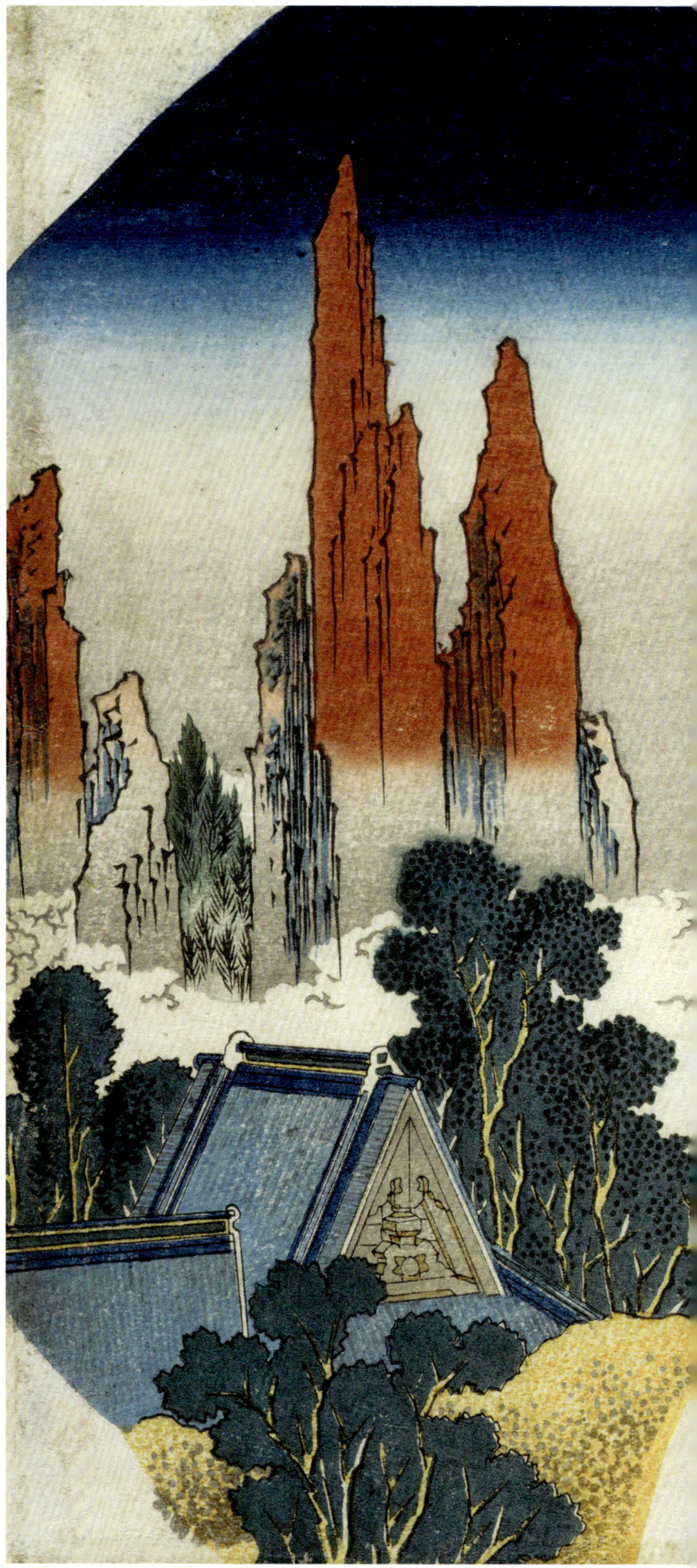

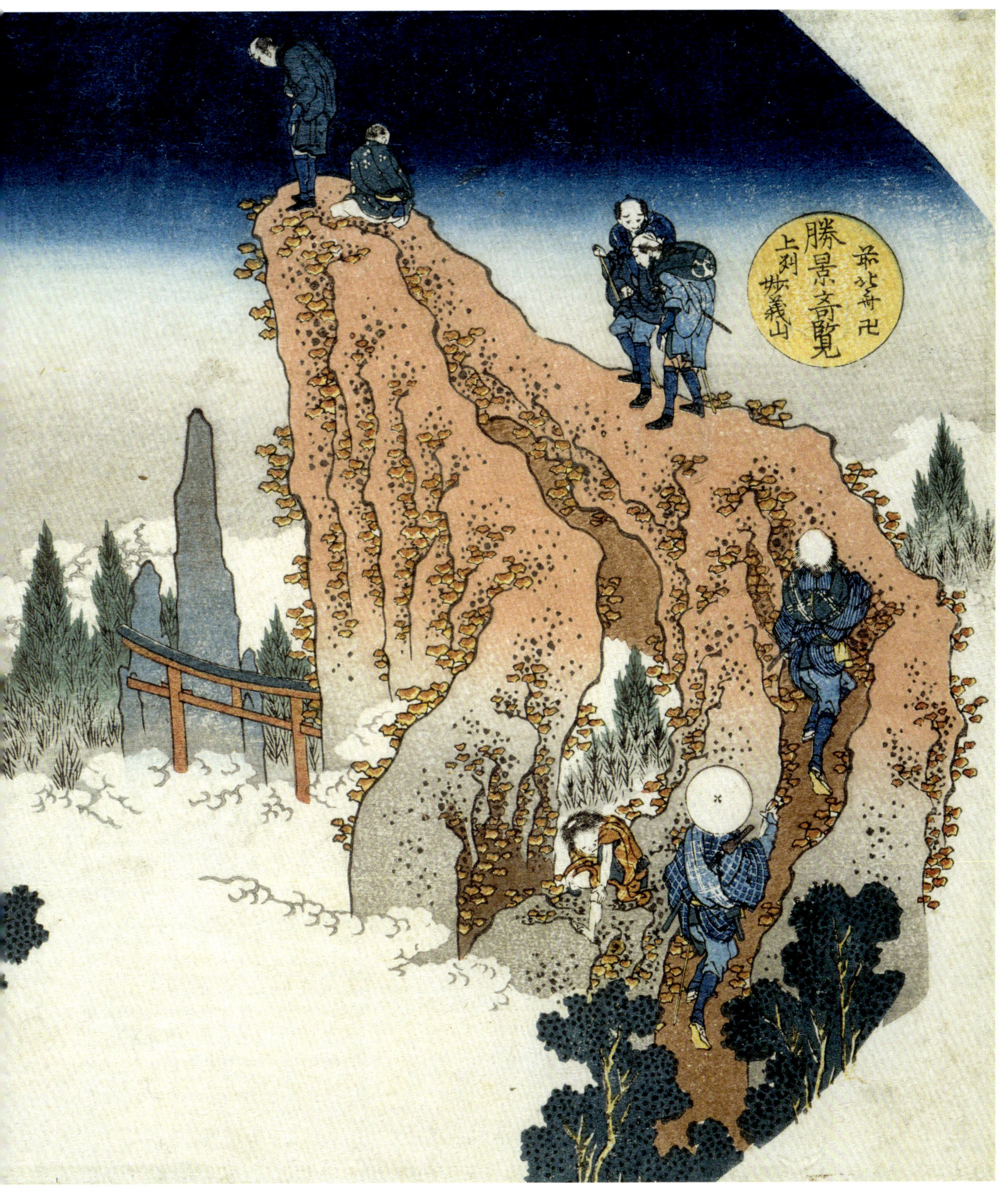
前北斎卍
勝景奇覧
上州妙義山

30 | **The Falling Mist Waterfall at Mount Kurokami in Shimotsuke Province**
(*Shimotsuke Kurokamiyama Kirifuri no taki*)
from the series *A Tour of Waterfalls in Various Provinces* (*Shokoku taki meguri*), about 1832

The set of eight vertical prints in the series *A Tour of Waterfalls in Various Provinces* are Hokusai's best-known landscape designs after the *Thirty-Six Views of Mount Fuji*. The waterfalls are not necessarily famous; instead, their selection seems to have been motivated by a desire to present the greatest possible variety. Hokusai's interest in assorted forms of waterfalls is hinted at on the last pictorial page of the first volume of *Hokusai manga*, published in 1814, which shows four small vertical scenes of streams and rapids of different configurations, but his ideas were not fully realized until the introduction of Prussian blue. As in the *Views of Fuji*, the outlines of the designs are printed in blue rather than black; the waterfalls themselves are described by combinations of dark blue, light blue, and unprinted white.

The Kirifuri Waterfall is one of the three most famous waterfalls in the area of Nikkō, the location of the Tōshōgū Shrine, famous for its elaborate buildings and their beautiful natural setting. The figures admiring the falls are most likely pilgrims traveling to or from the shrine. Hidden in their costumes are several references to the publisher, Nishimuraya Yohachi. The hat held by a figure at the upper right has the character "Ei," as in the house name Eijudō, and a similar hat belonging to the kneeling figure at the lower edge has a stylized version of the character "ju." The bundle on the back of the standing figure next to him has the publisher's trademark of a stylized mountain plus the lucky triple-comma symbol.

Signature: Saki no Hokusai Iitsu hitsu
Publisher: Nishimuraya Yohachi (Eijudō)
Woodblock print (nishiki-e); ink and color on paper
38 x 25.7 cm (14 15/16 x 10 1/8 in.)
William Sturgis Bigelow Collection, 11.19718

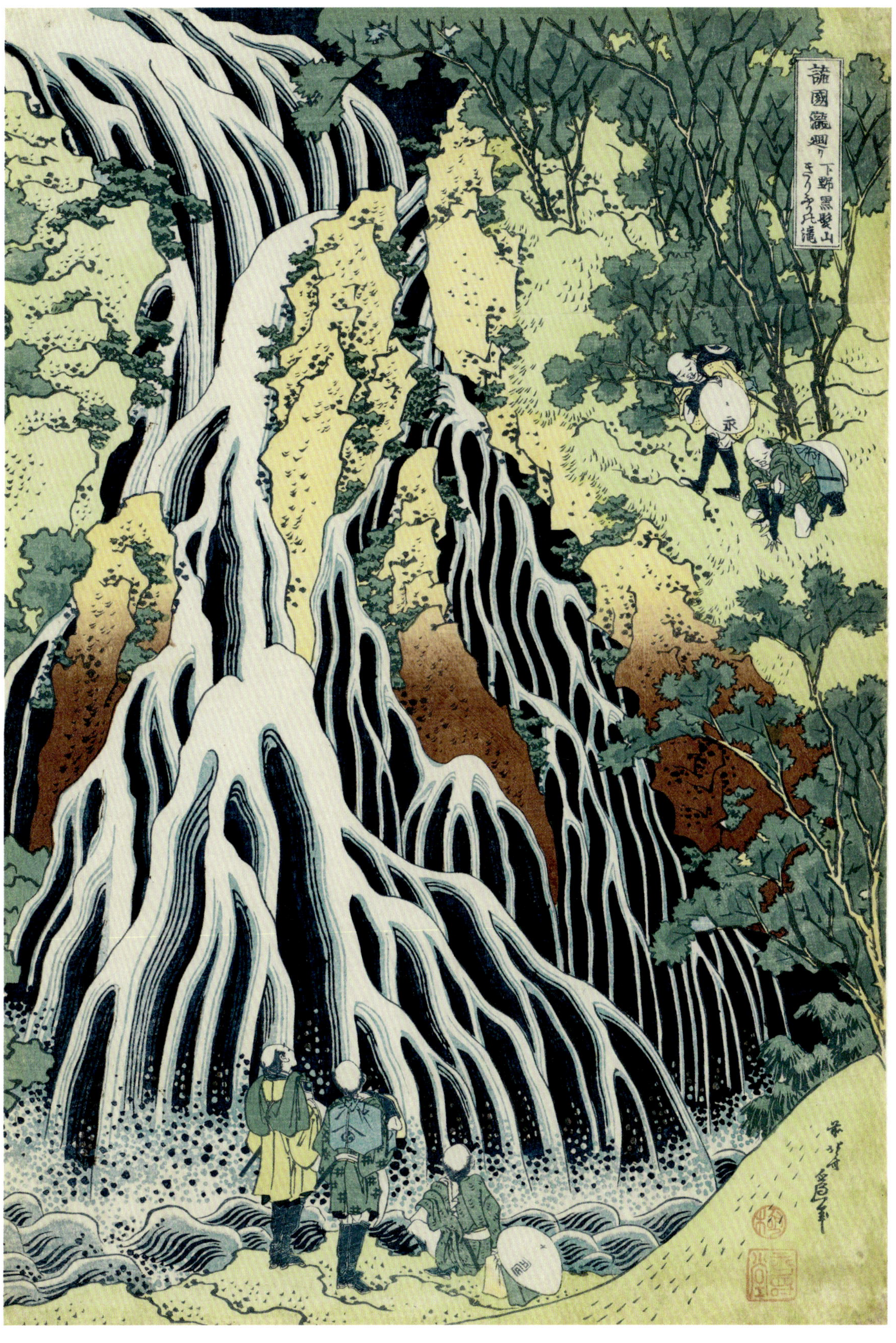
諸國瀧廻り
下野黒髪山
きりふりの滝

31 | **The Amida Falls in the Far Reaches of the Kisokaidō Road** (*Kisoji no oku Amida-ga-taki*) from the series *A Tour of Waterfalls in Various Provinces* (*Shokoku taki meguri*), about 1832

Located near the town of Shirotori, now part of Gujō City in Gifu Prefecture, this impressive waterfall was named for the vision of Amida Buddha, the Buddha who presides over the Western Paradise, once seen here by a priest. Almost two hundred feet tall, the waterfall looks much the same today as in Hokusai's print, except that the opening from which the water gushes is irregular in shape. Either the formation was rounder in Hokusai's time, or he may have deliberately exaggerated the shape to suggest the halo of Amida Buddha in the priest's vision. The convenient ledge to the left, on which two gentlemen enjoy a picnic prepared by their servant, also seems to be Hokusai's invention.

In addition to altering these physical aspects of the landscape, Hokusai adjusted the perspective to increase the impact of his design. The stream above the falls would not normally be visible when looking directly at the waterfall itself, but Hokusai has tipped up the ground plane at the top of his picture so that the round opening through which the water flows is filled by a decorative rippling. This stylized depiction of the water within the circular opening shows the influence of the Rinpa school of painting, a school with which he had been temporarily affiliated in the 1790s.

Signature: Saki no Hokusai Iitsu hitsu
Publisher: Nishimuraya Yohachi (Eijudō)
Woodblock print (nishiki-e); ink and color on paper
38.2 x 25.9 cm (15 1/16 x 10 3/16 in.)
William Sturgis Bigelow Collection, 11.17545

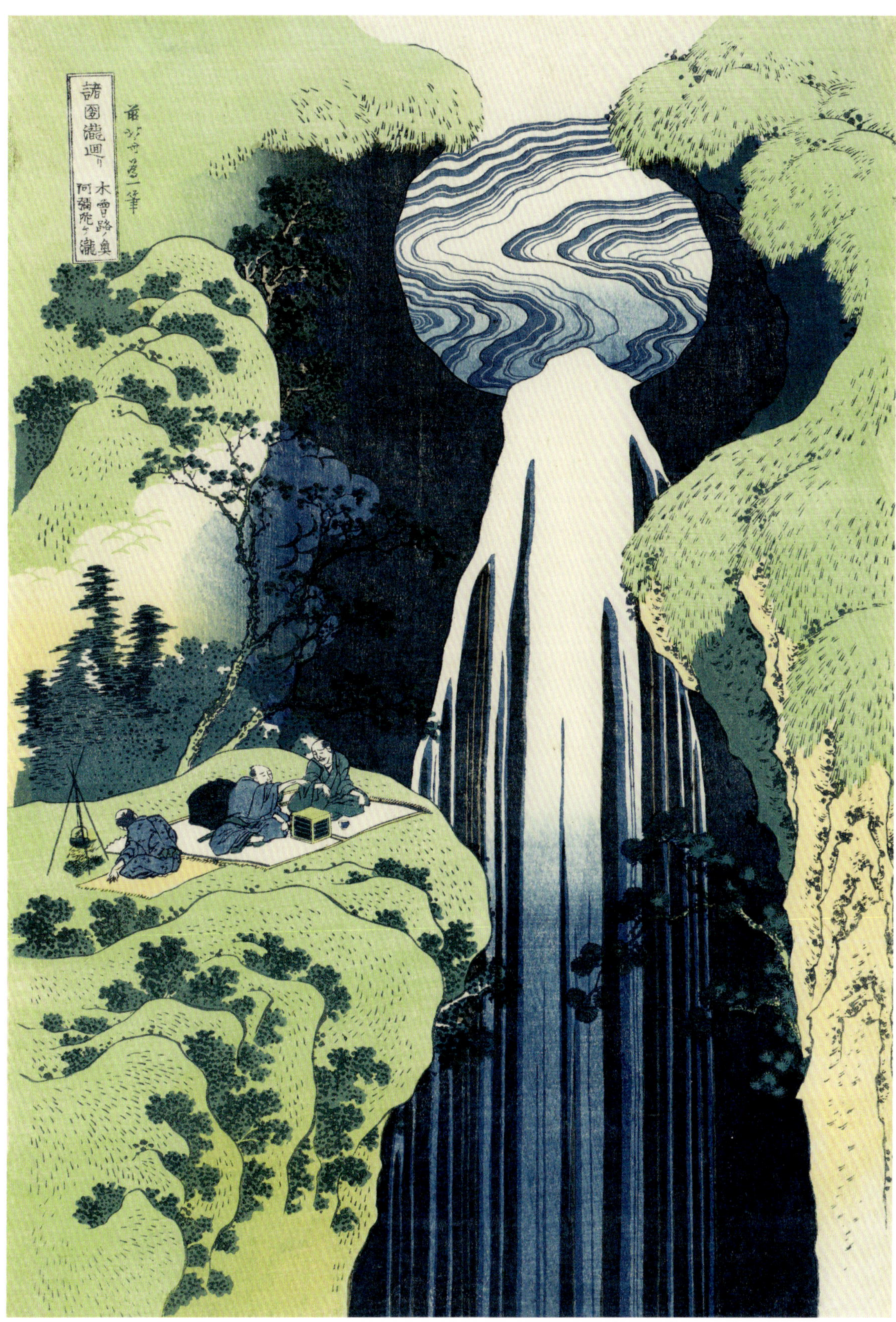
諸國瀧廻り
木曽路ノ奥
阿彌陀ヶ瀧

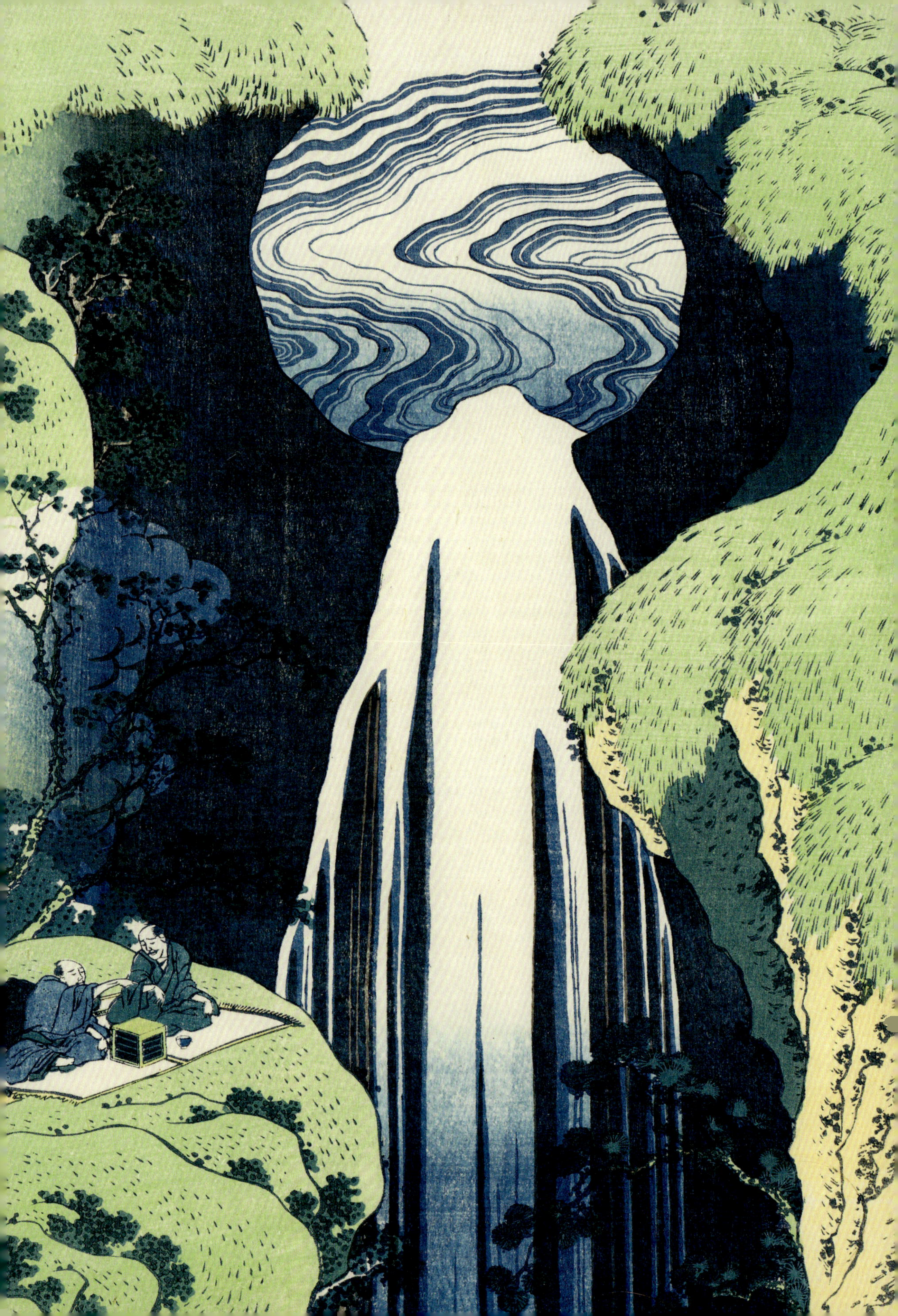

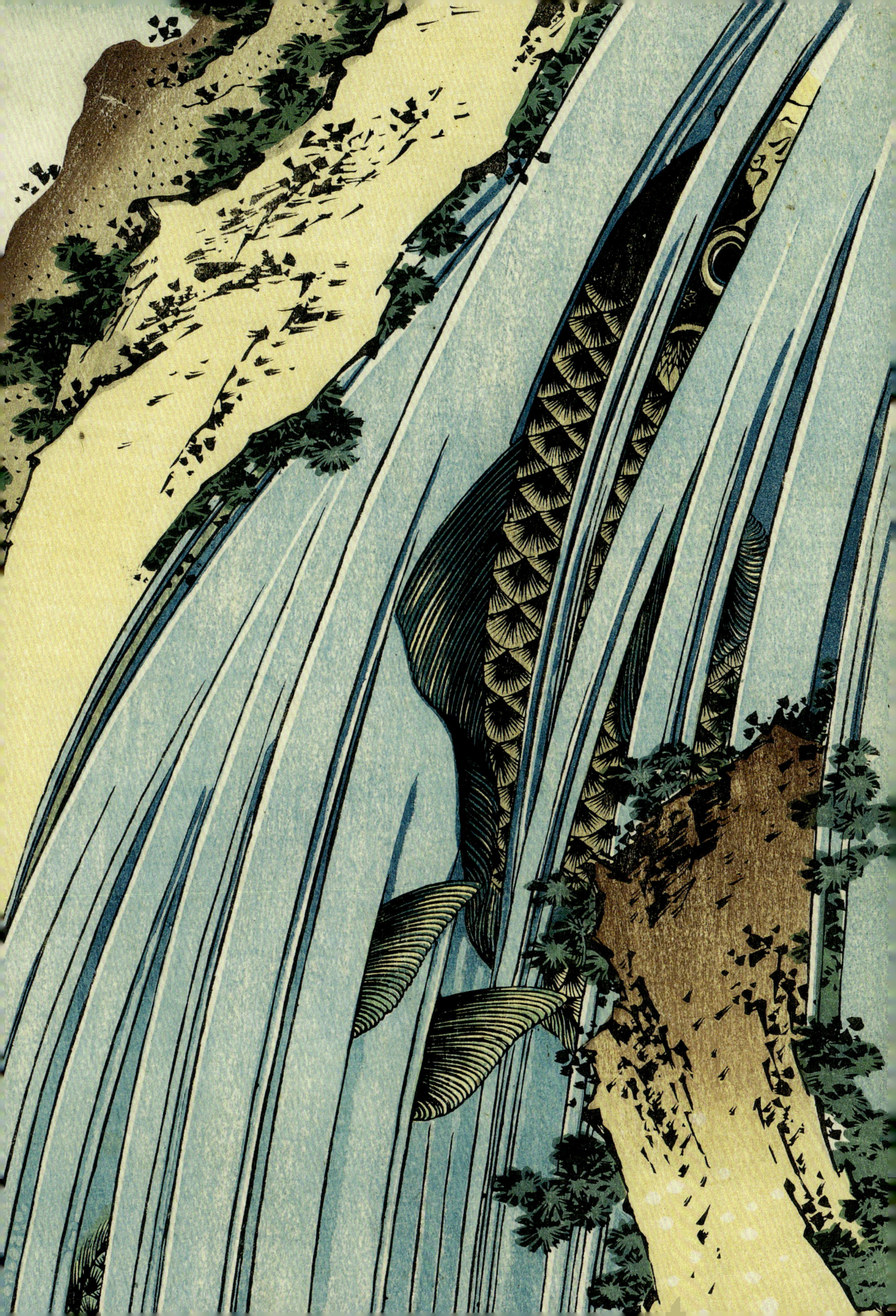

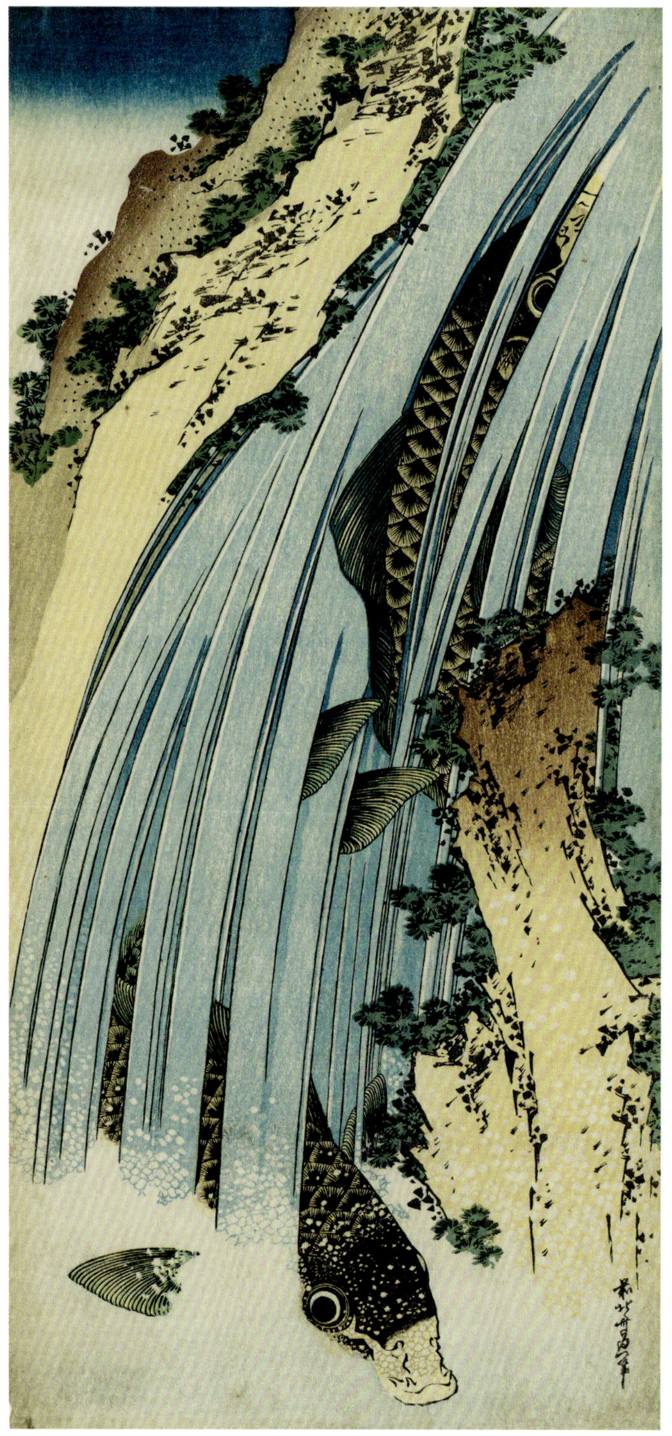

32 | **Two Carp in Waterfall**, about 1834

Like some other freshwater fish, carp swim upstream to spawn in the spring. They are known as powerful swimmers and can even jump over barriers. According to Chinese folklore, a carp that could swim up the Yellow River as far as Longmen, and leap up over the falls there, would turn into a dragon. In both China and Japan, a carp swimming upstream became an auspicious symbol of success as a result of great effort, and the subject was depicted in many paintings. Hokusai's version of this theme is unusual because he shows not only a carp swimming up the waterfall, but also a second carp at the bottom of the fall who seems to be swimming downstream. Is this carp waiting for its turn to ascend the falls or perhaps deciding to go in another direction altogether? The second carp adds an interesting element of narrative ambiguity to the familiar theme.

The print is from an untitled series of five probably published at the end of 1833 for the New Year holiday season of 1834. Although the prints lack titles, they are believed to be a set because of their identical signatures and their similarities of format and subject matter. Their size and their auspicious themes—horses and hawks for martial valor, turtles and cranes for longevity, and carp for persistence leading to success—would have made them elegant New Year decorations, a less expensive substitute for hanging scroll paintings.

Signature: Saki no Hokusai Iitsu hitsu
Woodblock print (nishiki-e); ink and color on paper
52 x 23.7 cm (20 ½ x 9 5/16 in.)
William Sturgis Bigelow Collection, 11.19647

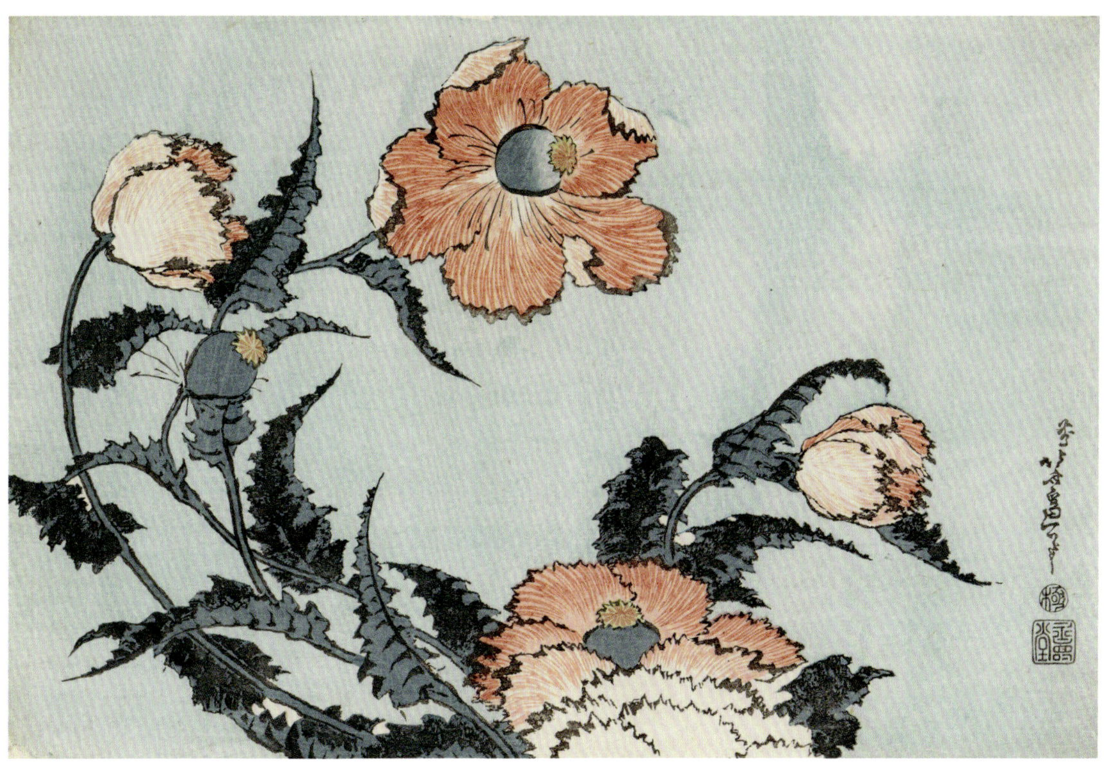

33 | **Poppies** from an untitled series known as *Large Flowers*, about 1833–34

Just as the great success of *Thirty-Six Views of Mount Fuji* made landscape an important print genre for the first time, the untitled series known as *Large Flowers* did the same for bird-and-flower prints. Like landscapes, bird-and-flower prints had previously been a minor subject within ukiyo-e, but Hokusai elevated them to the status of a major genre, and his lead was soon followed by other artists such as Hiroshige. Bird-and-flower painting had developed in China during the Song dynasty and was appreciated by the educated elite throughout East Asia. Hokusai's close-up views of flowers are strongly influenced by the printed illustrations in Chinese painting manuals such as the *Mustard-Seed Garden Painting Manual* (*Jieziyuan Huazhaun* in Chinese, *Keshien gaden* in Japanese). His skillful depictions of flowers in his own book illustrations and color prints were extremely influential in turn among Western artists; the Art Nouveau movement in particular was indebted to works such as the *Poppies.*

This striking design is often considered the finest composition in the *Large Flowers* series. The curve of the poppies as they bend in a strong wind has been compared to the curve of *The Great Wave* in the *Thirty-Six Views of Mount Fuji.* Since horizontal images in Japanese art are normally read from right to left, both of these left-to-right curves create a sense of surprise and drama for the viewer.

Poppies in Japan (and elsewhere) were most often enjoyed not as garden plants or potted plants but as wildflowers filling entire fields with their colorful blooms. Hokusai's extreme close-up implies a viewer lying on the ground among the poppies, looking up at especially fine blossoms against the blue sky and feeling the breeze that makes them bend so gracefully.

Signature: Saki no Hokusai Iitsu hitsu
Publisher: Nishimuraya Yohachi (Eijudō)
Woodblock print (nishiki-e); ink and color on paper
26.2 x 38.4 cm (10 5/16 x 15 1/8 in.)
William Sturgis Bigelow Collection, 11.17594

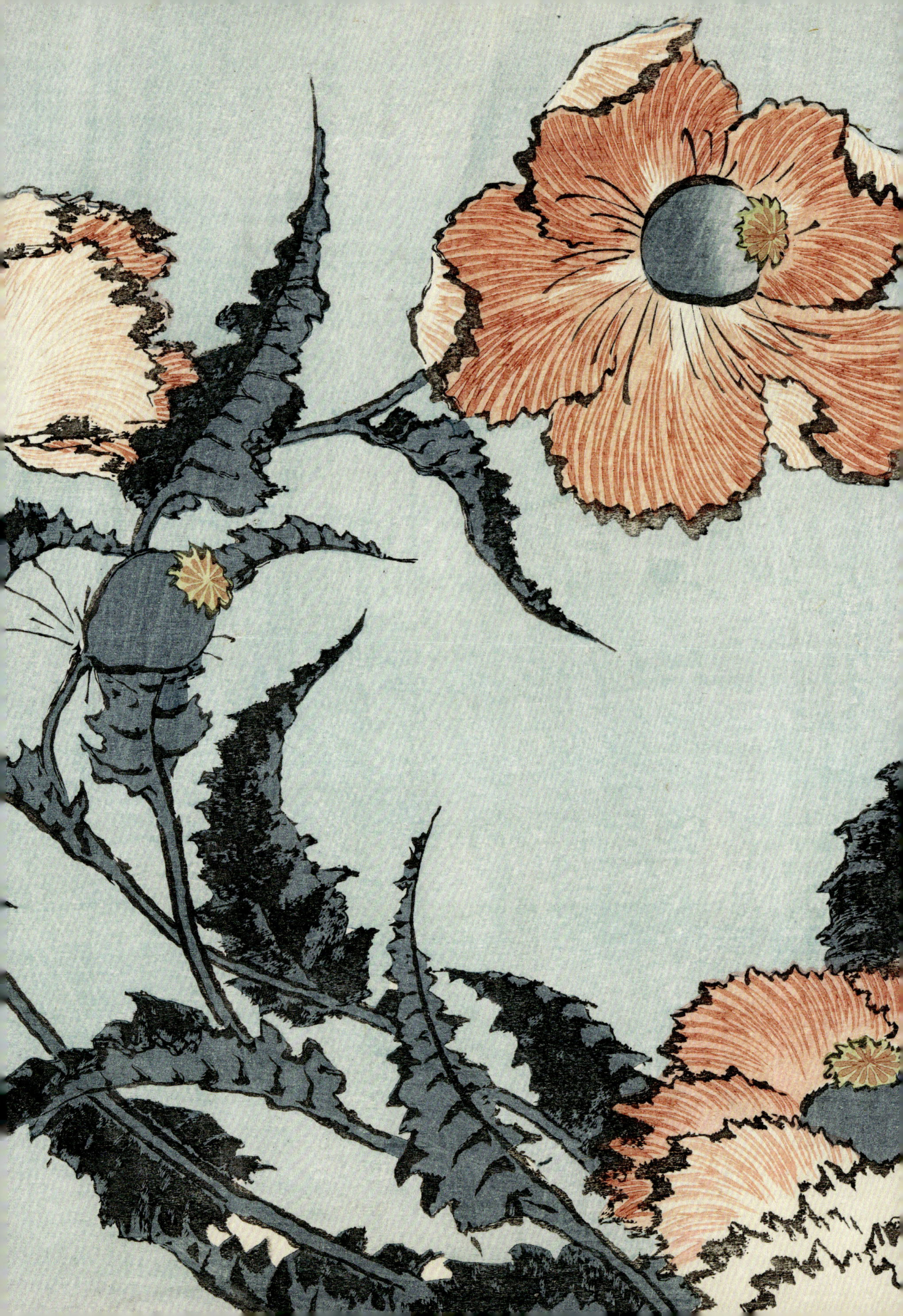

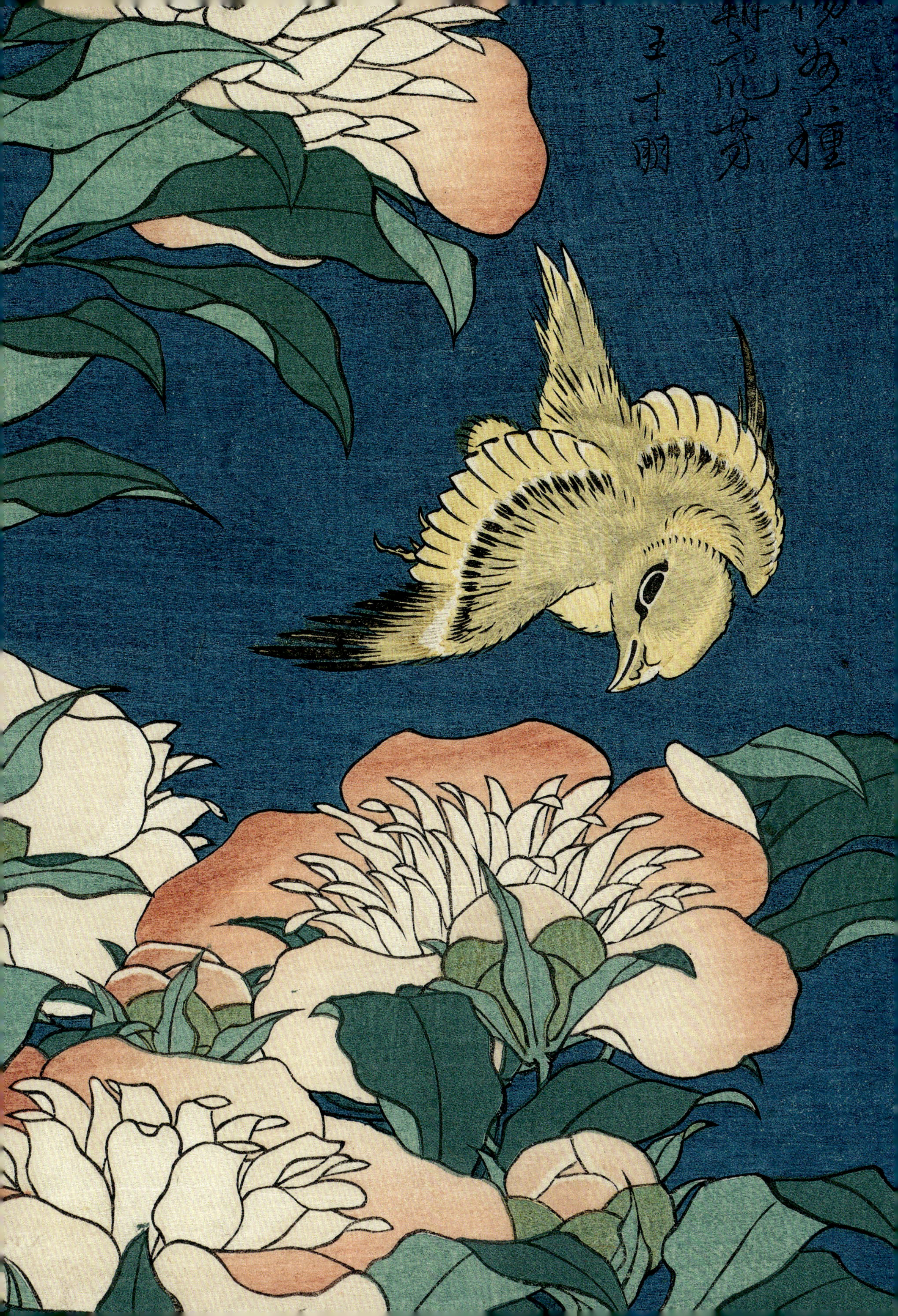

34 | **Peonies and Canary** (*Shakuyaku, kanaari*) from an untitled series known as *Small Flowers*, about 1834

The untitled series of bird-and-flower designs that has been nicknamed *Small Flowers* can be dated to about 1834 by an advertisement that appeared in a book published at New Year: "Pictures of flowers and birds in the *shikishi* format, with brilliant colors." The ten designs in the series were printed two at a time, on a standard-size ōban sheet, and then cut apart into half-size chūban prints that are almost the same size as the prestigious square *shikishi* format used for traditional album paintings and privately commissioned surimono prints. Each print is inscribed with either a Chinese or a Japanese poem. As advertised, the colors are indeed brilliant, all the more effective because of the small, jewel-like format.

In East Asian languages, a clear distinction is made between tree peonies and herbaceous peonies, the type shown here. According to a Chinese saying, tree peonies were at their finest in Luoyang, in northern China, and herbaceous peonies in Yangzhou, to the south. The Chinese couplet inscribed on the print is by the Northern Song dynasty poet Wang Shipeng (1112–1171) and reads: "The Yangzhou peony with its thousand leaves, supreme among the fragrances of spring." The brilliant yellow canary is an exotic songbird that originated in the islands of the Atlantic, was domesticated in Europe in the seventeenth century, and was imported to Japan by Dutch traders during the Edo period. Hokusai spells out the name of the foreign bird in phonetic *katakana* characters, "ka-na-a-ri."

Signature: Saki no Hokusai Iitsu hitsu
Publisher: Nishimuraya Yohachi (Eijudō)
Woodblock print (nishiki-e); ink and color on paper
26 x 19.2cm (10 1/4 x 7 9/16 in.)
William S. and John T. Spaulding Collection, 21.10228

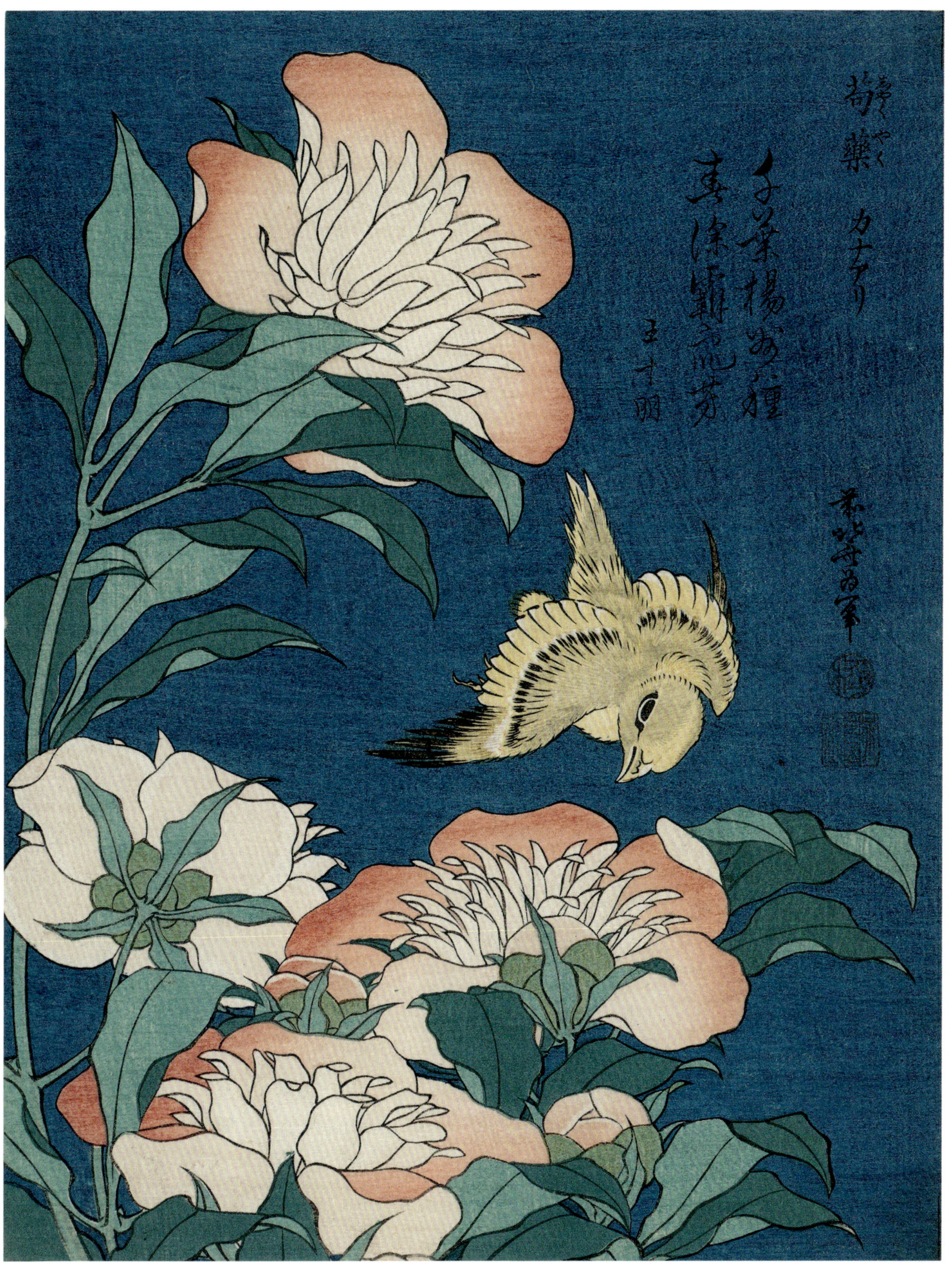
芍薬 カナアリ
前北斎為一筆

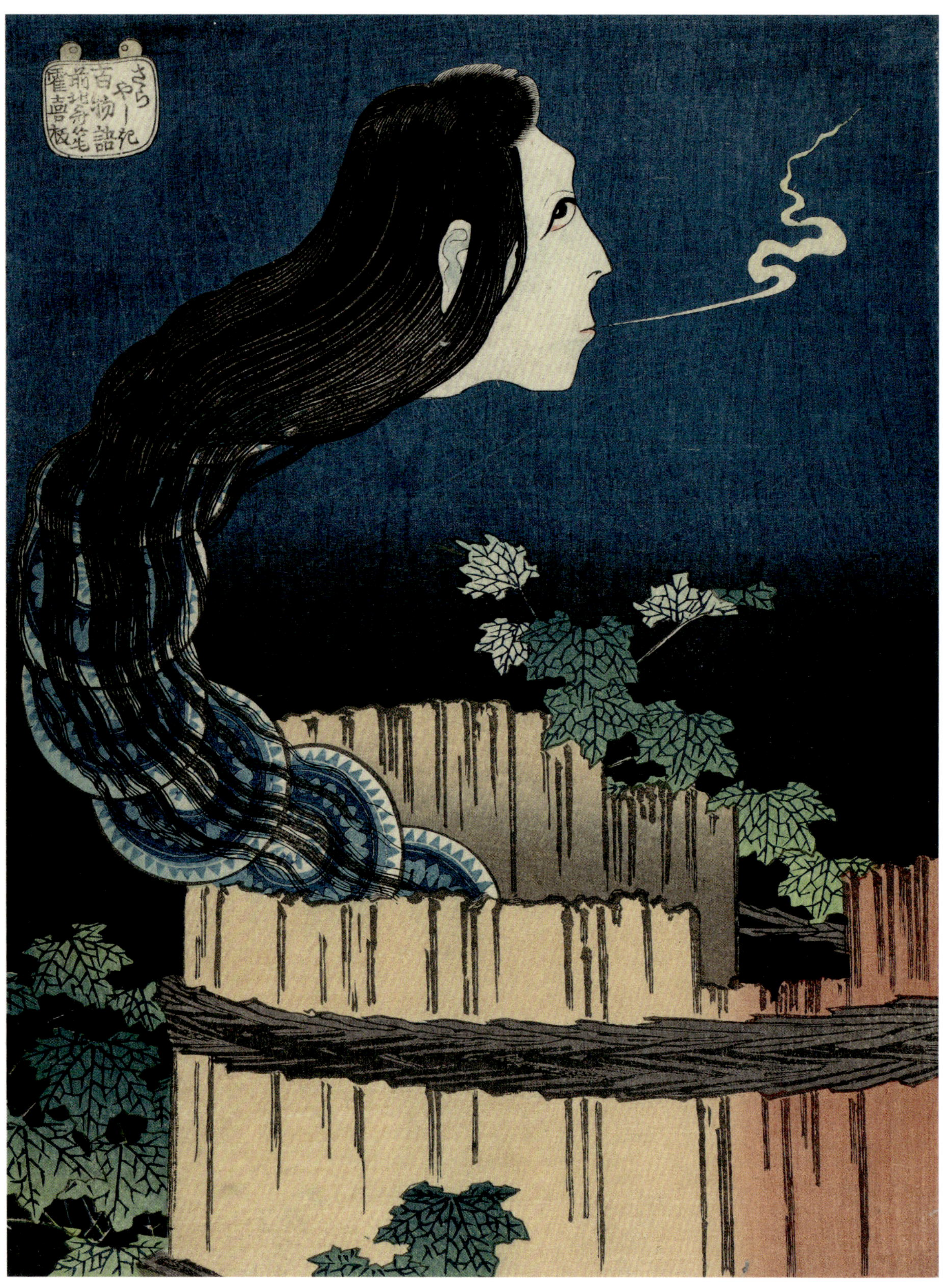
さらやしき
百物語
前北斎為一筆
鶴喜板

35 | **The Mansion of the Plates** (*Sara yashiki*) from the series *One Hundred Ghost Stories* (*Hyaku monogatari*), about 1831–32

Throughout his career, Hokusai was noted for his imaginative renditions of the ghosts and monsters that featured in many traditional Japanese tales and were incorporated into current novels and Kabuki plays as well. The title of this gorgeously colored small series refers to a popular game of telling ghost stories at night and gradually extinguishing the lights as the stories were told, also the subject of one of Hokusai's early perspective prints. The series title suggests that there could have been as many as one hundred prints, but in fact only five designs are known.

The story "Mansion of the Plates" was a traditional tale told in several parts of Japan. In 1741 it was made the subject of a musical narrative and was subsequently dramatized in various Kabuki plays, becoming very well known. The story tells of the unfortunate maidservant Okiku, who accidentally broke a precious porcelain plate that was part of a set belonging to her employer. The young woman either committed suicide by throwing herself into the well or, in some versions of the story, was killed by the enraged master of the mansion, who then threw her body into the well. There is even a Kabuki version in which the wicked master secretly broke the plate himself to frame Okiku after she refused his lecherous advances. Night after night, Okiku's ghost rose from the well and counted the plates in a ghostly moan, "One . . . , two . . . , three . . . ," with a horrible shriek when the count came up short.

The ghost of Okiku is generally drawn as a white-clad figure rising from the well in an eerie mist, but in Hokusai's clever, unusual version, it is the plates themselves that rise from the well one after another and make up the snakelike neck of the ghostly head.

Signature: Saki no Hokusai hitsu
Publisher: Tsuruya Kiemon (Senkakudō)
Woodblock print (nishiki-e); ink and color on paper
23.7 x 17.6 cm (9 5/16 x 6 15/16 in.)
William S. and John T. Spaulding Collection, 21.10236

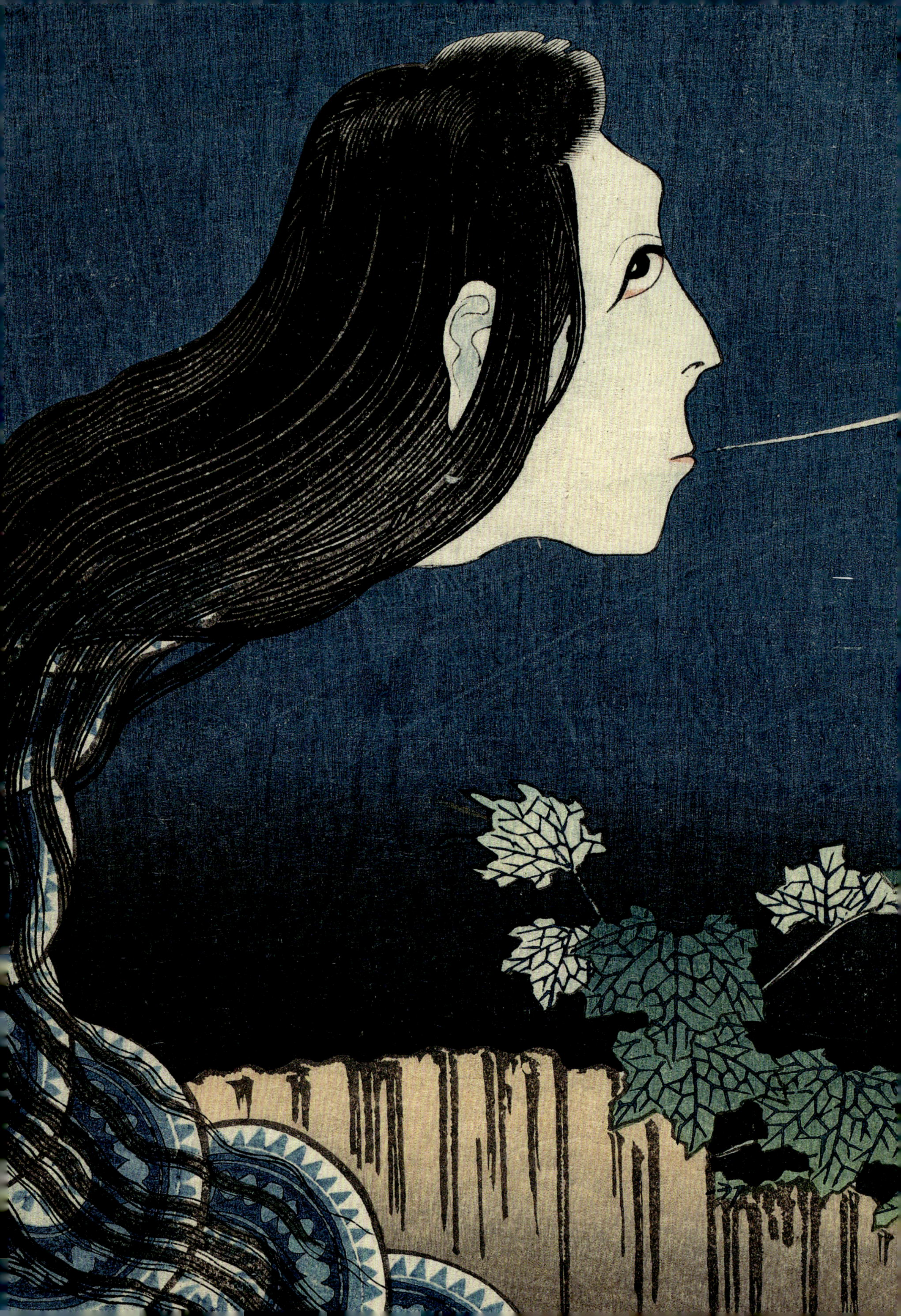

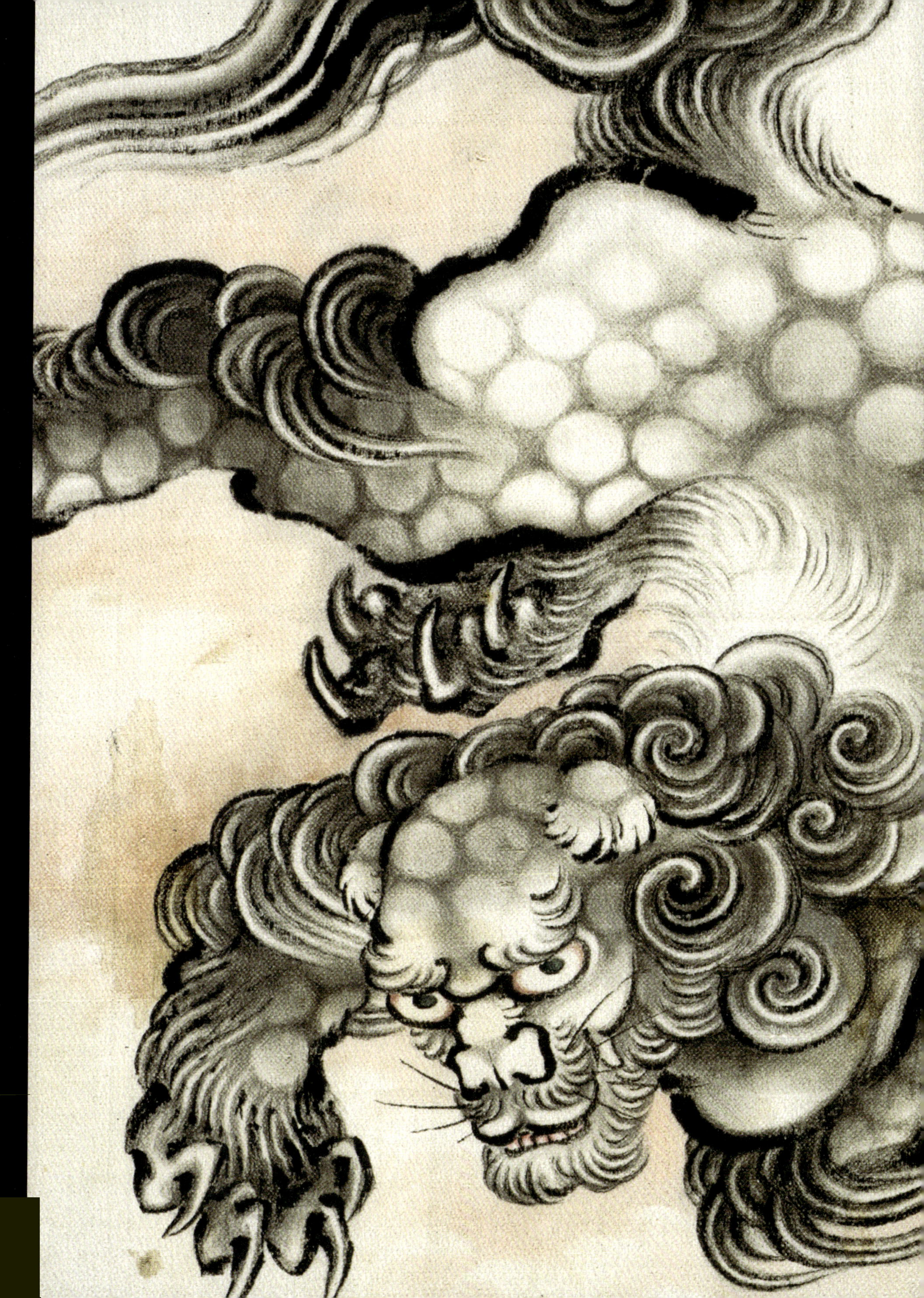

36 | **Mythological Chinese Lion**, 1844

The square format and silk fabric of this gorgeous painting identify it as a *fukusa*, a cover for a formally presented gift. A gift or gifts would be placed on a fine wood or lacquer tray, draped with the fukusa, and presented to the recipient. After duly admiring the presentation, the recipient was expected to return the tray and fukusa, but occasionally high-ranking officials took advantage of their power to keep the entire presentation assemblage as well as the gift itself. In the case of a fukusa as beautiful as this one, the temptation is obvious.

The combination of lions and peonies was a favorite in Edo-period Japanese visual arts and even in the Kabuki theater, where dancers sometimes performed in long red or white wigs to imitate the magical lions said to have appeared to a Japanese monk who visited China to study Buddhism. In fact, lions were not native to either China or Japan; their closest natural habitats were northern India and Persia. In those areas, they were symbols of royalty, and so they were used in Indian Buddhist art to honor the teachings of the Buddha. They are especially associated with Manjusri (in Japanese, Monju), the bodhisattva of wisdom. When Buddhism was transmitted to China, the symbolic lions came too, but their appearance diverged further and further from zoological accuracy as they were drawn by artists who had never seen the animals. What they lost in realism, however, they gained in magnificence, as artists such as Hokusai drew creatures filled with mystical power.

For over a year, in 1842 and 1843, Hokusai drew a lion every day as a good-luck charm, in the hope that he would continue to enjoy his long life and good health. His signature on this painting, "Brush of Manji, the Old Man Mad about Painting, aged eighty-five," further indicates his pride in his advanced age. Eighty-five of over two hundred surviving drawings were pasted into an album entitled *Daily Exorcisms* (*Nisshin joma*). The last drawing in the album, made at the end of 1843, shows a lion in a similar pose to the one shown here.

The exquisitely detailed peonies that make up the decorative border of the fukusa are thought to have been painted by one of Hokusai's pupils, possibly his daughter Ōi, who was a highly talented artist in her own right.

Signature: Gakyō rōjin Manji hitsu, yowai hachijūgosai
Fukusa; silk plain weave with ink and color
66.6 x 71.6 cm (26 1/4 x 28 3/16 in.)
William Sturgis Bigelow Collection, 22.398

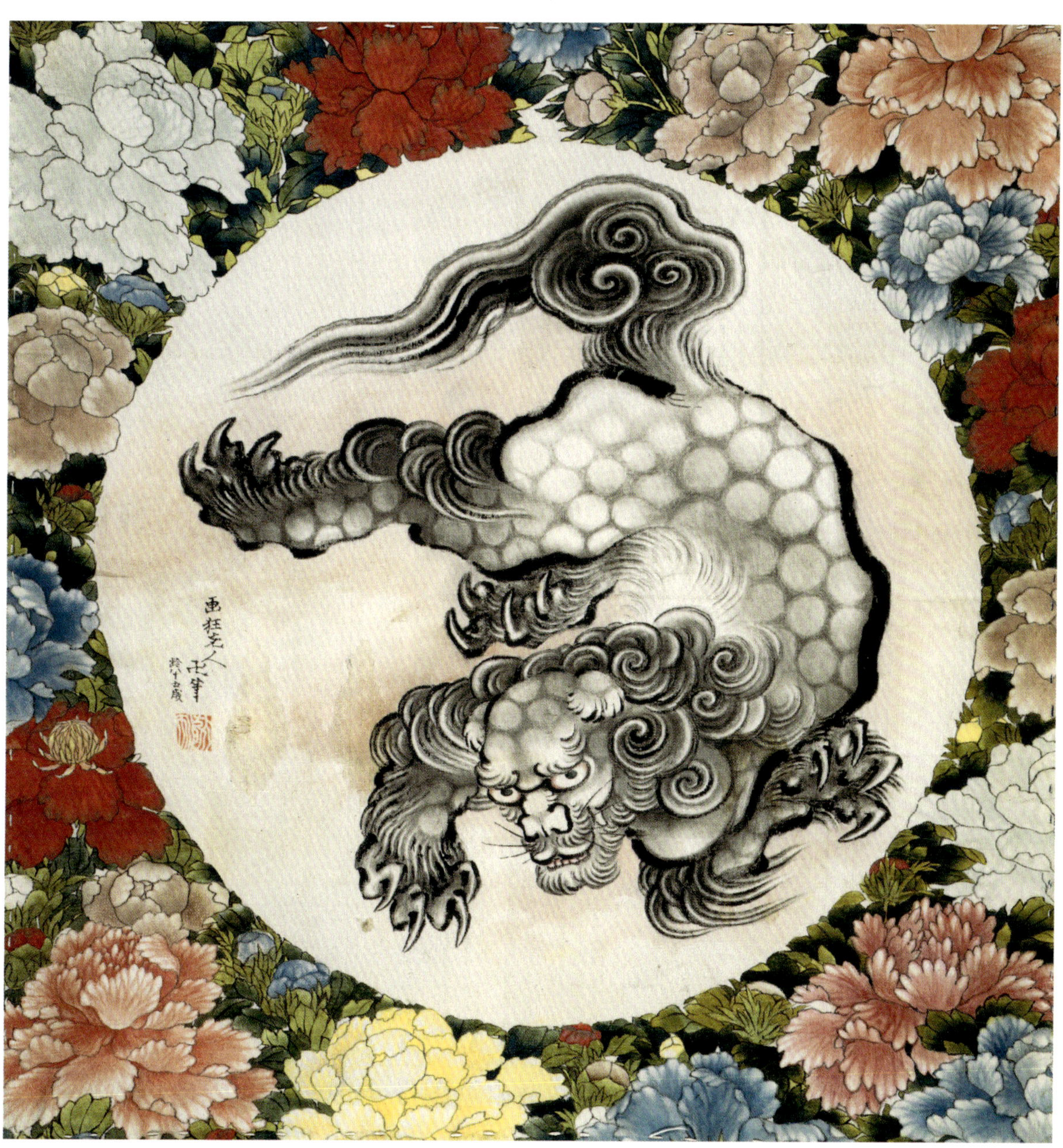
画狂老人卍筆
齢八十五歳

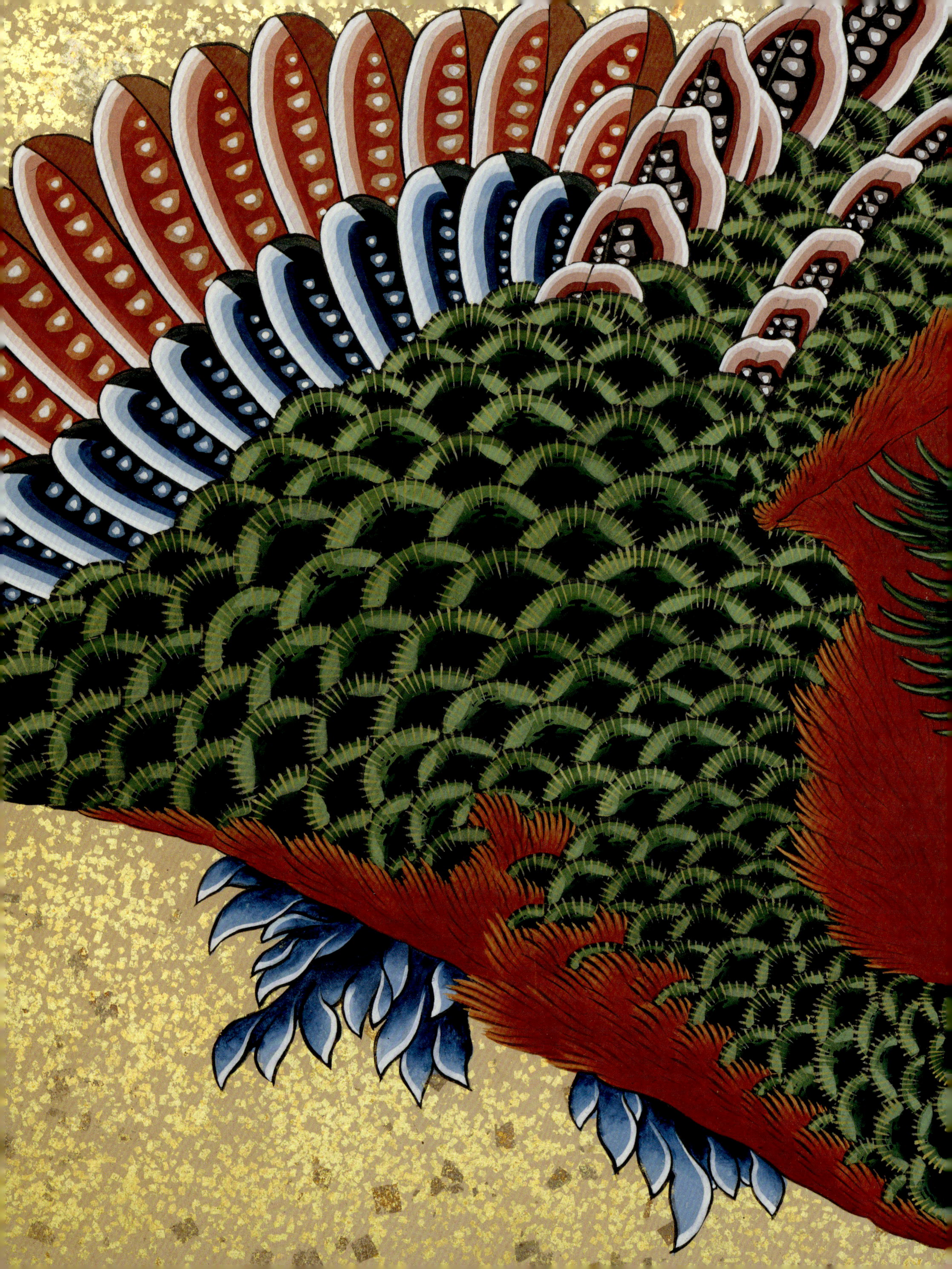

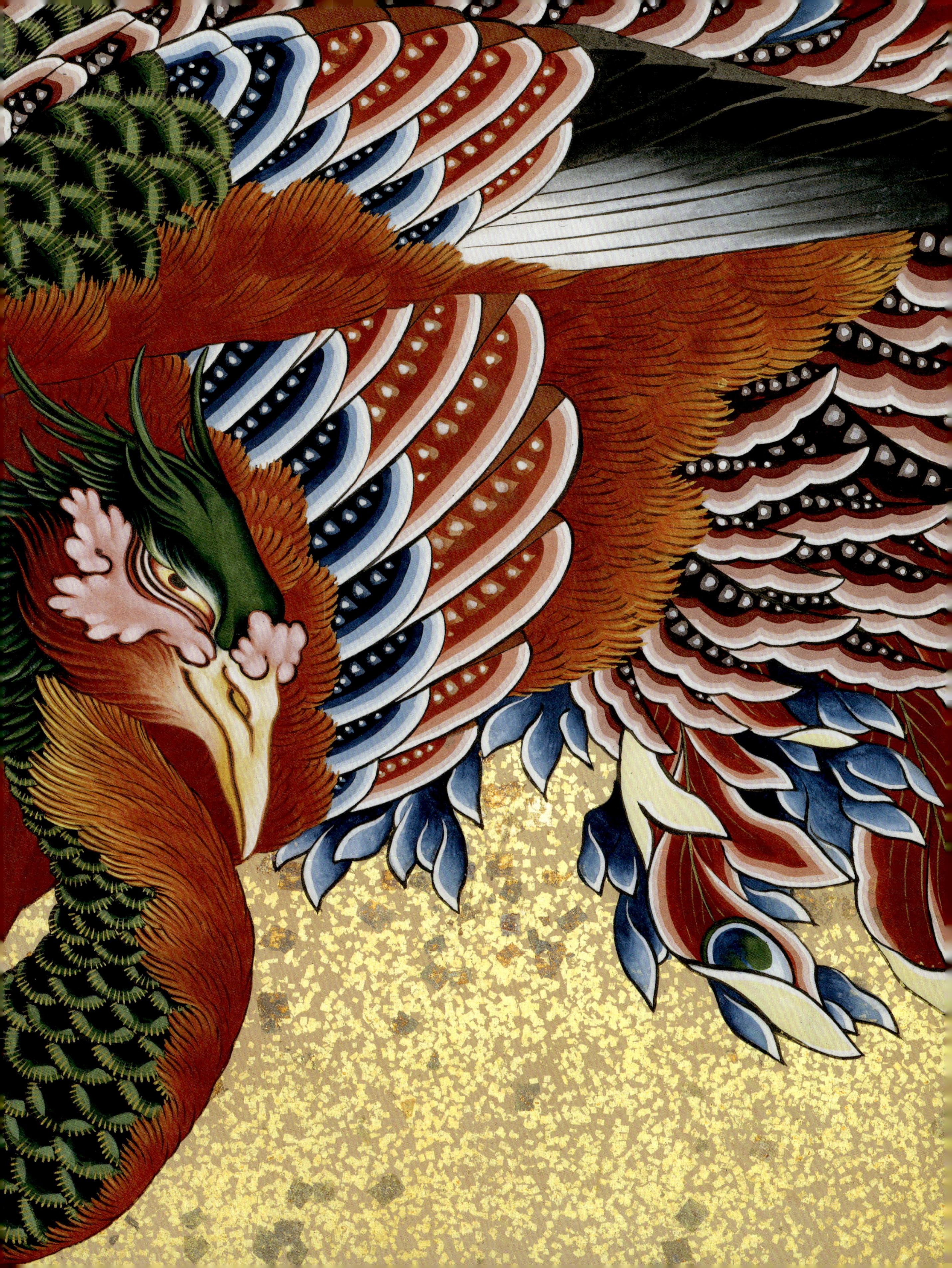

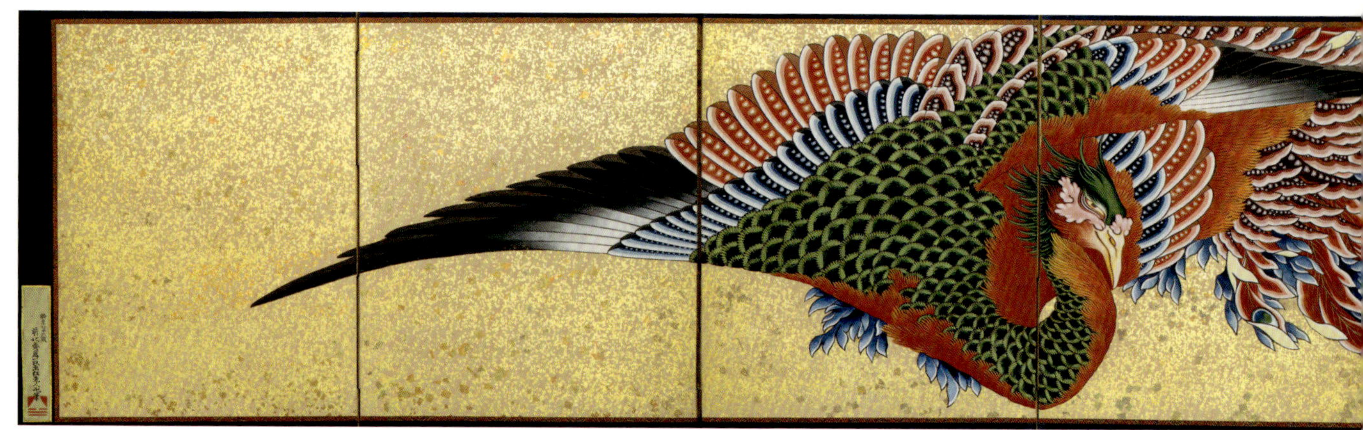

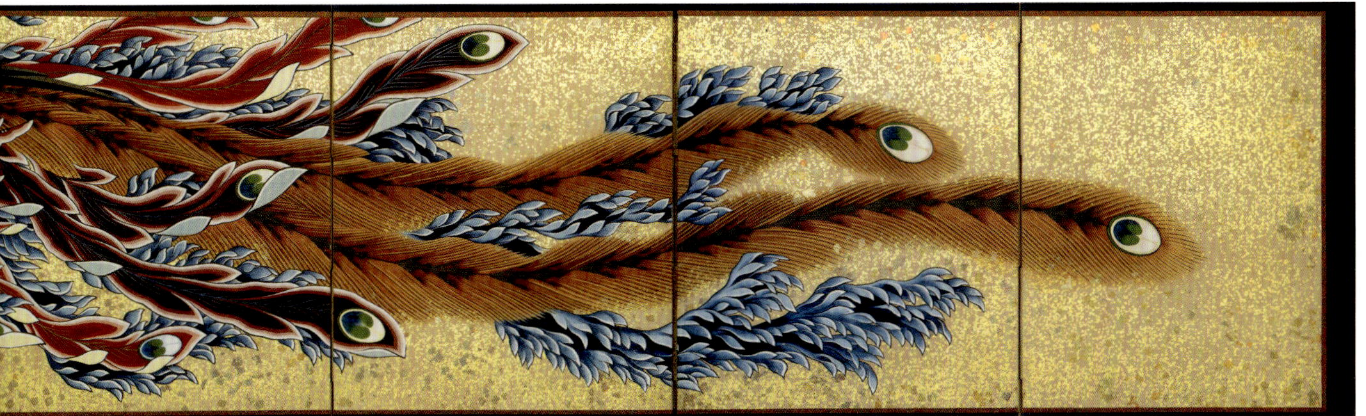

37 | **Phoenix**, 1835

The gorgeous mythical bird known as *hō-ō* in Japanese is a frequent subject in East Asian painting. Its name is generally translated into English as "phoenix," although its lore is quite different from that of the Western phoenix. In ancient China it was a miraculous, auspicious creature that appeared during periods of good government to signify the approval of Heaven. In later dynasties, it was sometimes used as a symbol of the empress, or femininity, and paired with a dragon, symbolizing the emperor, or masculinity.

Hokusai made numerous drawings and paintings of phoenixes, adapting their shape to the requirements of each project. He seems to have developed his own way of representing the fabulous bird, which he depicted as resembling an even more brilliantly colored peacock, but with a double row of feather "spines" down its back and a variety of feathers clustered together in its magnificent tail. He then contorted the shape of the bird as necessary to fit the format of a particular painting.

For this long, low folding screen, the bird's right wing is extended across the lefthand panels of the screen, with its body gracefully twisted so that its long tail floats through the air to the right, balancing the outstretched wing. The green feathers of the right wing merge with the plumage of the bird's body, while the left wing is seen edge-on. The compositional balance, enhanced by a wide range of brilliant colors, is so pleasing that anatomical consistency is irrelevant.

A screen such as this one was known as a pillow screen and was arranged around the bed (in Japan a bed was not a piece of furniture but an arrangement of thick quilts spread on tatami matting) to protect sleepers from drafts. This unusually fine example may have been a lavish wedding present, or it may have been a decoration for a well-appointed brothel; several such establishments are known to have had large wall paintings of phoenixes (see cat. 2).

Eight-panel folding screen; ink, color, cut gold leaf, and sprinkled gold on paper
35.8 x 233.2 cm (14 1/8 x 91 13/16 in.)
William Sturgis Bigelow Collection, 11.7433

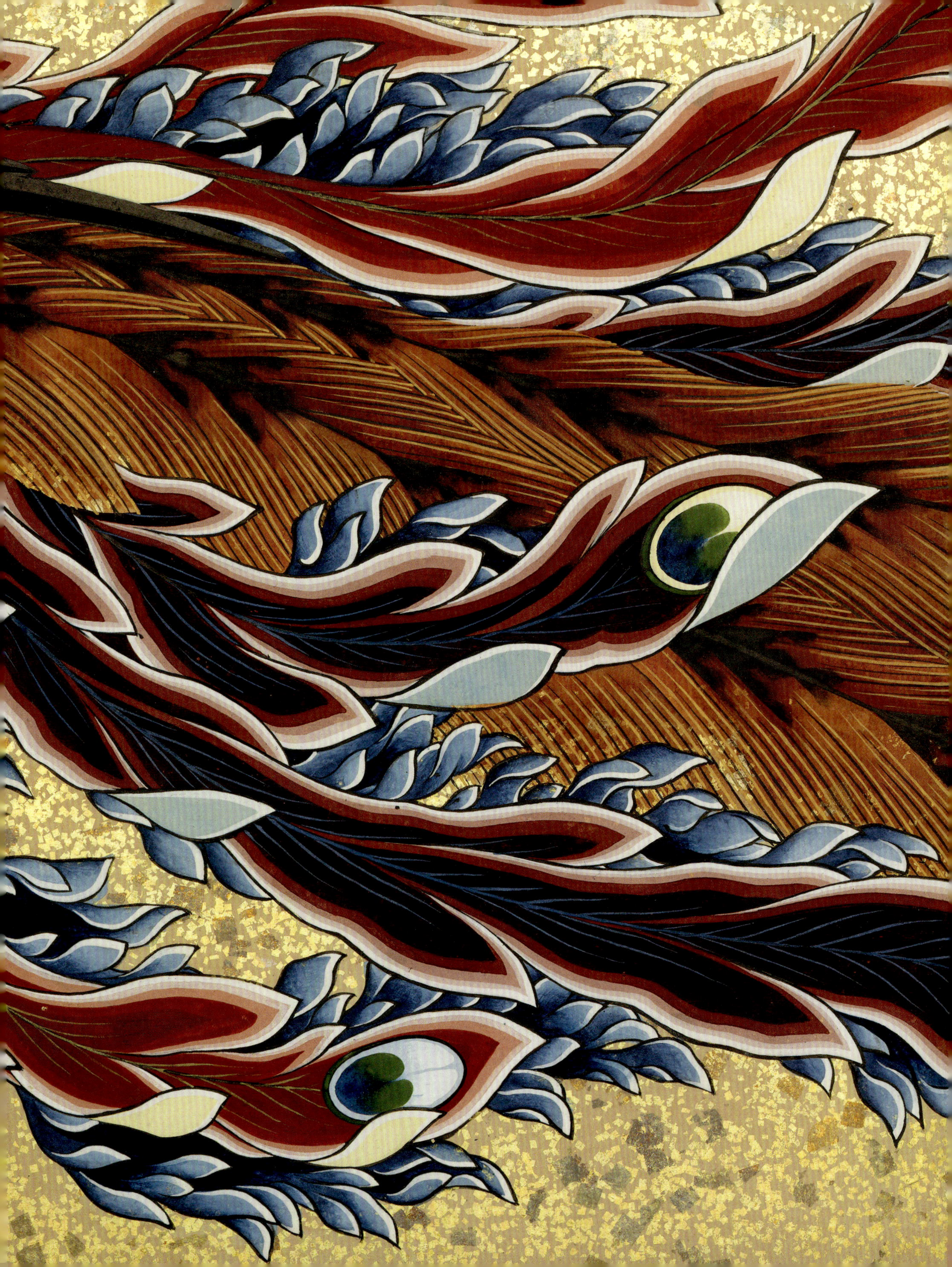

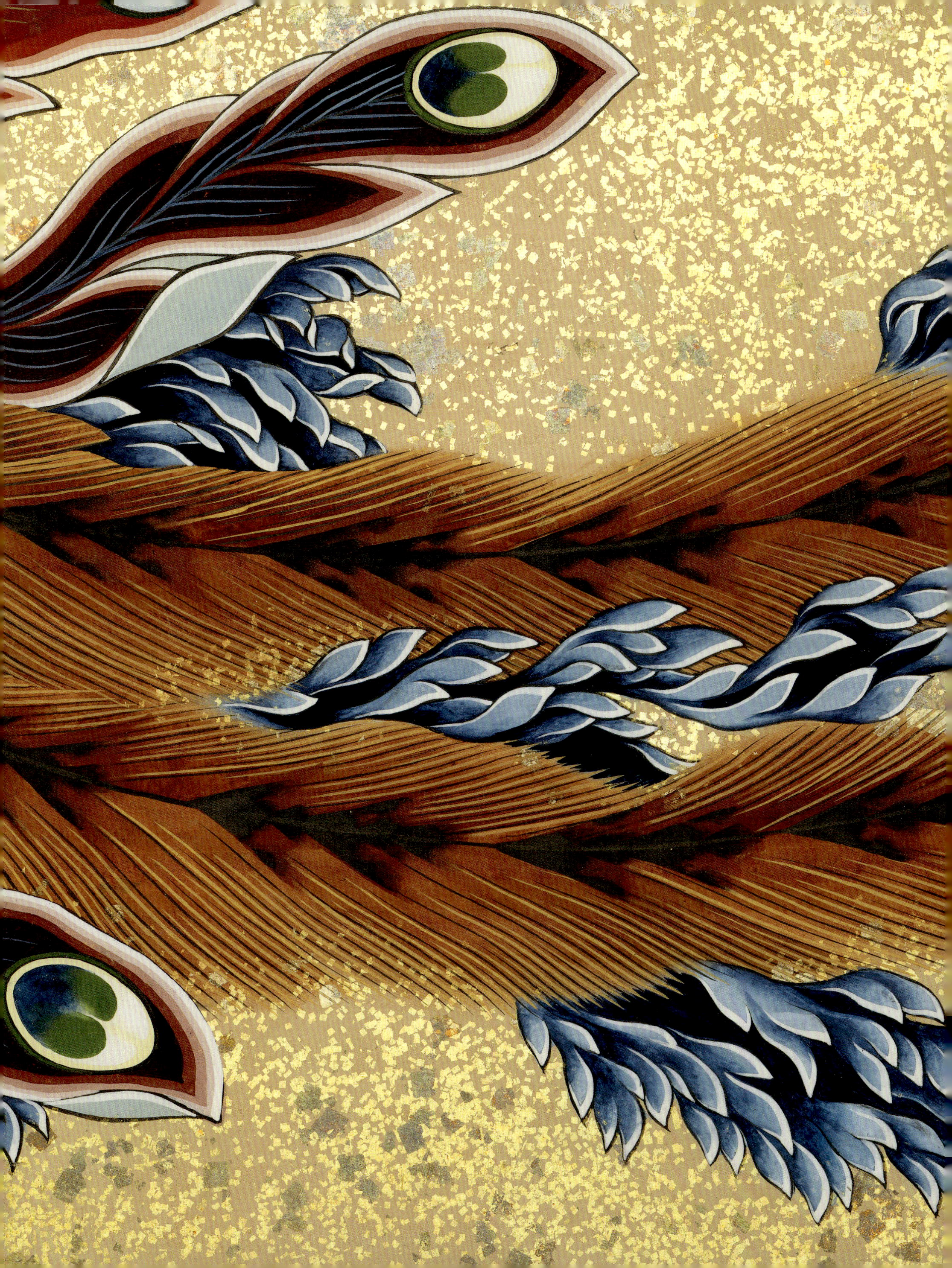

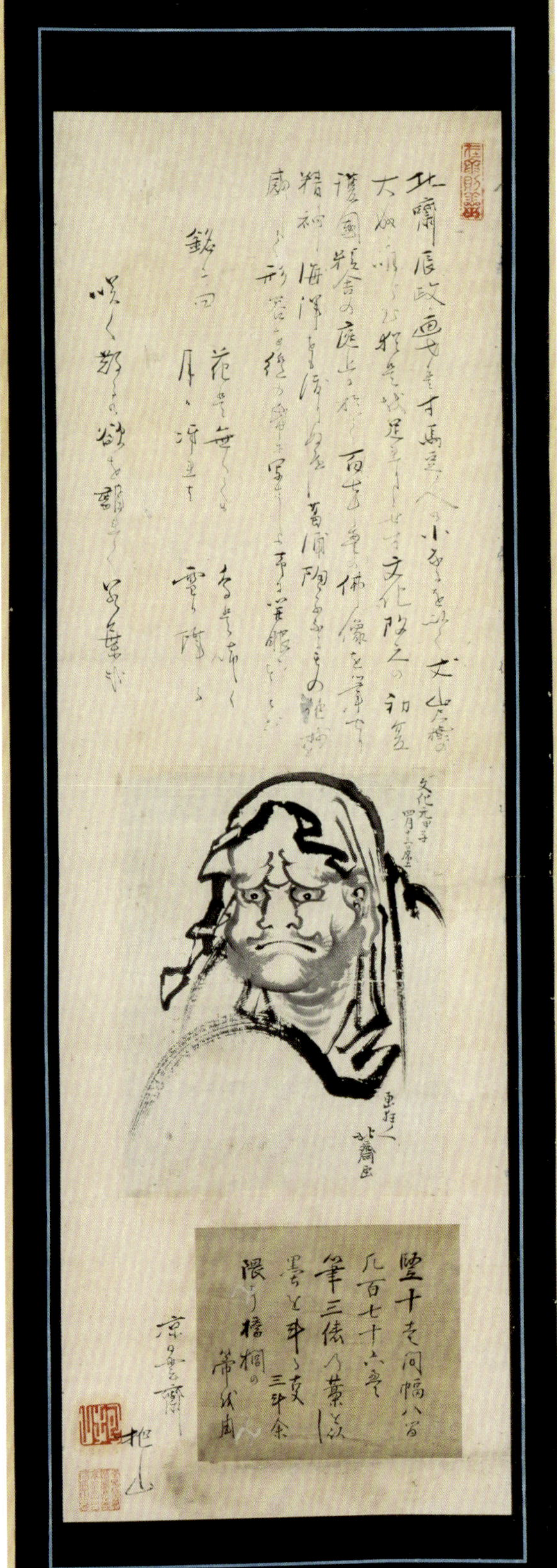

38 | **Picture of Daruma Painted at Gokoku-ji**, 1804

This modest sketch by Hokusai, mounted with explanatory texts by his admirers, records one of the master artist's most amazing feats: his painting of a gigantic image of Daruma (in Sanskrit, Bodhidharma), the founder of Zen Buddhism, before a large audience at the temple of Gokoku-ji in the Otowa district of Edo. The event took place at the beginning of summer, on the thirteenth day of the fourth lunar month, and was described in works such as *A Word and a Chat* (*Ichiwa ichigen*), a memoir by Ōta Nanpo (1749–1823), and *Annals of Edo* (*Bukō nenpyō*) by Saitō Gesshin (1804–1878).

A smaller sheet of paper, pasted below Hokusai's sketch, gives the statistics of the massive project. The painting measured about 66 feet by 48 feet, an area equivalent to 176 standard-size tatami mats (each about 6 feet by 3 feet), and used over fourteen gallons of ink. Brushes were made from the straw wrapping of three bales of rice, and palm-fiber brooms were also repurposed for painting. The calligraphic text that completes this scroll was written by Ryōtansai Hōzan at the request of Katsuho Tōshi and praises Hokusai in poetic language. The two individuals who used these pen names have not been identified, but probably they were involved with the staging of the event.

Hokusai repeated this remarkable performance thirteen years later, in Nagoya in 1817, during a visit to promote the ongoing serial publication of his multivolume, best-selling picture book, the *Hokusai manga*. His painting of Daruma at Nishikake-sho in Nagoya took an entire day to complete, with the help of his pupils, and was then hoisted by pulleys onto a scaffold for display. The event was so successful that Hokusai acquired a new nickname, Master Daruma (Daruma sensei). Back in Edo, he is said to have produced at least two more giant paintings in public performances: a horse painted in the Honjō area and an image of Hotei, one of the Seven Gods of Good Fortune, at Ryōgoku. Unfortunately, none of Hokusai's supersize works seems to have survived, so records such as this one are especially prized.

Signature: Gakyōjin Hokusai ga
Hanging scroll; ink on paper
84.6 x 27.2 cm (33 5/16 x 10 11/16 in.)
William Sturgis Bigelow Collection, 11.7438

文化元甲子
四月十三日席上

画狂人
北斎画

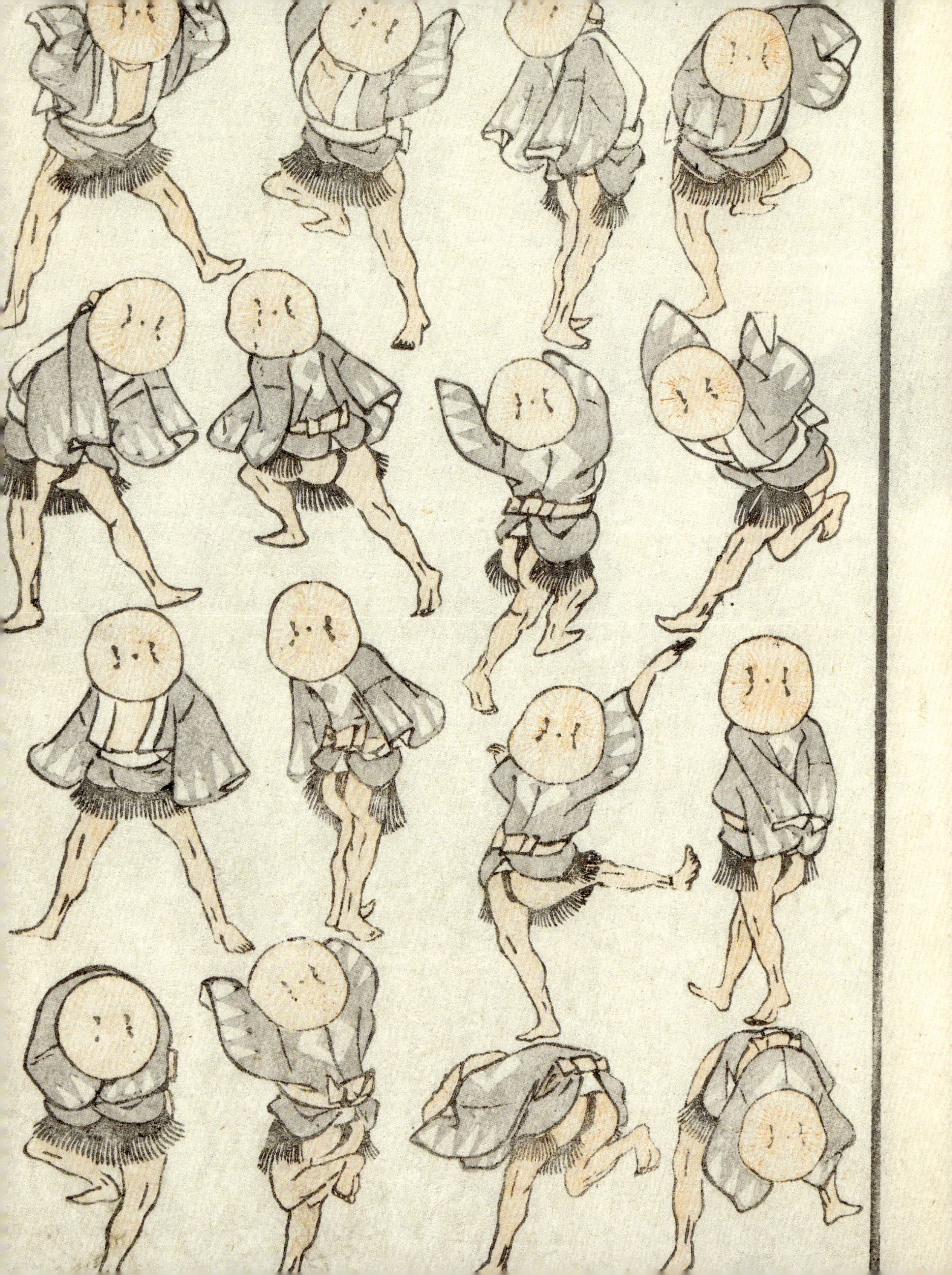

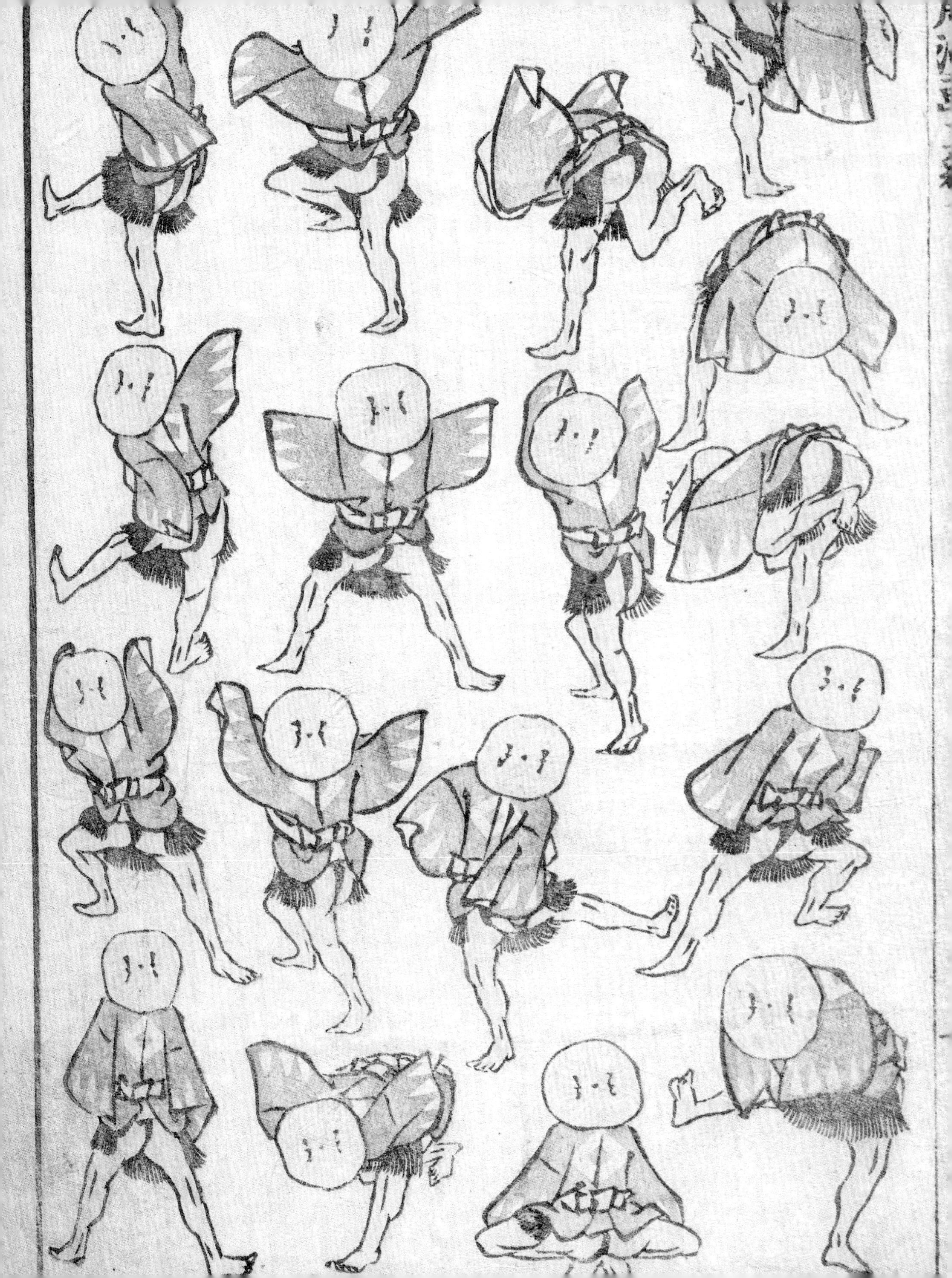

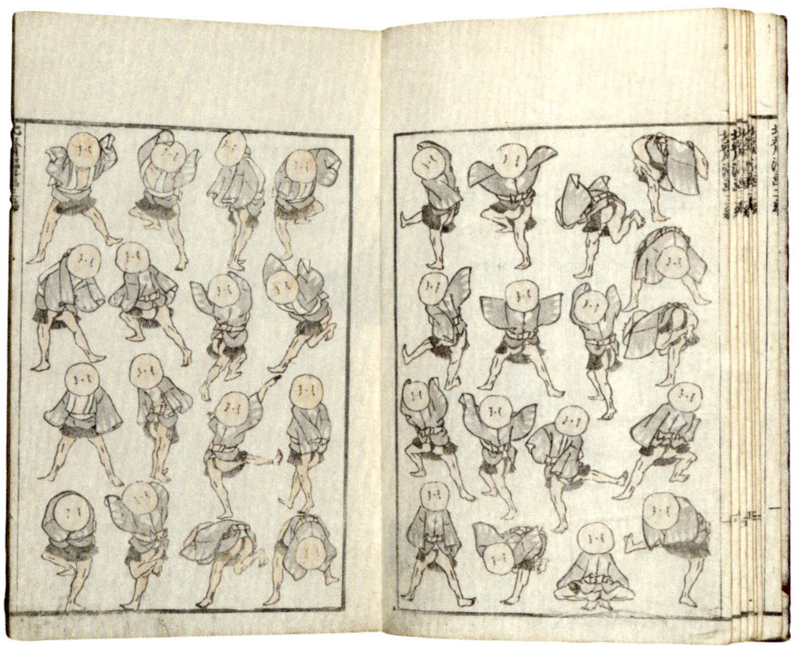

39 | **Hokusai Sketchbooks, Volume 3**
(*Hokusai manga sanpen*), 1819 or later

Hokusai's first great hit — the best-selling work that brought him stardom — was a series of printed picture books based on the sketches he drew for his pupils to copy. The books could be used as models for amateur painters or sources of information for craftsmen decorating objects of various kinds, or they could simply be enjoyed for visual amusement. The pictures have no particular theme or order, although there are sometimes several pages in succession devoted to a given subject. Part of the pleasure of viewing the books is a constant element of surprise: the next page may continue the subject shown on the page before, or it may introduce a completely new idea. Gods, humans, animals (real and imaginary), plants, landscapes, manmade objects, ghosts, and scenes from literature and history are all included.

According to the preface to volume 1, the idea for the book originated in 1812, when Hokusai visited the city of Nagoya as part of a trip to western Japan. Admirers in Nagoya collected assorted sketches by Hokusai and prepared them for publication as a book, jointly issued in Nagoya and Edo. The first volume appeared in 1814, with additional volumes published in quick succession, concluding with volume 10 in 1819. Much later, between 1834 and 1878, five more volumes were added to the series (although the last two are posthumous and are based on other, earlier books by Hokusai). No doubt the later volumes were attempts by the publishers to capitalize on Hokusai's ever-increasing popularity following the publication of his second great hit, the *Fuji* series, in the early 1830s.

All of the volumes in the series were reprinted many times, so dating the various editions is complicated. Volume 3 was first published in 1815; but this impression includes an advertisement for volumes 1 through 10 at the back of the book, which means that it must have been published in 1819 or slightly later.

The two-page spread illustrated here highlights Hokusai's talent for depicting figures in motion. A group of dancers, or perhaps a single dancer captured in a snapshot-like series of poses, performs the Sparrow Dance, a folk dance from the northeastern city of Sendai that imitates the fluttering movements of a sparrow. Today the Sparrow Dance is performed with fans, but in Hokusai's time a distinctive costume featuring a large, round hat was used for this popular amusement.

Publisher: Eirakuya Tōshirō (Tōhekidō)
Woodblock-printed book; ink and limited color on paper
Each page: 22.7 x 15.7 cm (8 15/16 x 6 3/16 in)
Gift of Mrs. Jared K. Morse in memory of Charles J. Morse, 1997.839

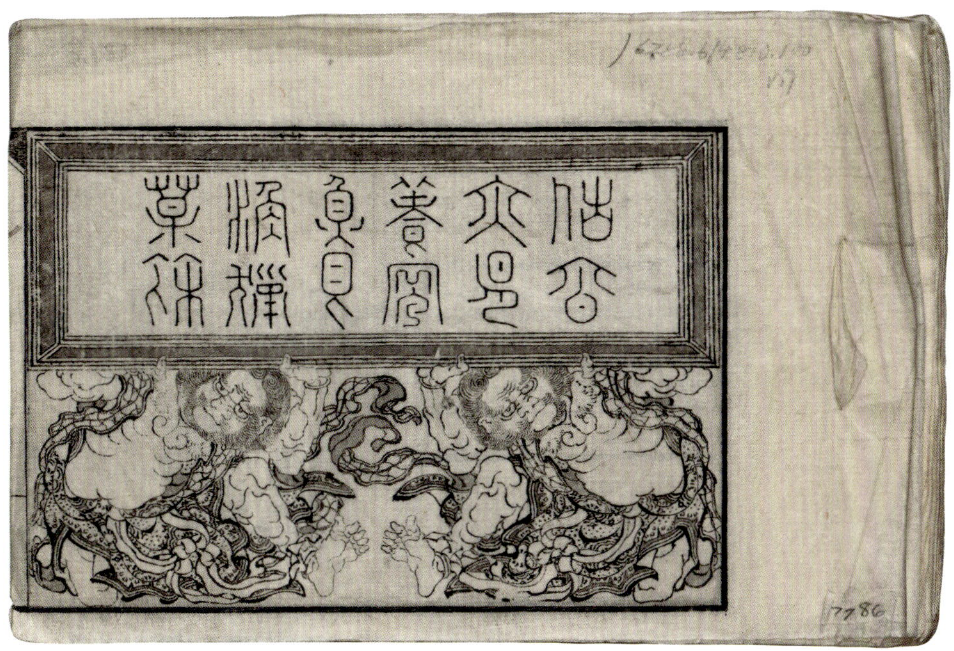

40 | **Drawings for a Three-Volume Picture Book**, about 1823–33

This untitled work consists of three volumes of finely detailed drawings for a picture book that was never published. There is no signature, but the drawing style matches Hokusai's from about 1823 to 1833. Volume 1 has a title page with muscular guardian figures, of the kind seen in Buddhist temple gates, holding a signboard that reads in decorative seal script: "Commerce, Trade, Sericulture, Sea Creatures, Fishing, Plants." Volume 2, titled *The Universe*, features astronomical deities and landscape features; and the untitled volume 3 shows buildings in landscape settings and people of various occupations.

Horizontal picture books were less common than those in the vertical format, but Hokusai did design several in the 1820s. One example, *Modern Patterns for Combs and Pipes* (*Imayō kushi kiseru hinagata*), was published by Nishimuraya Yohachi in 1823. In the back of the book are advertisements for other publications by Hokusai, including an otherwise unknown work called *Master Iitsu's Chicken-Rib Picture Book* (*Iitsu sensei keiroku gafu*). ("Chicken rib" is a classical Chinese literary expression for something that is trivial but nevertheless worthwhile, like the small but tasty bit of meat on a chicken rib.) According to the ad, this book had been planned since 1819 and included pictures of animals, birds, and plants, man-made objects, and astronomy and geography. The year 1819 most likely refers to the publication of volume 10 of the *Hokusai manga*, which at the time was intended to be the final volume of the set; it implies that the *Chicken-Rib Picture Book* is in some sense a continuation of the *Manga*.

Based on the similarity between the description in the advertisement and the contents of the drawings in these picture books, the close association of Hokusai with Nishimuraya Yohachi (later the publisher of the *Fuji* series), and the fact that the size and format of the booklets of drawings are very close to those of *Modern Patterns for Combs and Pipes*, art historian Seiji Nagata has suggested that these drawings were in fact intended for the *Chicken-Rib Picture Book*.

Drawings (hanshita-e); ink on paper
13.8 x 20.4 cm (5 7/16 x 8 1/16 in.)
Source unidentified, 1998.670.1–3

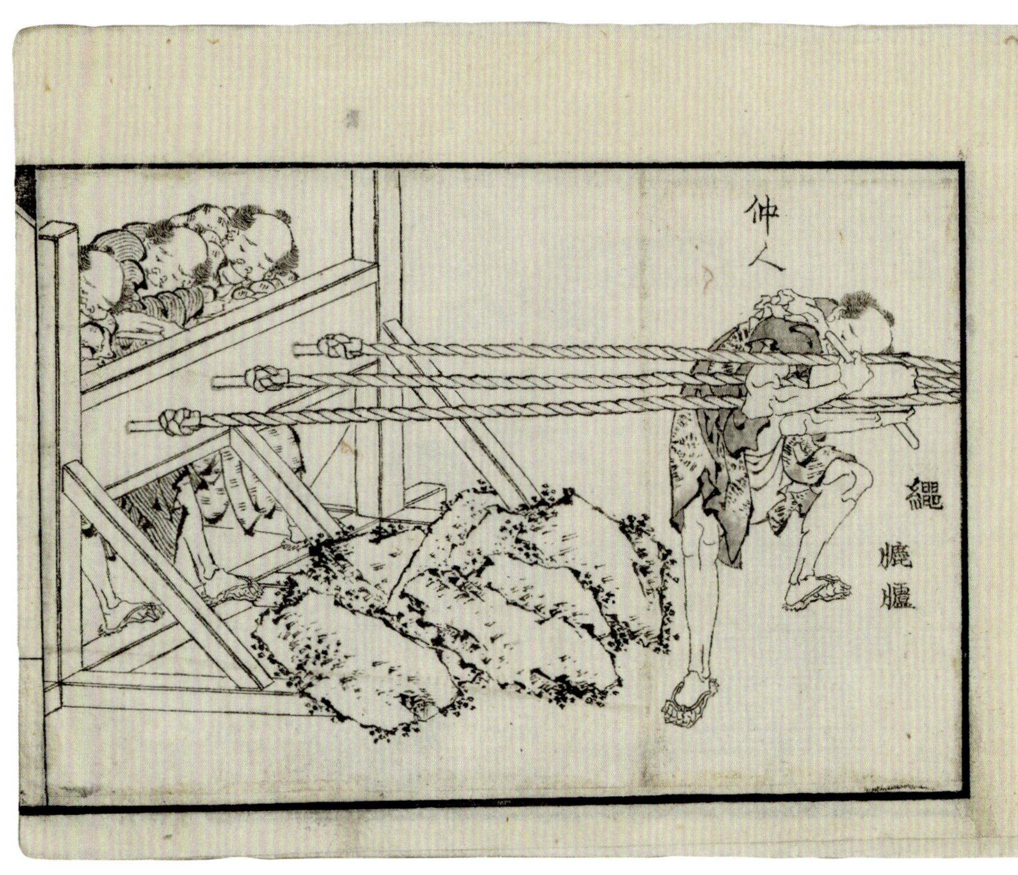
仲人
縋
臙臛

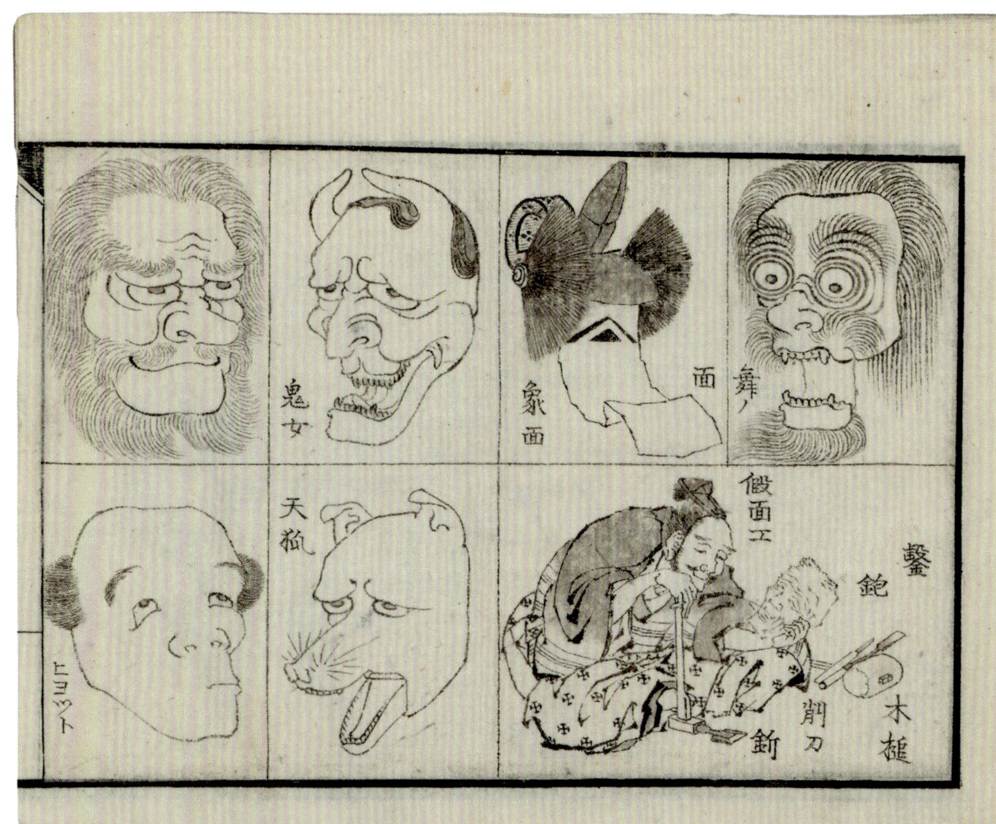
鬼女
象面
舞ノ面
ヒヨツト
天狗
假面工
鑿
鉋
木槌
削刀
釿

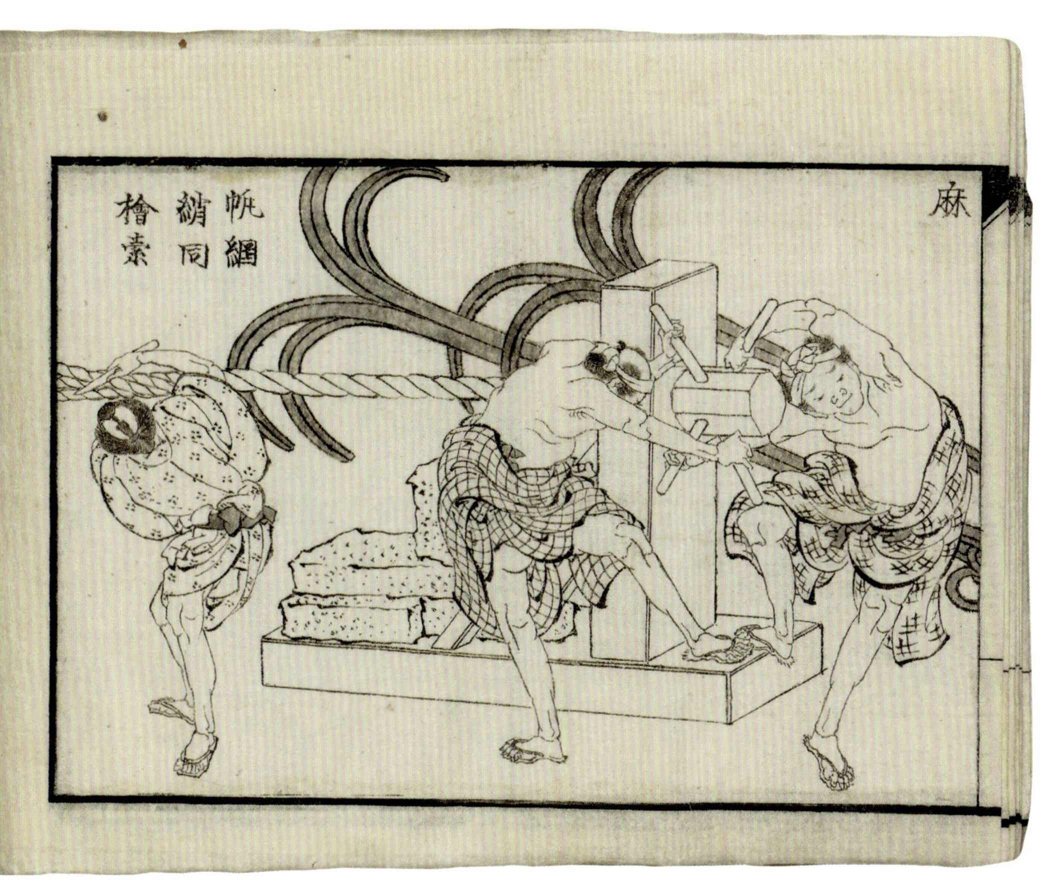
麻
帆綱
綃同
檜索

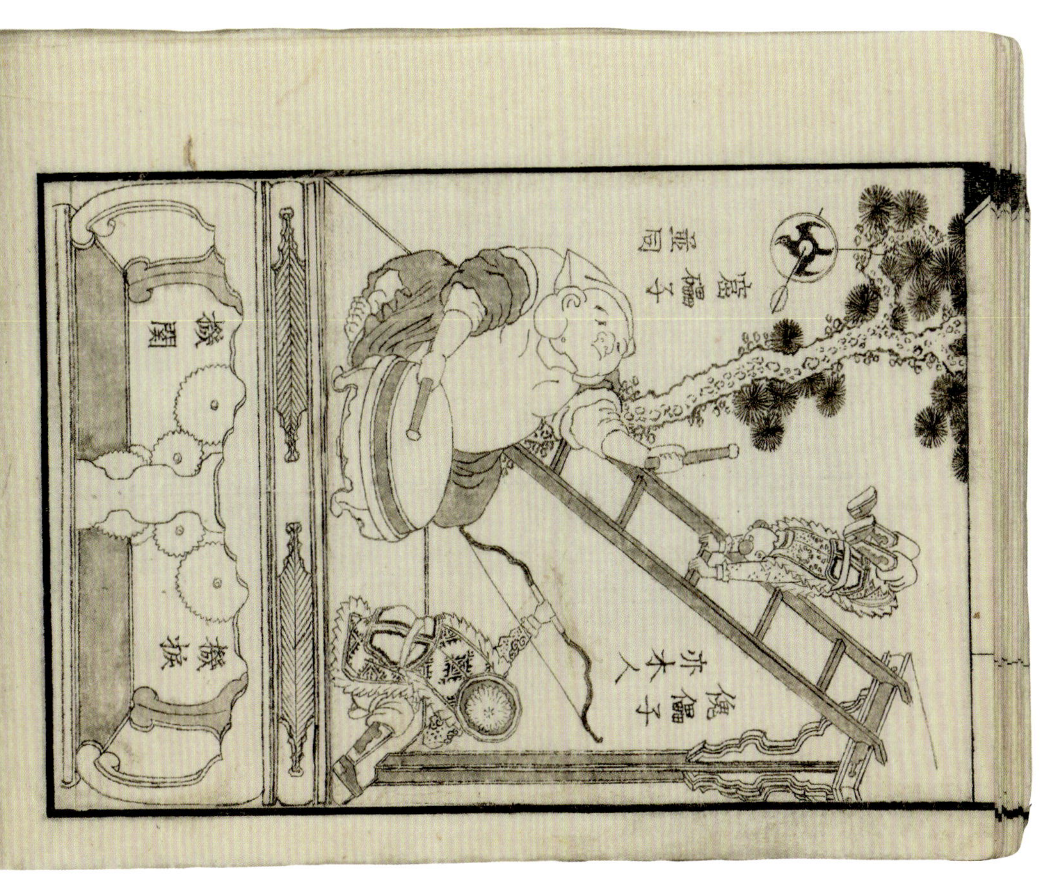

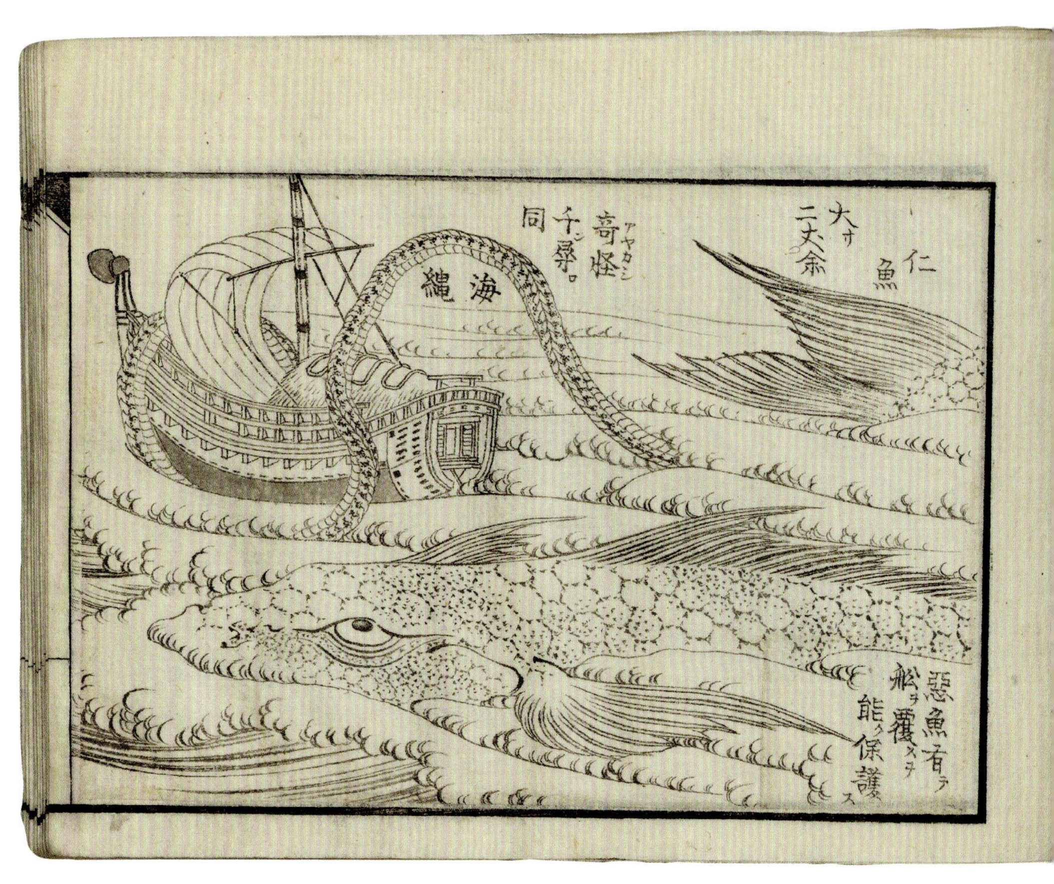
仁魚
大サ二丈余
海繩
奇怪
千尋ロ
同
悪魚有テ
船ヲ覆ヌテ
能ク保護ス

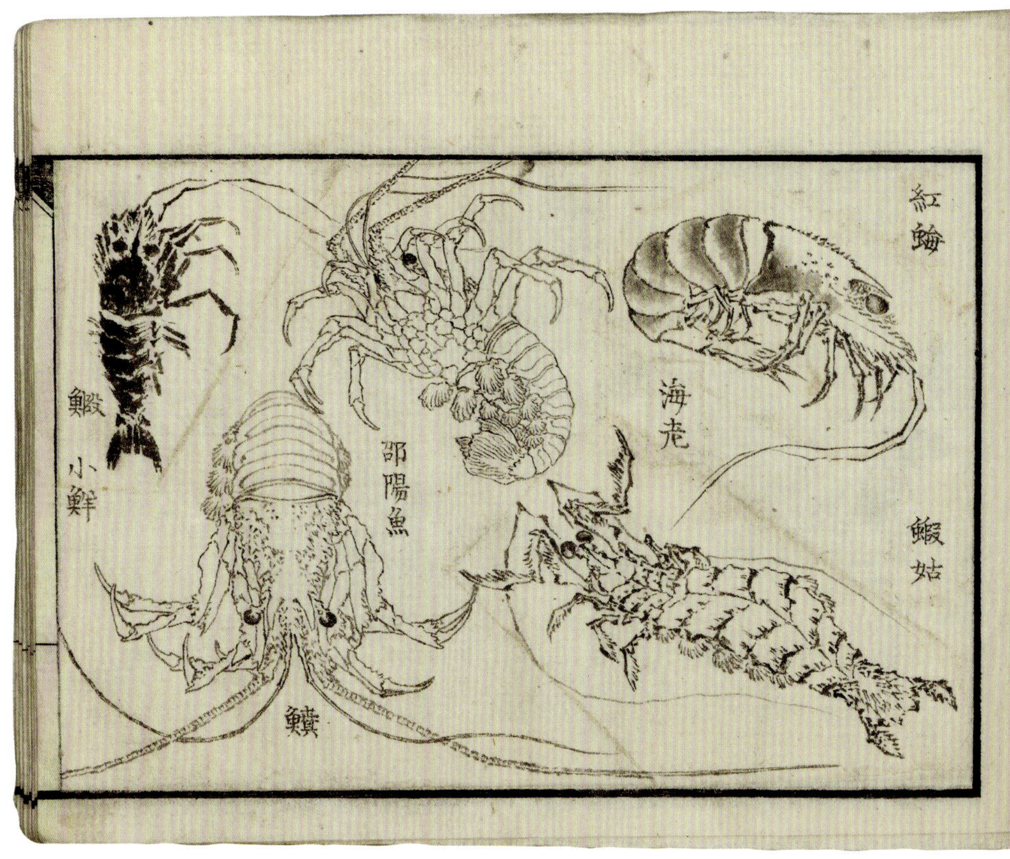
紅鯩
海老
鰕姑
部陽魚
鰕
小鮮
鱝

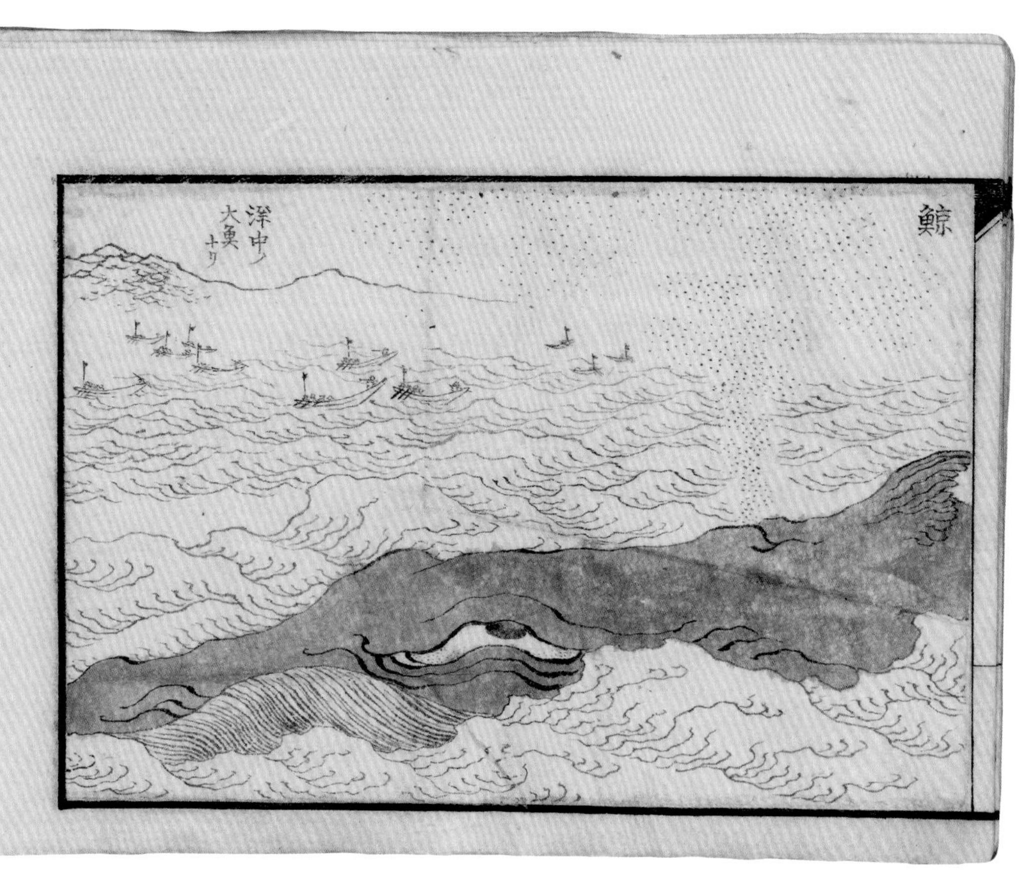
鯨
洋中ノ大魚ナリ

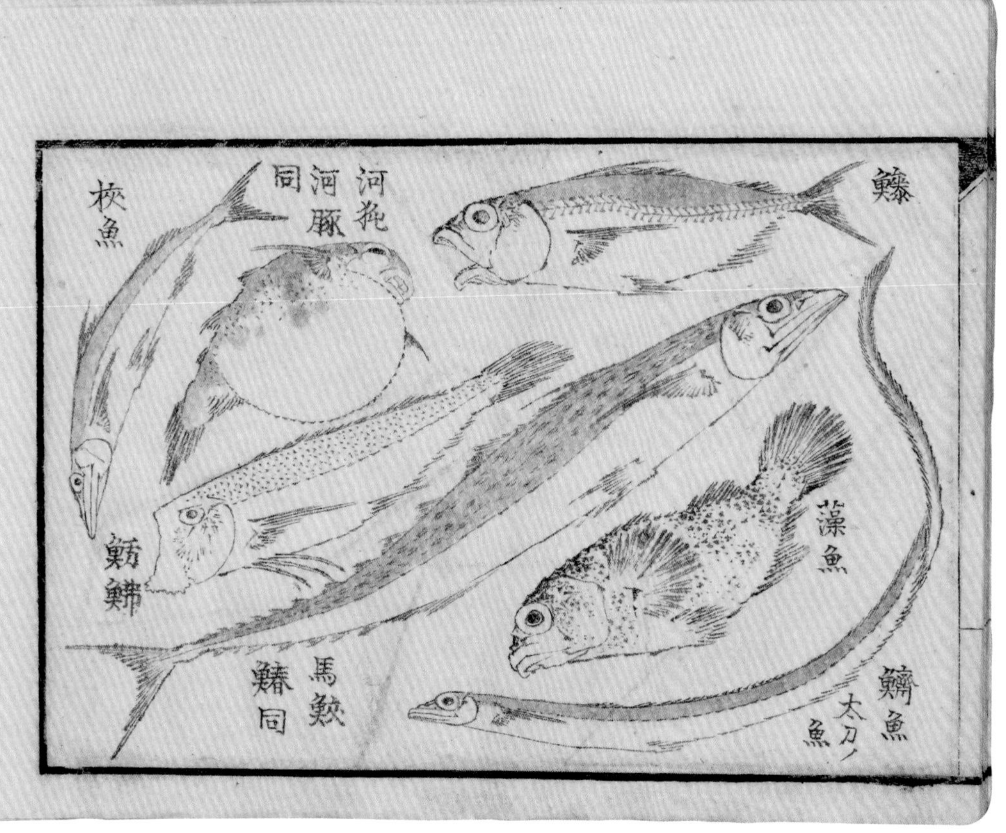
鰺
河魨
河豚同
梭魚
魴鮄
馬鮫
鰆同
藻魚
鱭魚
太刀ノ魚

41 | ***A Picture Book of Highway Bells***
(*Ehon ekirō no suzu*), about 1808–13

This full-color picture book is actually the second edition of what was originally an untitled series of single-sheet prints showing the fifty-three stations of the Tōkaidō (literally the Eastern Sea Road). The stations were towns that were designated by the Tokugawa shogunate as official highway rest stops, with inns and other facilities for travelers, on the great highway that ran between Edo in the east and Kyoto in the west. Printed guidebooks of the Tōkaidō Road had been available since the seventeenth century, but Hokusai seems to have been the first artist to design individual prints showing each of the fifty-three stations.

Between about 1804 and 1810, Hokusai designed seven different Tōkaidō series, all in small formats. The images generally focus on figures of travelers, but landscape elements sometimes appear also. This series is the largest of the seven. The first of Hokusai's Tōkaidō series was a set of surimono with kyōka poems, later reissued as commercial prints without the poems. The small formats of the other Tōkaidō series may have been inspired by the miniature scale of the first set, and perhaps also by the reluctance of publishers at this early date to commit to the expense of a large series of full-size prints. In the case of this series, the half-size designs were printed two to a sheet. For the second edition, shown here, the designs were not cut apart; instead, the sheets were folded in half and glued together at the edges to make a book.

About two decades later, in the early 1830s, the commercial feasibility of a full-size landscape series was demonstrated by the spectacular success of Hokusai's *Thirty-Six Views of Mount Fuji*. Inspired by Hokusai, the younger artist Hiroshige designed a full-size series of the *Fifty-Three Stations of the Tōkaidō*, which also became an enormous success, rivaling the *Fuji* series.

Publisher: Iseya Rihei (Kinjudō)
Woodblock-printed book; ink and color on paper
Each page: 23.3 x 16.3 cm ($9\frac{3}{16}$ x $6\frac{7}{16}$ in.)
Source unidentified, 1997.701.1–2

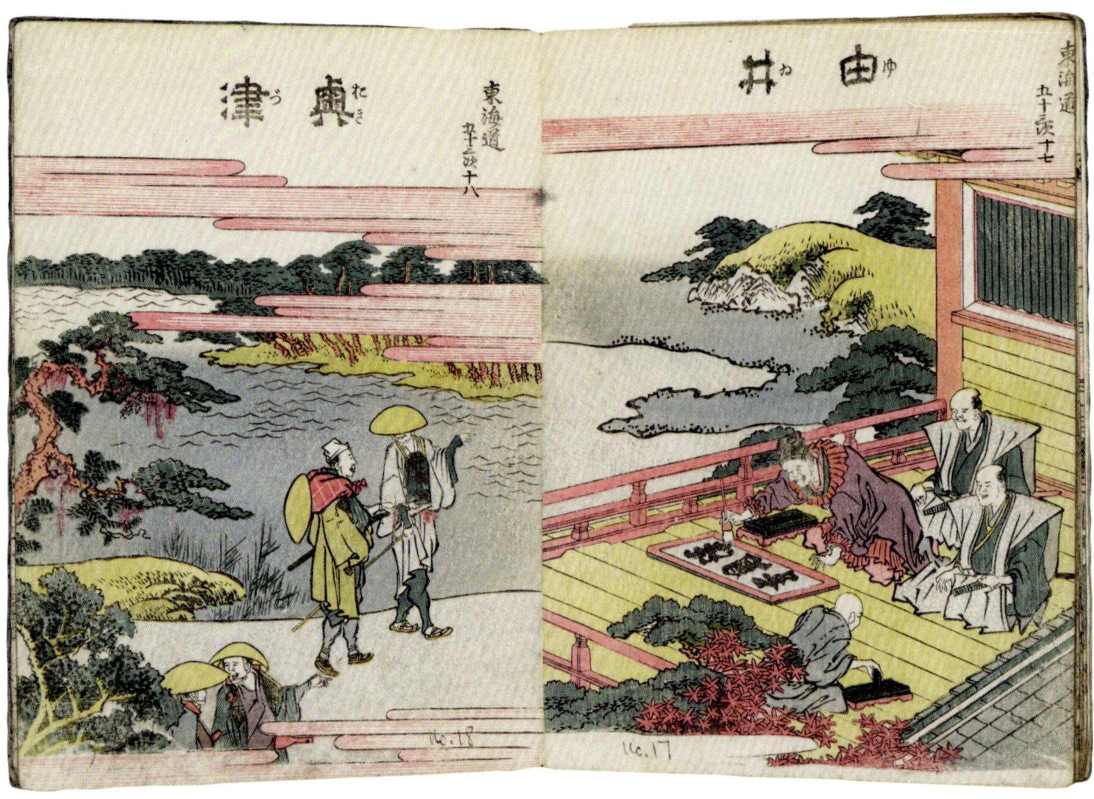

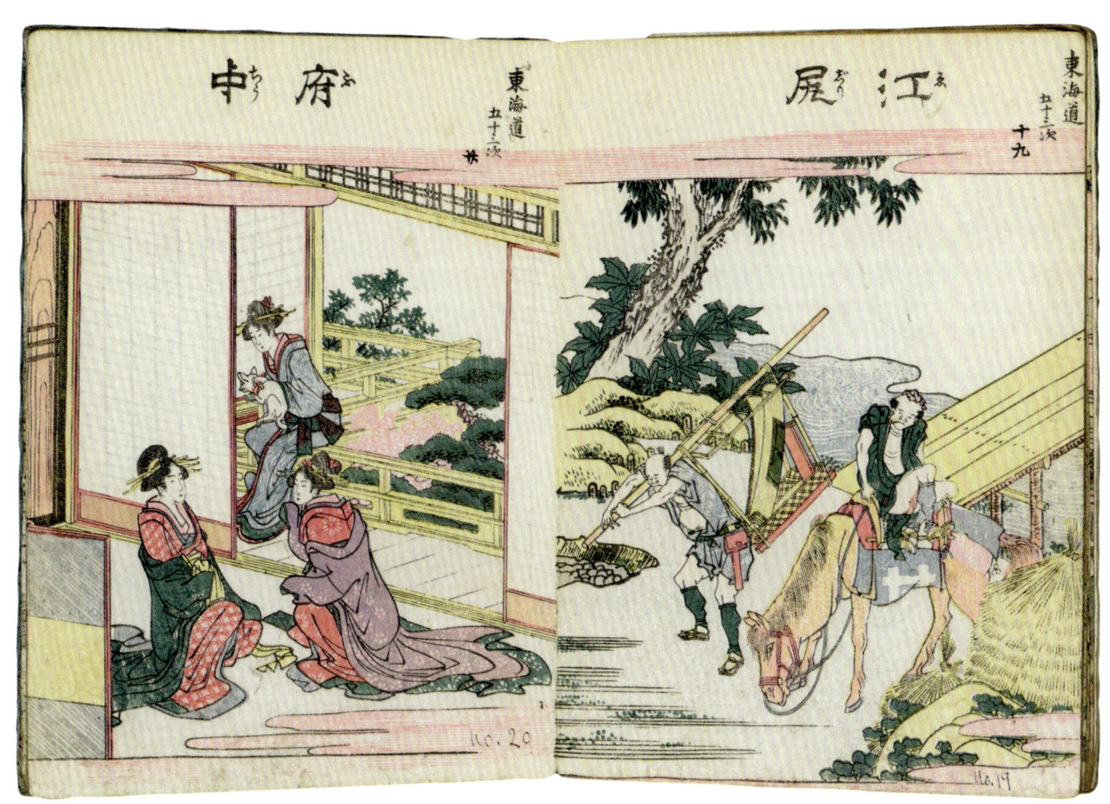
江尻
東海道
五十三次
十九
府中
東海道
五十三次
廿
no. 20
no. 19

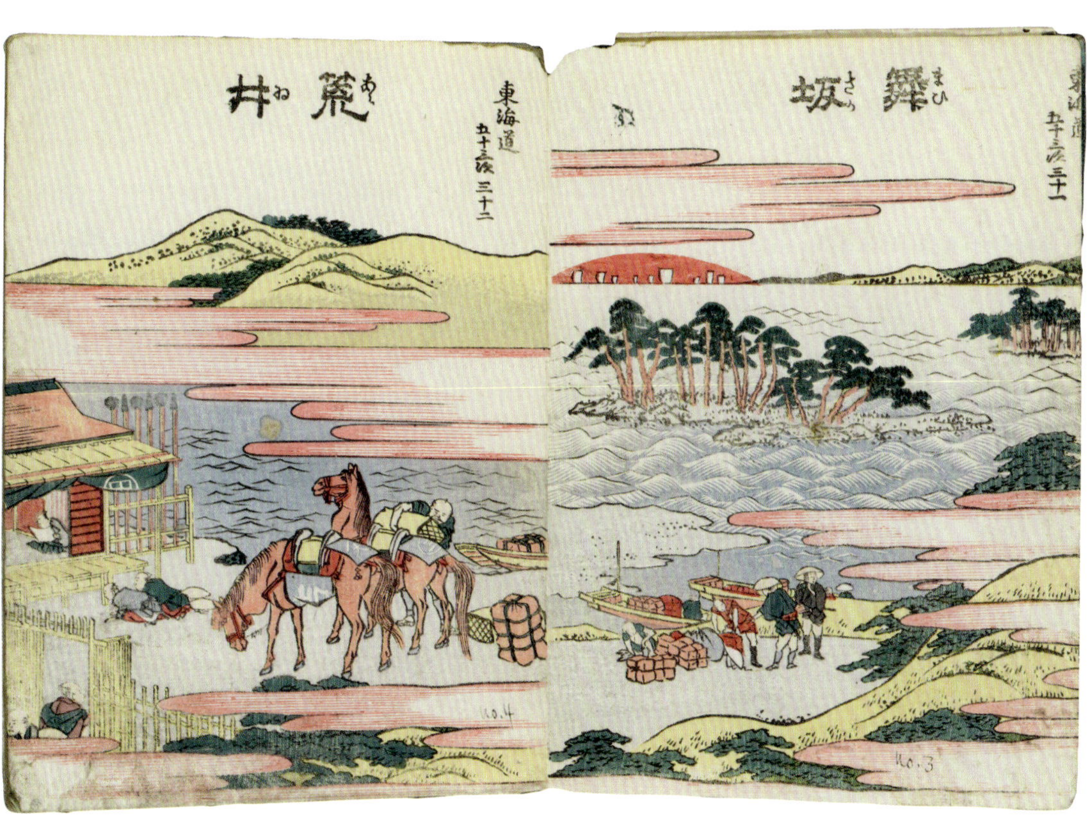
舞坂
五十三次三十一
荒井
東海道
五十三次三十二
no. 4
no. 3

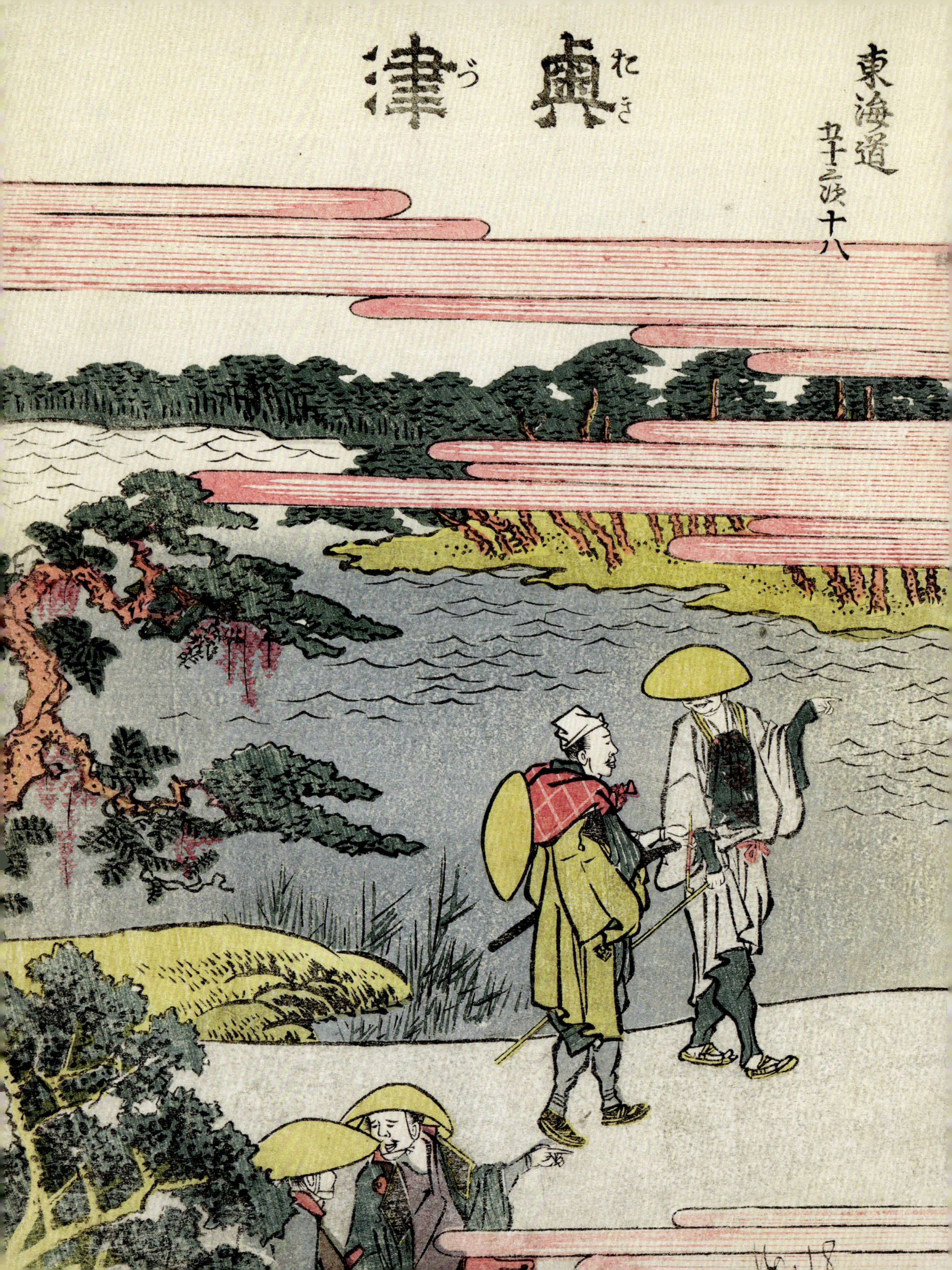
興津
東海道
五十三次 十八

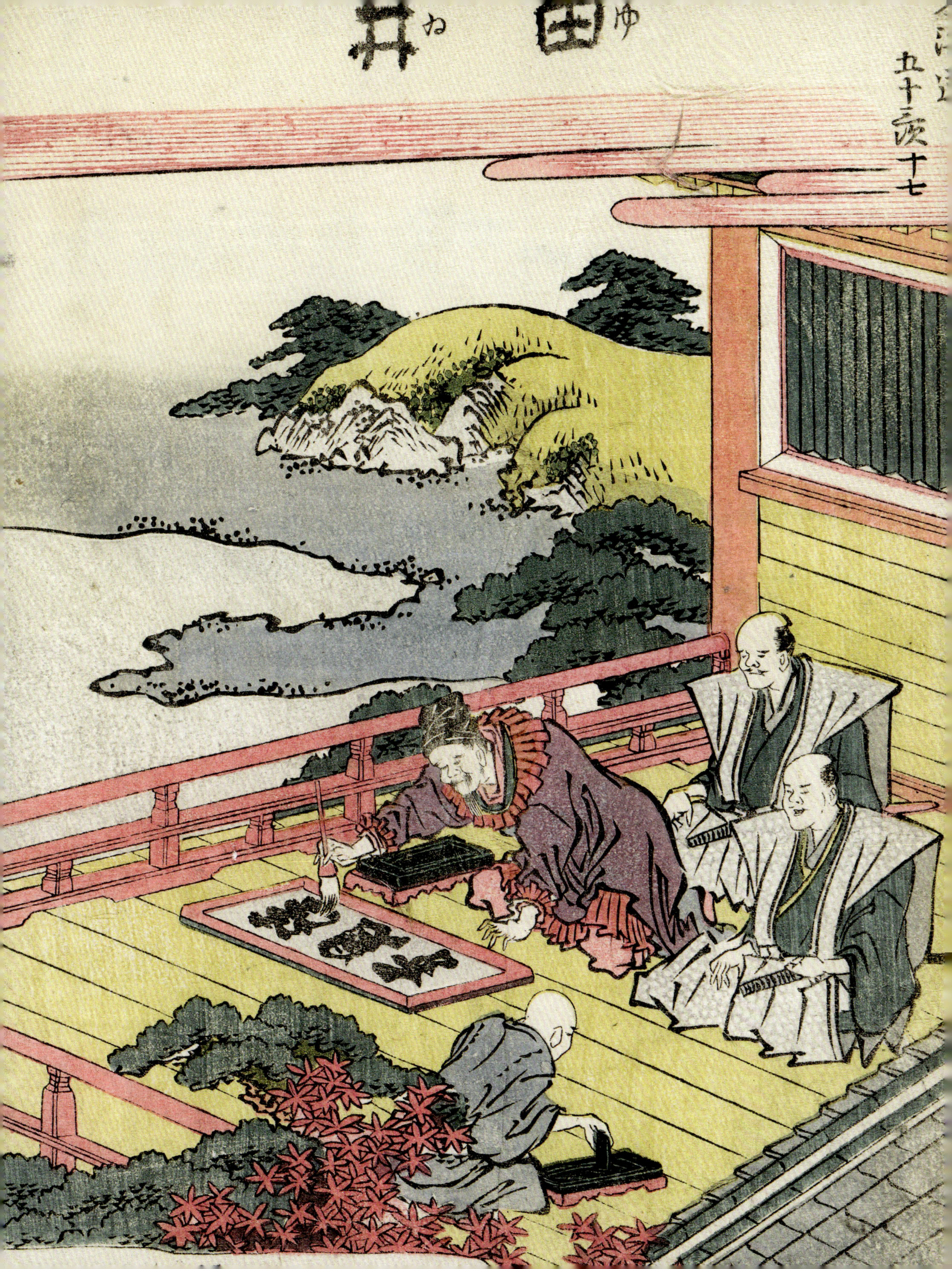
由井（ゆゐ）
五十三次 十七

42 | **Moonlit Night at Izumizaki**
(*Izumizaki yagetsu*) from the series *Eight Views of the Ryukyu Islands* (*Ryūkyū hakkei*), about 1832

The chain of islands that is now known as Okinawa, the southernmost prefecture of Japan, was formerly called the Ryukyu Islands, an independent kingdom. During the Edo period, the Ryukyu Kingdom maintained a tricky political balancing act by pledging itself as a vassal state to both the Chinese empire and the Satsuma domain in Kyūshū, Japan. Having supported the losing side in the dynastic struggle in 1644, the shogunate officially ignored the Chinese allegiance because Japan did not recognize the legitimacy of the ruling Qing dynasty, but it accepted the semi-independence of the Ryukyu Kingdom because an indirect connection to the Chinese government was potentially useful.

In 1719 a visiting Chinese diplomat selected eight especially attractive views in the vicinity of the port city Naha (now the prefectural capital) and wrote poems about them. A Chinese book on the Ryukyu Islands published in 1757 and reprinted in Japan in 1831 included illustrations of the poems. An embassy from the Ryukyu Kingdom, accompanied by an escort from Satsuma, visited Edo in 1832 and inspired numerous woodblock prints showing the procession of exotically dressed ambassadors, attendants, and musicians. Hokusai or his publisher must have had the idea of responding to the wave of popular interest in the Ryukyu Islands with a series of colorful landscape prints in the same format as his enormously successful *Fuji* series. Hokusai, who had never been to the Ryukyu Kingdom, based his designs closely on the previously published Chinese illustrations, adding color and details.

The stone bridge of Izumizaki was next to the Confucian temple in Kumemura, a center of Chinese learning in Naha. (The Shiseibyō Temple still exists today but has been rebuilt in a different location.) The book illustration Hokusai copied did not show the moon mentioned in the poem, but Hokusai added a full moon in the form of a white, unprinted area in the blue sky, with a cloud moving over its lower right corner.

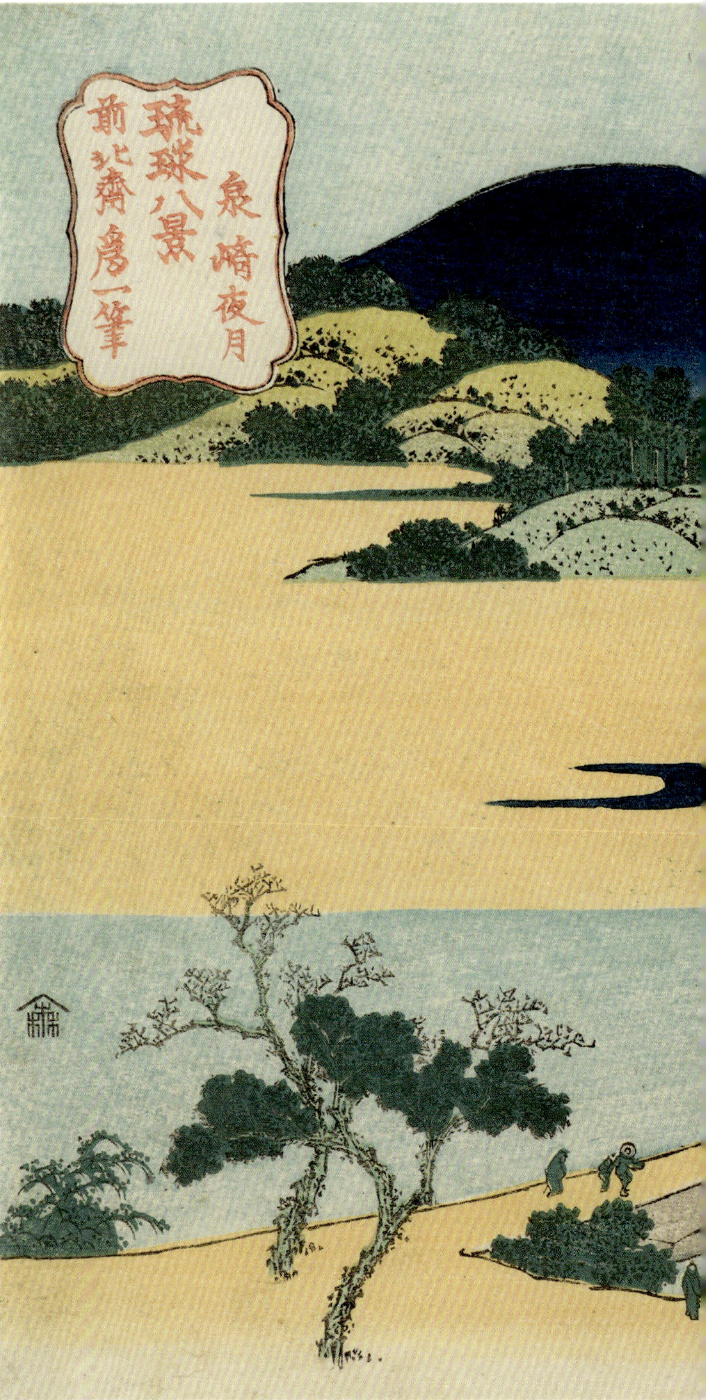

Signature: Saki no Hokusai Iitsu hitsu
Publisher: Moriya Jihei (Kinshindō)
Woodblock print (nishiki-e); ink and color on paper
26 x 37.6 cm (10 1/4 x 14 13/16 in.)
William S. and John T. Spaulding Collection, 21.6706

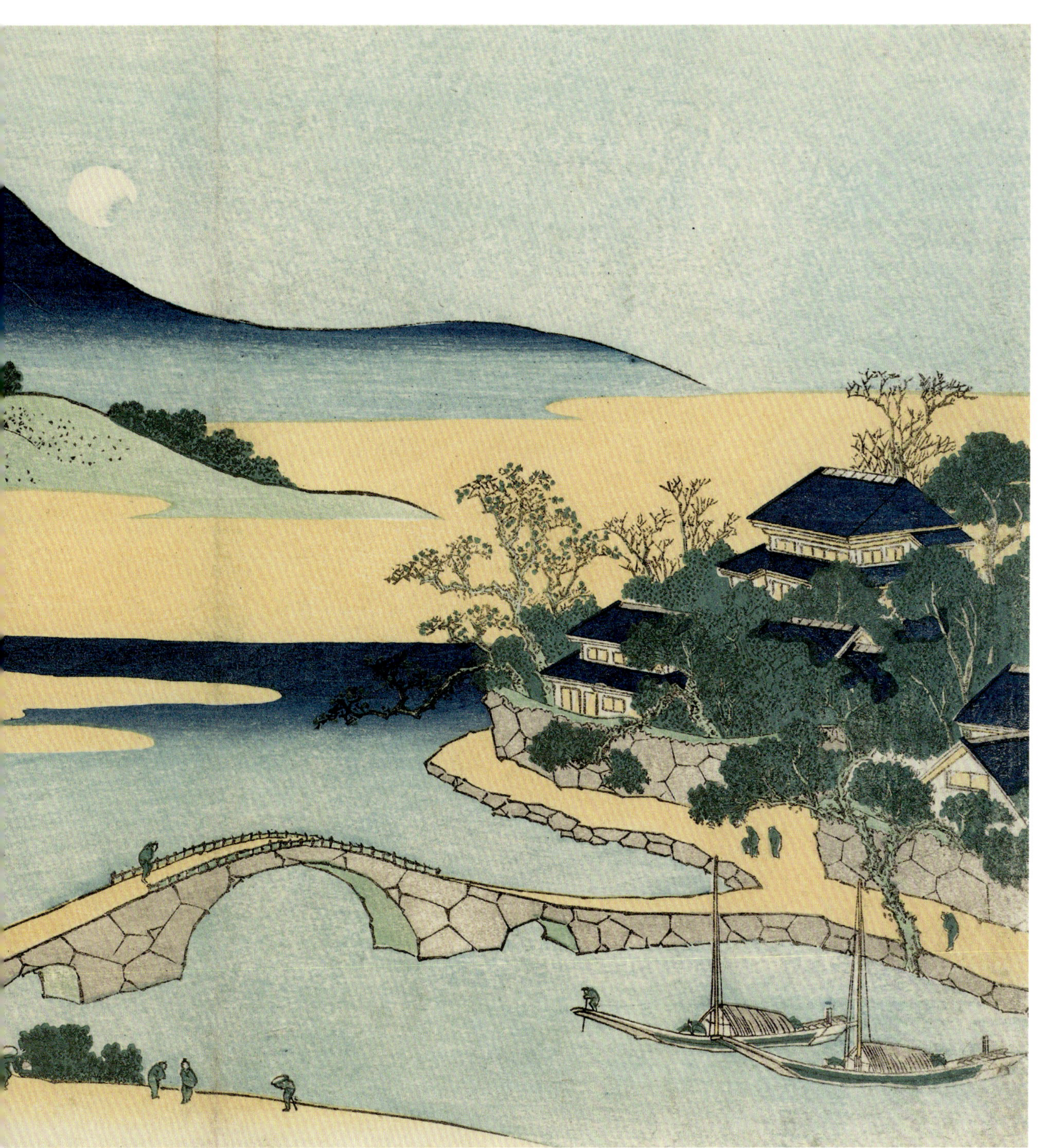

43 | **Descending Geese at the Sumida River** (*Sumida rakugan*) from the series *Eight Views of Edo* (*Edo hakkei*) on paper snack bags, about 1833

Most of the surviving examples of prints from the series *Eight Views of Edo* have been trimmed so that they look like ordinary, small-format prints, but originally each landscape was a decoration for a paper bag containing rice cakes, which were made in both sweet and savory flavors, corresponding to cookies and crackers. This impression, which has retained the entire front of the bag, features a rectangular panel reading "Finest Confectionery" in archaic seal-script calligraphy, placed just above the landscape in its chain-link frame. Lovers of Hokusai's work might have consumed great quantities of snack food in order to collect all eight scenes in the series.

The theme of Eight Views had been popular in Japanese art since the Muromachi period (1392–1568), when the motif of Eight Views of the Xiao and Xiang Rivers was one of the subjects of ink paintings imported from China and copied in Japan. Paintings of this subject were based on a set of eight Chinese poems describing specific sights in the Xiao-Xiang area, such as "Descending Geese on a Sandbar," "Autumn Moon on Lake Dongting," and so on. A Japanese version, the Eight Views of Ōmi (the scenic area around Lake Biwa, near Kyoto), with Japanese poems, was invented in 1500 and subsequently became the basis for many more Japanese versions of the Eight Views, including serious ones such as these scenes of Edo and amusing parodies such as the indoor *Eight Views of the Parlor* (*Zashiki hakkei*).

Signature: Saki no Hokusai Iitsu ga
Publisher: Akamatsuya Shōtarō
Woodblock print (nishiki-e); ink and color on paper
30.5 x 20.1 cm (12 x 7 15/16 in.)
William S. and John T. Spaulding Collection, 21.10234

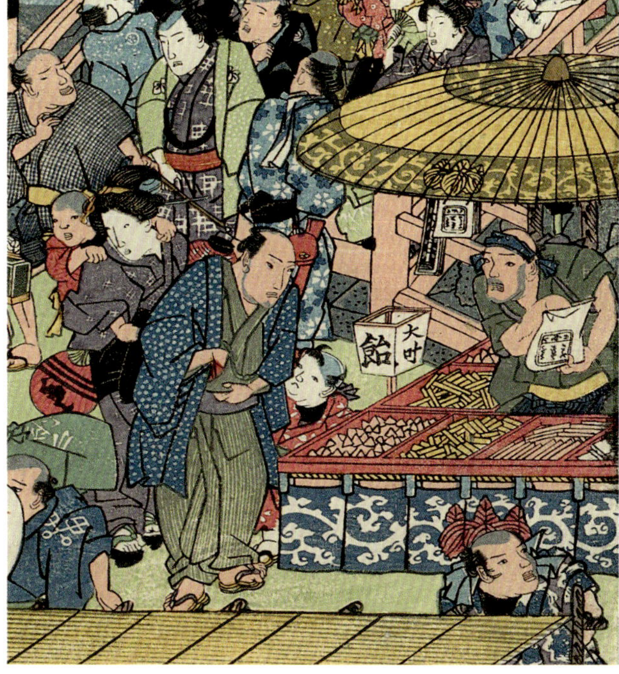

Fig. 7 | **In a detail from a panoramic view of a summer festival showing a father buying snacks for his family at a temporary outdoor stall, the vendor holds a paper bag similar to those once decorated by Hokusai. Utagawa Kunitora (working early 19th century), *Enjoying the Evening Cool at Ryōgoku Bridge in Edo: A Great Display of Fireworks* (*Edo Ryōgoku-bashi yūsuzumi ōhanabi no zu*), 1820s, woodblock print, triptych (overall): 38 x 76.5 cm (14 15/16 x 30 1/8 in.)**

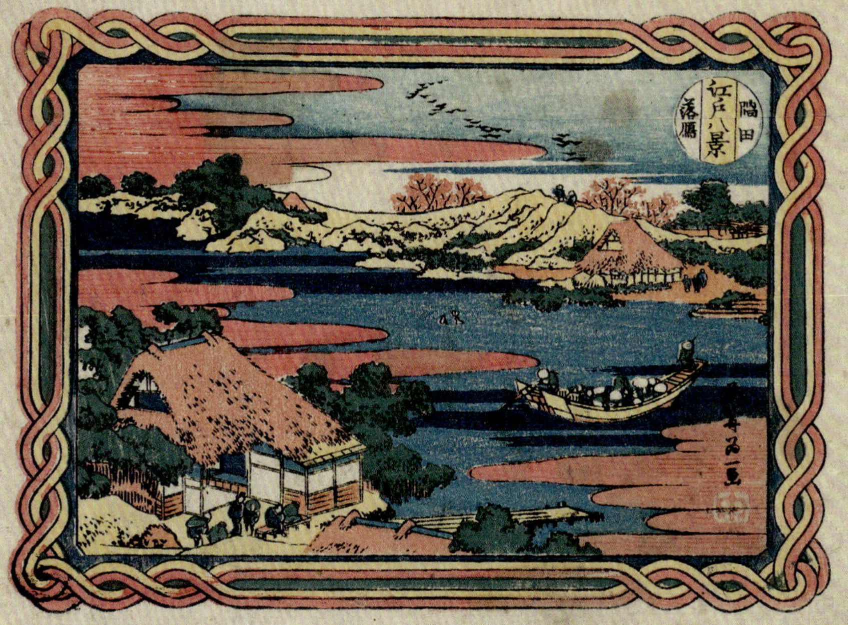
江戸八景
隅田
落雁

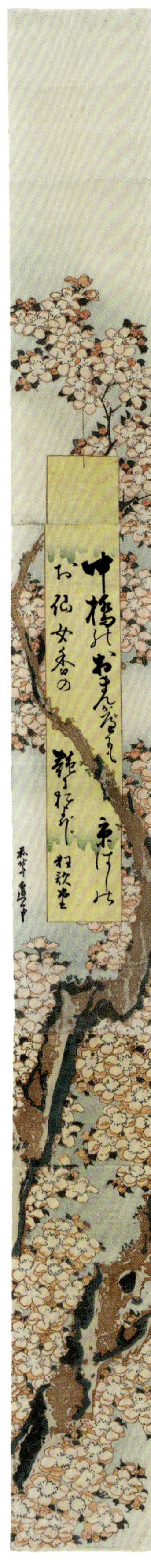

44 | **Flowering Cherry Branch with Advertisement for Senjokō**, about 1823–29

Prints in a long, thin, vertical format were known as pillar prints because they were intended to be hung on the stationary wooden pillars between the sliding paper panels of a Japanese room. Hokusai designed very few pillar prints, and this one, which is unusually elongated even for a pillar print, was almost certainly made as a special commission. The custom of adorning the branches of blossoming cherry trees with rectangular slips of decorated paper bearing poems in fine calligraphy dates back to classical times. In this case, however, the subject of the suspended poem is not the cherry blossoms but rather the cosmetic Senjokō (literally Fairy Lady Fragrance), a popular brand of the white face powder used by women and by Kabuki actors playing female roles. The poem is signed Kyōkadō, one of several pen names used by the kyōka poet Shikatsube no Magao (1753–1829), who also wrote comic fiction under the name Koikawa Sukimachi.

References to Senjokō appear in ukiyo-e prints and books throughout the 1820s and 1830s; the earliest known mention of it is in a book published in 1823. The powder was sold in paper packets at the Sakamoto store in Kyōbashi in Edo and was famous for the ubiquity of its advertisements, which included notices pasted on the walls of inns, tea shops, and other suitable public places; announcements in the backs of printed books, sometimes even two-page spreads; and product placement in the texts of books and in book illustrations and prints, associating Senjokō packages with beautiful women and noted actors. This massive advertising campaign apparently resulted from the fact that the proprietor of the Sakamoto store, Wada Genshichi, was also one of the official censors who approved books and prints for publication. It is not clear whether Wada pressured the artists, authors, and publishers to promote his product, or whether they spontaneously included it in their works as a gesture of goodwill toward someone whose approval was essential to their commercial survival.

This elegant advertisement, however, has no censor's seal, which means it was probably privately commissioned. It may have been intended as a promotional gift for customers who purchased large quantities of Senjokō in the hope that it would make them as beautiful as the cherry blossoms.

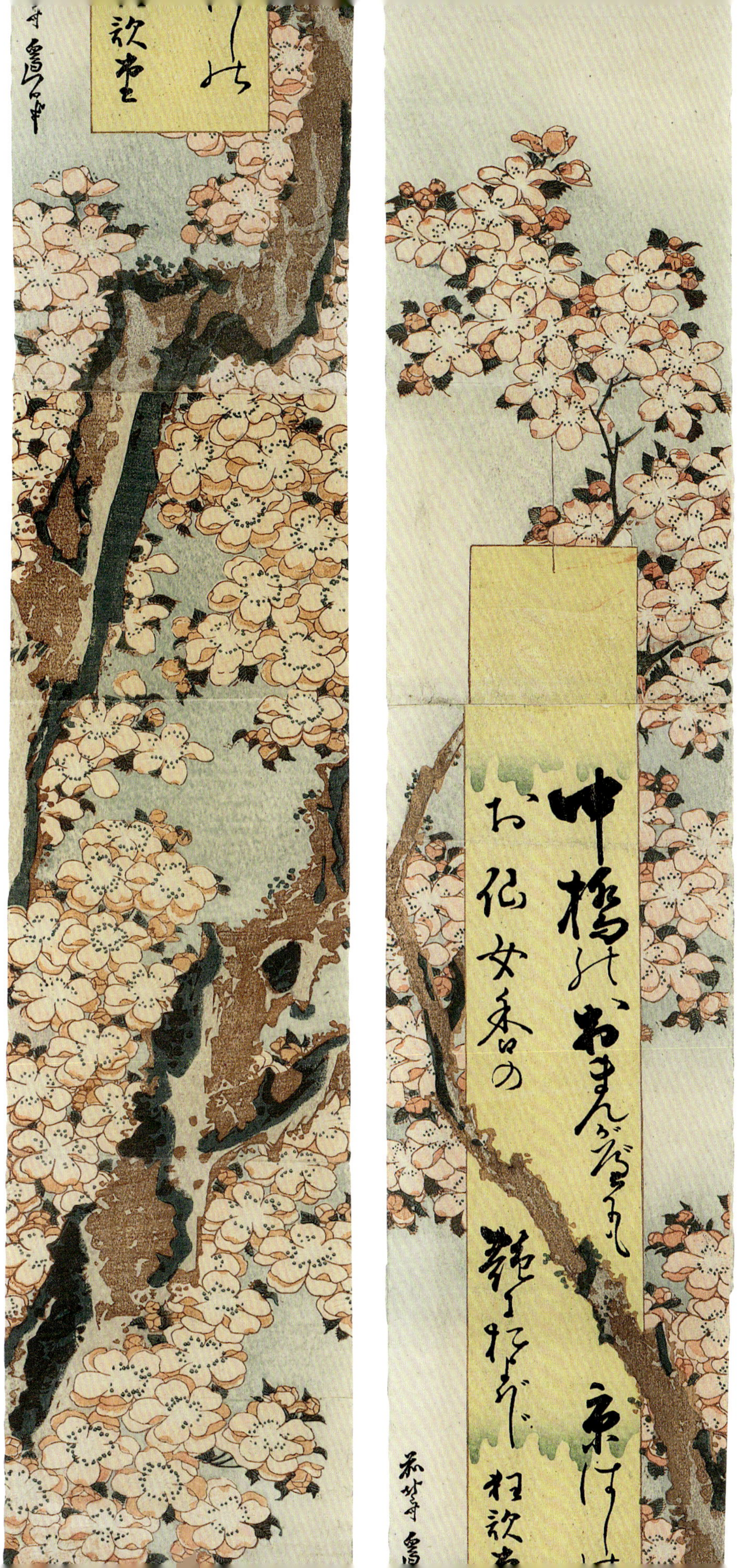

Signature:
Saki no Hokusai Iitsu hitsu
Woodblock print (nishiki-e);
ink and color on paper
115.8 x 10.2 cm (45 9/16 x 4 in.)
William Sturgis Bigelow Collection,
11.20403

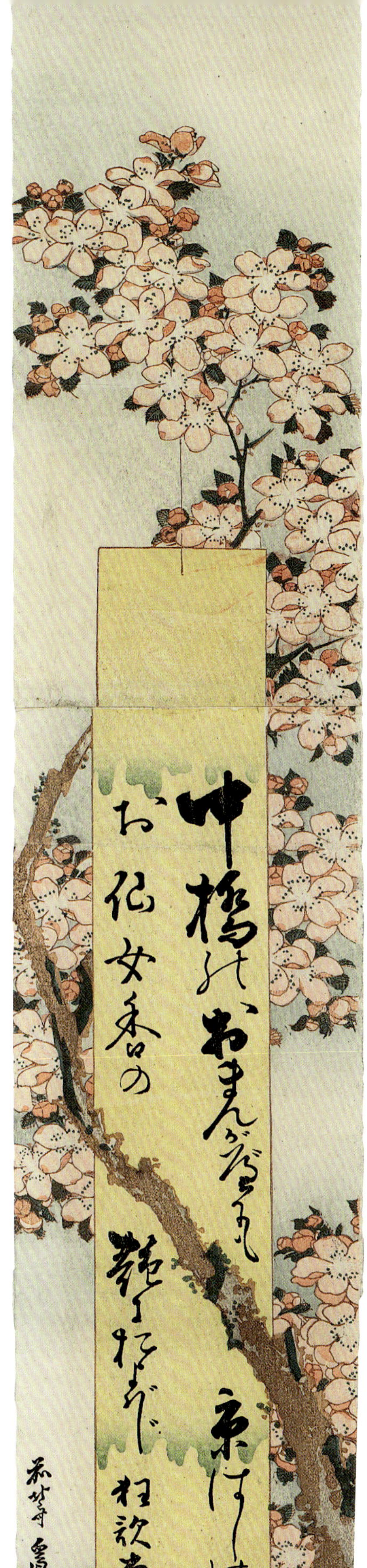

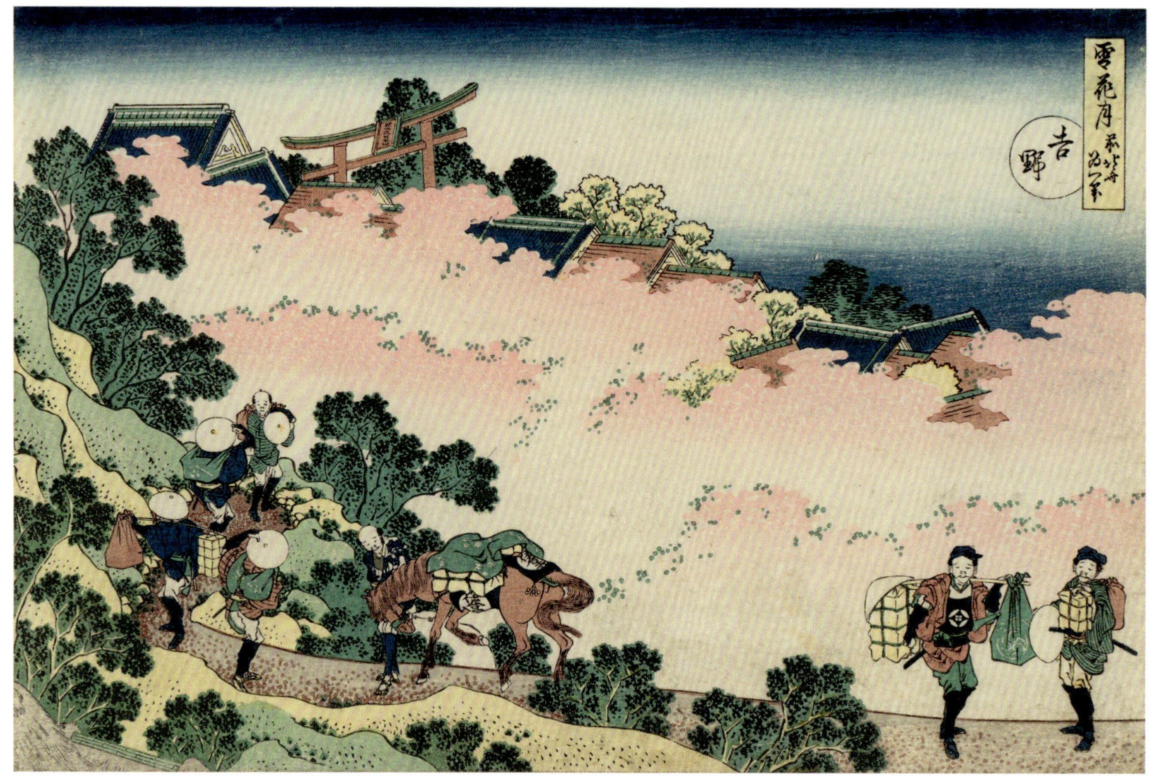

45 | **Cherry Blossoms at Yoshino** (*Yoshino*) from the series *Snow, Moon, and Flowers* (*Setsugekka*), about 1833

In Chinese poetry of the Tang dynasty, snow, the moon, and flowers were considered the three most beautiful things in the world, corresponding respectively to the seasons of winter, fall, and spring combined with summer. In ukiyo-e prints, the theme was often used as the basis for a series of three designs of subjects ranging from beautiful women to Kabuki actors to landscapes. Flowers were almost always interpreted as cherry blossoms, the most beloved of Japanese blooms.

For this series, Hokusai picked three especially beautiful and spectacular landscape scenes. The other two prints show snow on the Sumida River in Edo and the moon over Yodo Castle near Kyoto, so one might expect that the third scene would be related to the third of Japan's largest cities, Osaka. Instead, Hokusai chose to show the most famous cherry blossoms in all of Japan, in the mountains of Yoshino to the south of Kyoto. Even Edo residents who had never visited the area would have known of these cherry trees from the popular Kabuki play *The Thousand Cherry Trees of Yoshitsune* (*Yoshitsune senbon-zakura*), in which the twelfth-century general Yoshitsune and his followers hide from their enemies in the Yoshino mountains.

Hokusai shows not just a single tree or grove of trees, but an entire mountain valley full of cherry trees, blossoming in such profusion that their branches and trunks cannot even be seen, and the valley seems to be filled with a dense cloud of flowers. The publisher's trademark can be faintly seen on the green bundle carried on a pole at the lower right, and the trappings of the packhorse are marked with the expression *Shiawase yoshi*, a good-luck wish for a safe journey.

Signature: Saki no Hokusai Iitsu hitsu
Publisher: Nishimuraya Yohachi (Eijudō)
Woodblock print (nishiki-e); ink and color on paper
25.4 x 37.2 cm (10 x 14 5/8 in.)
William S. and John T. Spaulding Collection, 21.6713

46 | **Sei Shōnagon** from the series *A True Mirror of Chinese and Japanese Poetry* (*Shika shashin kyō*), also called *Imagery of the Poets*, about 1833

The large, eye-catching prints in this series could serve as elegant home decorations in place of more expensive hanging-scroll paintings. They are thought to have been designed between the *Thirty-Six Views of Mount Fuji* and the *One Hundred Poems Explained by the Nurse*, but many questions remain. Ten prints from the series are known, but since the series title gives no number, it is uncertain how many designs may have been planned.

The poems illustrated in the series are from both Chinese and Japanese sources. In this print the figures are Chinese, but the verse is by the Japanese court lady Sei Shōnagon, who often alluded to Chinese history and literature in her witty writings. Her famous poem, number 62 in the anthology *One Hundred Poems by One Hundred Poets*, reads: "Although, still wrapped in night / the cock's false cry / some may deceive, / never will the Barrier / of Meeting Hill let you pass."*

The false cry of the cock refers to a story from the Chinese classical work *Records of the Grand Historian* (*Shiji* in Chinese, *Shiki* in Japanese), which tells how, in 289 BC, Lord Mengchang (Mōsōkun in Japanese) was held prisoner by the king of Qin, the grandfather of the first emperor of China. He and his retainers made their escape, pursued by the king's army, but were blocked at the frontier by a gate that was closed until dawn. One of the retainers imitated the crow of a cock so skillfully that roosters in the neighborhood also began to crow. The gate was opened, and the fugitives escaped. Sei Shōnagon, however, declined a gentleman's romantic interest in her by sending him this poem, hinting that in her case tricks will not work and the Barrier of Ōsaka ("Ōsaka / au saka" was a standard poetic pun for "hill of lovers' meetings") will remain closed.

Signature: Saki no Hokusai Iitsu hitsu
Publisher: Moriya Jihei (Kinshindō)
Woodblock print (nishiki-e); ink and color on paper
51.2 x 22.4 cm (20 3/16 x 8 13/16 in.)
William Sturgis Bigelow Collection, 11.19644

*Translated by Joshua S. Mostow

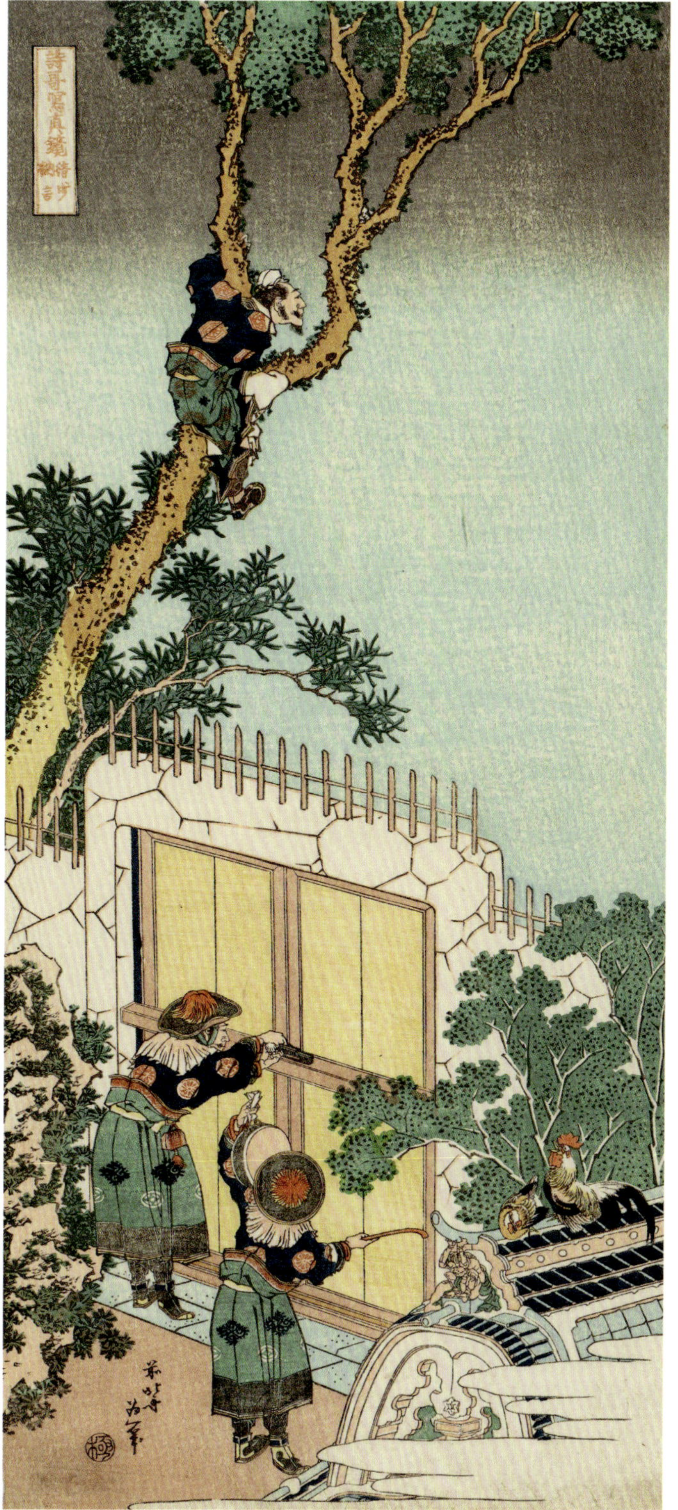

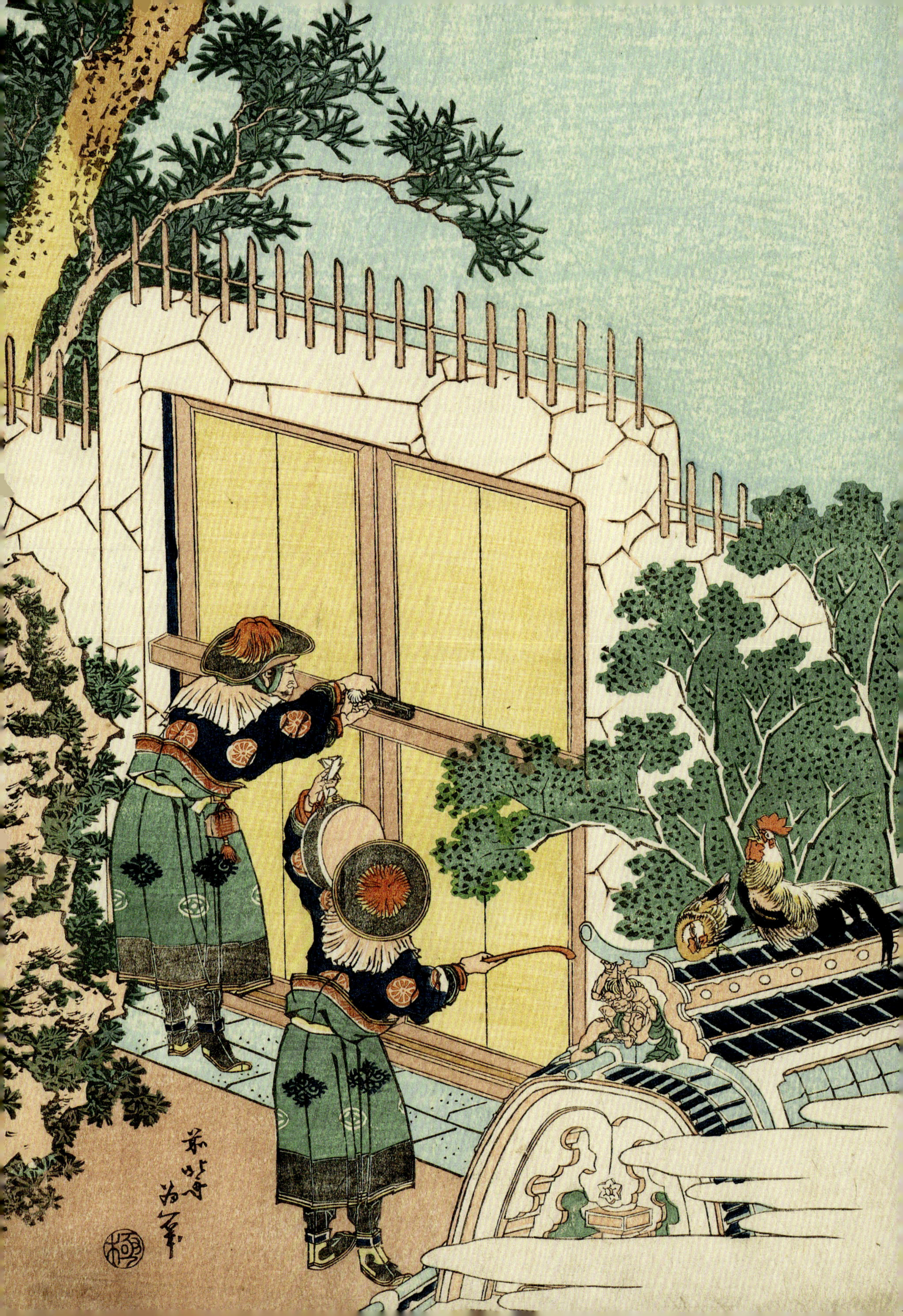

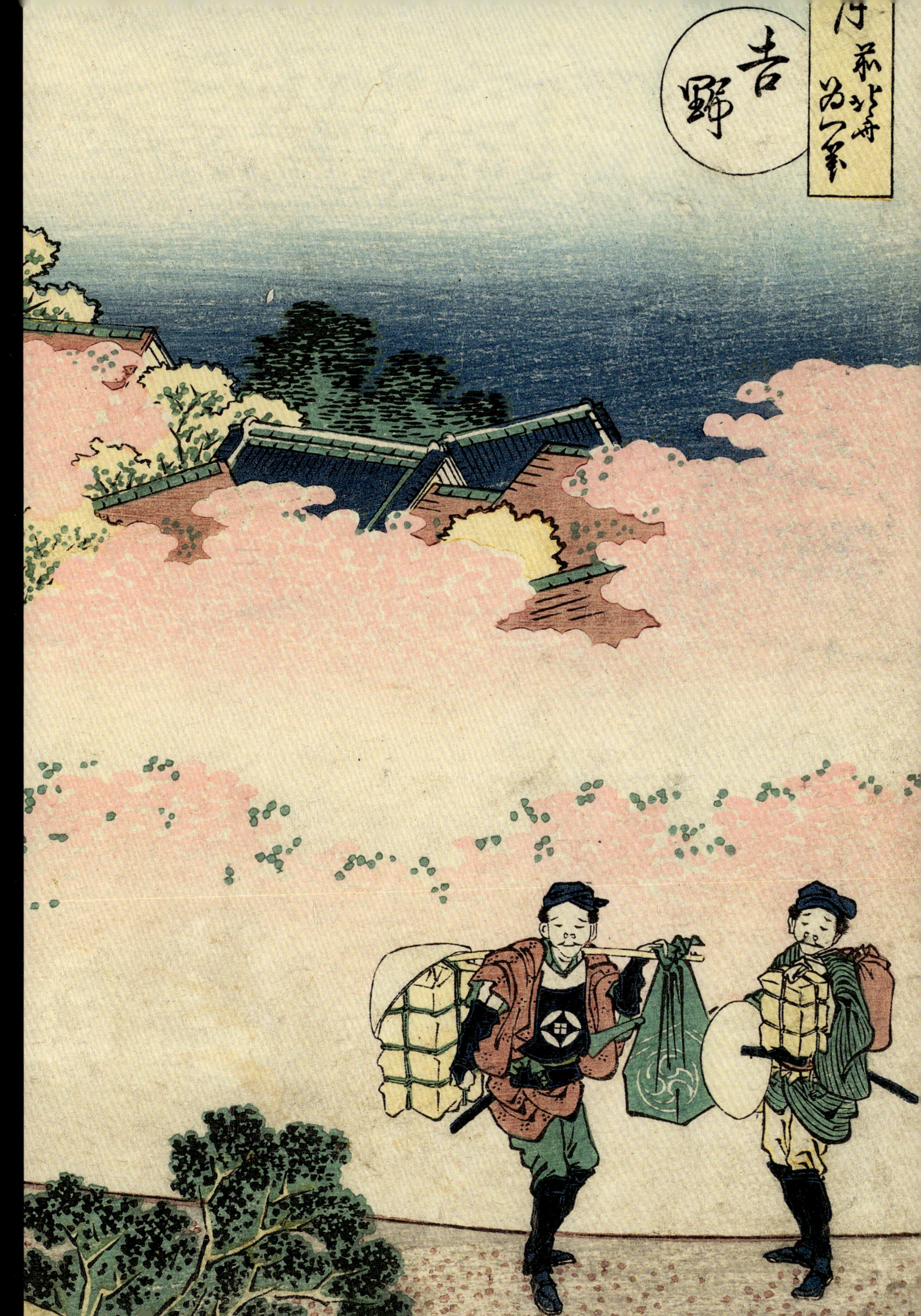
吉野

47 | **Poem by Ono no Komachi** from the series *One Hundred Poems Explained by the Nurse* (*Hyakunin isshu uba ga etoki*), about 1835

48 | **Poem by Ono no Komachi** from the series *One Hundred Poems Explained by the Nurse* (*Hyakunin isshu uba ga etoki*), about 1835

The uncompleted series *One Hundred Poems Explained by the Nurse* was the last of Hokusai's ōban landscape series and the most colorful. Although shades of blue, green, and yellow continue to predominate, many of the designs prominently feature red or red-brown as well. The word "uba" in the title can mean either a wet nurse or an old woman: in either case, a woman who might explain famous poems to children although she herself is not an expert on classical literature. Some of the prints show the scene described by the poem or the circumstances of its composition, while others update the scene to Hokusai's era and employ puns and other indirect allusions.

The series was first advertised in a book published in the spring of 1835 and may have been timed as a celebration of the six hundredth anniversary of the compilation of the beloved anthology *One Hundred Poems by One Hundred Poets* (*Hyakunin isshu*) by Fujiwara Teika in 1235. The first five designs in the series, representing the poets numbered one, two, three, six, and nine in the anthology, were issued by Nishimuraya Yohachi of the Eijudō publishing house, the publisher who had worked with Hokusai on the *Fuji* series.

Ono no Komachi, poet number nine in the anthology, was not only revered as one of the Six Poetic Immortals, whose works typified classical Japanese poetry, but was also said to have been the most beautiful woman in Japan when she was young. The example of her poetry selected for the anthology reads: "The color of the flowers / has faded indeed / in vain / have I passed through the world / while gazing at the falling rains."*

Hokusai's visual explanation of Komachi's poem has been expanded into a busy scene of village life on a fine spring day. The concept of color is suggested by two women spreading dyed cloth onto a drying board after it has been washed. The small cherry tree in the center of the picture is in full bloom, but the figure of a man sweeping the path beneath the tree indicates that some blossoms have already fallen. Directly under the tree, with her back turned to the viewer, is the most important figure of all: an old woman leaning on a cane who represents Komachi herself. The diagonal line of her bent back echoes the angle of the tree trunk. She looks up toward the blossoms as if contemplating the evanescence of both natural beauty and human beauty.

In addition to the finished full-color print, the MFA also owns a key block print, which includes the black outlines of the picture and the registration marks used to align the paper. In the printmaking process, this black outline block would have been carved first, using the artist's original drawing as a pattern. Impressions taken from it, like the one shown here, would then have been used to carve a separate block for each color, with identical registration marks on each block. A comparison of the key block and the finished print reveals the importance of color to the impact of the completed work.

47
Signature: Saki no Hokusai Manji
Publisher: Nishimuraya Yohachi (Eijudō)
Woodblock print (nishiki-e); ink and color on paper
24.9 x 37.2 cm (9 13/16 x 14 5/8 in.)
William Sturgis Bigelow Collection, 11.30177

48
Signature: Saki no Hokusai Manji
Woodblock print (key block); ink on paper
27.4 x 39.3 cm (10 13/16 x 15 1/2 in.)
William Sturgis Bigelow Collection, 11.17529

*Translated by Joshua S. Mostow

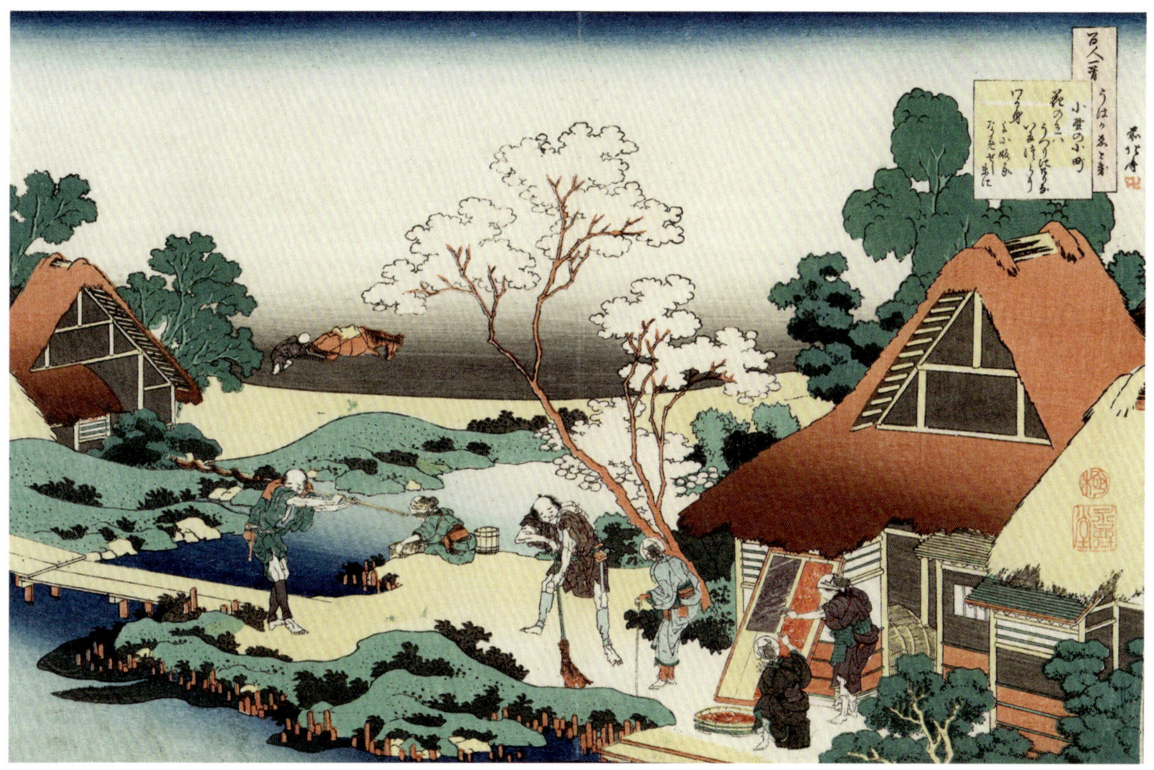

47

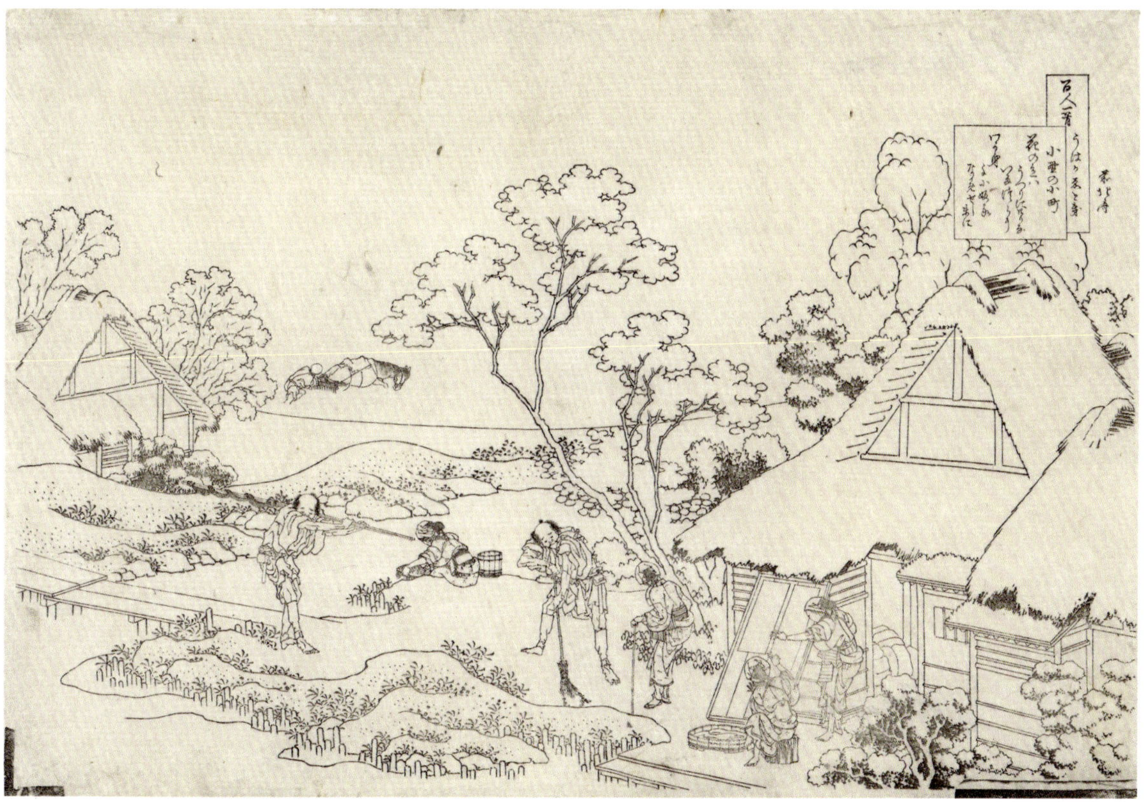

48

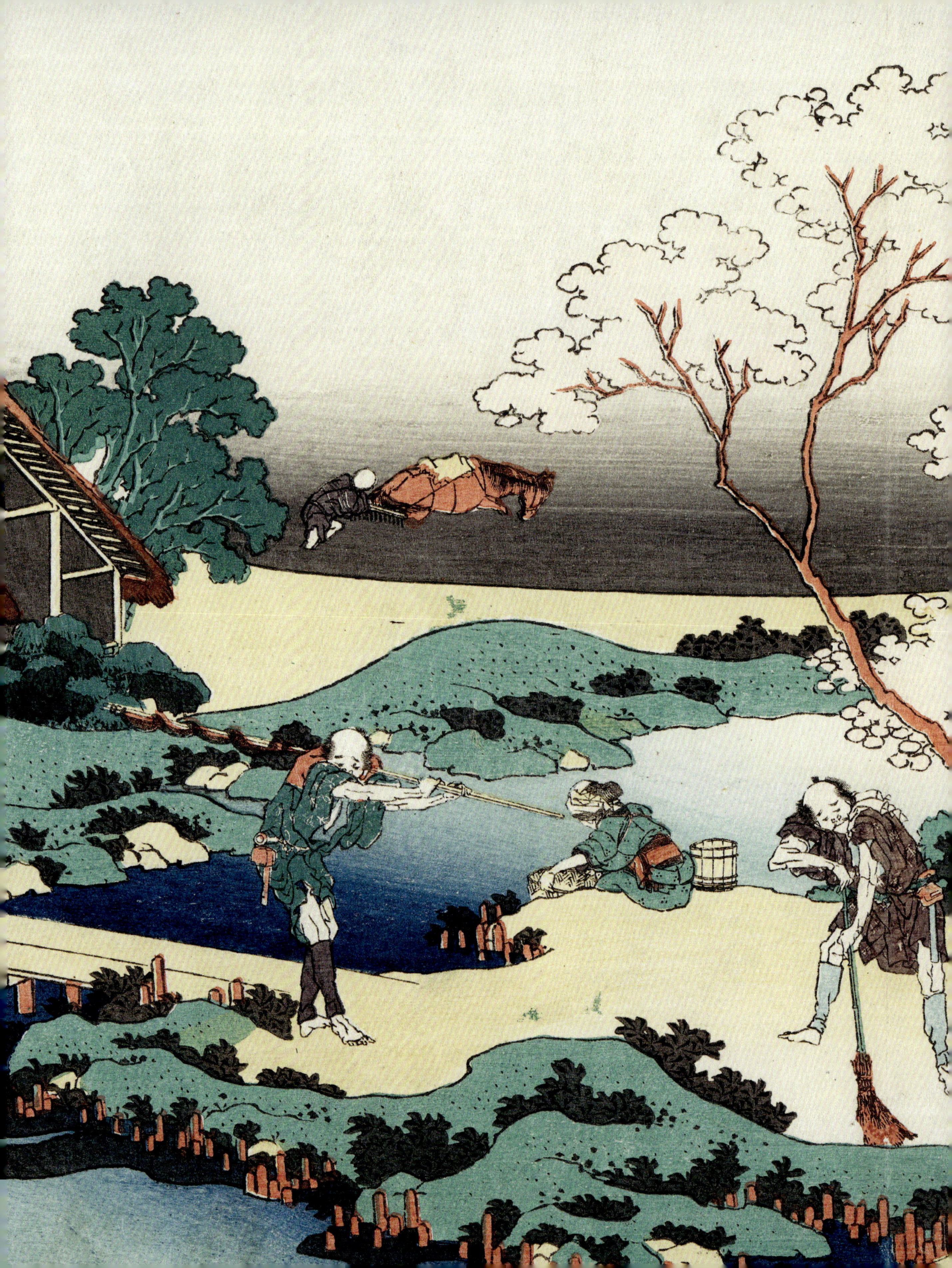

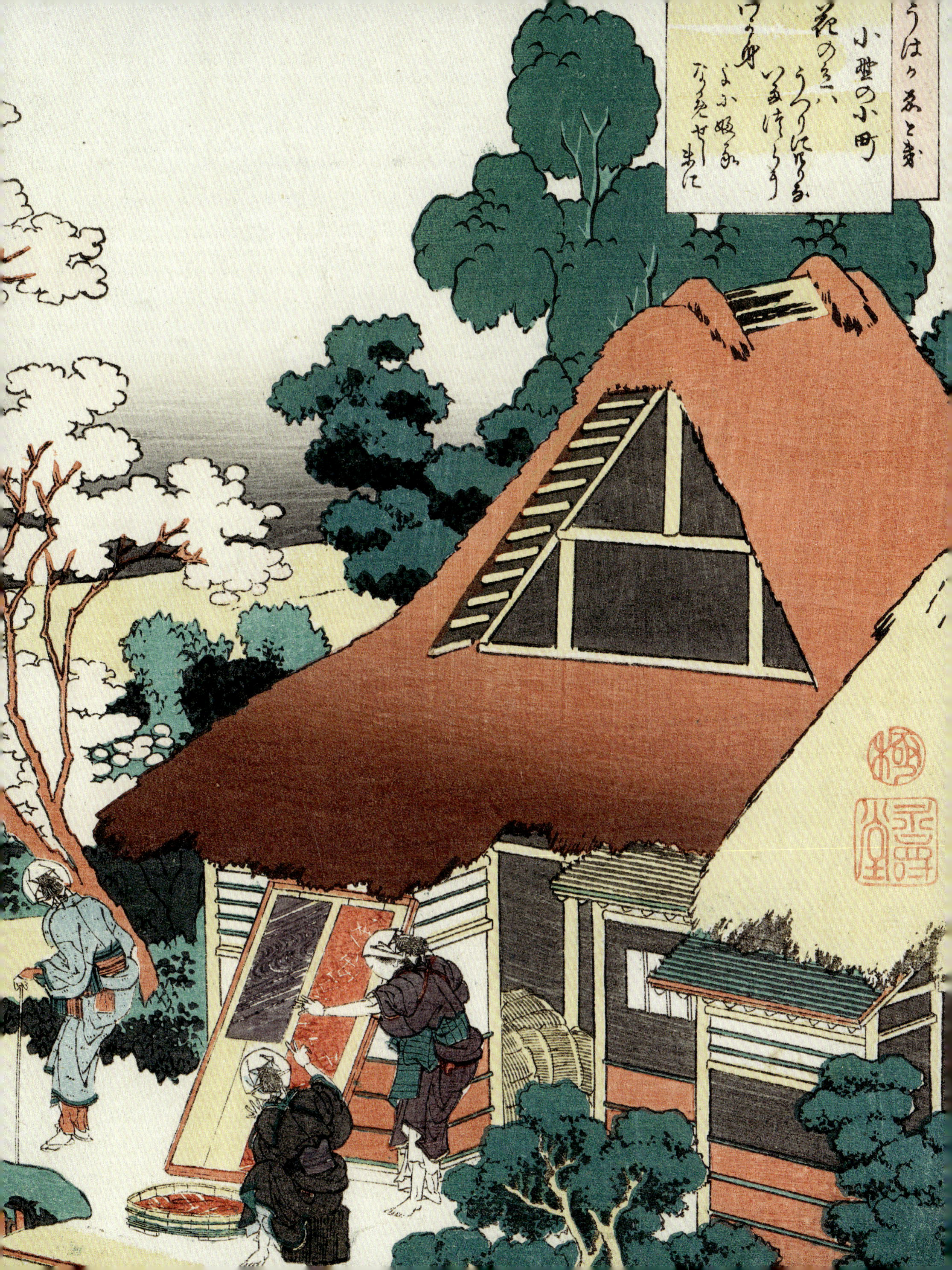
小野の小町

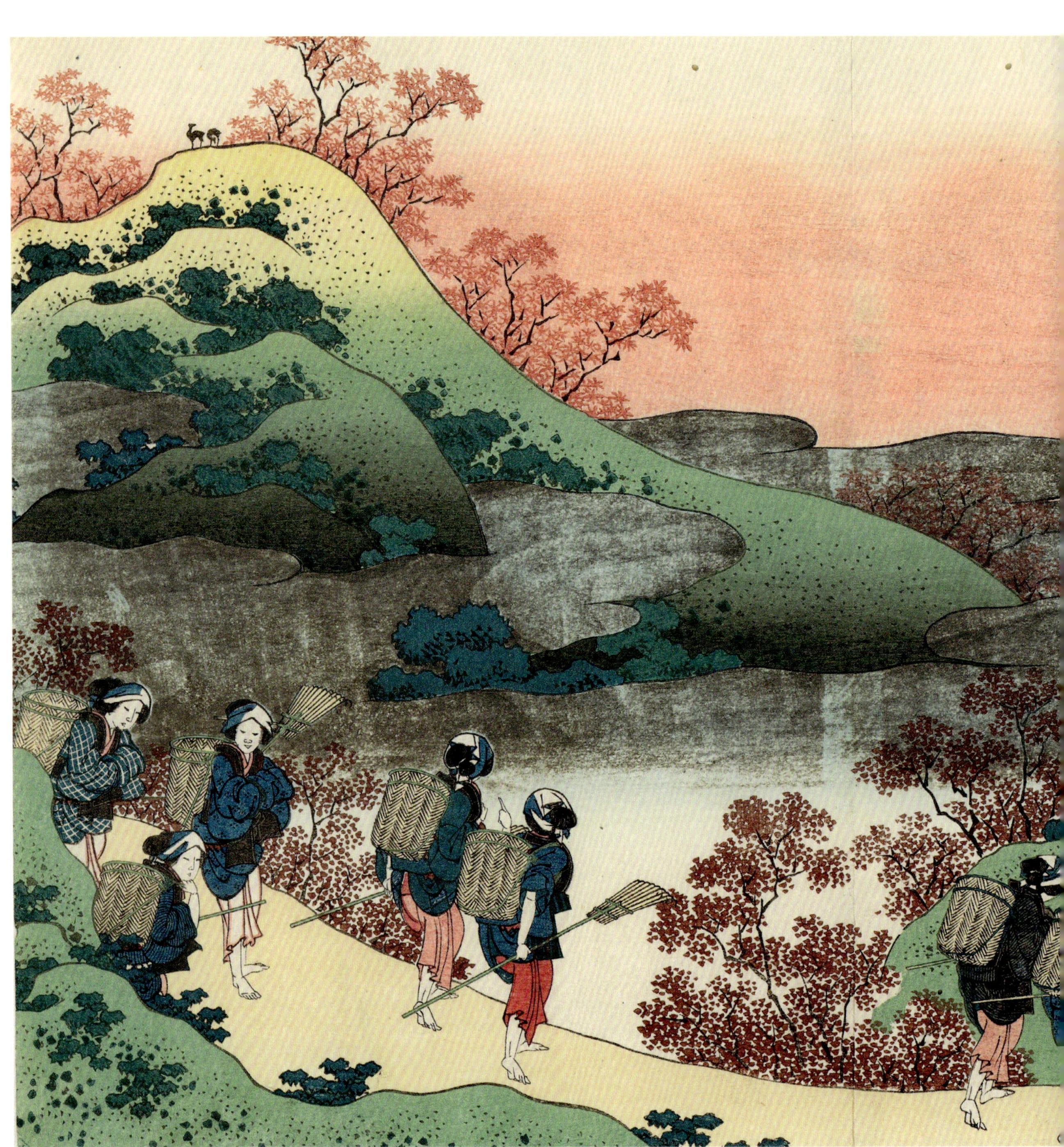

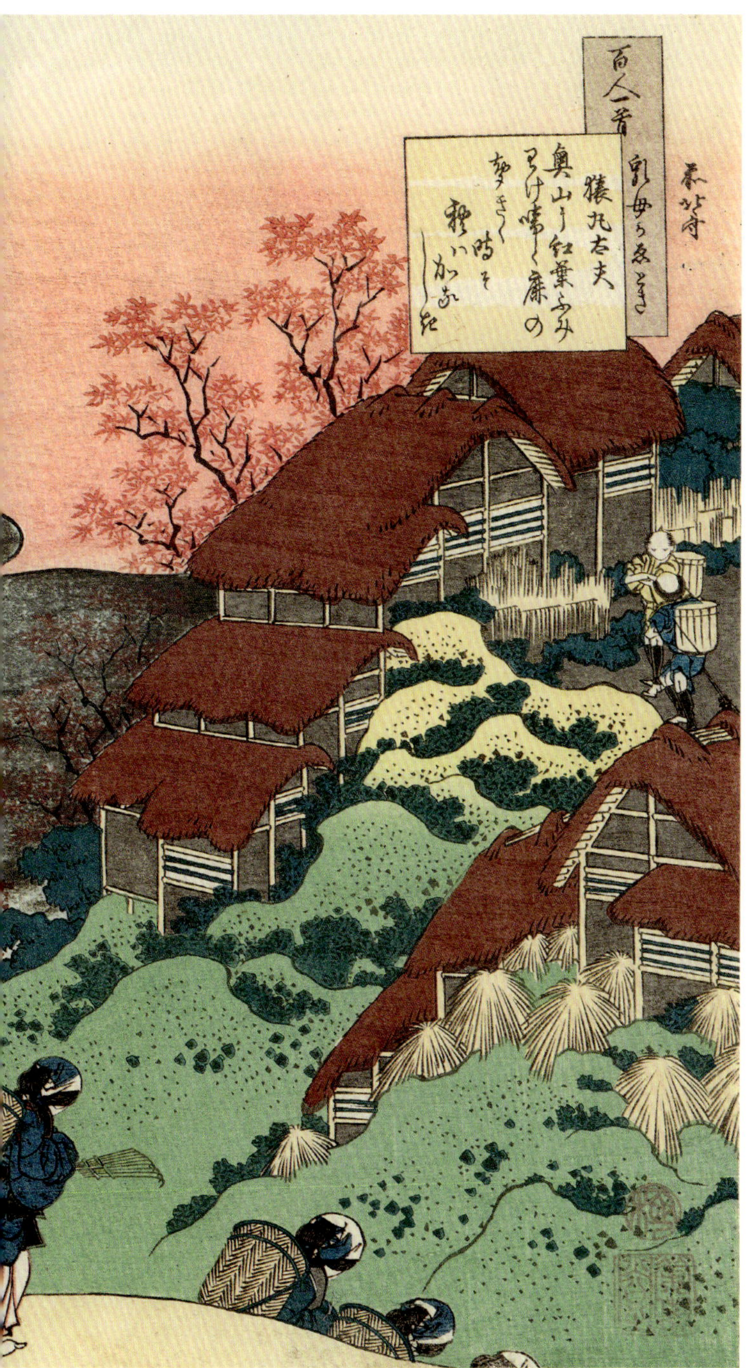

49 | **Poem by Sarumaru Dayū** from the series *One Hundred Poems Explained by the Nurse* (*Hyakunin isshu uba ga etoki*), about 1835

This beautifully colored design, with its red maple leaves and sunset sky, is a straightforward depiction of the scene described in the fifth poem in the *One Hundred Poems* anthology. The verse by Sarumaru Dayū reads: "When I hear the voice / of the stag crying for his mate / stepping through the fallen leaves / deep in the mountains—then is the time / that autumn is saddest."* Instead of the expected ancient courtiers, however, the people who hear the deer's lonely cry are a group of women from a mountain village returning home at sunset after a day gathering herbs and mushrooms. The viewer's eye follows their trail from left to right, toward the village where the men await them, and then around in a circle to the distant hilltop at left where the deer calls out for his own mate, before spiraling back into the mist-filled valley as the imagined deer's cry resonates throughout it.

Following the publication of the first five designs in the *One Hundred Poems* series by Nishimuraya Yohachi in 1835, twenty-two additional designs were published over the next year, but they have a slightly different "Eijudō" seal, which suggests a change had occurred in the publishing house. The most likely explanation is that Nishimuraya Yohachi went bankrupt as a result of the economic depression that struck Japan at that time, and his business continued under the same house name, but with another publisher, probably Iseya Sanjirō. The series ceased publication after the second group, including this print, was released, although Hokusai probably completed all of the drawings. A total of ninety-one designs are known, but only twenty-seven were published as completed color prints.

*Translated by Joshua S. Mostow

Signature: Saki no Hokusai Manji
Publisher: Iseya Sanjirō (Eijudō)
Woodblock print (nishiki-e); ink and color on paper
24.7 x 37 cm (9 3/4 x 14 9/16 in.)
William Sturgis Bigelow Collection, 11.30181

50 | **Li Bai Admiring a Waterfall**, 1849

51 | **Li Bai** (*Ri Haku*) from the series *A True Mirror of Chinese and Japanese Poetry* (*Shika shashin kyō*), also called *Imagery of the Poets*, about 1833

Li Bai (701–762) is considered one of the greatest Chinese poets of all time. Along with his close friend Du Fu (712–770) and other contemporaries, he contributed to making the Tang dynasty a golden age of Chinese culture. His famous quatrain on the waterfall at Mount Lu reads:

Sunlight streams on the river stones.
From high above, the river steadily plunges —
three thousand feet of sparkling water —
*the Milky Way pouring down from heaven.**

In this work, completed in the last year of his life, Hokusai attempted to achieve in painting what Li Bai had done in poetry: to capture the awesome beauty of the torrent of water pouring over the great falls. His fascination with the depiction of falling water culminates in this painting.

About fifteen years earlier, Hokusai had designed another view of Li Bai gazing at the waterfall of Mount Lu as part of his large-format print series *A True Mirror of Chinese and Japanese Poetry*. In the print, it is the poet himself who is the focus of interest as Hokusai explores the nature of inspiration; in the painting, the viewer is invited to experience that inspiration personally.

Both works feature a detail that is typical of Hokusai's sense of humor: one small servant boy in the painting, and two in the print, can be found clinging to the robes of the master. Li Bai was known not only for his genius but also for his fondness for alcohol; many of his poems deal with the pleasures of wine. According to legend, he drowned when he fell out of a boat in a drunken attempt to embrace the reflection of the moon. Apparently the little boys are working to keep their master on his unsteady feet and to prevent him from toppling into the waterfall that he contemplates so raptly.

*Translated by Sam Hamill

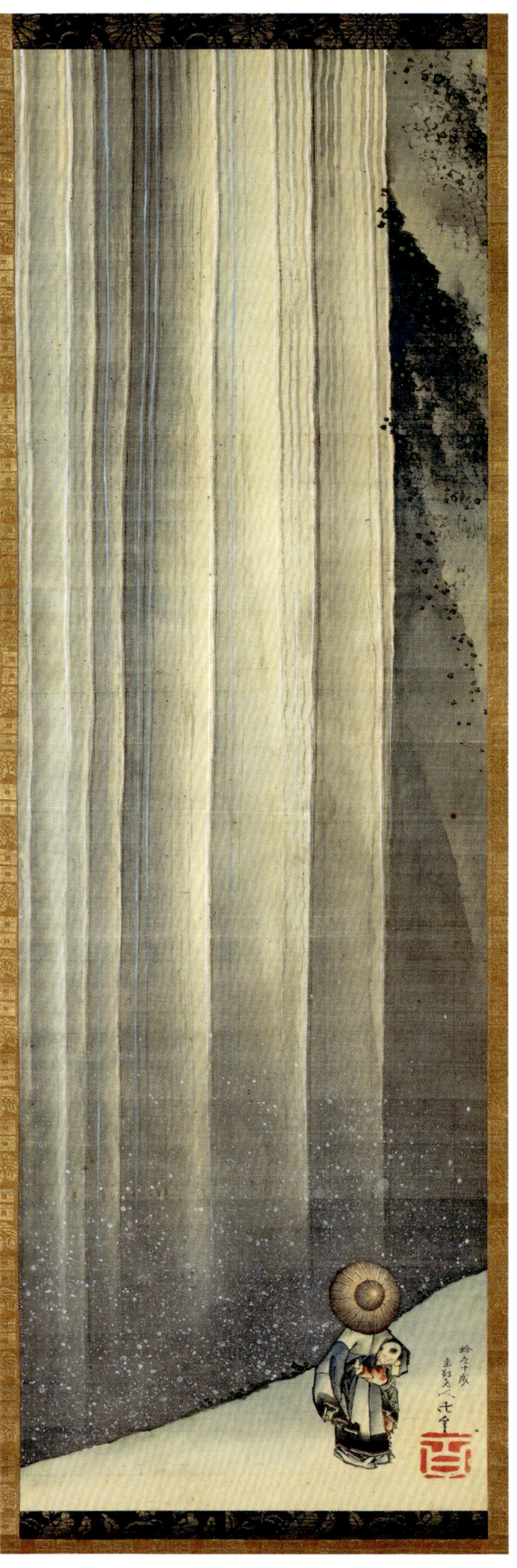

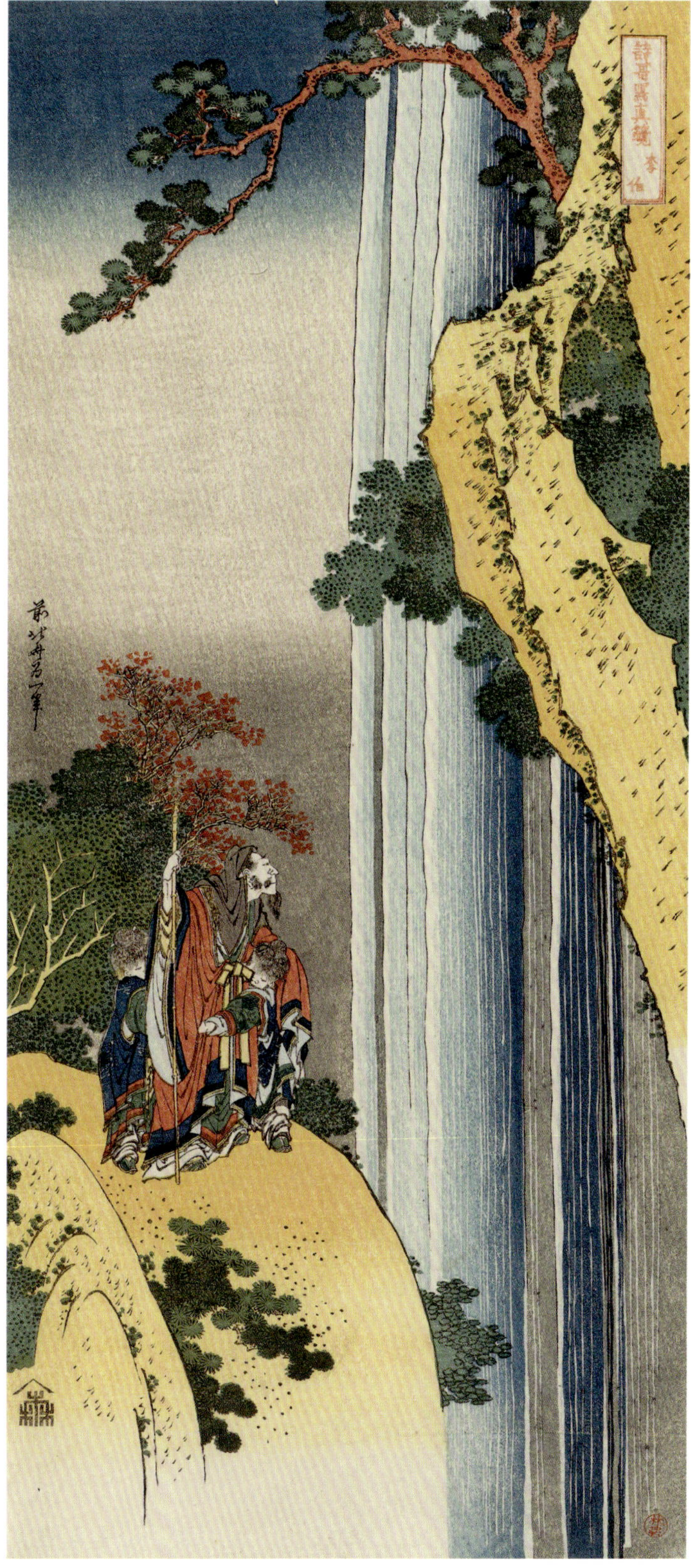

50
Signature:
Yowai kyūjūsai Gakyō rōjin Manji hitsu
Hanging scroll; ink and color on silk
93.4 x 30 cm (36 3/4 x 11 13/16 in.)
William Sturgis Bigelow Collection, 11.7452

51
Signature: Saki no Hokusai Iitsu hitsu
Publisher: Moriya Jihei (Kinshindō)
Woodblock print (nishiki-e);
ink and color on paper
50.9 x 22.4 cm (20 1/16 x 8 13/16 in.)
William S. and John T. Spaulding Collection,
21.6669

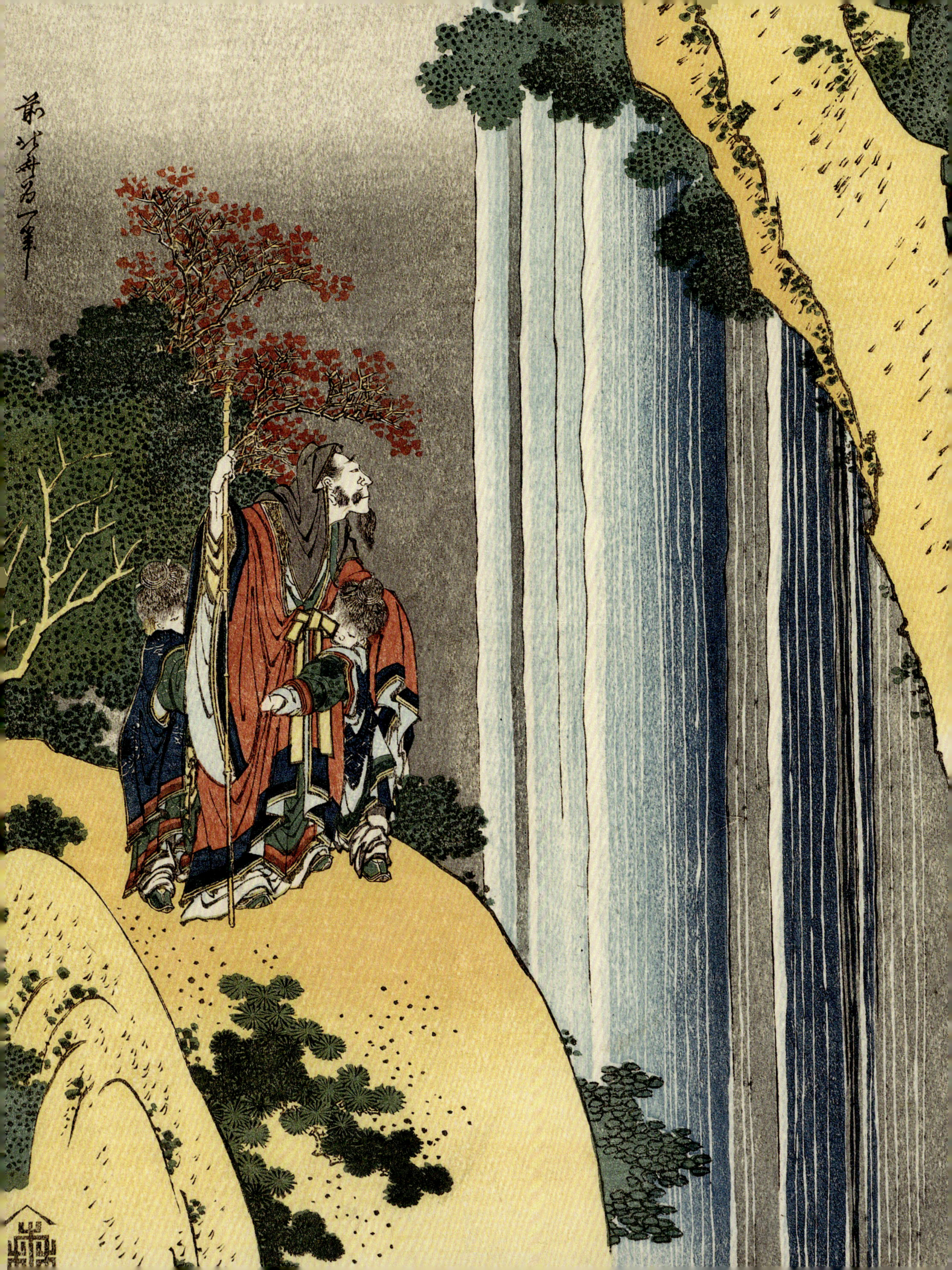
前北斎為一筆

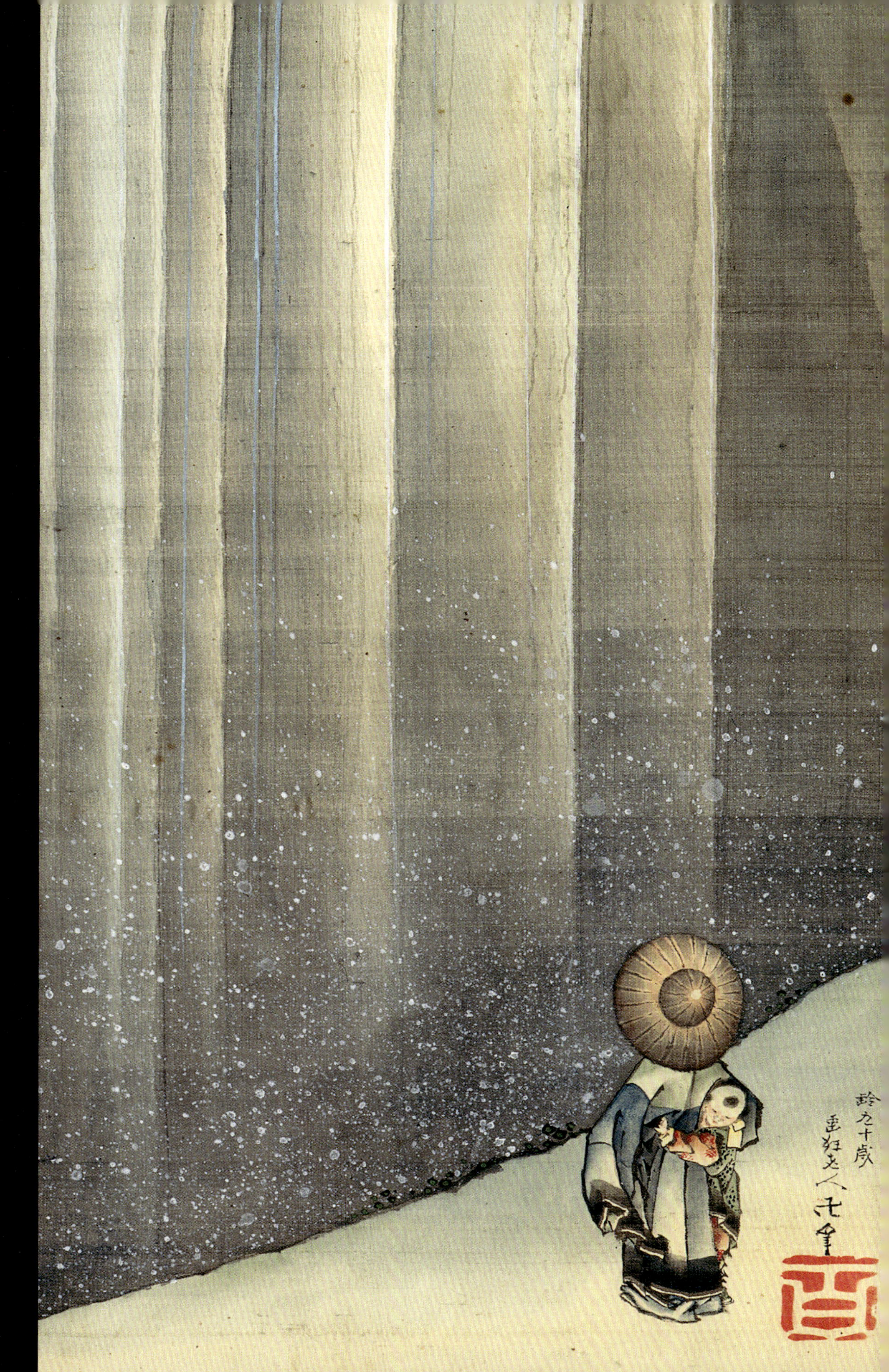

齢九十歳
画狂老人卍筆

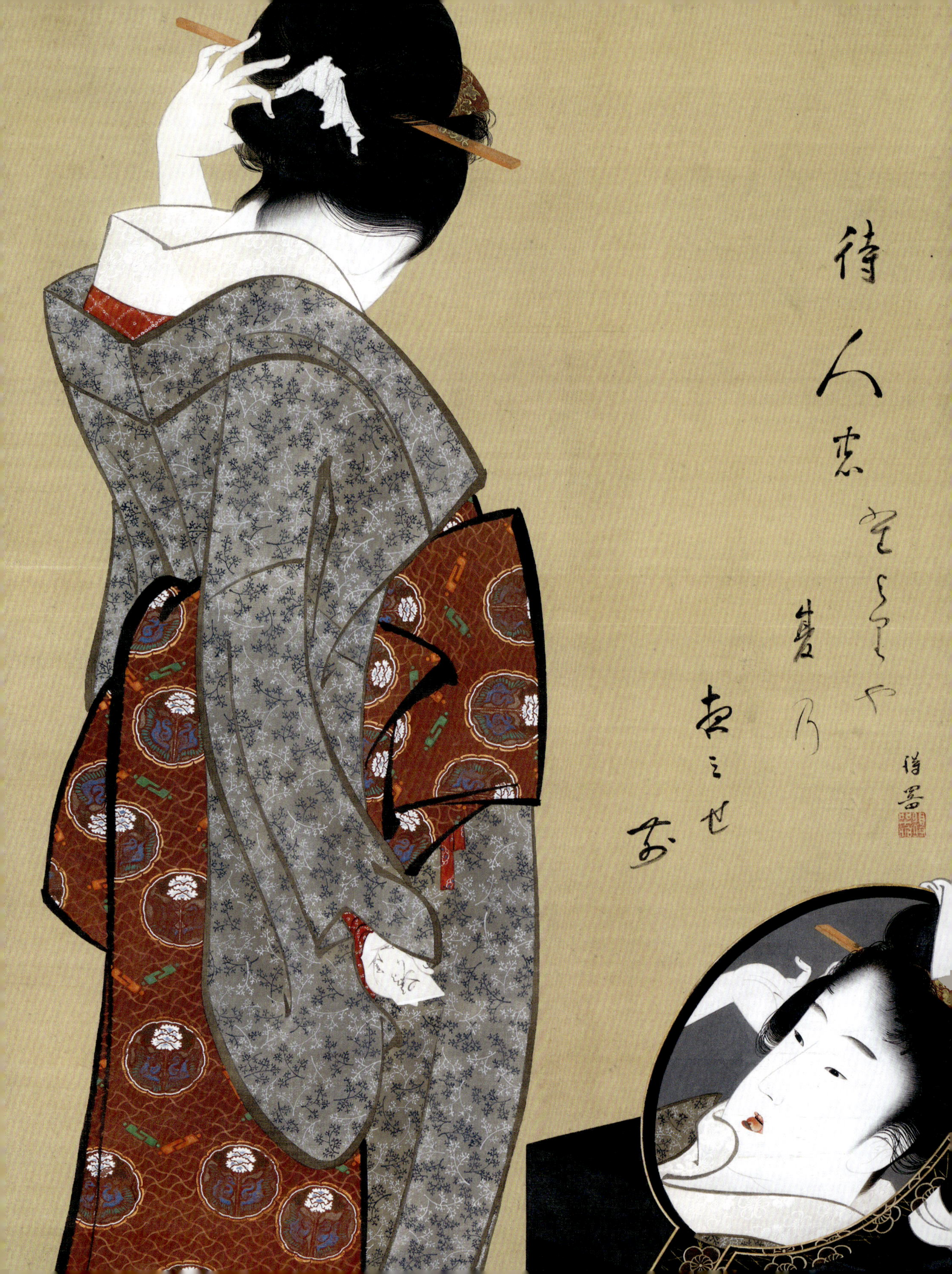

BRUSH AND BLOCK: HOKUSAI OBSERVED

Hokusai's art manifests a singular mastery of materials and techniques that infuses his work with a rare vitality. There is compelling evidence that prior to his formal training under the renowned painter and print designer Katsukawa Shunshō, Hokusai worked as a woodblock carver from his mid- to late teens.[1] If this is true, Hokusai gained practical experience in print production uncommon for a painter or even a print designer of his time. Such intimate knowledge of the block carver's craft might have stimulated the lively dialogue between painting and printmaking that continued in Hokusai's work throughout his life. One could say that his paintings share aspects of prints and that his prints share aspects of paintings, and that in many cases his paintings show a printerly understanding and his designs for prints show a painterly awareness. Three pairs of paintings and prints illustrate this ingenious and often playful feature of Hokusai's art especially well.

In a painting from 1805, an elegant woman gazes into a mirror while adjusting her coiffure (fig. 8). Meanwhile, in a printed frontispiece from an 1801 book, a group of servants with robes aflutter carry supplies for an outing (fig. 10). Although many other ukiyo-e painters also paid great attention to the depiction of clothing, in both of these works, which were created when Hokusai was in his forties, the artist depicted the waved structure of silk crêpe de chine fabric in an unusually tactile manner. He departed from a conventional two-dimensional portrayal by creating a three-dimensional texture using a technique more frequently seen on rigidly mounted screen paintings. He built up thick, reticulated lines of white pigment that

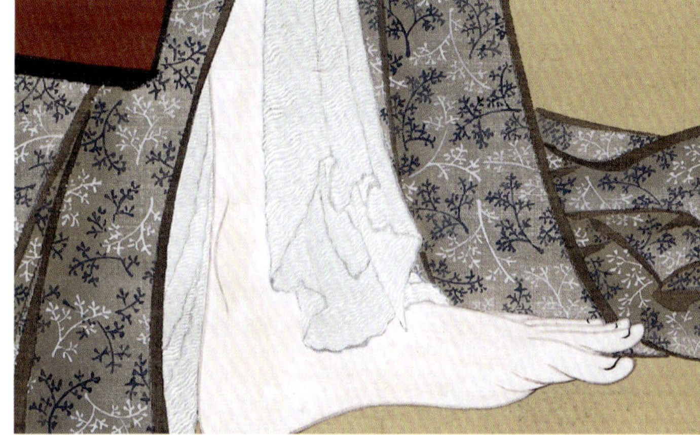

Fig. 8 (opposite) and fig. 9 (above) | **Details of cat. 1, *Woman Looking at Herself in a Mirror*, about 1805, hanging scroll, 138.7 x 57.5 cm (54 5/8 x 22 5/8 in.)**

stand out in relief against the pale blue background and perfectly imitate the irregularly raised surface of this type of fabric (fig. 9).

Virtuosic use of embossing, or blind printing, lends dimension to the fabric's distinctive rippled surface in the printed version. This effect was created when the printer carefully pressed the paper into deep grooves carved into the woodblock with a baren or rounded tool (fig. 11).[2] Throughout his career, Hokusai worked with several publishers, notably Nishimuraya Yohachi and Iseya Sanjirō of the firm Eijudō. These publishers played an important role in the production, visual appearance, and distribution of

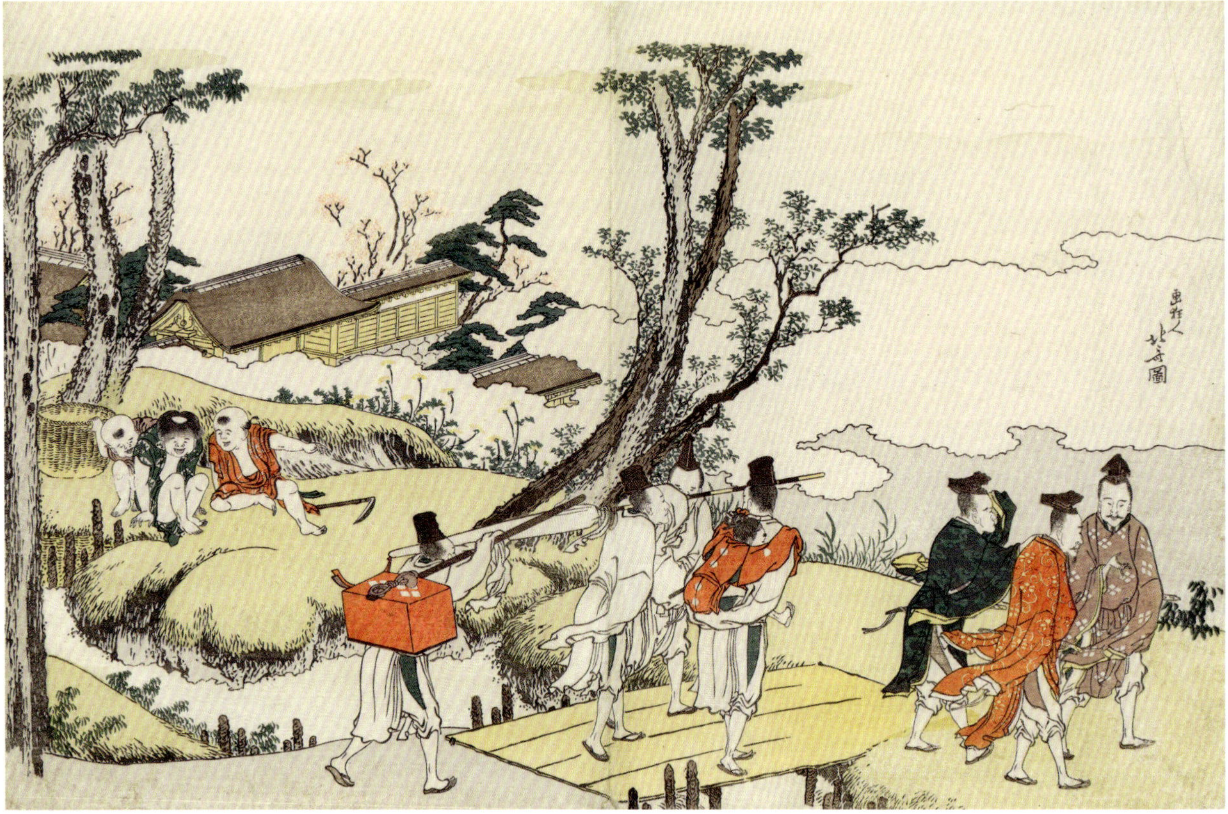

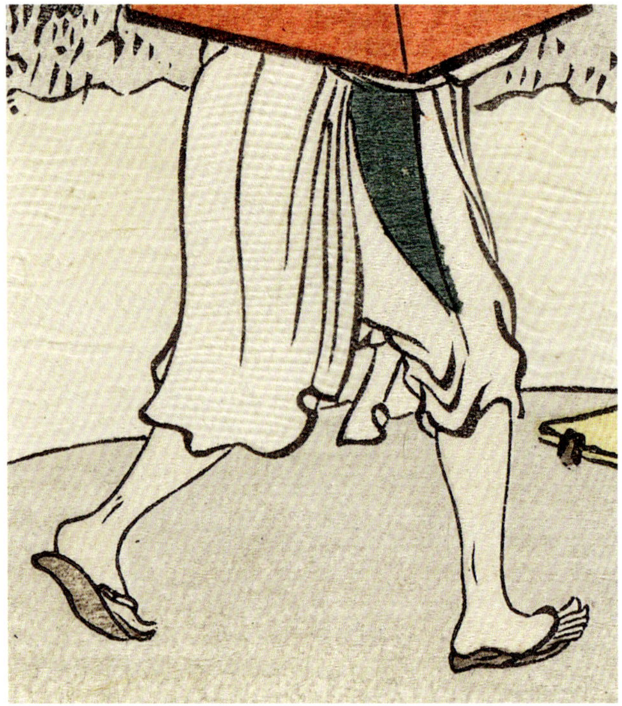

Fig. 10 | ***Courtiers Returning from a Picnic*, frontispiece by Hokusai from the book *The Thirty-Six Immortal Women Poets (Nyōbō sanjūrokunin uta-awase)*, illustrated by Chōbunsai Eishi (1756–1829), 1801, woodblock-printed book, 25.3 x 18.7cm ($9\frac{15}{16}$ x $7\frac{3}{8}$ in.)**

Fig. 11 | **Detail of above**

the prints he designed. Within the world of printmaking, it was often the publisher who commissioned the artist to create an image and coordinated its transformation into a print under the hands of skilled artisan block carvers and printers. Although the extent of Hokusai's involvement in the production of particular prints is not known, given his apprenticeship as a block carver, their final appearance may have benefited from his input on how to best utilize the skills of the carvers and printers. This collaboration with his publisher could have affected the choice and manner of color application, as well as the use of special effects such as embossing, burnishing, scattered bits of shell, and metallic pigments.

To capture the sheen of the oiled and carefully dressed hair of the painted figure, Hokusai mixed extra animal glue binder into his carbon black pigment and picked out the strands in fine, lustrous lines. More unusually, he used the same technique to emphasize the rich, polished surface of the black lacquered cosmetic box at the woman's feet (fig. 12). In printing, this glossy effect is often achieved by burnishing rather than by adding glue binders. A printer can lend a glossy surface to select areas of a design by carefully rubbing the print's front with a hard, smooth tool while it is placed over sections of the block's relief. Hokusai's deluxe surimono print *Duck, Abalone Shell, and Parsley*, for example, displays portions that were burnished after all the colors had been printed in order to convey the sheen of *mitsuba*, a type of Japanese parsley, and to distinguish the complex coloration of a drake mallard's head from its body's plumage (fig. 13).

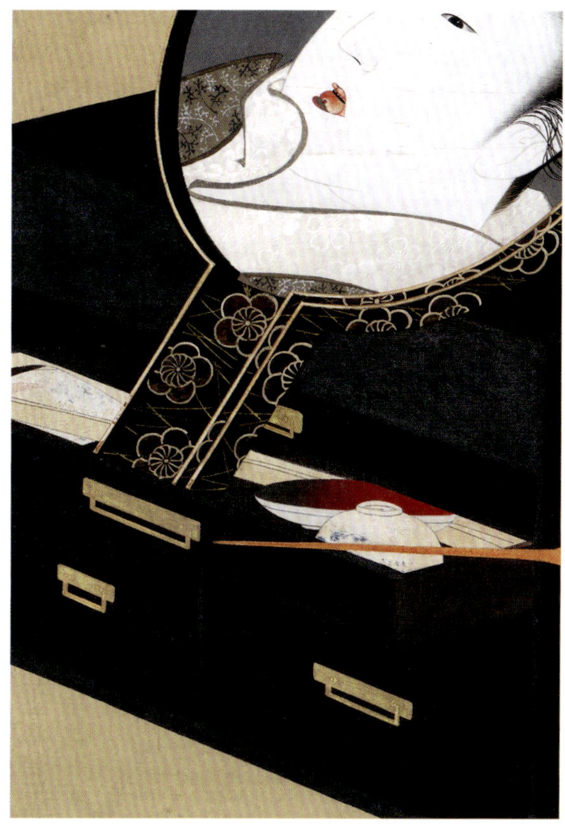

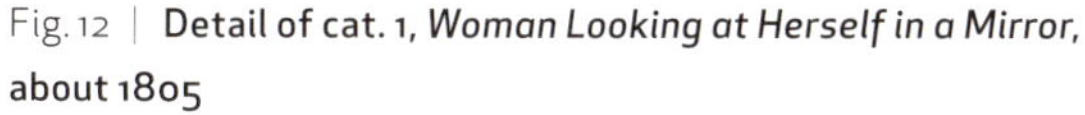

Fig. 12 | **Detail of cat. 1, *Woman Looking at Herself in a Mirror*, about 1805**

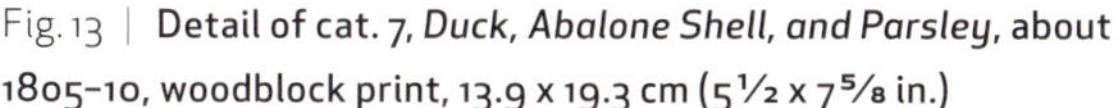

Fig. 13 | **Detail of cat. 7, *Duck, Abalone Shell, and Parsley*, about 1805–10, woodblock print, 13.9 x 19.3 cm (5½ x 7⅝ in.)**

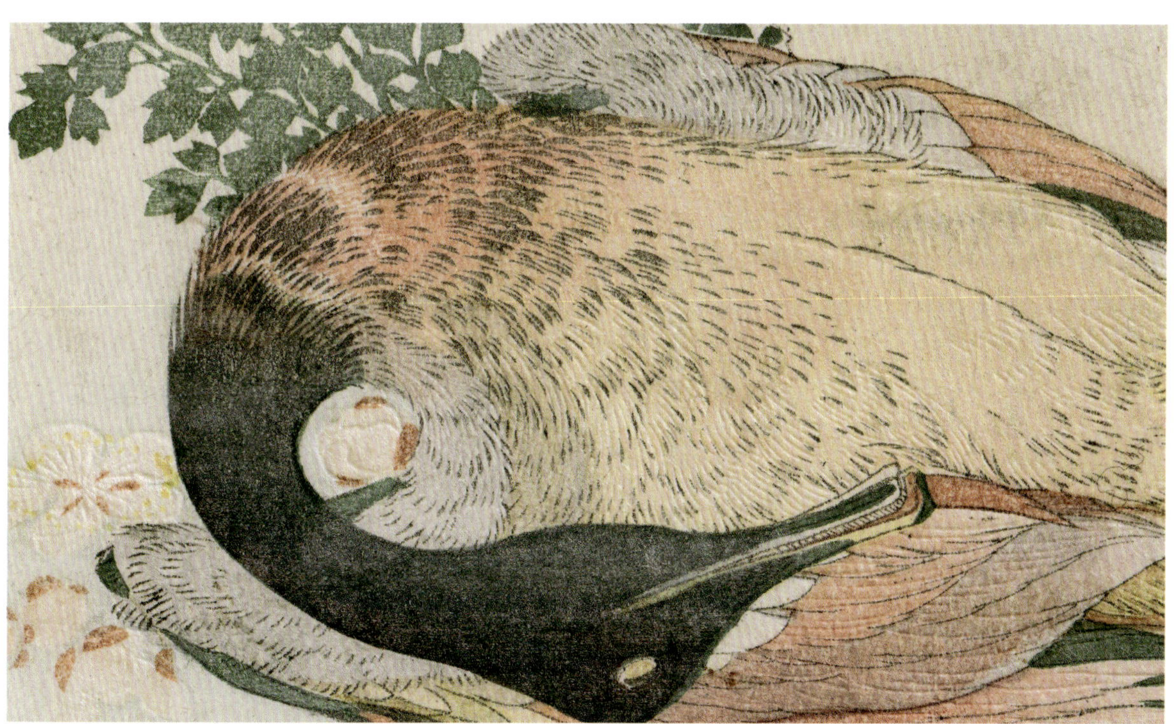

Hokusai was an acute observer of the natural world and had a lifelong fascination with optical effects.[3] *Willow and Crows*, created nearly forty years after *Duck, Abalone Shell, and Parsley*, presents a perceptive painted treatment of plumage in its depiction of a flock of crows fluttering about a windswept willow. Rather than using glossy paint, as he did in the painting of a woman looking in a mirror, Hokusai touched the dense, matte black of the birds' bodies with a thin layer of coarse blue pigment that catches the eye at various angles and reproduces the gleam of their refractive plumage (figs. 14 and 15). In the print, which presents a still life of ingredients waiting to be turned into a New Year feast, the layers of thinly printed color, starting with pale blue and followed by green, orange, and dark gray shading, on the drake's head are finished with burnishing in order to cleverly approximate the feathers' iridescent qualities, as noted earlier. But this naturalism did not stop with simply emulating the real world; the final step in this luxurious print's production was to brush a thin film of glue on the inner surface of the printed abalone and scatter genuine bits of the lustrous polychromatic shell (fig. 16).

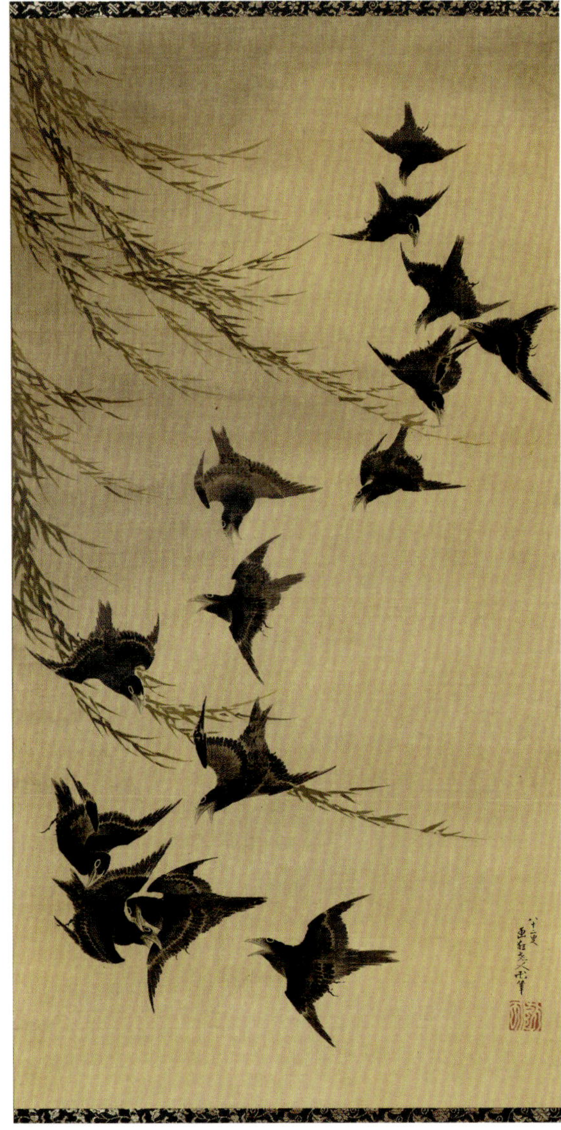

Fig. 14 | ***Willow and Crows* (*Yanagi ni karasu zu*), 1841, hanging scroll, 84.7 x 42.5 cm (33 3/8 x 16 3/4 in.)**

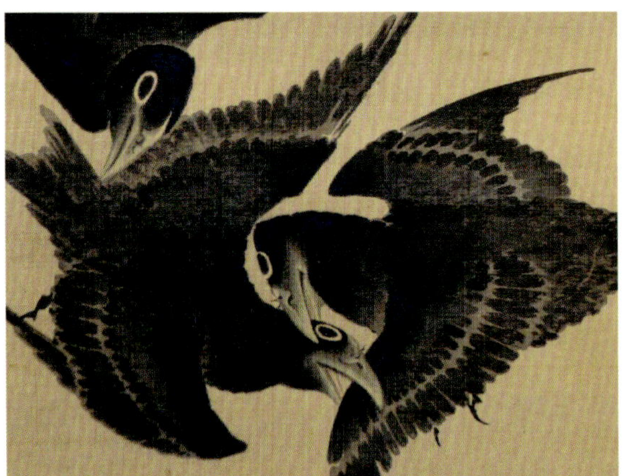

Fig. 15 | **Detail of above**

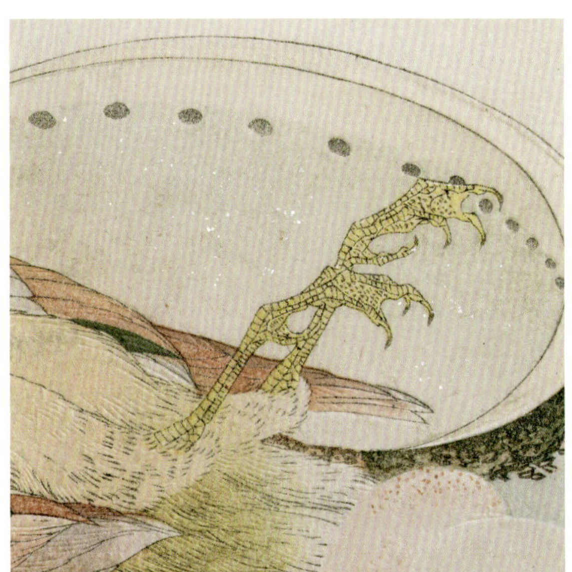

Fig. 16 | **Detail of cat. 7, *Duck, Abalone Shell, and Parsley*, about 1805–10, woodblock print, 13.9 x 19.3 cm (5 1/2 x 7 5/8 in.)**

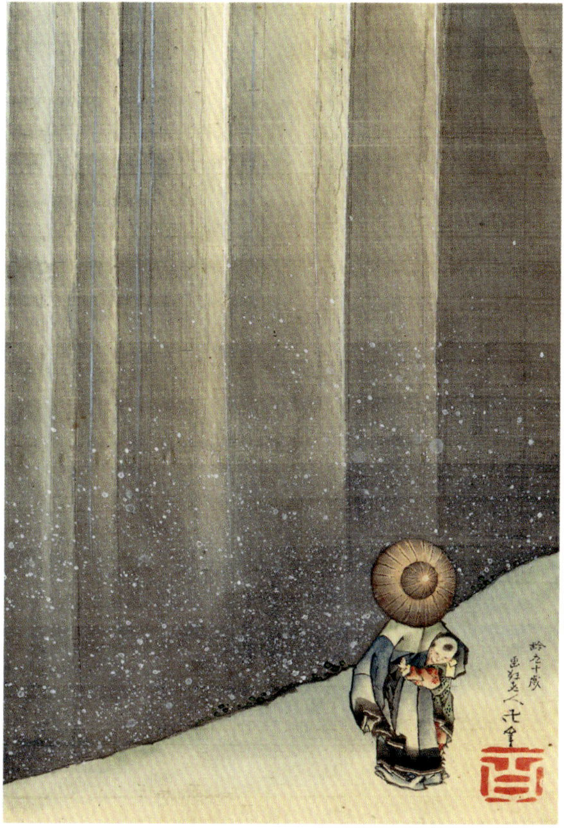

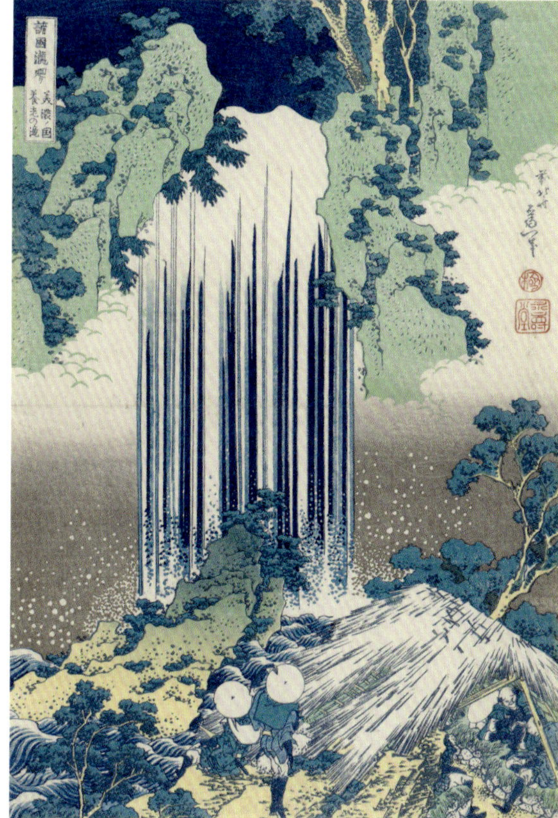

Fig. 17 | **Detail of cat. 50, *Li Bai Admiring a Waterfall*, 1849, hanging scroll, 93.4 x 30 cm ($36\frac{3}{4}$ x $11\frac{13}{16}$ in.)**

Fig. 18 | ***The Care-of-the-Aged Falls in Mino Province* (*Mino no kuni Yōrō no taki*) from the series *A Tour of Waterfalls in Various Provinces* (*Shokoku taki meguri*), about 1832, woodblock print, 36.7 x 24.3 cm ($14\frac{7}{16}$ x $9\frac{9}{16}$ in.)**

In the 1849 painting *Li Bai Admiring a Waterfall* and the print *The Care-of-the-Aged Falls in Mino Province* from nearly two decades earlier, cascades of water plummet into a dance of mist and spray (figs. 17 and 18). Both painting and print feature the vertical drop of a waterfall, which descends into a gray mist flecked with spray that creates a barrier between the falls and the foreground. However, the view is truncated in the painting, whereas the print also shows the origin of the falls and surrounding rocks, moss, and foliage. Spanning the years from his early seventies to the end his life, these waterfalls exemplify Hokusai's transcendence of the traditional boundaries between painting and print as well as his ability to exploit the characteristic qualities of the blue pigments.

Analysis carried out in the MFA's Scientific Research Laboratory has confirmed the presence of traditional indigo in addition to imported synthetic Prussian blue pigment in both the painting and the print.[4] Though indigo and Prussian blue can each yield very dark shades, the former can have greenish or reddish undertones, depending on plant source and manufacture, whereas the latter is considered brighter.[5] Each also has different material qualities. Indigo can be coarse and may not mix well, whereas Prussian blue is made of fine particles that combine easily with binders and other colors to produce even tones. In the painting, Prussian blue is used for the thin washes found on the figure's clothing and for the foliage on the rocky crags located at the right, where it has been more heavily applied. Prussian blue, with its brighter tone, seems to have been selected to bring these parts of the composition forward. These areas stand out from the waterfall, which is painted in tones of indigo that has been mixed in

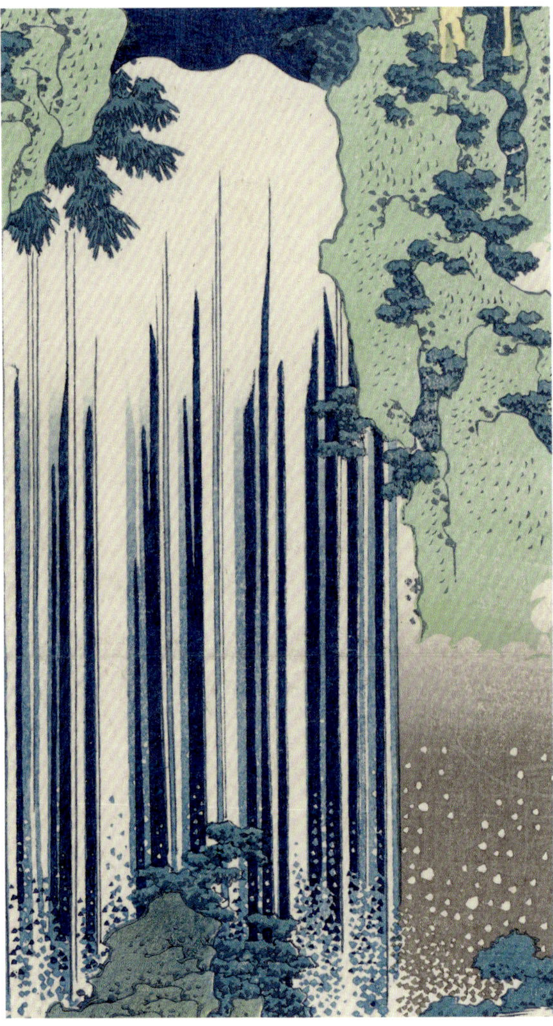

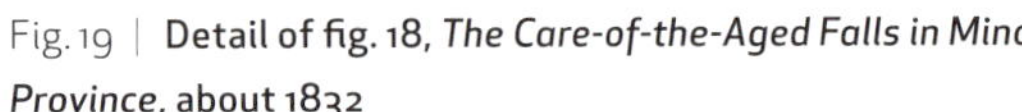

Fig. 19 | **Detail of fig. 18, *The Care-of-the-Aged Falls in Mino Province*, about 1832**

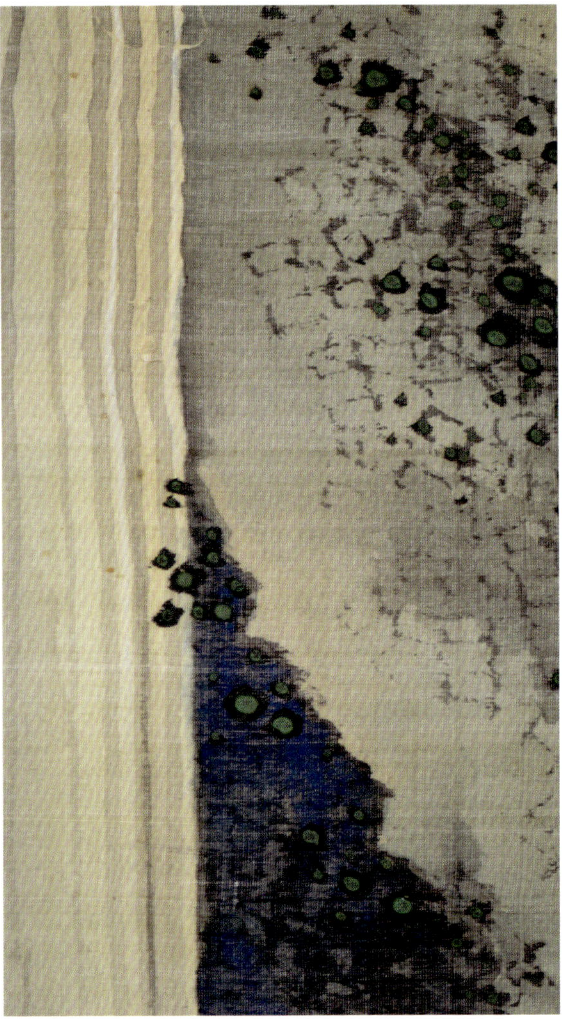

Fig. 20 | **Detail of cat. 50, *Li Bai Admiring a Waterfall*, 1849**

part with white or applied as a wash. The use of both blues, one for the advancing figure of Li Bai and the other for the receding waterfall, contributes to the success of the spatial relationships within the composition.

Prussian blue's bright tone can be found in the patch of sky above the print's falls, in the water's flows, waves, and spray, and mixed with orpiment yellow for the green foliage on the crags and trees (fig. 19). The comparatively duller indigo is used for the outlines and the clothing of the foreground figures, causing these elements of the composition to recede. The strategic contrast of the pigments dramatically focuses this composition on the falls itself and encourages viewers to become one with the anonymous figures looking upward in awe and wonder at the power of the falls.

Hokusai used two printerly techniques in the painting. To create the foam at the foot of the falls, he spattered white pigment onto the silk surface of the painting. To control the extent of the spray, he cut a stencil of paper to protect the figures on the bank in the foreground, which has the added effect of visually throwing this part of the composition into relief. The artist also used monoprint stamping to convey the texture of the rocky cliff at the upper right (fig. 20). Unusually, instead of painting with a brush, he dipped a rectangular object into paint, perhaps a small block of wood, and repeatedly impressed it to achieve a craggy, rough effect.

The exuberant play of color and blank paper in the print's waterfall and the spray at its base mimics painting techniques. Flanking either side of the falls is a gray mist formed with a method known as *o-bokashi*, which, in this case, involved rubbing a broad moistened brush over thickly applied color and guiding it upward to print graduated tones that become increasingly pale.[6] Because this effect is created by manipulating color directly on the block, similar to applying color to paper or silk when painting, each impression of this print is unique in much the same way that a painting is unique. Irregular circular gouges carved into the same block leave the underlying paper free of the gray mist and transform these areas into droplets of spray. To lend volume to the falls, light blue vertical cascades of water were printed with a technique akin to that used to print the gray mist. Toward the upper reaches of the falls, their color gradually fades into the paper's tone and contrasts sharply with the overlapping cascades of evenly printed dark blue. Each cascade disassembles into a jumble of light and dark blue spray. In some cases, flecks of paper or light blue peek out from under voids in the dark blue; in others, spray originates from raised areas of the block printed over blue as well as blank paper. This complex succession of colors printed uniformly, colors printed using o-bokashi to create graduated tones, and paper left in reserve emulates the layering that is often found in paintings.

As seen in these three pairs of works, which collectively span the course of his career, Hokusai was a versatile master of both painting and print design. Though the use of certain techniques and materials found in his art was not unique, he was particularly adept at incorporating elements from each discipline, always moving effortlessly between painting and print design. Hokusai once wrote that he sought to "reach a divine level of understanding" as an artist, so that "every dot and line" in his own work can be seen to "be alive."[7] His extraordinary mastery of materials and techniques enabled him to do just that.

JOAN WRIGHT
Bettina Burr Conservator, Asian Conservation

PHILIP MEREDITH
Higashiyama Kaii Conservator of Japanese Paintings

1. Seiji Nagata, "Hokusai's Artistic Career and Topics for Research," in Ann Yonemura et al., *Hokusai* (Washington, DC: Freer Gallery of Art and Arthur M. Sackler Gallery, Smithsonian Institution, 2006), 2:1–7.
2. The paper used for traditional color woodblock printing is made from *kōzo*, a variety of the paper mulberry plant that is cultivated in Japan. The paper of the highest quality used for traditional woodblock printing is known as *hōshō gami*. Its long, supple fibers give it remarkable strength and absorbency. These features allow the paper to undergo multiple printings without being damaged.
3. Timon Screech, "Hokusai and the Microscope," in Ann Yonemura et al., *Hokusai* (Washington, DC: Freer Gallery of Art and Arthur M. Sackler Gallery, Smithsonian Institution, 2006), 2:329–339.
4. Analysis conducted by Michele Derrick and Richard Newman in the MFA's Scientific Research Laboratory, using x-ray fluorescence (XRF), ultraviolet (UV) fluorescence, infrared microspectroscopy, and Raman microspectroscopy.
5. Marco Leona and John Winter, "The Identification of Indigo and Prussian Blue on Japanese Edo-Period Paintings," in *Studies Using Scientific Methods: Pigments in Later Japanese Paintings*, vol. 1, ed. Jennifer Alt (Washington, DC: Freer Gallery of Art, Smithsonian Institution, 2003), 57–81.
6. For a full description of how o-bokashi is created, how it can vary, and how it differs from uniform printing (*tsubushi*), see Tōshi Yoshida and Rei Yuki, *Japanese Print-Making: A Handbook of Traditional and Modern Techniques* (Rutland, VT: Charles E. Tuttle, 1966), 68, 76–77.
7. "At one hundred, I may reach a level of divine understanding, and if I live a decade beyond that, everything I paint—every dot and line will be alive. I ask the god of longevity to grant me a life long enough to prove this true." Katsushika Hokusai, *Hokusai: One Hundred Views of Mount Fuji*, introduction and commentary by Henry D. Smith II (New York: George Braziller, 1988), 7.

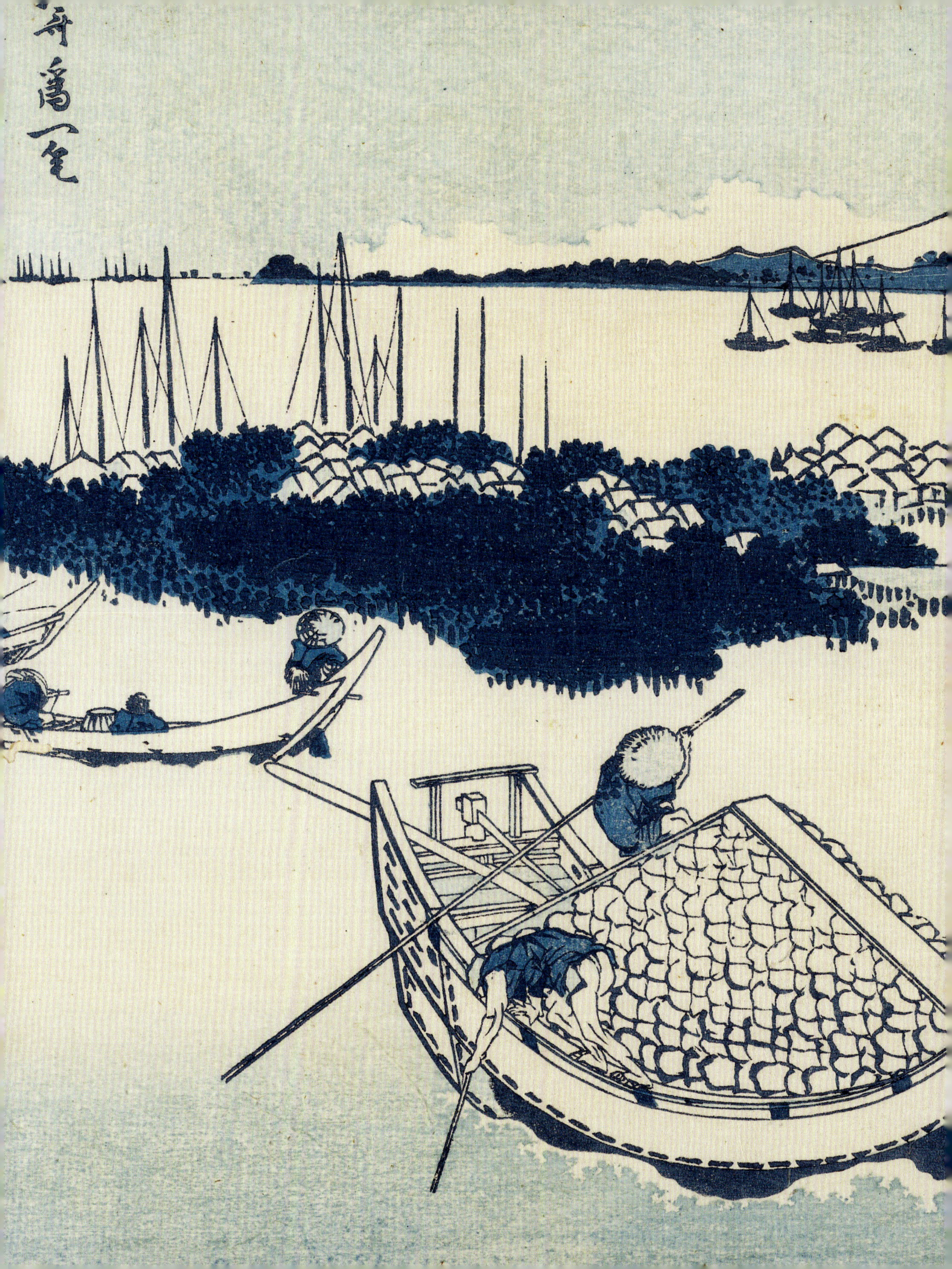
斎為一筆

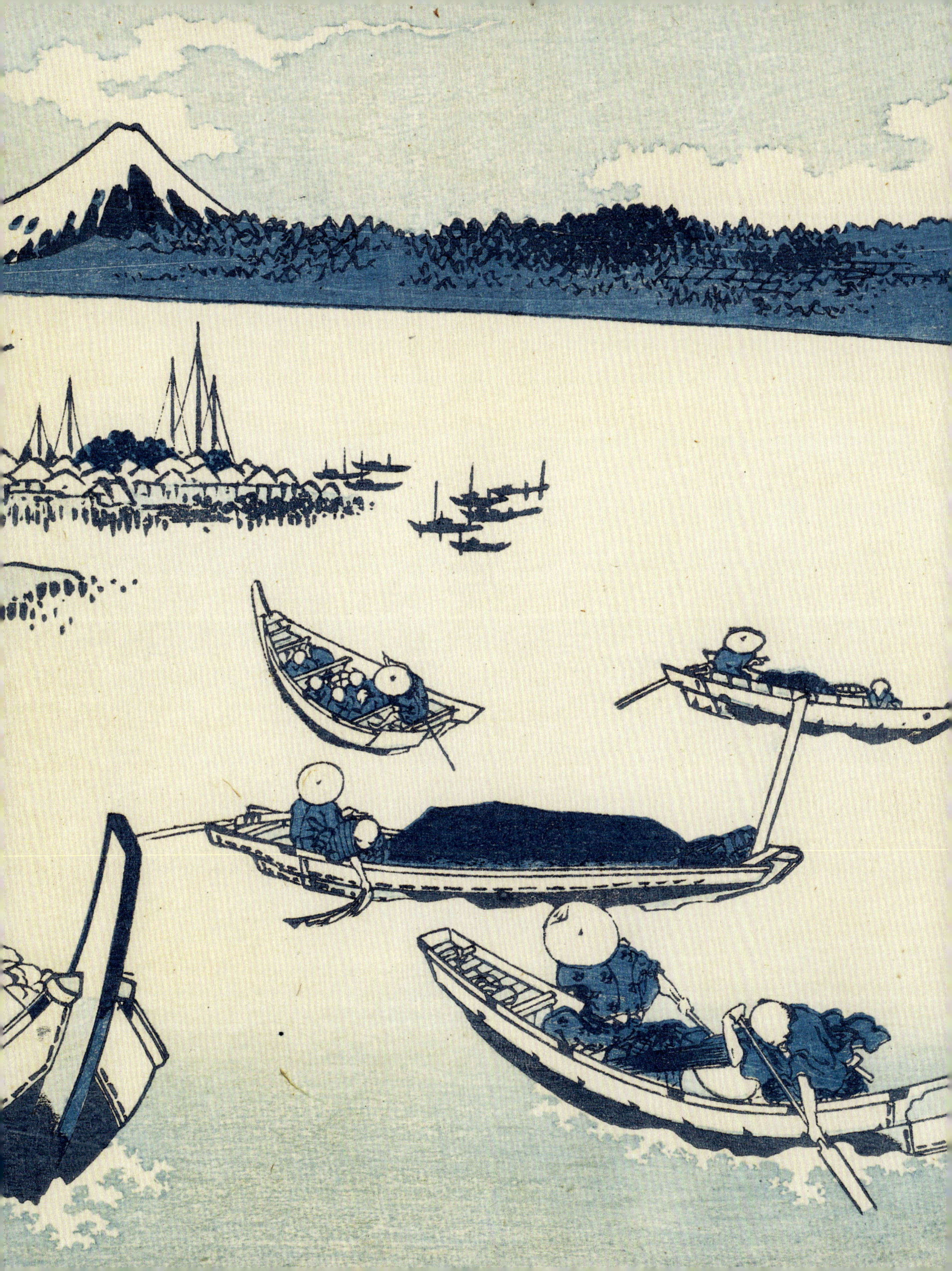

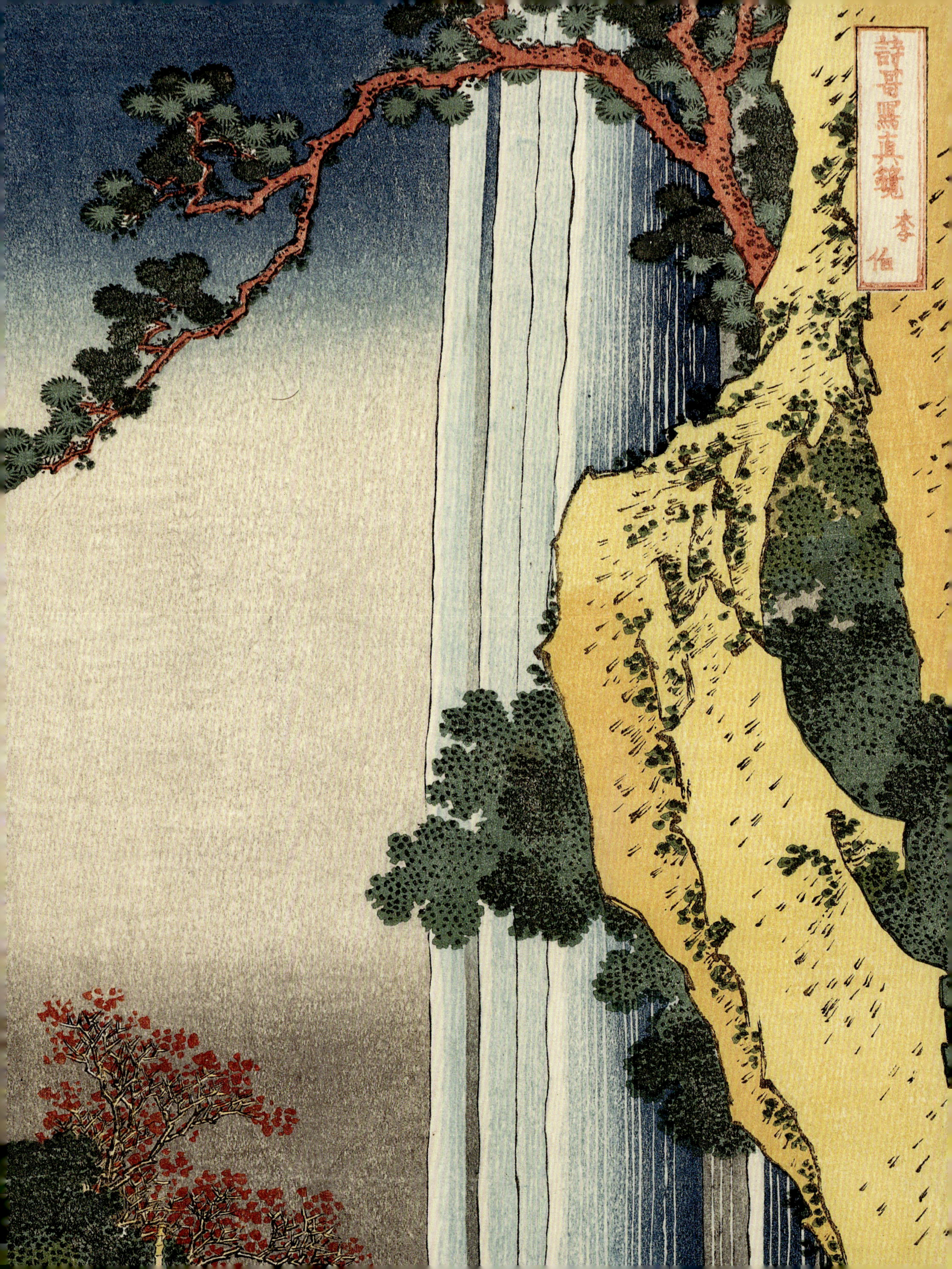
詩哥寫真鏡
李伯

FURTHER READING

Barrett, Timothy. *Japanese Papermaking: Traditions, Tools, and Techniques*. New York: Weatherhill, 1983.

Calza, Gian Carlo, ed. *Hokusai*. London: Phaidon Press, 2003.

Calza, Gian Carlo, with John T. Carpenter, eds. *Hokusai Paintings: Selected Essays*. Venice: The International Hokusai Research Centre, 1994.

Carpenter, John T., ed. *Hokusai and His Age: Ukiyo-e Painting, Printmaking, and Book Illustration in Late Edo Japan*. Amsterdam: Hotei Publishing, 2005.

Clark, Timothy. *Hokusai's Great Wave*. London: The British Museum Press, 2011.

Forrer, Matthi. *Hokusai*. With texts by Edmond de Goncourt. New York: Rizzoli, 1988.

———. *Hokusai: Bridging East and West*. Exh. cat. Tokyo: Nihon Keizai Shimbun, 1998.

———. *Hokusai: Prints and Drawings*. Exh. cat. London: Royal Academy of Arts, 1991.

Guth, Christine M. E. *Hokusai's Great Wave: Biography of a Global Icon*. Honolulu: University of Hawaii Press, forthcoming.

———. "Hokusai's Great Waves and the Maritime Turn in Japanese Visual Culture." *Art Bulletin* 93, no. 4 (December 2011): 468–85.

Hillier, Jack. *The Art of Hokusai in Book Illustration*. Los Angeles: University of California Press, 1980.

———. *Hokusai: Paintings, Drawings and Woodcuts*. Oxford: Phaidon Press, 1955.

Hughes, Sukey. *Washi: The World of Japanese Paper*. Tokyo: Kodansha International, 1978.

Jett, Paul, John Winter, and Blythe McCarthy, eds. *Scientific Research on the Pictorial Arts of Asia: Proceedings of the Second Forbes Symposium at the Freer Gallery of Art*. London: Archetype Publications and Freer Gallery of Art, 2005.

Kanada, Margaret Miller. *Color Woodblock Printing: The Traditional Method of Ukiyo-e*. Tokyo: Shufunotomo, 1989.

Katsushika Hokusai. *Hokusai: One Hundred Views of Mount Fuji*. Introduction and commentary by Henry D. Smith II. New York: George Braziller, 1988.

Keyes, Roger. "'My Master Is Creation': Prints by Hokusai Sōri (1795–1798)." *Impressions* 20 (1998): 38–51.

Lane, Richard. *Hokusai: Life and Work*. New York: E. P. Dutton, 1989.

Meech, Julia, and Jane Oliver, eds. *Designed for Pleasure: The World of Edo Japan in Prints and Paintings, 1680–1860*. Seattle: Asia Society and Japanese Art Society of America in association with University of Washington Press, 2008.

Morse, Anne Nishimura, et al. *Drama and Desire: Japanese Paintings from the Floating World, 1690–1850*. Exh. cat. Boston: MFA Publications, 2006.

Morse, Peter. *Hokusai: One Hundred Poets*. New York: George Braziller, 1989.

Nagata, Seiji. *Hokusai: Genius of the Japanese Ukiyo-e*. Translated by John Bester. Tokyo: Kodansha International, 1995.

Nagata, Seiji, et al. *Hokusai*. Exh. cat. Tokyo: Nihon Keizai Shimbun, 2005.

Nagata, Seiji, Sarah E. Thompson, et al. *Hokusai from the Museum of Fine Arts, Boston*. Exh. cat. Tokyo: Nihon Keizai Shimbun, 2013.

Narazaki, Muneshige. *Hokusai: The Thirty-Six Views of Mount Fuji*. Translated and adapted by John Bester. Masterworks of Ukiyo-e. Tokyo: Kodansha International, 1968.

Reigle Newland, Amy, ed. *The Hotei Encyclopedia of Japanese Woodblock Prints*. 2 vols. Leiden: Hotei Publishing, 2006.

Rosenfield, John M. *Extraordinary Persons: Works by Eccentric, Nonconformist Japanese Artists of the Early Modern Era (1580–1868) in the Collection of Kimiko and John Powers*. Cambridge, MA: Harvard University Art Museums, 1999.

Screech, Timon. *The Western Scientific Gaze and Popular Imagery in Later Edo Japan: The Lens within the Heart*. Cambridge: Cambridge University Press, 1996.

Stratis, Harriet K., and Britt Salvesan, eds. *The Broad Spectrum: Studies in the Materials, Techniques, and Conservation of Color on Paper*. London: Archetype Publications, 2002.

Van Rappard-Boon, Charlotte, and Lee Brushke-Johnson. *Surimono: Poetry and Image in Japanese Prints*. Leiden: Hotei Publishing, 2000.

Watanabe, Toshio. *High Victorian Japonisme*. Swiss Asian Studies 10. Bern: Peter Lang, 1991.

Yonemura, Ann, et al. *Hokusai*. Washington, DC: Freer Gallery of Art and Arthur M. Sackler Gallery, Smithsonian Institution, 2006.

Yoshida, Tōshi, and Rei Yuki. *Japanese Print-Making: A Handbook of Traditional and Modern Techniques*. Rutland, VT: Charles E. Tuttle, 1966.

FIGURE ILLUSTRATIONS

Fig. 1
Quick Lessons in Simplified Drawing, Part One (*Ryakuga haya-oshie, shohen*), 1812
Woodblock-printed book; ink on paper
Each page: 18.4 x 13 cm ($7\frac{1}{4}$ x $5\frac{1}{8}$ in.)
Source unidentified, 1997.895

Fig. 2
Quick Lessons in Simplified Drawing, Part Two (*Ryakuga haya-oshie, kōhen*), 1814
Woodblock-printed book; ink on paper
Each page: 18.6 x 13.2 cm ($7\frac{5}{16}$ x $5\frac{3}{16}$ in.)
Source unidentified, 1997.896

Fig. 3
Newly Published Board Game of a Journey to and from Kamakura, Enoshima, and Ōyama (*Kamakura Enoshima Ōyama shinpan ōrai sugoroku*), 1820s
Signature: Saki no Hokusai litsu zu
Publishers: Nishimuraya Yohachi (Eijudō), Tsuruya Kiemon (Senkakudō), Jōshūya Jūzō (Kinjūdō)
Woodblock print (nishiki-e); ink and color on paper
62.2 x 43.2 cm ($24\frac{1}{2}$ x 17 in.)
William Sturgis Bigelow Collection, 11.19654

Fig. 4
Extraordinary Persons of Japan (*Nihon kijin den*), illustrated by Utagawa Kuniyoshi (1797–1861), about 1845
Author: Hanagasa Bunkyō (1785–1860)
Publishers: Suharaya Mohei et al.
Woodblock-printed book; ink on paper
Each page: 22.6 x 14.2 cm ($8\frac{7}{8}$ x $5\frac{9}{16}$ in.)
Source unidentified, 1997.957

Fig. 5
Fuji in Mist (Muchū no Fuji) from volume 1 of *One Hundred Views of Mount Fuji* (*Fugaku hyakkei*), 1834
Publishers: Eirakuya Tōshirō (Tōhekidō), Nishimuraya Yohachi (Eijudō), et al.
Woodblock-printed book; ink on paper
Each page: 22.5 x 15.5 cm ($8\frac{7}{8}$ x $6\frac{1}{8}$ in.)
Gift of Mrs. Jared K. Morse in memory of Charles J. Morse, 1997.809.1–2

Fig. 6
Express Delivery Boats Rowing through Waves (*Oshiokuri hatō tsūsen no zu*), about 1800–5
Signature: Hokusai egaku
Woodblock print (nishiki-e); ink and color on paper
18.5 x 24.5 cm ($7\frac{5}{16}$ x $9\frac{5}{8}$ in.)
William S. and John T. Spaulding Collection, 21.6678

Fig. 7
Utagawa Kunitora (working early 19th century)
Enjoying the Evening Cool at Ryōgoku Bridge in Edo: A Great Display of Fireworks (*Edo Ryōgoku-bashi yūsuzumi ōhanabi no zu*), 1820s
Publisher: Yamamotoya Heikichi (Eikyūdō)
Woodblock print (nishiki-e); ink and color on paper
Triptych (overall): 38 x 76.5 cm ($14\frac{15}{16}$ x $30\frac{1}{8}$ in.)
William Sturgis Bigelow Collection, 11.36852a–c

Figs. 8 and 9
Details of cat. 1
Woman Looking at Herself in a Mirror, about 1805
Signature: Dokuryū Kukushin Hokusai ga
Hanging scroll; ink, color, gold, and mica on silk
138.7 x 57.5 cm ($54\frac{5}{8}$ x $22\frac{5}{8}$ in.)
William Sturgis Bigelow Collection, 11.7424

Fig. 10
Courtiers Returning from a Picnic, frontispiece by Hokusai from the book *The Thirty-Six Immortal Women Poets* (*Nyōbō sanjūrokunin uta-awase*), illustrated by Chōbunsai Eishi (1756–1829), 1801
Publisher: Nishimuraya Yohachi (Eijudō)
Woodblock-printed book; ink and color on paper
Overall: 25.3 x 18.7cm ($9\frac{15}{16}$ x $7\frac{3}{8}$ in.)
Source unidentified, 1997.386

Fig. 11
Detail of above
Courtiers Returning from a Picnic, 1801

Fig. 12
Detail of cat. 1
Woman Looking at Herself in a Mirror, about 1805

Fig. 13
Detail of cat. 7
Duck, Abalone Shell, and Parsley, about 1805–10
Signature: Gakyōjin Hokusai ga
Woodblock print (surimono); ink and color on paper
13.9 x 19.3 cm ($5\frac{1}{2}$ x $7\frac{5}{8}$ in.)
William Sturgis Bigelow Collection, 11.16798

Fig. 14
Willow and Crows (*Yanagi ni karasu zu*), 1841
Signature: Hachijūnisō Gakyōjin Manji hitsu
Hanging scroll; ink and color on silk
84.7 x 42.5 cm (33 3/8 x 16 3/4 in.)
William Sturgis Bigelow Collection, 11.7421

Fig. 15
Detail of above
Willow and Crows, 1841

Fig. 16
Detail of cat. 7
Duck, Abalone Shell, and Parsley, about 1805–10

Fig. 17
Detail of cat. 50
Li Bai Admiring a Waterfall, 1849
Signature: Yowai kyūjūsai Gakyō rōjin Manji hitsu
Hanging scroll; ink and color on silk
93.4 x 30 cm (36 3/4 x 11 13/16 in.)
William Sturgis Bigelow Collection, 11.7452

Fig. 18
The Care-of-the-Aged Falls in Mino Province (*Mino no kuni Yōrō no taki*) from the series *A Tour of Waterfalls in Various Provinces* (*Shokoku taki meguri*), about 1832
Signature: Saki no Hokusai Iitsu hitsu
Publisher: Nishimuraya Yohachi (Eijudō)
Woodblock print (nishiki-e); ink and color on paper
Vertical ōban: 36.7 x 24.3 cm (14 7/16 x 9 9/16 in.)
William Sturgis Bigelow Collection, 11.25226

Fig. 19
Detail of above
The Care-of-the-Aged Falls in Mino Province, about 1832

Fig. 20
Detail of cat. 50
Li Bai Admiring a Waterfall, 1849

Details
p. 1: from cat. 1; pp. 2–3: cat. 42; pp. 4–5: from cat. 34; p. 6: cat. 45; pp. 24–25: cat. 49; pp. 164–65: cat. 19; p. 166: cat. 51; p. 169: cat. 41; p. 171: cat. 29; p. 172: cat. 2; p. 176: from cat. 45

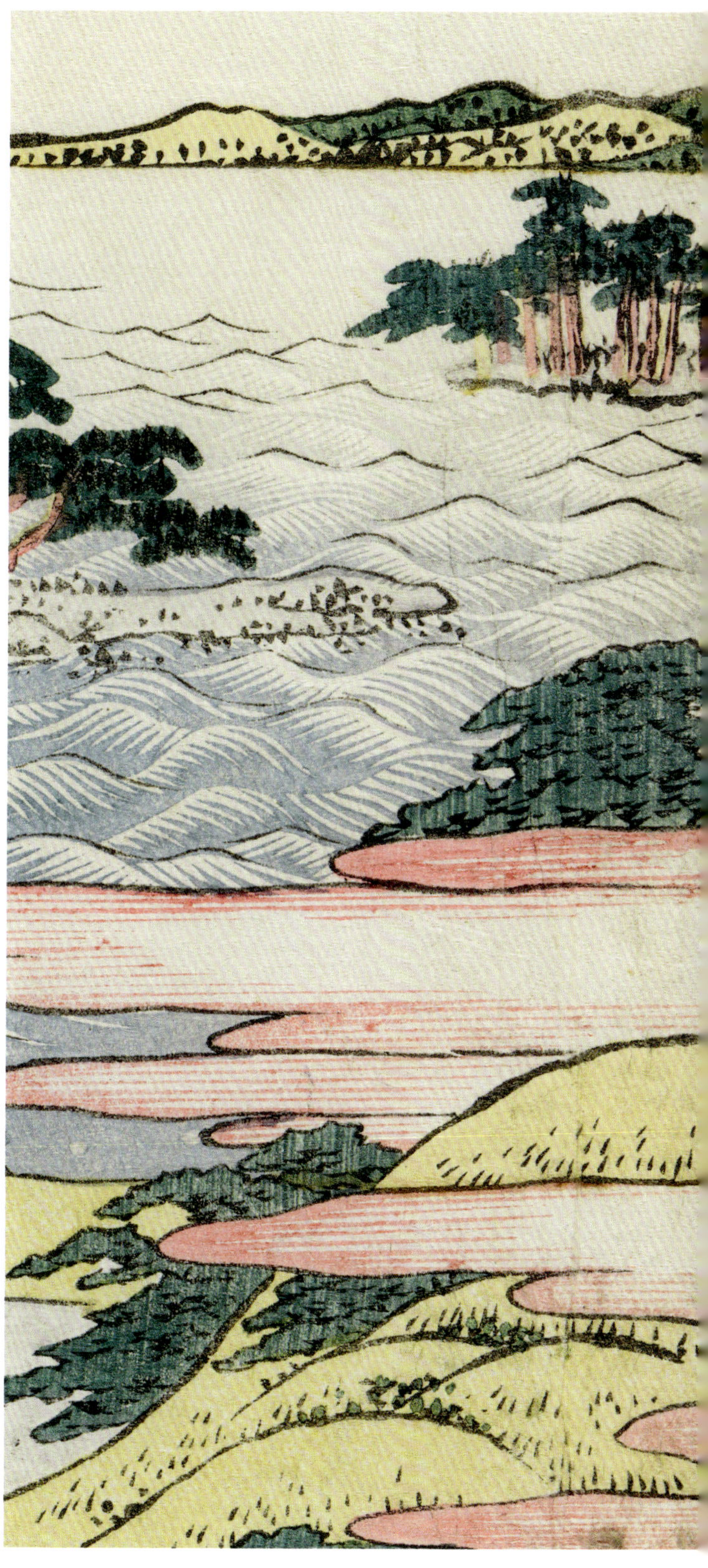

ACKNOWLEDGMENTS

First and foremost, I am deeply grateful to my two co-curators on the exhibition that inspired this book: in Japan, Seiji Nagata, Director of the Katsushika Hokusai Museum of Art, and in Boston, Anne Nishimura Morse, William and Helen Pounds Senior Curator of Japanese Art. Seiji Nagata, one of the world's leading authorities on Hokusai, has worked with the MFA on three traveling exhibitions of our Japanese prints. As a fitting culmination to the series, the Hokusai show will be on view at home as well as in Japan. Anne Morse has contributed her encyclopedic knowledge of Japanese art in general and of the MFA collection in particular, as well as invaluable advice on organizing and presenting a large-scale exhibition.

The intellectual content of this book has been greatly enhanced by the work of the curators at the venue museums in Japan: Yasumasa Oka, Akira Tsukahara, and Noriko Katsumori of the Kobe City Museum; Chika Kagami of the Nagoya/Boston Museum of Fine Arts; and Tomomi Shigematsu of the Kitakyushu Municipal Museum of Art. Additional contributions were made by Atsuko Okuda, Makoto Takemura, and Mika Negishi of the Sumida City Cultural Promotion Foundation, and by editor Yuriko Iwakiri.

In Boston, our conservators have actively pursued scientific research on the materials and methods used by Hokusai, and some of their findings are discussed in an essay in this book, co-authored by Joan Wright, Bettina Burr Conservator, Asian Conservation, and Philip Meredith, Higashiyama Kaii Conservator of Japanese Paintings. The appearance of the works of art owes much to the skill of the Asian Conservation Studio at the MFA, headed by Jacki Elgar, Pamela and Peter Voss Head of Asian Conservation. I am thankful for the dedication of Joan Wright, Hsin-Chen Tsai, Elyse Driscoll, Sarah Kelly Gurney, John Robbe, Philip Meredith, Jacki Elgar, Tanya Uyeda, and Kimberley Nichols.

Curatorial efforts were supported by Jane Portal, former Matsutaro Shoriki Chair, Art of Asia, Oceania, and Africa; Kelsey Mallet; and Ellen Takata. I am also grateful to Pamela Parmal, Department Head and David and Roberta Logie Curator of Textile and Fashion Arts.

In MFA Publications special thanks are due to Emiko K. Usui, Anna Barnet, Terry McAweeney, Christopher DiPietro, and Susan Marsh.

Finally, I would like to mention the Japanese Print Access and Documentation Project (JPADP), which has facilitated our many recent exhibitions of Japanese prints. The Project accessioned, rehoused, photographed, and published on the MFA website the entire collection of more than fifty thousand Japanese prints. Thanks are due to an anonymous American donor, an anonymous Japanese donor, and the State Street Bank for providing funding for the Project; and to the dozens of MFA staff and volunteers, too numerous to mention individually, who carried it out.

SARAH E. THOMPSON
Assistant Curator for Japanese Prints
Museum of Fine Arts, Boston

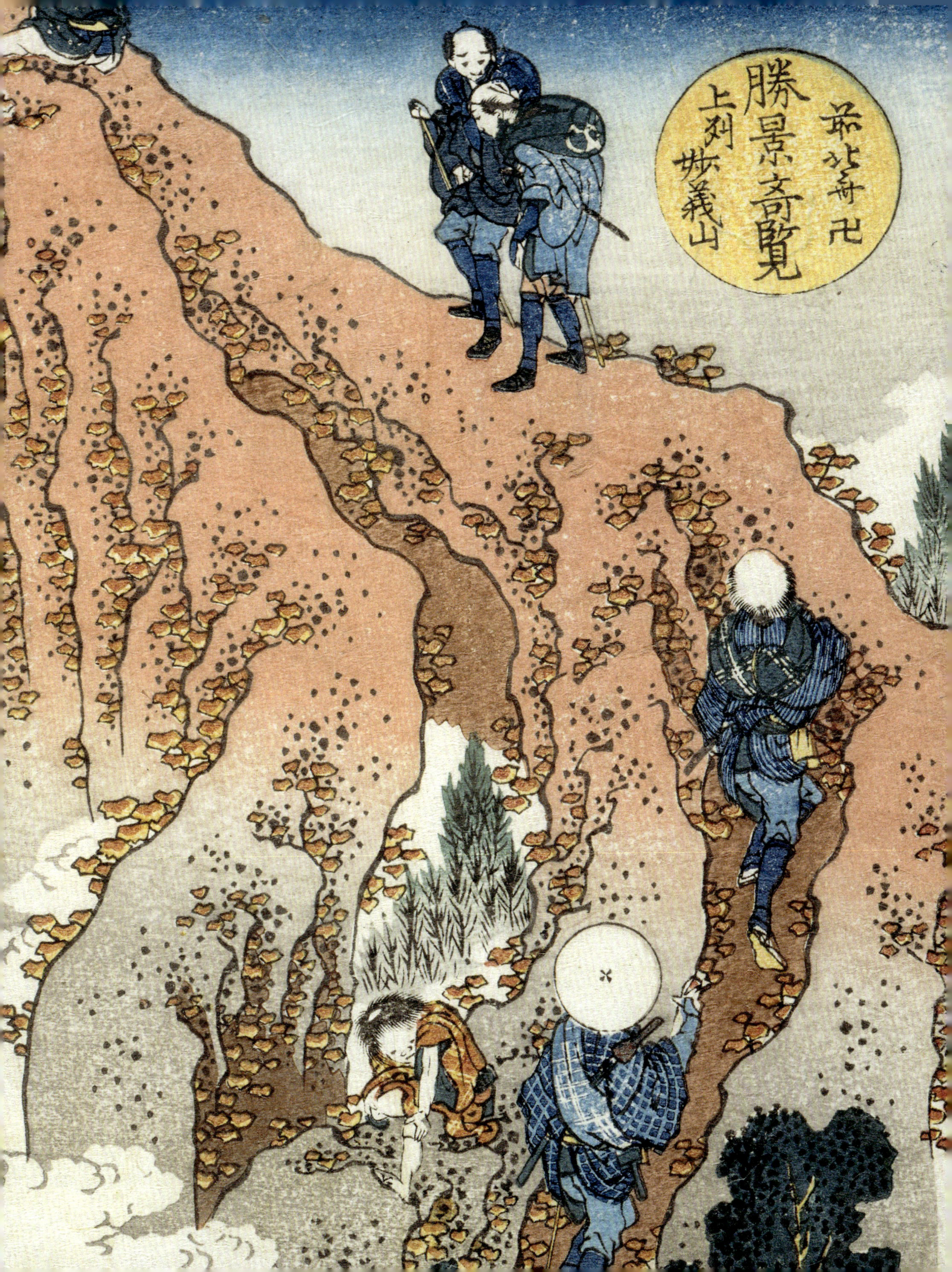

前北斎卍
勝景奇覧
上州妙義山

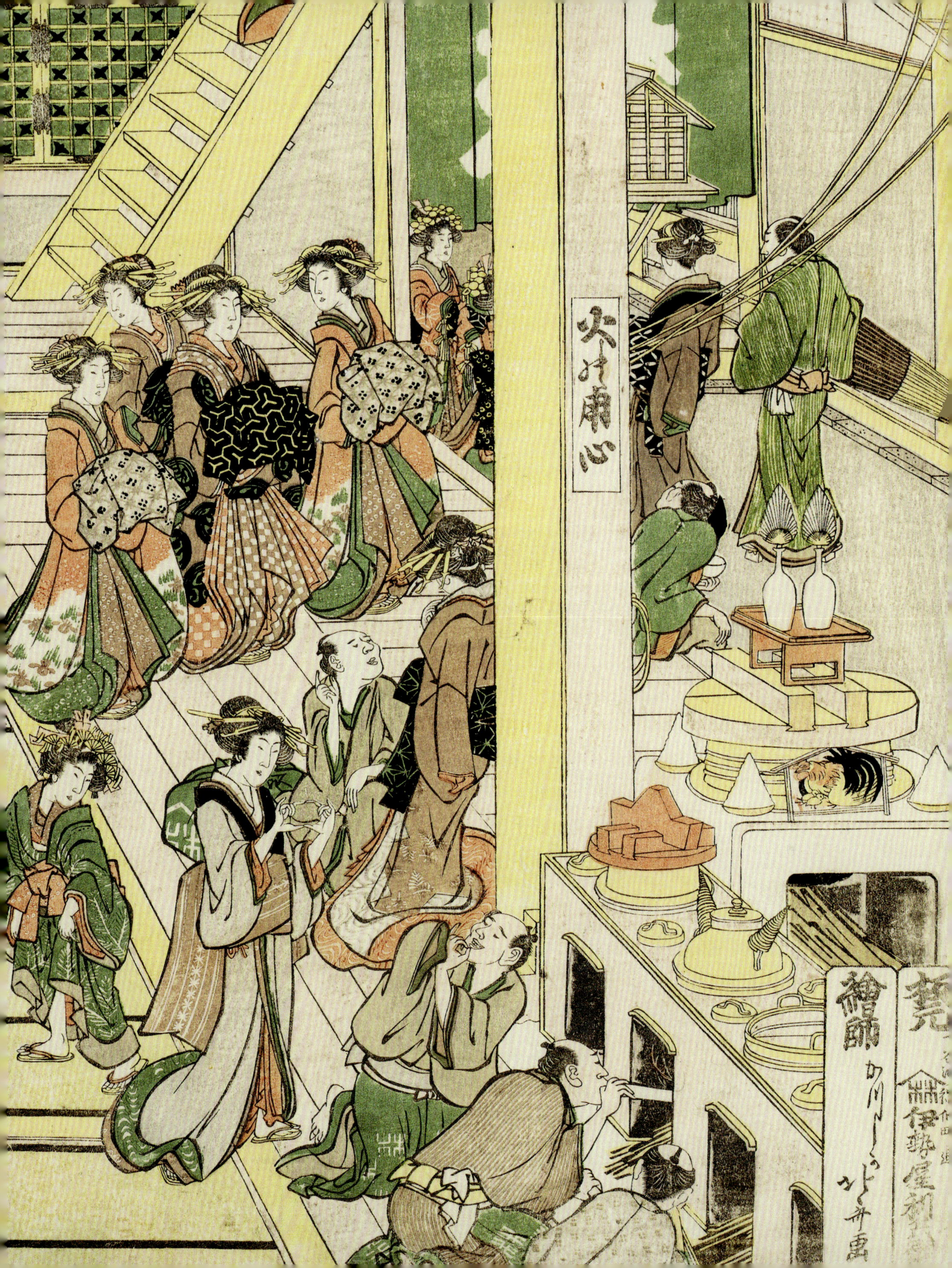
火の用心
絵師 かつしかほくさい画
売
伊勢屋利兵衛

INDEX

Page numbers in **bold** refer to illustrations. All works are by Hokusai unless otherwise indicated.

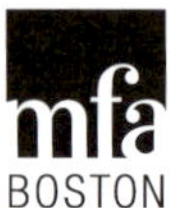

MFA Publications
Museum of Fine Arts, Boston
465 Huntington Avenue
Boston, Massachusetts 02115
www.mfa.org/publications

This book was published in conjunction with the exhibition *Hokusai*, organized by the Museum of Fine Arts, Boston, from April 5, 2015, to August 9, 2015.

Generous support for the exhibition was provided by the Jean S. and Frederic A. Sharf Exhibition Fund.

Generous support for this publication was provided by the Andrew W. Mellon Publications Fund.

ISBN 978-0-87846-825-6

Library of Congress Control Number: 2014955012

While the objects in this publication necessarily represent only a small portion of the MFA's holdings, the Museum is proud to be a leader within the American museum community in sharing the objects in its collection via its website. Currently, information about more than 330,000 objects is available to the public worldwide. To learn more about the MFA's collections, including provenance, publication, and exhibition history, kindly visit *www.mfa.org/collections*.

For a complete listing of MFA publications, please contact the publisher at the above address, or call 617 369 3438.

Case cover: Detail of cat. 37, *Phoenix*, 1835

All illustrations in this book were photographed by the Imaging Studios, Museum of Fine Arts, Boston, except where otherwise noted.

Grateful acknowledgment is made to the copyright holders for permission to reproduce the following texts:

p. 42: Yukinoya Torikane poem from John T. Carpenter, ed., *Hokusai and His Age: Ukiyo-e Painting, Printmaking, and Book Illustration in Late Edo Japan* (Amsterdam: Hotei Publishing, 2005). Reprinted with permission.

p. 143: Sei Shōnagon poem from Joshua S. Mostow, *Pictures of the Heart: The* Hyakunin isshu *in Word and Image* (University of Hawai'i Press, 1996). Reprinted with permission.

p. 146: Ono no Komachi poem from Joshua S. Mostow, *Pictures of the Heart: The* Hyakunin isshu *in Word and Image* (University of Hawai'i Press, 1996). Reprinted with permission.

p. 151: Sarumaru Dayū poem from Joshua S. Mostow, *Pictures of the Heart: The* Hyakunin isshu *in Word and Image* (University of Hawai'i Press, 1996). Reprinted with permission.

p. 152: Li Po, "Waterfall at Lu-Shan," from *Crossing the Yellow River: Three Hundred Poems from the Chinese*, translated by Sam Hamill. Copyright © 2000 by Sam Hamill. Reprinted with the permission of The Permissions Company, Inc., on behalf of Tiger Bark Press, www.tigerbarkpress.com.

Edited by Anna Barnet
Copyedited and proofread by Dalia Geffen
Designed by Susan Marsh
Typeset in Apex New by Matt Mayerchak
Production by Terry McAweeney
Printed and bound at Graphicom, Verona, Italy

Distributed in the United States of America and Canada by
ARTBOOK | D.A.P.
155 Sixth Avenue
New York, New York 10013
www.artbook.com

Distributed outside the United States of America and Canada by
Thames & Hudson, Ltd.
181A High Holborn
London WC1V 7QX
www.thamesandhudson.com

SECOND PRINTING
Printed and bound in Italy
This book was printed on acid-free paper.

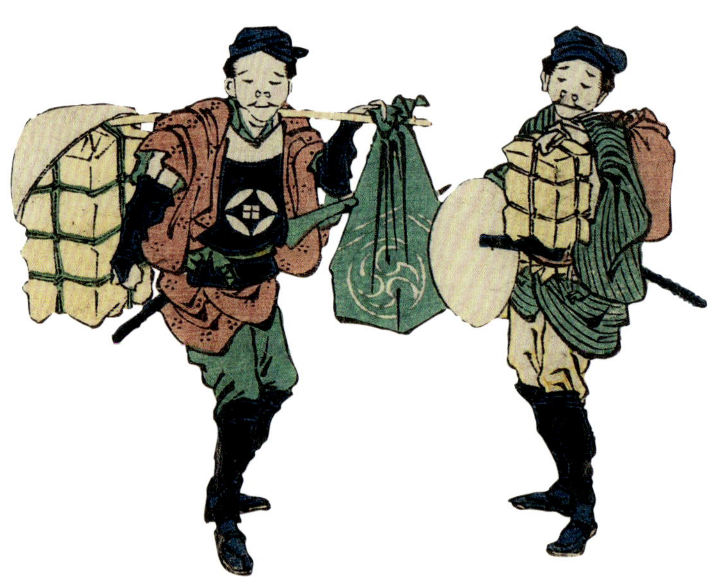